ASPECTS OF GREEK AND ROMAN LIFE

General Editor: the late H. H. Scullard

* * *

THE FAMILY IN CLASSICAL GREECE

W. K. Lacey

THE FAMILY
IN CLASSICAL
GREECE

W. K. Lacey

CORNELL UNIVERSITY PRESS
ITHACA, NEW YORK

© 1968 Thames and Hudson

First published 1968 by Cornell University Press.
First published, Cornell Paperbacks edition, 1984.

International Standard Book Number 0–8014–9274–2
Library of Congress Catalog Card Number 68–14817
Printed in the United States of America

The paper in this book is acid-free and meets the guidelines for permanence and durability of the Committee on Production Guidelines for Book Longevity of the Council on Library Resources.

CONTENTS

LIST OF ILLUSTRATIONS

PREFACE

THE FAMILY IN GREEK HISTORY is a subject which has hitherto not found favour among historians. There is no book on the subject—in English at least—and in the customary students' text-books the family receives short shrift; the authors all omit the word 'family' altogether from their index, or admit it only with reference to the Homeric period. The larger-scale works, L. Whibley's *Companion to Greek Studies*, and the *Cambridge Ancient History*, remain equally uninformative.

This book is an attempt at an introduction to the subject; it has many intentional omissions, and no doubt a number of unintended ones, but this is inevitable in a short outline of what is in fact the most central and enduring institution of Greek society. City-states rose and fell, democracy and oligarchy fought, foreign conquerors came and went, but the family remained stubbornly entrenched as the fundamental institution of the Greeks. This book, however, only attempts to deal in any detail with the family in the archaic and classical ages, the great era of the city-states, because there was in these ages, and in these alone, a relationship of peculiar closeness and complexity based essentially on the fact that the *polis* was no more and no less than the sum total of its families. Another volume will be required to study the Greek family outside the city-state and the Graeco-Roman family of the period following the Roman conquest of the Greek lands.

The all-pervading role of the family has the result that there is scarcely any topic in Greek civilization in which the family is not concerned; this has imposed the need for a rigorous selectivity, especially in quoting from predecessors' work. I have in most cases acknowledged the work in which I first came across the point in question, even when the author was not the first to make it, and I have at all times, when faced with the choice of an English or a foreign author, quoted the English, on the ground that his work is more likely to be accessible to students, and that students are more likely to use it. The exceptions to this rule mostly affect works whose bibliography is too meagre to enable a student to pursue his own enquiries further. Where, however, there is a general consensus based on a reliable ancient author, I have confined my references to the ancient source.

Among the intentional omissions in this book are large-scale references to Greek Tragedy. An introductory preface is no place for an extended discussion, but I have taken the view that Athenian audiences did not suppose that figures on the tragic stage were normal human beings living in normal family circumstances. What the characters say therefore has no independent value for telling us about society, though very often it will support what we know from other sources to be true. Comedy, on the other hand, was about normal human beings in comic situations; it is therefore always potentially useful. Fragments of comedy, however, as of tragedy, are unreliable as evidence; as the anthology of Stobaeus shows, they can be selected to 'prove' almost anything.

Another intentional omission is the distinction between Demosthenic and 'Demosthenic' speeches; were any speech in the Demosthenic corpus demonstrably much later than the great orator's lifetime, the distinction would be meaningful, but this has never been shown. What is more important than identifying the actual author is to remember that, whoever wrote any speech, all those who spoke in Greek law-courts were prepared to be liars, and that habitual liars will be good liars, so that their lies must have sounded plausible to the audience to whom they were addressed (an Athenian one in almost every surviving case); the exact truth of what orators say has therefore also not been considered in this book.

Almost all questions in Greek history have been, and many still are, the subject of extended debate; this is hardly surprising when the small quantity of evidence and the large number of workers, and of approaches attempted, are taken into consideration. In general, I have tried to indicate areas of disagreement which seemed most important for the family, and to cite views divergent from that which I have taken when these seem to be reasonable alternatives, but I have not entered into exhaustive discussion of theories which seem to me to be based on wholly false premises, such as a matriarchal organization of society.

The spelling of Greek, and of Greek names, presents a perpetual problem; the approach I have taken is not consistent, but conforms to the practice of this series, and attempts to be helpful. All authors, familiar or not, I have spelt as in Liddell and Scott's Lexicon (LSJ), 9th edition. Other personal names have generally been anglicized except when to do so would be misleading, as with Pindarus, tyrant of Ephesus, or when the traditional spelling is positively misleading, or to use it would compel readers who know no Greek to mispronounce the name. Familiar names are in their familiar form. Hence, for example, I use Pericles and Lycurgus, and Penelope, not Penelopeia; I use Solon and Plato, but prefer Dracon to Draco and Cleisthenes to Clisthenes. All place-names have been anglicized except for the names of places like Pylos and Melos, in which I have retained the Greek -os. The cult names of deities have been left in their Greek form, like Zeus Ktesios. In pronouncing names, -ou is pronounced as in 'you', except in the final position, when -ous is as in 'owe us'; similarly -aus is as in 'slay us', but -eus may be either as in 'use' (noun), or as in 'see us'.

I have declined to translate a number of Greek words whose customary English equivalent is inexact or positively misleading, and sometimes so bathetic as to leave the reader perplexed as to how any language could have tolerated such dreadful jargon. I have thought it better to provide a short glossary of words commonly used, and to attempt to explain the various shades of meaning where this is appropriate in the text.

This book began as a course of lectures for the Classical Tripos in Cambridge; no doubt this will be evident to the reader. That it is not much more evident owes a very great deal to Mr G. T. Griffith and Dr M. I. Finley, from whom I have had a vast amount of good counsel and helpful criticism. They will not agree with all I have said, but they have saved me from many more avoidable errors and forced me to look afresh at a large number of questions.

All dates are BC except when otherwise stated.

GLOSSARY

Anchisteia Close relationship; hence the group of kinsmen acknowledged by law for purposes such as the succession to a deceased person's estate.

Andreia Cretan word, equivalent to *syssitia* (q.v.), but also with family connotations. See Chapter VIII. Singular *andreion*, though this form is not found in the ancient sources.

Cleruch An Athenian given a holding of land by the state outside Attica, whether he actually lived there or was merely an absentee landlord. A cleruchy is a group of cleruchs.

Deme English form of *demos*, people; also a local unit within Attica (and possibly elsewhere) used in classical times as the group for maintaining the register of citizens.

Dokimasia Preliminary examination undergone by all Athenians at the time of their enrolment as full citizens, and the chief (perhaps all) magistrates before they were admitted to their office.

Engye Betrothal agreement, essential preliminary to legal marriage in classical Athens, except for *epikleroi*.

Enktesis The right to own land and other real property; its grant was equivalent to a grant of citizenship.

Ephebos Young citizen undergoing two years of military training. Plural *epheboi*. *Ephebia* was the organization for conducting the training.

Epidikasia Legal action before the Athenian Archon to claim the right to marry an *epikleros* or to gain possession of an estate which lacked an established heir. *Epidikos* means liable to claim by *epidikasia*.

Epikleros Girl (or woman) without living brothers at the time of her father's death. See Chapter VI. Plural *epikleroi*.

Genos (plural *genē*) Two meanings. 1 A group of families claiming descent from a common (usually heroic) ancestor. 2 Family, in a wide and general sense, like the English word. *Gennētai* are fellow-members of a *genos*.

Hetaira A female companion, usually a euphemism for a high-class prostitute. *Hetairos*, the masculine form of the word, usually lacks the sexual implication,

12

meaning a comrade, often in arms or in an aristocratic or oligarchic association. A *hetaireia* is an association of *hetairoi*.

Homoios   Like or equal, hence a Spartan full citizen, or Spartiate.

Hoplite   A fully-armed infantry soldier.

Kleros (also *klaros*, plural *kleroi*; *klaroi*)   An allotment of land, also the estate of a deceased person, hence *epikleros* means a girl who transmitted one to her children.

Kyrios (feminine *kyria*)   The person who has the legal power to dispose of the property or to manage the affairs of a person who is not fully his (or her) own *kyrios*, such as woman or a minor. Hence *kyrieia* is full ownership or headship of a family.

Liturgy   A form of taxation (especially in classical Athens) imposed on the richer citizens; the most frequent was the trierarchy, q.v., but many public spectacles and festivals were financed by liturgies.

Medism   Supporting the Persian side in the struggles with the Greeks.

Metics   Greeks who lived more or less permanently in a city not their own, in which they did not have citizen-rights; metics were therefore *xenoi*, q.v.

Neodamodeis   Inferior citizens in Sparta, Chapter VIII, note 42.

Orgeones   Associations in Athens, probably akin to members of craft-guilds.

Oikos   A family, including its property as well as its human members, also the group in which an Athenian citizen was registered in his phratry and perhaps in his deme also, Chapter IV. Plural *oikoi*. *Oikeioi* means members of the *oikos*, but the meaning is sometimes stretched to mean kinsmen generally.

Phratry   A group in Athens of obscure origin, but great importance, at least in the social field, Chapter I. Members of a phratry were *phrateres*.

Stasis   Political strife within a city-state.

Syssitia   Spartan men's messes, also found in other cities. Singular *syssition*, not found in the ancient sources.

Temenos (plural *temenē*)   A parcel of land set aside for the service of a god or spirit, or (in early times) for a king or other leader.

Thetes   Athenians too poor to own a suit of armour, and hence unable to serve in the army; they rowed in the fleet.

Thiasos   Association in Athens smaller than the phratry; membership was not always hereditary.

Trierarch   Citizen, especially Athenian, taxed by being made responsible for equipping a trireme (warship), and (sometimes) commanding it on service, though this was often done by deputy. *Trierarchy* is the office of trierarch, sometimes shared by two or more trierarchs.

Xenos (also *xeinos*, *xsenos*)   An outsider admitted into a closed society, used both of visitors to a family circle and of foreigners allowed to reside in a city not their own, Chapter I (fin.) and Chapter V, note 86, q.v. for *proxenos*. Plural *xenoi*, *xeinoi* etc.

Zeugitai   The hoplite class at Athens.

CHAPTER I

THE FAMILY
IN THE CITY-STATE

THE CHARACTER OF THE OIKOS

ARISTOTLE BEGAN his work on Politics[1] by stating that it is necessary to break down communities into their smallest parts in order to understand the different characteristics of each. The smallest unit of the state is the family, the *oikos*, which is comprised of the three elements, the male, the female and the servant. The servant is defined as that which comes under the rule of another to obtain security; to Hesiod, says Aristotle, this is the plough-ox (the servant of the poor), to political man (i.e. man of the *polis* or city-state) it is his slave. Male and female have a natural instinct to procreate themselves successors, says Aristotle, an instinct common also to all living creatures, and this introduces into the family a fourth element, the children.

A further essential element in the *oikos* was its means of subsistence; that Aristotle agreed that this was so is proved both by his statement that the members of an *oikos* are those who feed together,[2] and by his subsequent remark that some call the obtaining and management of possessions the whole of household management.[3] An *oikos* that could not support its members was, to the Greeks, no *oikos* at all.

An *oikos* without children was also not fully an *oikos*.[4] Every Greek family looked backwards and forwards all the time. It looked backwards to its supposed first founder, and shared a religious worship with others with a similar belief; it also looked forwards to its own continuance, and to the preservation for as many future generations as possible of the cult of the family which the living members practised in the interest of the dead. The son of a house was therefore (in the best period of the Greek *polis*) under a strong obligation to marry and procreate an heir for the *oikos* in order to keep the *oikos* alive, and he himself both felt that obligation and, so far as we can see, acted upon it. The other requirement, however, that the *oikos* must be able to support its members, was also not forgotten. No Greek would have accepted the idea that every man has a right to marry and beget children if he wants to; marriage was for those who could afford it. Consequently, when a father's *oikos* was not large enough to provide a livelihood for several sons, some of them would leave it to seek their fortune away from home, enlisting as mercenary soldiers or as sailors, or establishing for themselves a new home as members of a colony when their own (or another) city called for volunteers.[5]

An *oikos* was therefore a living organism which required to be renewed every generation to remain alive; it supported its living members' needs for food, and its deceased members' needs for the performance of cult rituals. A childless *oikos* was visibly dying—no man's life-span is all that long—so we may well appreciate the joy with which a child, and especially the first-born son of a family, was received.

THE INDIVIDUAL AND THE OIKOS

The relationship between individual and *oikos* exhibits considerable variations in the different ages and communities of the Greek world. In the Homeric world the individual hero (the only class for which we can say anything significant) was wholly responsible for it, and wholly in command of it, in so far as his power enabled him to be.[6] In the *polis* communities of old Greece, the ancestors' land, and their tombs, which were the evidence of their ancient ownership and the object of the family's cult, provided strong unifying bonds within which the individual lived as a member of his *oikos*. Here too every *oikos* was itself a member of one or more larger groups, the clan (*genos*), the phratry, the tribe (*phyle*), the deme, whose members were fully members of the *polis*. Membership of these larger units was secured through membership of an *oikos*, so that the individual was never free of the units to which he belonged. In the colonial settlements, especially in Ionia and Sicily, however, the individuals who went

1 Zeus, the father of the Olympian gods, was particularly associated with family religion. On this second-century stone relief, found near Corinth, he sits enthroned at the right; by him stands a goddess, presumably Hera, his wife. At the altar under a sacred tree tied with a sash stand a father, mother and child, while to the left stand other members of the family, and beyond the tree a memorial *stele* is visible, surmounted by two figures who presumably represent deceased relatives. The top of the stone is carved to suggest a roof (*cf.* Pls. *2*, *3* and *31*).

2, 3 Aristarche (above) and [Aris]toboule record their families' worship of
Zeus Meilichios in a shrine near Athens; note the cornucopia (below), symbol
of plenty, and the pig, the customary offering (Xenophon, *Anab.* VII, 8), which
stands ready for sacrifice.

out were freed from their ancestral *oikoi* by their emigration, and
however successful the attempts to foster the spirit of unity and
civic-consciousness may have been, the web of family tradition
and *oikos*-membership was never so strong, since it was not rooted
in *oikoi* (lands and houses in particular) and cults which the families
felt had been vested in them by right of descent from some
mythical, heroic founder.[7]

This lack of cohesiveness in society had two principal results:
it made these city-states much less exclusive than those of the
motherland, but it also made them politically much less stable,
with the result that they came frequently under the rule of tyrants.
Syracuse, for example, despite the dreadful experiences of the
tyranny of Dionysius I and his successors (405–344), remained less
than thirty years under the constitutional rule established by
Timoleon before it again came under a tyranny, that of Aga-
thocles, in 316.[8] Regular features of these and similar tyrannies
were transplantations of whole populations, expulsions of old
citizens, and enrolments of new ones, who were often non-Greek
mercenaries, and redistributions of lands, houses and other
property which formed an essential part of the *oikoi* of the civic
communities of old Greece. Settling down into a homogeneous
and reasonably cohesive society always remained, therefore, a task
whose accomplishment tended to elude them.

In earlier times, other Greek communities in Southern Italy and
Sicily had tried to compensate for their lack of deep roots in the
soil by establishing codes of law and quasi-religious or philosophical societies which provided the cohesive element in the
state. Zaleucus of Locri in Italy is reputed to have been the first
compiler of a code of laws in the Greek world; this was perhaps
in the mid-seventh century BC. Another famous lawgiver was
Charondas of Catana, whose laws were also used in Rhegium and
other towns of this area; those which have survived in our
ancient sources[9] are much concerned with the family, though they
are said to have covered other fields of law as well. He probably
worked in the sixth century BC, earlier than the philosopher
Pythagoras, who came to Croton towards the end of that century.[10] Croton was then a town which already had a flourishing

school of medicine and physical culture, but it was under the cohesive discipline of the Pythagorean societies that it rose to its greatest prosperity and success, in the first half of the fifth century.

Politically, these and most of the other city-states of this area were aristocratic, as were the cities of the Aegean world from which came the greatest of the individualistic poets—Lesbos, whose society lives for us in the poetry of Alcaeus and Sappho in the early sixth century,[11] and Paros, the home of Archilochus at least one generation earlier, whose bastard birth was no doubt ultimately responsible for his rejection as a suitable husband for Neoboule, whose hand he had been promised.[12]

In sharp contrast with these individualists, however, stand the roughly contemporary poets of mainland Greece, Theognis and Solon, the former proclaiming in Megara the ideals of an aristocratic society which had lost its monopoly of political power,[13] while Solon in Athens sought to justify his new code of laws, with its transfer of ultimate responsibility for justice from the family to the city's magistrates, by advocating the familiar aristocratic ideal that every man should know his place;[14] the ancient leaders of the state should lead it, the mass of the people should accept an underprivileged position, though one in which their rights were supported by the force of law. In these and other mainland communities the process of emancipating the individual from his family units was very slow indeed, as was the loss of political power by the old aristocratic families even in Athens, the most democratic of these states, whose leaders, with the single exception of Themistocles, were drawn from the noble families until the death of Pericles in 429.[15] This age (the last half of the fifth century) was, however, also the age of the Sophists, those itinerant teachers who came to mainland Greece, and Athens in particular, from both the Aegean and the western Greek worlds. They offered a challenge to all the old accepted codes of behaviour and values, and their influence, combined no doubt with the divisive effects of the Peloponnesian War (431–404), perhaps set in motion that greater individualism which is the mark of the fourth century, and against which Plato wrote his *Republic* and *Laws*.[16] The end of the independence of the city-states at the hands of the Macedonian monarchy at the end of that century also swelled the tide of individualism, and the Hellenistic Age (*i.e.*, after Alexander's death in 323) reveals a much greater freedom of action for individuals in relation to their families, and a much lessened sense of responsibility towards them, as towards the state also. The tightly-knit corporation of the city and the unity of the family were closely interdependent, and were the basis and the product of the greatest age of the city-states. Therefore (to return to Aristotle) the study of the family is the study of two relationships: the *oikos* as an independent unit, especially the relationships of the free members,[17] and the *oikos* as a constituent unit of the larger units out of which the city-state, or *polis*, was composed.

THE OIKOS AND ITS KYRIOS

Greek society was (and is) patriarchal: the master of the *oikos* was the head of the family, its *kyrios*, as its governor, governing the slaves as master, the children as a sort of king because of their affection for him and his greater age, his wife like a political leader, differing from normal political leadership only in that this relationship does not involve change of leaders, as self-governing states normally change their leaders, but the husband is always the head of the family.[18]

Headship of a family, *kyrieia* (κυρίεια), and the status of *kyrios* (κύριος), is an important feature of all Greek family life. In Homer it is taken for granted, in democratic Athens it is defined by the lawyers in certain aspects; even in Sparta it is implied in the status of full citizen, *homoios* (ὅμοιος), of Spartiate rank, above thirty years old, who alone was allowed a share in political life, and to set up house and live with his wife.

Only a man could be *kyrios* of a family. This is not to say that women could not look after a man's property when he was absent on military service or abroad, whether for trade or state service. Obviously they could; we can quote as examples Penelope in Homer, who managed at least to prevent Odysseus' house being taken over during his absence, or the trierarch of the Demosthenic speech numbered XLVII,[19] who left his wife in

charge of his estate close by the Hippodrome. Nor does it mean
that when a man died his widow did not look after his possessions
until his heir was established, or until the guardian to his children,
if they were minors, had taken charge of their property. For such
periods women were said to be in control of possessions, *kyria*,[20]
(κυρία), but these periods have the essential quality of the temporary, pending the return of the actual *kyrios*, or the establishment of a new one in possession of the property. Such a position
does not convey the right to make decisions regarding the disposal of property, especially disposal of the essential element in
the property of the *oikos*, its *kleros* or allotment of land. Before
the Hellenistic Age, only at Sparta do we hear that the women
had the power in their husbands' absence to dispose even of real-
estate,[21] and here, as elsewhere also, only daughters had the right
of succession to the usufruct of their father's property for their
lifetime clearly established by law, and the right and duty to
transmit it to their children.

THE OIKOS AND ITS LANDS

As the *polis* never ceased to rest on an agrarian basis,[22] so the
family's lands always remained of fundamental importance. It is
commonly supposed, both from what traces of early systems of
land-holding survive, and from the practices adopted when
colonial settlements were made,[23] that land—arable land, that is—
was initially divided into *kleroi* which were allotted to the various
heads of the kinship-groups of the settlers, except for lands designated as *temenē* (singular *temenos*) which were in later times dedicated to the gods, but in primitive times were allocated to the
chief, who was also the priest and claimed heroic—*i.e.*, semi-divine
—status. Whether or not such *kleroi* were or had ever been equal
is unknown; it was a principle of democratic propagandists that
they should be equal, but it is much more likely in an early aristocratic age that the division was unequal.[24] Aristotle declares that
'in many cities it was not even lawful to sell the *kleros* which had
first been allocated'[25] (*sc.* to a family); clearly this rule was designed to prevent undue accumulations of land by individuals.
Aristotle also speaks of instances at Corinth and Thebes[26] where

it is said that the number of *oikoi* was by law to be prevented from falling. In Athens, it is generally agreed, the rule that land was not to be alienated from a kinship-group lasted into historical times, though the point at which it became possible to alienate it is disputed, various dates from Solon[27] to the Peloponnesian War being proposed.[28]

Certainly, as N. G. L. Hammond has pointed out,[29] Thucydides believed that in 431 the rural population of Attica was living on the land which they had occupied for many generations, and inalienability of land may be the best explanation of how it came about that neither the Alcmaeonidae, banished after the Cylonian conspiracy in the seventh century, nor Peisistratus' exiled opponents became impoverished in their exile a century later (nor, we may add, did Peisistratus himself). Exile in the fourth century automatically carried with it confiscation of goods and lands. On the other hand, the careful provisions of the law on ostracism, first used in 488,[30] in which it was specified that property should not be confiscated, carry the suggestion that in the early fifth century an exile existed in which property would be confiscated. The fact that land was in general not alienated before 431 cannot be taken to mean that it could not be.

Inalienability of land, however, is a limitation on the power even of a *kyrios*. It is also a reminder that modern notions of ownership may be misleading, and suggests that we should not look on the *kyrios* of an *oikos* as an individual owner, but as the present custodian of what belongs to his family, past, present and, if he is successful in procreating a son, future.[31] In consequence, even when it was legal to dispose of ancestral land, it was deemed disgraceful to do so. In Plato's will there is a marked contrast between his treatment of his ancestral farm and the one he bought.[32] To be a man who sells ancestral land is an insult used by politicians,[33] and the same allegation is used as a consideration detrimental to an opponent in law.[34] The presence of family tombs on land was certainly one reason, but civic duty and the maintenance of the *oikoi* was undoubtedly another. Moreover, in *polis*-communities only a citizen of the *polis* was entitled to own land in the domain of the *polis*;[35] the only exceptions to this rule were a few specially privileged aliens who were explicitly granted this right (known as *enktesis*, ἔγκτησις). It therefore follows that minors always had to have a guardian if their father had died before they were of age to assume the *kyrieia* of their property, and that every woman had to have a *kyrios* all her life.[36] Frequently—before her marriage, while she was married, and when she had been widowed but had an adult son—a woman's *kyrios*, and the *kyrios* of the property which had been set aside for her maintenance were the same person, but when a widow was left with an infant son, his guardian was custodian of the property, since it was held in trust for her son, who would ultimately inherit it, while control of her personal status (*i.e.*, whether she was remarried or not) reverted to her own family's *kyrios*.

Women did not in the fullest sense own landed property at any stage in Greek history (except in Sparta),[37] but there were occasions on which a man had only female children; when this disaster occurred, the Greeks' interest in maintaining the continuity of the families was so great that they arranged for such girls to be married to their nearest agnatic relative (a father's brother—*i.e.*, an uncle—if possible) in order to re-establish the family in the next generation. Such girls were in Athens given the name of *epikleros* (ἐπίκληρος), a word sometimes mistranslated as 'heiress'.[38] Heiress and *epikleros* do not correspond, since an *epikleros* never owned 'her' property, in that it was not within her power to dispose of it except through a child; conversely, however, it could not legally be alienated from her as long as she lived.[39] The arrangements for the marriage of an *epikleros* were therefore of the deepest concern both to her relatives and to the state, and at Athens at least and at Gortyn in Crete and elsewhere we can prove the existence of elaborate legal provisions to ensure that a lack of sons did not cause a family to become extinct, and that the future of girls without brothers was not simply left in the hands of their father's kinsmen.

Men without natural heirs could also adopt sons. We do not know how early this was possible in Athens, but there are traces in Homer,[40] so that it may have been admissible from the earliest times. An adopted son, however, was also not wholly *kyrios* of the *oikos* he inherited, since he could dispose of it only by begetting a son, and not by will. There is also some evidence[41] that at Athens an *oikos* did not become registered in the name of an adopted son until he had begotten a son and registered him in the *oikos* of his adoptive father, thus providing two generations of successors to the *oikos*.

Women's inability to own property and to dispose of it also had the result that households consisting of one woman or a group of women and no men were virtually unknown;[42] households therefore often included elderly women who were either in the master's *kyrieia* or put themselves under his protection. That this was very common is certain, and it was further encouraged by law, since in Athens at least children were legally obliged to maintain their parents in their old age.[43] The fact that her husband's mother was living in the house cannot always have been welcome to a young wife, and Plato at least thought that it was undesirable,[44] but it did help to prevent one of the great social problems of modern times—the loneliness of the old.

THE OIKOS AND THE LARGER UNITS IN THE STATE

Beyond the *oikos* to which a man belonged lay the wider kinship-groups, the *genos* (in the plural *genē*), or clan, and the phratry, or brotherhood. What the origins of these groups were we do not know; members of the same *genos* traced their pedigree back to a common ancestor, but it was freely acknowledged even in ancient times[45] that the members of the same *genos* (*gennētai*) were not necessarily kinsmen, and that outsiders had been admitted.

It was perhaps as a result of this that there were almost social class-divisions amongst the *gennētai*. There were noble houses who provided in settled conditions the political leadership of the *genē*,[46] and who held the hereditary priesthoods, and probably considered themselves to be the genuine lineal descendants of the ancestor-hero; they were known in Athens as *Eupatridae*.[47] Some *gennētai* were also known as *homogalaktes*—sharers of the same milk; there is no agreement among scholars about what this implies. If it meant 'sharers of the same mother's milk', then it must mean the highest of the high-born, who were descended not merely from a common father but also from a common mother, the principal wife no doubt.[48] It is nowadays more usually thought to have described some sort of foster-brother,[49] or outsider brought into the family and participating there in the sacrifice of milk which belonged to the cult of the family hearth.[50]

The defence of the family against *force majeure* was perhaps the principal motive for incorporating outsiders into *genē*.[51] That this was so is suggested by the fact that *genē* appear to have been amongst the early military subdivisions of the Athenian state in the opinion of the author of *Ath. Pol.*,[52] from whom it descended into the lexica of late antiquity, such as that of Harpocration.

Genos, however, is an elusive term; besides the wider group of nominal kinsmen the *genos* also included a man's actual kinsmen, those within the legally acknowledged kinship-group. The Greek for next of kin is 'the nearest in *genos*'[53] and succession to men who lacked sons was always determined in terms of the *genos*, preference being given to those who were descended through the male line. This must suggest that in the settlement-age the groups who settled the Greek countryside and divided up the agricultural land believed themselves to be related to one another, though whether this relationship was one of actual kinship or the sort of kinship described by the lexicographers (above) is impossible to discover.[54]

An *oikos* also belonged to a phratry. The origins of phratries are also obscure; they appear once in Homer[55] as unmistakably military units, and they appear in a fragment of *Ath. Pol.* as the military unit larger than the *genos*.[56] Phratries have been explained as local self-defence groups,[57] or as the oldest unions of a number of families,[58] but the military group, the 'blood-brotherhood', seems to be a more satisfactory explanation for two reasons, one philological, the other sociological. Philologically *phrater* (φράτηρ) is a form of the Indo-European word for brother by blood, one born of the same parents (as in Latin, for example, the word is *frater*), yet nowhere in the Greek dialects is *phrater* used in this sense;[59] it is always used to mean a member of the same phratry, and different words were adopted for brothers by birth. In society the evidence comes from the rules about exacting penalties from homicides, the first field of law, perhaps, in which in the most primitive times rules had to be established under which the various family-groups could regulate their relationships.[60] In Athenian law the duty of avenging a violent death (or securing purification) was laid on the *oikeioi*, the members of the *oikos*, failing whom it fell not on the *genos*, but on the phratry,[61] despite the fact that the phratry played no part in determining the succession-rights to the *oikos* of the deceased. In historical times, however, in Athens the phratries had become associated with the *oikoi* and the (locally determined) demes, whose rolls comprised the citizen-registers, and for military purposes had been supplanted by groups of comrades (*hetaireiai*),[62] or sharers in the tent (σύσκηνοι),[63] and, when the classes of *epheboi* (young soldiers) were organized (not certainly before the fourth century),[64] the companies of men who had trained together between the ages of eighteen and twenty.

THE OIKOS IN RELIGION

All Greek social groups were also religious unions, whose management lay in the hands of the head.[65] In Athens, the cult of the *oikos* itself with its *kleros* of land, the local group of which the *kyrios* of the *oikos* was head, was that of Zeus Herkeios, and many aspects of family religion are associated with Zeus[66] (*Pls. 1–3*). The cult of the family as part of the *genos*, or more probably of all the families of all the *genē* corporately (since each *genos* also had its own individual ancestor-hero), was that of Apollo Patroös.[67] The cult of the phratries, also common to all, was that of Zeus Phratrios, for which each phratry had its own altar at which the sacrifices were performed.[68]

When a citizen became a candidate for one of the higher magistracies (or perhaps all offices) he was required to answer the question 'have you an Apollo Patroös and a Zeus Herkeios, and where are their shrines?'; this part of the *dokimasia* (δοκιμασία), or preliminary scrutiny of magistrates,[69] appears to be ancient, and there is no doubt that membership of associations which owned these cults was proof of genuine Athenian citizenship—Socrates for example was proud of belonging to them.[70] On the other hand, it appears not to have been necessary to have a Zeus Phratrios, a fact which militates against the assertion that phratry-membership was necessary for full citizenship.[71]

The common gods of all the *kleroi*, *genē* and phratries, however, were a feature of democratic societies: Aristotle in the *Politics*[72] mentions the amalgamation of private cults as one means of making a *polis* more democratic, but the families provided the origin of the state cults, and their cults continued to exist beside the state cults. The state had its own shrines of Zeus Herkeios (in the forecourt of the Mycenaean palace on the Acropolis, under the sacred olive tree) and Apollo Patroös (in the Agora),[73] but private shrines of *genē* to Apollo Patroös are known,[74] and it is clear from the lexicographers[75] that shrines of Zeus Herkeios were to be found in individuals' courtyards; the failure of the archaeologists to find them is therefore not surprising. In the case of the phratries, the Demotionidae for example had their own altar to Zeus Phratrios on the ancestral site of Decelea,[76] and their own festival days besides the state festival of the Apatouria.[77] In other cases the state simply took over the family festivals, leaving the original priestly families in charge of the cult.[78]

KINSHIP AND THE OIKOS

The organization of city-states, however, required that kinship should be legally defined; in Crete, at Gortyn, the successive kin-ship-groups entitled to inherit from a man or woman who had died are enumerated in respect of movable property, preference being given to direct lineal heirs, then to collateral relations in order of proximity of common parents; ultimately 'those of the household who compose the *klaros*'—that is, those associated with the real property, even if not kin by any direct descent—become the heirs to the movables.[79]

In Athens the democracy had by the fourth century defined the limits of kinship recognized by the law to children of first cousins;[80] this kinship-group, *anchisteia* (ἀγχίστεια), was the group which was entitled, in due order, to succeed to vacant estates, and had legal duties and responsibilities in case of death within the group, especially if it was death by violence; the *anchisteia* was obliged to bury its own dead, and to seek vengeance, or at least purification, for the violent death of any of its members. This *anchisteia* was also the limit chosen by Plato in his Republic as suitable for similar duties in cases of homicide, and may have been general in the Greek world.[81] Unfortunately, however, its interpretation, at least by the orators, is rather loose, and 'son of a first cousin' is also used to describe the son of a father's first cousin, who is of course a second cousin to the person spoken about or the speaker himself; whether this confusion is a mere matter of successful legerdemain by the orators, or a genuine doubt, is a matter on which there is no absolute certainty, and some disagreement among scholars.[82] We cannot say how early this definition began; it may well be post-Solonian and date from the period of the Peloponnesian War (late fifth century) which broke up many of the old compact local kinship-groups,[83] and caused heavy losses of citizens, including whole families in the plague,[84] and the contemporary growth of the passion for litigation. A possible—and perhaps more likely—date, however, is the time when the liberation of the individual *oikoi* from their *genos* made a definition of the limits of the kinship-group highly desirable— that is, in Solon's day, in the early sixth century.

THE OIKOS AND THE LAW

As in all primitive societies, the most important kinship-groups among the Greeks of the age of settlement were those of the most important families, whether their 'importance' lay in their military leadership or priestly functions, or (most usually) both.[85] Communities remained essentially tribes until the interrelationships of the kinship-groups, and of the individuals within these groups, came under the regulation of a law which was not just the monopoly of the noble, priestly families, but was known —or at least knowable—to all. This common knowledge of the law was the foundation of the city-state; the dawn of Greek history in the seventh and sixth centuries BC is therefore the age of the lawgivers, so-called:[86] part of their work was political—the establishment of a constitution containing a political structure— but most of it was concerned with establishing a code of laws;

that is, they tried to establish rules by which the claims of different families in their relations with other families could be regulated. These claims, like those regulated by all codes of laws, fell broadly into the two classes of property-claims and claims concerning persons. Property-claims include especially those concerning land and houses, real-estate, and the rights to acquire, own and transmit it to successors—claims, in fact, which affect primarily the family's means of subsistence. In claims concerning persons the family was concerned both because injury to persons might affect a family's ability to maintain itself (for example through the disabling of the breadwinner) and because its religious ties and honour might be affected, as for example in cases of murder, rape or seduction. Honour in this last sense certainly had religious undertones, but it had also practical, political consequences as well, since in city-states (Sparta excepted of course) a child not born in wedlock had no kinship rights or claims over property belonging to the family of its mother. The bastard, and the state of bastardy, are important subjects in Greek law, and so, in consequence, are rape, seduction and virginity. The vital importance of the family for the state is well illustrated by the fact that all legal cases affecting the family in Athens were classed as public and not private;[87] that is to say, it was open to any person, not merely the injured party, to take the initiative in prosecuting a suspected offender, and the prosecutor was in most cases also exempt from the statutory penalties which were normally attached to a prosecutor who failed to convince one-fifth of the jury. In a state which lacked a public prosecutor it is hard to think of more active steps which could have been taken to ensure that the family was fully protected in its rights by the law.

THE OIKOS AND ITS XENOI

An *oikos* also included outsiders who had a right to come in, or whom the master of the house accepted into the *oikos*. These may be said to have been of two classes, those who came into the *oikos* in order to serve it, and by their labour to help to sustain it, and those who came in only on a temporary basis, as visitors. The former comprised principally the slaves and the animals which worked on the farm and the beasts of burden, the latter the *xenos* (plural *xenoi*), a word which is the Greek for both host and guest. The act of sharing house and board made the slave fully a member of the family;[88] in fourth-century Athens, and probably from very much earlier, a slave was made a member of the family ceremonially by having nuts and dried fruits scattered over him by the mistress of the house when he came into it, a ritual which also greeted the bride when she first entered her husband's house.[89] Slaves were initiated into the cult of the family's gods, and normally took part in the family's religious festivals.[90] The plough-ox too was regarded as an intrinsic part of the family, as Aristotle says.[91] This statement cannot be taken too literally, nor as having that meaning in the fullest sense, but that there was a very strong bond of fellow-feeling between a peasant and his oxen is attested by the fact that the Athenians would never sacrifice a ploughing-ox, nor one which had been harnessed (*sc.* to a cart)— it was regarded as 'a farm-worker and a partner in the labours of men',[92] and it is shown on the stage in the touching scene in Aristophanes' *Acharnians* when the peasant comes onto the stage to recover his lost plough-oxen.[93]

The *xenoi* were a part of the Greek idea of the family, and fair treatment of (and respect for) their *xenoi* was among the 'unwritten commandments' upon which the ethical standards of the *polis* were based, 'that you should honour the gods, your parents and your *xenoi*'.[94] *Xenoi* were hereditary among the noble families, accustomed to travel away from their homesteads for trade, interest or even piracy and war, and to a lesser extent the same was doubtless true of humbler folk; it was considered scandalous to injure one with whom you had shared in table and salt,[95] while to give shelter to a traveller from another city was a virtuous act, often (in myth) bringing reward to the doer, while to turn away a suppliant at the altar was an act that called down divine vengeance.[96]

The importance of the *xenos* in the Homeric poems is particularly great, no doubt because of the aristocratic society they portray, and that society must be first considered, not least because of the fact that Homer was the basic educational medium in Greece, and hence the institutions and ideas of the society he portrayed cannot but have been influential in shaping Greek thought in a way in which the historical Mycenaean society did not.

CHAPTER II

THE FAMILY
IN HOMERIC SOCIETY

THE UNITY OF THE OIKOS

IN THE SOCIETY of the Homeric poems,[1] the ambitions, hopes, desires and fears of the heroes are centred in their families, who are included in numerous instances where wishes for good and for ill are expressed. Thus Odysseus thanked Alcinous for his hospitality and for the arrangements for his return home in the words, 'When I return, may I find my good wife at home and my dear ones all safe and sound, and may you who remain here bring happiness to your families, your good wives and your children; may the gods give you every kind of blessing and no harm strike your people'.[2] Similarly, in the curses invoked upon the side which breaks the treaty while Paris and Menelaus duel, their families were involved; both the armies pray 'Whoever first shall do violence to this sworn treaty, as this wine is poured out in sacrifice, so may their brains be split, theirs and their children's alike, and may their wives be subjected to others'.[3] Similarly, to curse Phoenix his father prayed that he should be childless for ever, thus destroying his hopes for posterity, whereas Elpenor, imploring Odysseus not to leave him unburied, adjured him 'by your wife, by your father, by Telemachus your son'.[4]

That the family should continue to flourish economically is equally an object of the deepest concern; Menelaus can say 'Easy it is to recognize the son of a man to whom Zeus has given success in marriage and begetting sons, even as now he has given to Nestor all his days, and the gift of a green old age prospering in his house, and that of having sons who are both intelligent and warriors of the highest rank'; and 'to attain a green and prosperous old age and to bring up a fine son' had been Odysseus' prayer to the gods.[5]

33

Peleus, father of Achilles, it is said, had both good gifts and bad from the gods; 'though he outdid all men in good fortune and wealth and, though a man, secured a goddess to wife, yet the gods inflicted evil even upon him in that he begot only one son fated to die young'.[6] Achilles himself expressed his grief for Patroclus in terms of the worst things he could imagine: 'Nothing worse than this could I suffer, not if I should hear of my father's death . . . nor though it was my beloved son who is being brought up in Scyros . . . I had trusted that I should be the only one to perish, but that Patroclus . . . should bring Neoptolemus to Phthia and show him everything, my treasure, my servants and my great hall with its high roof'.[7]

Death itself on the other hand was regarded as not so terrible, especially if it was death with honour. It is true that Hades is a gloomy, depressing place, without the joys of even the hardest human life,[8] but for a hero death in the act of saving his family and its livelihood was bearable. Hector can say 'But fight, all of you, by the ships; and if one of you is struck by bolt or spear and meets the doom of death he must die; it is no disgraceful thing for a man to die in defence of his country; but his wife will be left safe behind and his children, with his house and his lands secure if the Achaeans sail home in their ships'.[9] The fate of a captured city conjures up the most dismal pictures in the Homeric poems. In the story of Meleager, the hero was deaf to the entreaties of his father and mother and brothers and his companions and friends for whom he felt most affection; he would not go out and fight until his wife, Cleopatra, 'begged him with tears and recited to him all the tragic sufferings which fall upon men whose city is taken in war—they kill the menfolk, fire consumes the citadel and other men bear off the children and the buxom married women'.[10]

It is when we compare sentiments like these with the urgings to patriotism from the orators and dramatists of the city-states, who include—as for example Aeschylus does in *Persae* 403–5— along with children and wives the altars of the city's gods, and the ancestors' tombs, that we can appreciate how completely family-centred the society of the Homeric poems is. Not even the wider family groupings seem to have much importance, for,

4 The plaster friezes on a Late Minoan sarcophagus provide a contrast between the white-armed women worshippers and the darker colour used to represent the male piper. As a crowned woman dressed in typical Minoan style approaches, blood is flowing from the neck of the trussed bull on the table. A woman, perhaps a priestess, wearing a shorter skirt which appears to be made of an animal's skin, is officiating at the altar. Other white-armed women are seen in *Pls. 14, 22*, both of the sixth century.

5, 6 Large Attic burial vases (5 ft. high) of the eighth century reveal their aristocratic owners' interests. The frieze above suggests a love of chariots, horses and warfare. Between the chariots warriors battle with swords and spears; the figures on the right with their strange shield may represent the 'Siamese twins' mentioned by Homer, who describes similar encounters, except that in the *Iliad* the throwing-spears are usually discharged before swords are drawn. The holes in the frieze must have been made by the owner, and are not part of the original design. Below, a figure in a shroud lies on a bier. The mourners are stylized without distinction of age or sex except for the child standing next the bier, and, below it, two men on stools are distinguished from the two skirted women sitting on the ground.

though it appears at times that it is good to have kinsmen for vengeance or support, it is clearly implied that the succession of distant kinsmen to one's possessions was a serious misfortune to be avoided by all possible means, and a man's clan as a body with corporate aspirations and corporate religious bonds seems quite foreign to the Homeric world.[10a]

PARENTAGE OF HEROES

The immediate, conjugal family, however, was not a Homeric hero's only concern; his parentage was equally important. All heroes of any standing are known by their patronymic, some by their patronymic almost as often as they are by their own name,[11] and we know the grandfathers of many as well. This is true of many minor figures also, even those who are introduced only to be killed.[12] Beyond these normal limits, there are several longer genealogies. Glaucus can trace his lineage back five generations, though he has little knowledge beyond his grandfather Bellerophon, and acknowledges amongst his collateral relatives only his first cousin Sarpedon. Aeneas can go back seven generations, but Erichthonius, six generations back, is the only distant ancestor who is more than a name; Aeneas' collateral relatives are recognized back to the fourth generation, but this recognition of such distant relatives is both unusual, and probably appears here with the specific object of showing Aeneas' possible claim to kingship in Troy on the deaths of Hector and Priam.[13] Greeks apparently always stop at their great-grandfathers; this is probably connected with the customarily accepted limitation of the family—the wider kinship-group acknowledged for legal purposes—to those who shared a common great-grandparent,[14] but it must also be remembered that Homeric heroes liked to trace their descent back to a god, beyond whom genealogy would not attempt to penetrate; Achilles was two generations only from Zeus, as was Idomeneus.[15] Not all heroes, however, trace their descent back to the gods; in Homer neither Diomedes nor Telemachus does so, nor does the prophet Theoclymenus; in his pedigree the hereditary gift of prophecy is most stressed, since this was its most important element, and the proof of his credentials.[16] The assertion of a claim to status by pedigree is the likeliest explanation of the growth of catalogue poetry (in which genealogies played a large part), as the hereditary leaders of the aristocratic age in Greece sought to establish their claims to rule by prerogative of descent from the ruling gods.[17]

ASSERTION OF HEROIC STATUS

Pride in lineage was also an element which made the Homeric hero feel obliged to behave in a heroic way. Odysseus bade Telemachus 'not to shame his father's race, who of old have always excelled in might and manly courage at all times'; Hippolochus' parting instructions to Glaucus were similar.[18] Personal honour as a hero, an *agathos*,[19] however, made the same demands, as Hector remarked to Andromache;[20] and when Nestor adjured the Greeks to be brave he bade them 'put *aidos* in their hearts and remember their families, children, wives, possessions, parents'.[21]

The claim to be a hero, an *agathos*, depended in the first place upon family, but high birth was not enough; to sustain the claim other qualifications were required, the principal one being the strength and fighting ability necessary to protect a hero's family and possessions from would-be marauders, and perhaps also the ability to augment his possessions by plunder.[22] For the individual hero this meant the ability to take vengeance in person upon individuals who molested him and his *oikos*; for the *basileus*, one of the higher chiefs, there was in addition the ability to marshal other heroes to support him in larger-scale struggles, and a man's rank in the hierarchy of heroes depended on the number and the quality of his following.

Apart from the *Catalogue* in Book II of the *Iliad*,[23] the story of Telemachus' assertion of his status in *Odyssey* 2 and 4 demonstrates this. The suitors of Penelope did not deny his claim to be master of his house, and hence a member of the circle of *agathoi*, but he came to be regarded as a threat to them only when he summoned an assembly, denounced the suitors and raised himself a following with which he manned a ship and sailed off to Pylos and Sparta in defiance of the wishes of the suitors. The calling of the assembly was itself important, for this prerogative appears to have been confined to the king, since we are told it had not happened since Odysseus left, but it was not the essential action which proved Telemachus' claim to status, as he acknowledged when he agreed with Antinous and Eurymachus that the claim to the mastership of his house and to the kingship were not indissolubly linked.[24] The essential action, the one which drove the suitors to determine to kill him, was his raising a following in defiance of their wishes —and his doing it in person (or appearing to do so, since in fact, the bard says, it was Athene in the guise of Telemachus who did it).[25] Moreover, the quality of his following was important; when Antinous asked Noëmon 'who are the young men ($\kappa o \hat{v} \rho o \iota$) in his following? Are they the pick of Ithaca or are they his own labourers ($\theta \hat{\eta} \tau \epsilon s$) and thralls?' clearly he expected to hear that it was the latter. When Noëmon replied that his young followers 'are the best of the people after ourselves', Antinous and Eurymachus were at once thrown into consternation, and initiated their plot to kill Telemachus.[26]

MARRIAGE PATTERNS

Marriage connexions were therefore frequently sought by Homeric heroes with a view to securing additional military strength for their following, and hence for the defence of their *oikos*. A great chieftain's daughters were sought with gifts, which are sometimes represented as being very large in the case of the greatest chieftains' daughters (who by convention at least were also particularly beautiful), but a great chieftain could also obtain a following by bringing warriors into his house in order to secure their services, and often giving them wives of a quality appropriate to their martial prowess.[27]

These two motives apparent in the selection of a mate created a variety of marriage-patterns. Fathers of daughters gathered round them warrior sons-in-law, like Priam, who had twelve sons-in-law who lived with their wives in his palace, and Hector is alleged by Sarpedon to have claimed that he could hold Troy without levies of troops or allies, alone, with his brothers and his sisters' husbands.[28] Great kings might also make promises of marriage to warriors in return for their services, as Priam did to

Othryoneus in a bargain in which the suitor took the initiative, or as Agamemnon, taking the initiative himself, promised a daughter to Achilles after the war. Others who were given a bride by a father for their valour include Bellerophon and Odysseus' imaginary Cretan, while Odysseus himself was offered Nausicaa by Alcinous because he had made such a remarkable impression.[29] Cisses, who it appears had no son of his own, sought to obtain an heir by bringing up his grandson Iphidamas and marrying him to his second daughter; but it was in vain, since he came to Troy and fell to Agamemnon's spear. The fact that when Homer tells of his death, he suggests that Iphidamas had been a suitor, giving gifts and making promises, merely reveals a piece of bardic forgetfulness.[30]

Another similar marriage-pattern appears where the father of a hero goes out to obtain his son a bride; Menelaus did this for Megapenthes, his son, and Achilles claims that his father would seek a bride for him if he went home from the war—'there are plenty of Greek girls, daughters of chieftains who command fortresses; I shall marry which of them I desire'. We note that his father would take the initiative, but the choice lay with Achilles; also that it is assumed that any prospective father-in-law would be happy to give his daughter to Achilles, and that the girl's views are nowhere mentioned.[31]

Another pattern is when a father gives a daughter to a great chieftain to be one of a number of wives; this pattern seems to be restricted to Troy, and to Priam's numerous wives; Altes gave his daughter to Priam as a wife, and the bard specifically states that she was not the only wife, and that Altes gave many gifts with her.[32]

The remaining two patterns, marriage by capture, and marriage by contest, may be seen as variations on the pattern of the bride-groom seeking a bride; examples of the former are Briseis (on whom see p. 42), also Helen and Clytemnestra (Klytaimnestra), both of whom were genuinely married to their adulterous husbands Paris and Aegisthus. Melampus obtained Pero by winning the contest set by Neleus her father, though oddly enough he did not marry her himself, but gave her to his brother to marry;[33]

Penelope decided to select her second husband by her contest of the bow, though whether this was a plot with Odysseus, as claimed by Amphimedon, an attempt to diminish the cost to Odysseus' *oikos*, a challenge to her suitors to prove themselves the equal of Odysseus (Penelope's ostensible reason),[34] or a mere reflection of her dislike of all of them, is far from clear.

MARRIAGE GIFTS

In the first of these marriage-patterns—that in which a suitor comes to sue for a chieftain's daughter in order to take her to his own home—and in that one alone, we find the suitor offering *hedna* (gifts).[35] *Hedna* are customarily (*e.g.* in *LSJ*) translated as 'bride-price', and in Homeric society the heroes are said to have purchased their wives; this theory has been disproved,[36] and it now seems clear that to the Homeric heroes weddings were, like all other social occasions, occasions on which gifts were exchanged.

At weddings the bride herself naturally formed a large part of her parent's gift, especially if she were outstanding in birth, looks, intelligence or skill, or any combination of these.[37] But when the bridegroom was sought by the bride's father, then the bridegroom's contribution of himself, whether for his services or for his family's aid, was the more valuable, and we hear of no *hedna*.[38] A girl (or woman) of particularly great talents and qualities would be the object of competition, and we hear of suitors competing with gifts, especially in the *Odyssey*, and for Penelope's hand.[39] However, it should be noted that whenever *hedna* for Penelope are mentioned it is assumed that she will go to her new husband's house, and her new husband will not move into hers (or rather Odysseus').[40]

WIVES, CONCUBINES, BASTARDY

Since Homeric heroes held such views as these about the nature and purposes of marriage, it is not surprising that they were prepared to breed warrior sons from more than one wife, and that in consequence the line between wife and concubine was extremely fine, and marriage was essentially a question of fact and not of law.

Fear of the anger of an important father-in-law might secure a wife's position, as fear of his wife is said to have restrained Laertes from sleeping with Eurycleia in her youth, but Agamemnon can claim to prefer his captive concubine Chryseis to Clytemnestra, and it was Amyntor's preference for a concubine which led to his quarrel with Phoenix.[41] In the *Odyssey*, Helen's failure to give Menelaus a son resulted in his begetting a son from a slave concubine, and it is clear that it was this son who was going to inherit his father's position in Sparta.[42]

Briseis provides the clearest evidence of the ability of a warrior to call whom he would his wife; not only is she called 'wife', (ἄλοχος) and not 'mistress' (παλλακίς), though this word is harder to fit into a Homeric hexameter, but she was not even Achilles' only bed-mate at Troy; yet Achilles could say to the embassy 'are the Atreidae the only men who love their wives (ἀλόχους)? Any fine and sensible man loves and cherishes his wife (τὴν αὐτοῦ), even as I loved Briseis with my whole heart, captive of the spear though she is'.[43] And in her lament for Patroclus Briseis could tell how he used to console her: 'Not even when swift Achilles slew my husband and sacked the city of Mynes did you (Patroclus) allow me to lament, but always said you would make me the noble wife of glorious Achilles, and sail with me to Phthia and celebrate my wedding with a feast to the Myrmidons'. From this we must understand that Achilles could make her his acknowledged wife by public recognition of the fact and proclaiming it before his own people.[44] And from this we must conclude that marriage was a *de facto* state, and a man and a woman living together in an *oikos* and openly proclaiming their marriage were effectually married, and there was no law either to limit a man's choice or to prescribe a definite period for the marriage.

No doubt it was also the need for warriors which enabled well-born unmarried mothers not merely to keep their male children, but even to obtain husbands from among the upper class.[45]

In the *Odyssey* there may be some change of attitude as there is a change of viewpoint (see note 1); the bastard Megapenthes is introduced rather apologetically as Menelaus' prospective heir, and the criticism of Clytemnestra for her bigamous marriage to

Aegisthus is much harsher than that accorded to Helen in the *Iliad* for hers to Paris,[46] though Homer always regards the action of both as discreditable.[47] Ares' seduction of Aphrodite was also clearly disgraceful;[48] but, being gods, Ares and Aphrodite could not be put to death, the fate of the adulterer who in classical times in Athens was caught in the act.

It may be thought that the poet's attitude towards the other girls in the *Odyssey* who had been seduced was because they were not of the heroic class, and their lovers were not gods, and that fornication with a bond-woman was interfering with a master's property, but there can be no doubt that in the *Odyssey* the poet sees fornication as a clear sign of moral turpitude in a woman.[49] Examples include Eumaeus' Phoenician nurse, who stole Eumaeus and some treasure when she eloped with her lover, and came to a bad end on the ship.[50] The dozen maids who sleep with the wooers 'dishonour the house of Odysseus' and 'brought reproaches down upon Telemachus and Penelope'; their departure from the house at night made Odysseus 'growl and snarl like a bitch who snarls threateningly as a stranger passes by while she stands guard over her puppies', while he compared his feelings with how he had felt as he watched the Cyclops devour his men.[51] Their punishment duly followed the slaughter of the wooers, who are themselves said 'to commit evil deeds by raping the maids'.[52]

It is also clear that the wooing of Penelope is wrong because it is not known that her husband is dead—she would do wrong to remarry both in her own estimation and in that of the people, and the suitors do wrong to woo her, as Odysseus says both in his disguise as the beggar and when he has revealed himself as ready for revenge.[53] But it cannot be doubted that Penelope is represented as having the power to remarry; in his parting instructions Odysseus told her not to wait for him beyond a certain time, but to marry if he had not returned. 'When you see my son with a beard sprouting on his chin, marry whomsoever you please, and leave your home'.[54] Such a marriage, though bigamous to our way of thinking, would have been perfectly in accordance with Homeric custom as seen in the case of Paris and Helen, since marriage was a *de facto* state.[55]

KYRIEIA IN HOMERIC SOCIETY

The wooing of Penelope also reveals Homeric custom about the headship of the family (its *kyrieia*).[56] While Telemachus had no following and hence lacked the status of a hero, and Odysseus was not known to be dead, Odysseus remained head of his family, and Penelope's *kyrios* in consequence as long as she stayed in his house; it was possible, however, for her to return voluntarily to her father and re-enter his *kyrieia*.[57] When Telemachus was old enough and capable of claiming the *kyrieia* of Odysseus' house, he had the right to send Penelope back to her father, though this would involve paying recompense, or he could allow her to stay on in his house. But if Odysseus was proved dead, and Penelope in consequence a widow, Telemachus would have full power to dispose of her in marriage as her *kyrios*. At least part of the confusion in the *Odyssey* over Penelope's remarriage is caused by the lack of agreement between the speakers as to who is Penelope's *kyrios*, because it depends on whether or not Odysseus is dead, and whether or not Telemachus is of heroic status.[58]

Daughters, however, did not wholly lose contact with their own families at marriage: their own families maintained an interest in them, and they in their families; we find Andromache's grandfather ransoming his daughter, Bellerophon being sent to Anteia's family for punishment, and, most strikingly, the curse put upon Meleager by his mother for killing her brother.[59]

PROPERTY OF THE OIKOS. GIFTS

The wooing of Penelope is also associated with the wasting of the assets of Odysseus' house; Homeric heroes have sometimes been the butt of critical comment for their concern with their property, but it should be remembered that if a hero failed to protect his property, it involved not merely his financial ruin and loss of face or status, but starvation, or near-starvation for the whole family alike. Consequently, a sufficient livelihood is one of the criteria for the maintenance of an honourable status, and a great king like Odysseus is pictured as having enormous wealth in flocks and herds.[60] Any hero who thinks of his wife and children also thinks of the possessions which will support them,[61] and it is clear from a number of passages that even a noble family which had not the power to defend its possessions might be the prey of the more powerful. The household of Telemachus in the *Odyssey* is the principal example (*Odyssey, passim*), but parallels may be found in Achilles' statement that it is only fear of himself that protects his father, or the fate which Andromache saw in store for her orphan son after Hector's death—other men will filch his corn-lands and he will be refused food at the feasts of the warriors.[62]

Possessions had to be both sought and hoarded; they had also to be given away as gifts to other heroes, and in the self-valuing society of the Homeric poems a man set a value on himself by the gifts which he gave, the equal of which he expected to receive in return.[63] The gods 'took away the wits' of Glaucus when he exchanged his golden armour for that of Diomedes which was bronze; on the other hand Telemachus was urged to make a fine present to Athene (disguised as Mentes) on the ground that he would not lose by the exchange.[64] But status also exacted gifts from others, as Thersites said to Agamemnon: 'Your huts I know are full of bronze, and there are many specially chosen women in them, whom of course we Achaeans always give you first whenever we take a fortress-town', etc.[65]

Women too gave gifts, but almost always the things that they themselves or their women had made;[66] Helen gave Telemachus a fine robe for his bride, Arete chose the clothes to be put in Odysseus' box, a bride's reputation, it is said, depends on the clothing she gives her bridegroom's escorts.[67] On a humbler level Penelope gave Eumaeus a set of clothes when he went out onto a farm and promised the beggar new clothes if she believed him, but when, in the contest of the bow, she went on to offer him weapons, she was rebuked by Telemachus. Such things were in the sole disposal of the *kyrios* of the *oikos*.[68]

PROPERTY. SUCCESSION

Also in Homer we find the idea of property as being of two classes, lands and houses on the one hand, and slaves, animals and movables on the other. In the *Odyssey*, nobody ever denies

Telemachus' right to succeed to Odysseus' *oikos*,[69] though they were prepared to deny him the effective use of it; it is only in the event of his death that they will divide up the possessions and provisions and give his house to Penelope's new husband;[70] they assumed, of course, that Odysseus was dead. Similarly we may compare the threats to Athene disguised as Mentor when she was supporting Odysseus in the battle in the hall (where Agelaus threatens death for Mentor himself, expulsion of his sons from their hall, and prohibition of his womenfolk from the city streets, but not confiscation of his *oikos*), with Odysseus' oath that the suitors will not be spared, 'not even if you were to give me your whole family estates, both what you now have and anything you get from any source'—that is to say 'not even if you were to become beggars', the most extreme possible demand.[71]

Succession to property was through descent; there are no wills in Homer. Descent normally means descent to sons, but it can also mean descent to daughters' husbands[72] assuming that they are strong enough to maintain their position against possible rivals. Achilles can jeer at Aeneas that he cannot hope, even by killing Achilles, to become ruler of Troy because Priam has sons of his own, but when Diomedes slew both Xanthus and Thoas distant relatives divided their aged father's inheritance.[73] Homer stresses particularly strongly the loss to their families of only sons, or of all the sons;[74] a twice-repeated phrase speaks of sons 'who did not repay their rearing', and we hear of the ransom which Dolon's father would be happy to pay for him, he being the only son in a family of six.[75]

THE LIFE OF THE FAMILY

The life of the family is generally portrayed romantically in the Homeric poems, especially in the *Odyssey*, though there are exceptions,[76] like the curses upon Meleager or Phoenix. The marvellous joy which Odysseus felt on sighting Phaeacia was 'like that of children watching their father recover from some fell disease'; so the family's joy at a warrior's homecoming is vividly pictured: 'Nor is Tydeus' son aware that he who fights with the gods is not long of life, nor do his children chatter around his knees when he has come home from war and grim battle'.[77] In the *Odyssey*, Eumaeus provides two romantic pictures of his mistress's treatment of her thralls,[78] and the whole story of Nausicaa is similarly romanticized.

Homer's women are not portrayed as being entirely home-keeping—Andromache for instance 'might have gone to visit her relations', similes provide a flirtation outside the walls of Troy and housewives quarrelling in a street; the shield of Achilles showed housewives standing at their doors to watch a wedding and women assisting in the defence of a city wall,[79] an activity acknowledged alike by the military writers and the practice of classical times. Nevertheless, women are called by the stock-epithet λευκώλενοι (white-armed), as Minoan art represents them in yellow paint and not dark ochre like the men[80] (*Pl. 4*), nor does Homer provide a picture of equality between the sexes, or the possibility of women's participation in public life. Even Penelope was bidden to withdraw from the room by Telemachus on two occasions on which he asserted his control over the house, the first when he decided to call an assembly, the second when he asserted his rights to the disposal of the bow—'do you go into the *oikos* and see to your handicrafts (ἔργα), your loom and your distaff, and bid your maids push on with the work; discussion (μῦθος) shall be the concern of men, of all, and of myself above all; for I am he who has power of control (κράτος) in this house'.[81]

DEATH AND BURIAL. VENGEANCE

When a man had died, his funeral rights lay with his family; wife and mother and son and father took the principal parts, but there are many variations,[82] based very often on the actual state of the family or the point of the struggle reached in the poem.

Much stress is laid on the proper ceremonies, which conveyed honour if done splendidly, as were Patroclus' and Achilles',[83] and respect if properly conducted;[84] it should be noted, however, that funeral ceremonies could be conducted without the body, as would have happened in the *Odyssey* had Telemachus ascertained that his father was dead.[85] Not to bury a body was of course to disgrace the dead, and failure to recover a deceased comrade's corpse a disgrace to his surviving kinsmen and friends;[86] 'the dogs (or the vultures) will get your body' is the last taunt in many a Homeric duel.[87] But a seemly limit to mourning was expected, even for a brother or a son.[88]

Vengeance for a death was a matter for the family; this applied to those slain in battle, where a brother boasts that it is good to leave kin (γνωτόν) to exact vengeance, and Andromache fears that her son may be killed by the relative of someone whom Hector slew;[89] it applied perhaps more emphatically to those murdered, whether by accident or otherwise, as Nestor told Telemachus: 'How good a thing it is for a son to survive a man who is perished, as he (Orestes) too took vengeance upon his father's murderer', etc.[90]

There are traces of judicial systems in which a man may, by making payment to the relatives of the deceased man, obtain their pardon, and continue to live in his own community, but the dispute portrayed on the shield of Achilles suggests that the relatives did not have to accept the proffered payment. Odysseus assumed that if he killed the suitors in Ithaca he would have to fly the country,[91] and though the majority of references imply that it was the relatives who took vengeance,[92] in at least two places popular opinion, it is clearly envisaged, would be brought to bear.[93] The punishment was the same as that imposed by angry relatives—exile. Most of the exiles in the Homeric poems are, in consequence, murderers, or at least homicides.[94]

EXILE AND XENOI

The choice of exile as a self-imposed punishment for murderers is an interesting reflection of the economic basis of the family system of the Homeric poems; an exile could not maintain or protect his family, and, unless he had special skills, as a warrior like Patroclus or a prophet like Theoclymenus, he was unlikely to lead a long or happy life.[95] The exile is one kind of outsider, stranger (xenos or xeinos), who may be found in the Homeric family; he was accepted in return for services. Other outsiders regularly accepted are the skilled craftsmen, such as 'a prophet, a doctor, a spearmaker, or a minstrel'.[96]

THE FAMILY IN HOMERIC SOCIETY

Humbler folk may be given their food and clothing in return for work; Irus ran messages for the suitors; Telemachus says the beggar will work for him; Odysseus as the beggar claimed to be too old to earn his living by farm-work, though he took up a challenge from Eurymachus to do it. He then added: 'And if Zeus were to stir up some fighting from somewhere and I had a shield and two spears and a bronze helmet to fit over my temples, then you would see me in the thick of it amongst the leading champions'; clearly men at arms were another important category of outsiders, given food and clothing in return for their services.[97] Even the most transient outsiders, beggars and suppliants, can expect a bed and food if they can reach the master of the house,[98] and, if they bear good news, some reward like clothes and shoes and something for the road, but they cannot claim to be treated like real, noble visitors and *xeinoi*.[99]

Noble *xeinoi*, who could be either inherited from parents or ancestors or personally acquired, were both potential allies in war, and provided in their homes comfortable points of call for a noble when away from his own home whether for visiting, trade or piracy. In the *Iliad* Lycaon, we hear, was ransomed by a *xeinos*, who bought him from the master who had purchased him from his captor, but Axylus the 'hospitable host' was not saved from Diomedes by any of his old *xeinoi*. Diomedes and Glaucus, finding they are descended from fellow-*xeinoi*, refuse to fight one another;[100] in the *Odyssey*, in Phaeacia, Odysseus refused to box against his host.[101]

Odysseus, we hear, had a wide circle of *xeinoi* with whom he used to exchange visits, and it was as his father's son that Telemachus received a welcome at Pylos. So, guests arrived at Ithaca making claims on Telemachus, like Mentes or the 'Cretan'; Odysseus in disguise made a claim even on old Laertes; in Sparta Menelaus says that he and Eteoneus his squire must entertain strangers since they were often entertained on their journeyings.[102]

A typical blend of prudence and suspicion governed these rather complex relationships; the lack of a master in the house made Penelope neglect visitors,[103] it also caused Telemachus to put his guest in charge of a friend.[104] Suspicion of strangers at first acquaintance was not out of place in an age when traders and pirates were virtually indistinguishable, and at times the same people,[105] and force was regarded as a legitimate method of acquiring property,[106] and when even those who had arrived in peace were apt to leave with plunder, as Paris left with his host's wife and half his property, and a Phoenician trader with three goblets, a maidservant and the king's son. The obligation to say farewell to one's host was therefore not merely a social convention;[107] it was to make sure that the guest left with only what the host intended he should take with him.

Thus we see that the Homeric picture is of a society which was an association of self-supporting family-based units responsible to themselves and relying on themselves for their own protection and their economic survival. This produced a hierarchical society in which an individual's place in the society was determined first by his descent and the number of followers he could claim through his power and wealth,[108] but ultimately by his physical prowess and his ability to defend his inheritance. It is a society in which the warrior himself was the mainstay of the family whose continuance he could, and was obliged to, secure by the procreation of children to succeed him. To fail in this was a disaster, since it would not secure him protection in his old age, a proper burial or a name to hand down to posterity, for which last Achilles was prepared even to lay down his life.[109] At least as important as this, however, was the fact that the economic survival of the family depended on the hero's ability to obtain and sustain a livelihood, and for this his *oikos* and its defence alike were the fundamental necessities.

CHAPTER III

THE FAMILY AND
THE EVOLUTION OF STATES

THE CREATION OF CITY–STATES

THE SOCIETY PORTRAYED in the Homeric epics perished at some time between the tenth and ninth centuries and the seventh century, a period described by Thucydides as one of migration and settlement.[1] The societies that arose from the seventh century took the classical form, the city-state or *polis* (plural *poleis*). In their political organization *poleis* varied widely in the distribution of rights and privileges among the citizens, but they all had in common a determination to be their own masters, self-sufficient, responsible to themselves for their own defence, and living under their own code of laws.

Poleis were not created in one generation, nor even in two (except for some colonial settlements of historical times which were settled under the aegis of an already-existing city, and followed their mother-city's customs or laws, which they took with them). They grew out of a process known as synoecism, which varied widely from place to place, but was often attributed to a single powerful ruler or king (as Theseus was traditionally responsible for the synoecism of Attica).[2] When a number of groups of families became a *polis* is hard to define exactly, but communities can only be called truly unified *poleis* when something like a common code of laws came to be formulated and administered by the officers of the community, who were then able to settle disputes by means of judgements in a common court of law,[3] and regulate matters which had previously been governed by the separate (and possibly differing) customs of the individual families or villages.[4] Many communities, even *poleis*, continued to exist without a unifying legislature for long periods of time.

The process of forming *poleis* was accomplished much more quickly in some areas than in others. Physically, *poleis* tended to coalesce quickly where the need for local self-defence was great and drove the families together.[5] On the wide plains of Thessaly, however, a feudal system without *poleis* prevailed into classical times;[6] on both sides of the isthmus of Corinth (an area especially open to piracy), many *poleis* coalesced early in history. The need for self-defence ensured that settlements which were sent out as colonies to neighbouring lands always, from the date of their foundation, had a fortified rallying-point, and hence some sort of *polis*-system.[7] But, though self-defence was the *raison d'être* of a *polis*, it was characteristic of a *polis* that men did not carry arms on their daily business; it was a sign that a country was primitive if they did so.[8] The Greeks were very conscious of the difference between a blow with a fist or a stick and a blow with a spear or other weapon of war; the former was understandable, especially in defence of property, the latter showed intent to kill.[9]

In the field of civil law, however—the law governing property and a family's possessions—in general it is true to say that the more deeply-entrenched the old families were in a *polis*, the longer these families seem to have monopolized judicial and religious control, and the later was the introduction of the state's law,[10] which liberated the family *oikos* from its *genos*, and even the individual from his *oikos*.

Poleis varied greatly in the complexity of their family-structure, and in its rigidity. This arose from various causes; of these, one of the most important was the lands upon which the *polis* subsisted. One of the facts of Greek geography is that the rich 'deep-soiled' agricultural lands of the plains are not merely richer, but are very much richer than the hill-slopes.[11] For these lands, in the age of the migrations, men fought, and the richer the lands were the more often they were invaded, and the more often the population changed, says Thucydides.[12]

When a new wave of invaders arrived, the previous settlers, if they could not resist them, either fled or stayed as a subject population; in consequence, in the rich lands such as Laconia, Argos, Boeotia, Thessaly, and in Crete and in some places near the isthmus of Corinth, the early aristocracies were racially different from the labourers who worked in their fields, and from the poorer farmers, who worked on the hill-slopes or eked out what subsistence they could as shepherds on the higher mountain-pastures or as charcoal-burners or woodsmen[13] (the traditional poor men of European folk-tales).

The history of the settlement of Attica was, however, different —or so all Athenians, including Thucydides, believed. Attica, with its relatively poor agricultural land, was little invaded, and the fine defensive citadel on the acropolis with its water supply enabled the natives to resist invaders, so that the people of Attica, the Athenians, claimed to be the indigenous population, lacking these racial differences, and the landowners therefore claimed to have inherited their lands from a period of incredible antiquity.[14]

Athens and Attica were therefore different from most states of Greece, if Thucydides is right; and modern observers must therefore beware of regarding Athens as typical of all Greece.[15] The Dorian states of the isthmus of Corinth were perhaps more typical, paralleled as they are by the Thebans in their race-conscious attitude to Boeotia,[16] or by the Spartans and their exclusive community of 'equals' which excluded all non-Spartiates from any share in the government, or the racially-divided and class-conscious society revealed at Gortyn in Crete.[17]

OIKOS, GENOS AND THE CREATION OF LAW

All *poleis* were composed of a number of individual *oikoi*; the lands of an *oikos* were part of the *oikos*,[18] since, as we have already remarked, the means of subsistence were an essential part of the *oikos*. One of the important processes in the consolidation of *poleis* was the establishment of the *oikoi* as the units of the *polis*, independent, in the long run, of any *genos*, with the result that a man came to own his land (his *kleros*) because he had successfully established a claim as next of kin to the previous owner, either within a defined kinship-group or as the heir designated under a lawful will, or because he had purchased it, having the right to do so as a member of the *polis*, and not because he was the person entitled to succeed by virtue of kinship within a *genos* or some other unlimited family group.[19] It need hardly be doubted that ownership of land, or at least of holdings of the best agricultural land, was collective in early times, in the sense that the members of each *genos*, who shared responsibility for the defence of their lands, claimed the right to determine, under the leadership of the head of the *genos*, and by custom, who should succeed to a vacant or disputed piece of land.[20]

The object of the *genos* was its own permanent survival—that is, to ensure the defence of the *oikoi* which belonged to it, both the persons and the lands. Thus 'law' comprised taking vengeance upon outsiders who injured the *genos*, and expulsion from the *genos* of offenders against it;[21] 'he may die without anyone taking vengeance'[22] was the sentence of expulsion; 'we set no value on his life' the penalty; the man expelled became an outlaw, a wolf.[23]

Killing by an outsider provoked the wrath of his victim's whole *genos*; against a killer the *genos* stood solid, accepting no distinction between murder and homicide, and even justifiable homicide was sometimes punished in the same way, by exile or death.[24] Even in near historical times, in Sicyon, Isodemus, who killed his wife's paramour in the act of adultery, had to flee abroad (*c.* 600),[25] and the Alcmaeonidae in Athens were expelled for killing in defence of the state against a *coup d'état* (632, trad.).

The legal process in this latter case was that the relatives of the dead succeeded in proving that sacrilege had been committed: thereupon we are told that the whole Alcmaeonid clan, including the deceased, were cast out of Attica,[26] an expulsion which resulted in a standing feud between this *genos* and other noble houses. The important thing to note, however, is not so much the sentence, which may in fact not be correctly reported by our sources, as the existence of the court. The court of the Areopagus was the most ancient in Athens;[27] even into the fourth century it dealt with cases of intentional homicide, and its president, the Basileus (King), heard all cases of homicide, wounding and physical violence.[28] Thus, it is clear that arbitration between *genē* in cases of homicide was the earliest function of this *polis*-community.[29]

The Archon, the magistrate in Athens who acted as the guardian of the rights of property (especially land), Aristotle says, was unimportant in ancient times and appointed later than the Basileus and the Polemarchos, the ancient commander-in-chief:[30] this suggests that the *genē* themselves controlled the right to judge questions affecting property for some time after the judgement in cases of violence had become a matter for the *polis*. Still later[31] came the appointment of the *thesmothetai*, whose duty was to assemble the case-law of the community by recording (though not publishing) judgements. In Aristotle's day they still heard prosecutions for proposing illegal or disadvantageous laws.[32] We do not know the date of their appointment, but it preceded the first attempts to publish written laws; these are traditionally attributed to Dracon (621, trad.), about whom all that we know for certain is that he codified the laws dealing with homicide.[33] The codification of the civil law as accepted in classical times was attributed to Solon (594, trad.), though it is clear that even before his day there had been some penal regulations laid down by Dracon, since Aristotle mentions that the penalties established by Dracon were particularly severe.[34] Moreover, the *oikoi* had already gone some way towards becoming independent of their *genos*, since it is a mark of individual ownership of property (as distinct from corporate ownership by a group like a *genos*) that children, for example, can be sold for debt, or (in the case of women) for unchastity.[35]

It is probable, too, that the individual had, before Solon's day, already been made responsible for his acts, and that his *genos*, *oikos* and its property were protected from arbitrary vengeance by an injured party, as they are in the contemporary law from Elis.[36] This is suggested both by the existence of the statutory penalties mentioned above, and by Solon's law enabling 'anyone who wished' to take action on behalf of an injured party. This is usually taken to imply that previously there had been those entitled to do so (*e.g.* by virtue of kinship), and that the law had provided for redress in some form or other. Tradition, however, made Solon the Athenian lawgiver, except for the laws on homicide.

How far all this is literally true is probably irrelevant, but the process by which the law was created seems to be fairly typical. It seems normally to have required either a revolution or the threat of one, or a crisis of some sort, to bring about the appointment of a lawgiver either to codify what were the usual customs of the *genē*, or to publish the rules under which the magistrate was supposed to act.[37] In Athens the nature of the crisis which Solon had to deal with has been the subject of considerable discussion, but it is clear that the plight of the poor was at least the obvious symptom;[38] but in the states dominated by one race, or *genos*, as at Corinth, it was a tyrant, either Periander (Periandros) or his father, who, having overthrown the ruling families, codified, or revised and made public the city's laws under his personal rule (*c.* 625–585);[39] in Sparta the new (or revised) repressive legislation associated with Lycurgus was in response to the crisis of the second Messenian War (*c.* 640–620); in Mytilene civil war and military defeat led to the appointment of Pittacus (*c.* 600).[40] In the colonial settlements of Southern Italy and Sicily, where the earliest written codes were established, it was probably mainly the need to consolidate a heterogeneous citizen body which lacked a strong body of family tradition which was responsible for the codification, though their relative insecurity may have contributed to their feeling the need for consolidation.[41]

THE OIKOS AND ARISTOCRATIC SURVIVALS FROM HOMERIC SOCIETY

Lawgivers and tyrants alike provided breaks in the government of the *poleis* by their aristocracies, which remained the general rule; after the lawgivers the aristocrats did not disappear, but they ceased to hold unquestioned power, and after the revolution which had ended their monopoly of control they had to come under the law and discipline of the *polis*. They retained many of their ancient prerogatives, often in vestigial form; knights (*hippeis*) we know to have been the collective name of some ruling aristocracies and, before hoplite warfare started, wealthy cavalrymen normally formed the government.[42] In Athens *hippeis* monopolized the council before the time of Solon, and the chief offices till the

7   This vigorous scene from the upper frieze of a tall jug made in Corinth shows
the family in a hoplite battle-line. The family, or personal, emblems on the
shields of the phalanx on the right include several devices known also from
literature and coins. Skilful use of colour differentiates between the greaves
and helmets of the warriors and their darker flesh, particularly that of the
unarmed piper who gives the time to the marching troops. This may suggest
that the Spartans, who are known to have done so, may not have been unique
in marching into battle to the strains of the pipe. The backs of the shields are
also gaily decorated, but this may reflect the artist's love of colour rather than
any particular city's or family's armaments. The frieze is *c.* 2 in. high.

8-10 Athenians referred affectionately to their coins as 'owls'; on the obverse side appeared the helmeted head of Athene, on the reverse, the owl, an olive twig and the legend Athe(nians). Below, six earlier coins; one (top) from Miletus declares 'I am the badge of Phanes'; five 'heraldic' coins of Athens show the badges of various families. Bottom right, the incuse reverse type common to such early coins.

11, 12   After their great victory over the Carthaginians in 479, the Syracusans minted gold coins called 'demareteion', after Queen Demarete, and later, the very large (10 drachma) silver coins shown. The head (above), with dolphins and legend 'of the Syracusans', may not be her portrait, but it is peculiar to this series.

13–15 The long hair and lovely clothes of the wreathed youth with the flower (left) and the girls drawing water at the public fountain (above), details from sixth-century vases, contrast with the plainer garment of the reveller (below), who plays 'kottabos', a game whose object was to flick dregs from a cup into a jar placed at a distance.

16 A youth who has overindulged at a party is being consoled by an *hetaira*, whose concern for him is beautifully portrayed. Her hair, which is short and reddish, suggests that she is a slave from northern Europe; her vine-wreath indicates that she has been at the party too. The plainness of their dresses contrasts with the finery of 30 years earlier.

17 The wrestling-school, as the nakedness of both figures suggests, was the scene for homosexual approaches such as that shown here. The age of the man is shown by his beard; the youth, like those in *Pls. 13* and *15*, is at the age which the Greeks most admired, when the beard is still only a soft down.

18, 19 The riotous party of bearded men, beardless youths and *hetairai* dance to the music of a lyre and two pipes. Both the flute-girl and the girl with the cup (below) seem to be the centre of quarrels. The latter repels a bearded man who is trying to grab her cup; he is being abused by a cup-carrying youth. On the right the man with the stick is defending the flute-girl from the reveller who has his hand in her dress.

20 The small scale of Athenian trade is well shown on this jar (above) made about 500; a cobbler is cutting out a pair of shoes for a boy, who stands on the table. It is not certain whether the standing figure (right) is the boy's *paidagogos* or the owner of the shop, and the operative in consequence a slave. The former seems the more probable.

middle of the fifth century.[43] Elsewhere, *hippeis* was the name retained by the Spartan king's bodyguard;[44] in Euboea *hippeis* retained religious functions;[45] in Athens the noble, priestly families retained their prerogatives and some measure of respect right through the democratic period;[46] at Ephesus the Basilidae, at Miletus the Branchidae, once a ruling aristocracy, retained their powers in the religious sphere.[47] But in this sphere, too, the *polis* gradually took a more prominent part; it was characteristic of a tyranny (that of Peisistratus) that the worship of Dionysus, the peasants' god, was encouraged in Athens, along with the Eleusinian mysteries, in which no regard was paid to class-distinctions, even slaves being admitted.[48]

These *hippeis*, like the heroes in Homer, were horse-loving; they cultivated horse-breeding and racing with chariots besides fighting from horseback. Cavalry warfare as an art-subject is a feature of the aristocratic age;[49] funerals and processions are features of the art of the Geometric period[50] (*Pl. 6*). Family pride ensured that even when hoplite (infantry) warfare became normal, and foot-soldiers began to appear in art, the family heraldic emblems appeared on the shields of warriors depicted on vases in the seventh and sixth centuries[51] (*Pl. 7*), in marked contrast to the simplicity of the designs of some city-states, or the formidable zig-zag pattern of the Spartan phalanx.[52]

In Athens, too, where perhaps the family structure was even more deeply entrenched than elsewhere (above, p. 53), the early coinage was stamped with the heraldic badges of the nobles,[53] and it was not till the tyranny of Peisistratus that Athens had a city badge at all, the helmeted head of Athene, and the owl[54] (*Pls. 8–10*).

Almost all Greek states are aristocratic—*i.e.* ruled by noble families—when they emerge into history; the exceptions are those which emerge under the rule of a tyrant, but the tyrants' families, who were themselves frequently of noble birth, cultivated the same ideals of excellence as the aristocracies, ideals which stemmed ultimately from the self-valuation which was so important in Homeric society. Like the Homeric heroes, the aristocratic nobles cherished physical strength and engaged in athletic sports and hunting; they took the lead in promoting the national games at

Olympia and Delphi and elsewhere, where the only important qualification for entry was to be of free birth and pure Greek descent.[55] They also cultivated the more peaceful arts, music and dancing, indulged their taste for fine clothes and personal adornment and wore their hair long; the art of the sixth century implies a *jeunesse dorée* of upper-class sophistication and a love of the beautiful, of gay clothes and flowers and beauty in the young—especially boys—which is itself a testimony to their love of the beautiful[56] (*Pls. 13–15*). These nobles did not lack their critics, such as Tyrtaeus in Sparta and Xenophanes in Ionia[57] (sixth century) and there was a darker side to the picture; pride in birth could easily lead to snobbery,[58] love of finery to effeminacy,[59] admiration of beautiful boys to paederasty (*Pl. 17*), gatherings to spend a convivial evening in singing to drunken orgies[60] (*Pls. 16, 18, 19*), and a love of display often ended in absurd extravagance, especially in celebrating the two principal family festivals, marriages and funerals.

The Homeric self-valuation of the individual which led a man to make a show often led to great extravagance at these family festivals; Periander in Corinth,[61] Solon in Athens, Charondas and others[62] legislated against extravagance at funerals; the 'Lycurgan' funeral at Sparta was extremely unostentatious,[63] though whether this was an innovation or not we do not know. We hear of nobles' marriages being celebrated with great splendour; the marriage of Agariste, daughter of Cleisthenes of Sicyon, was certainly Homeric in its grandeur, and thoroughly aristocratic in concept; the suitors were 'those who thought themselves qualified in person and in birth', Cleisthenes watched their behaviour in the wrestling ring and at dinner, studied their accomplishments and characters, and made enquiries about their descent and family, and at the end of his year's entertainment he selected the two Athenians, and of these preferred Hippocleides because of his manly qualities (ἀνδραγαθία), and because he was by descent connected to the family of Cypselus of Corinth.[64] The marriage of the daughter of Antisthenes of Acragas in Sicily, though later in date, shows the same love of extravagant display in a rich and noble family.[65]

ARISTOCRATIC DYNASTIES

We hear of many more marriages, however, in which the political needs of the aristocratic family were considered; many ruling families such as the Bacchiadae at Corinth were endogamous;[66] according to Herodotus, one Bacchiad girl, Labda, was married outside the *genos* because she was lame and none of the Bacchiadae would marry her. When she gave birth to a baby, her kinsmen determined to suppress the child—Herodotus claims it was because of two oracles, but it is not necessary to believe this —and Labda herself regarded the visit of her kinsmen as nothing extraordinary. 'She thought that it was because of their kindly feeling towards the child's father that they had come' (Herodotus says) 'and put her baby in the arms of one of them.'[67] Most of the other aristocracies of which we know married within their own circle of political dynasts, and we need not doubt that, as at Sparta, wherever a small council is found as the main ruling body, it was drawn from an endogamous ring of noble families.[68]

Marriages to neighbouring rulers were also known from quite early times, especially in colonial settlements; some of these were royal marriages, as that of Damodice, daughter of the ruler of Cyme, to King Midas of Phrygia,[69] or the marriage of Melas, tyrant of Ephesus, to the daughter of Alyattes, king of Lydia, who himself had a Greek wife as well as a Carian; these were marriages in quest of military power of the sort seen in the Homeric poems.[70] Others were the result of Greek settlers going out to new homes without wives, as happened in the case of the bloody massacre at Miletus,[71] or in the apparently peaceful intermingling of races we find in southern Russia.[72]

Within Greece, tyrants frequently made alliances by marriage. Cylon, would-be tyrant of Athens, married the daughter of Theagenes, tyrant of Megara;[73] Aristocrates of Arcadia, who led the Messenians in the second Messenian War, had a daughter who married Procles tyrant of Epidaurus, whose daughter married Periander of Corinth;[74] the Argive noble Gorgilus had a daughter Timonassa who married successively Archinus the Cypselid ruler of Ambracia and Peisistratus of Athens.[75] The complexity of the intermarriages of the families of Gelon and Theron, tyrants of

Syracuse and Acragas at the beginning of the fifth century, almost defies analysis; Theron's daughter married successively Gelon and his brother Polyzelus; his niece married their third brother, Hieron; Theron himself married the daughter of Polyzelus, his son-in-law; this was presumably the child of a previous marriage and not his own grand-daughter.[76]

Other noble families, like the Alcmaeonidae of Athens, also had marriage and other connexions abroad; besides their marriage into the family of Cleisthenes of Sicyon, we know that they had relations at Sparta, a state which they traditionally represented in Athens.[77] Cypselus of Athens was also a grandson through his mother of the Corinthian Cypselus, and there is evidence from a number of states that outsiders of pedigree were admitted to citizenship in archaic times;[78] additional military strength would always be welcome. Ties of *xenia* also crossed the boundaries of the *poleis*, as had the ties of the Homeric princes; an example in a very 'heroic' vein is the treatment of Euaephnus of Sparta by Polychares of Messenia, who spared Euaephnus when he detected him cheating him because he was his *xenos* (says Diodorus), but when Euaephnus slew his son, he revenged himself in blood. The story of Glaucus of Sparta, whose uncertain honesty was punished by Apollo by a sentence of extinction for his race, also shows connexions of *xenia* extending across city-boundaries.[79]

ARISTOCRATIC WOMEN

The women of these aristocratic families enjoyed considerable freedom. The circle of Sappho was clearly well-educated,[80] and in Alcaeus' poems we hear of beauty-contests at a country shrine.[81] Aristocratic women are characterized by Semonides of Amorgos (b. 664) in his unattractive satire on women; they are like dainty mares, they dodge all chores, no milling or sifting of flour, no cleaning sewage out of the house, no getting sooty in the kitchen, always washing (two or three times every day) and rubbing on unguents, they wear their hair long and well-combed and smothered in flowers, a lovely picture for others to see but to their husbands they are a pest—unless one is a tyrant or king, people who delight in that sort of thing.[82] Pittacus the tyrant of

Mytilene was said to have been henpecked by his aristocratic wife, and many of the 'sages' advised marrying a woman of your own rank.[83] Some marriages were said to have been for love, as that of Periander and Melissa, and Peisistratus' daughter is said to have kissed her fiancé openly in the street in front of her mother; Semonides' good wife loves her husband and is loved by him into old age.[84] There is clear evidence that aristocratic women did not only practise the traditional crafts of wealthy women, elaborate embroidery, needlework and tapestry-weaving,[85] but they also travelled—with their husbands, for example, to the national shrines, the protection of which was expected to shield them from most of the perils of the journey.[86] They even took some part in politics, either unofficially and indirectly, as when the women of the Alcmaeonidae, we are told, sheltered some of the supporters of Cylon,[87] or more overtly, as when Demarete, daughter of Theron of Acragas, led the Syracusan women in sacrificing their gold jewellery to pay mercenary troops in the crisis of 479, and gave her name to the victory coinage (*Pls. 11, 12*).[88]

The value set on the women's honour may be illustrated from Solon's laws, which prescribed death for the adulterer caught in the act, and for the detected adulteress social banishment, by forbidding her to put on festival clothing or enter the public sanctuaries; anyone who met her was ordered to disgrace her publicly, stripping off her clothes and festive ornaments and beating her—only she was not to be maimed or killed.[89] All the early law codes of which we have any knowledge made provision for social excommunication of the adulteress, except that at Gortyn, where the code deals only in monetary penalties,[90] and at Sparta where there was no need for a law since there was no such thing as adultery, or so the Spartans claimed.[91] In public life, men's concern with their women's honour is well illustrated by the story of how Hipparchus, son of Peisistratus, avenged his defeat by Aristogeiton for the homosexual love of Harmodius by putting an insult on the sister of the latter; this was avenged in turn by the murder of Hipparchus. Abusing the honour of citizens by insulting behaviour (ὕβρις) towards boys and maidens is said to be a general cause for the downfall of tyrannies.[92] The capture of their children and their use as hostages played an important part in forcing Hipparchus' brother Hippias and his friends to surrender to their besiegers in 510.[93]

ARISTOCRATIC OIKOI IN POLEIS

Throughout the age of rule by hereditary aristocracies, however, the *polis* gradually encroached on the noble families, at different rates in different communities. Their display came to be not solely for their own satisfaction, but to stimulate political support by gaining popularity among their fellow-citizens, and the city-states responded. Olympic victors were thought to bring honour to the state as well as to themselves, so were granted free maintenance at public expense, and it is clear that they received other honours as well;[94] some even attempted to obtain political leadership on the strength of their success, as Cylon in Athens (632 trad.), or Philippus of Croton in Southern Italy (*c.* 510); in Croton too, Milon, who was six times Olympic victor (from 532), was general in the battle which resulted in the destruction of Sybaris.[95] Success in the games also was thought by many tyrants to make them respectable, as when Cleisthenes of Sicyon sought for a husband for his daughter Agariste after his Olympic victory; three of Pindar's odes are written for the victories of tyrants at Olympia,[96] and others commemorate tyrants' victories elsewhere. Even in the fifth century Alcibiades gained great renown for his (according to Plutarch) unique feat in entering seven chariots for the same Olympic games and obtaining first, second and fourth prizes;[97] by this action, Alcibiades claimed, he brought Athens into high repute.[98] Display sometimes took more practical forms; Alcibiades' father Cleinias had distinguished himself by captaining a trireme which he provided, and had equipped, and for which he had engaged a whole crew of 200 men at his own expense at the time of Xerxes' invasion;[99] Aristotle tells us that it was their patriotic expenditures in the Persian Wars which enabled the council of the Areopagus to gain political dominance in Athens thereafter.[100] Later in the fifth century, Cimon gained much political influence by his public services and private liberality,[101] and Nicias through the lavishness of his expenditures on behalf of the city and its religious observances.[102] Later still, Xenophon, that master of enlightened self-interest, exhibits a lively concern for his patriotic expenditures, and for the horse on which he would ride to battle.[103] In the fourth century the orators constantly back up their arguments, in political and private cases alike, by the public services they claim to have done,[104] and the city encouraged a competitive spirit by the prizes it awarded to the tragedies and other religious competitions and, in the navy, by prizes for the best ship, and the first to be ready for service when the muster was called.[105]

POOR FAMILIES

Of the poorer families in the aristocratic age little can be said. Hesiod (eighth century perhaps), it is true, poses as a poor man, and his farm was at Ascra, near Thespiae, on the hills to the south-west of the deep-soiled Boeotian plain, hence not a rich one, as Hesiod complains; yet he was not really poor.[106] His father, a trader, had had the means to buy the farm on which Hesiod made his living, which was itself less than a fair division of his father's estate by Hesiod's account.[107] From *Works and Days* it is clear that Hesiod lived in a community; cities (*poleis*) are punished for a man's evil deeds by war, famine and disaster;[108] the 'gift-devouring kings' who give crooked judgements, together with Hesiod's advice to avoid litigation, show some traces of a system of judgement or arbitration;[109] there are neighbours whose good opinion should be retained and who are a man's best stand-by,[110] but it is extraordinary how often the cutting off of the family or the wasting of the *oikos* is said to be the gods' punishment for evil.[111] Such offences were gaining wealth by underhand means, wronging a suppliant or stranger-guest (*xenos*), adultery with a brother's wife, wantonly maltreating orphans, abusing a father when he is old; family discord is said to mark the fifth (and worst) race of mankind.[112] However, despite the moralizing, the *Works and Days* may reflect the limited horizons of those less than comfortably off; limit your family to one son, as you can't afford more unless you live to be old (and thus accumulate extra wealth);[113] marry at the age of about 30 a neighbour's daughter, a virgin aged about 19, because then you will have friends close at hand if there's an emergency;[114] avoid rash adventures, and loose women;[115] all this reveals the mind of a man whose means force him to be careful of what he owns.

But Hesiod was not destitute; he advised against seafaring because it was too risky (it was a thing that poverty drove men to attempt),[116] he never considers sending his daughters out to work,[117] and the poem reveals people much poorer than he. Besides the household slaves, whom he takes for granted,[118] there are the labourer (*thes*) and the wool-worker (*erithos*), who are made part of the family for that part of the year for which they are useful, the *thes* for the ploughing season, and for the harvest, the *erithos* when the *thes* is put out of the house. 'Prefer one who has no child', says Hesiod.[119]

Who were these poverty-stricken women? They might have been widows, since orphans appear among those whom it is wrong to injure,[120] but they may equally well be the women-folk of the poor who 'with their wife and their children in bitterness of spirit seek for a livelihood among their neighbours who do not concern themselves with them'.[121]

These are the real poor, often hungry, who 'look wistfully to others' (for food), and suffer swollen feet, and whose hands become skinny through starvation and who go groping bent double over a stick in the cold of the winter. It is a fate which, to Hesiod, lies always close at hand, and could happen to anyone, so, he says, 'do not taunt the poor man with his poverty'.[122]

Political strife could easily make any man a penniless refugee,[123] but apart from these, very few of those not in the ruling classes ever appear outside the pages of Hesiod; a family of sculptors is known in Chios,[124] and we need not doubt that most of the skilled craftsmen's trades were carried on from father to son.[125] A diver is known at Scione, who taught his daughter to dive too; and Sappho can scorn a country-girl, and knows of a child goat-herd.[126] Otherwise we can only say that the poor talked, and that most men were concerned not to get a bad reputation, and we have a few insults from noble writers like Theognis (*c.* 600), who despised the low-born.[127]

THE OIKOI AS THE POLIS

However, once the individual and his private possessions had become recognized by law, the individual's *oikos* began to supplant the *genos* as the integral, organic unit of the *polis*. To the *polis* instead of the *genos* the family *oikos* began to look for protection from enemies for itself and for its lands, and to the *polis* in return the family *oikos* owed a variety of obligations. Conversely, since the existence of the *polis* depended on its ability to defend the *oikoi* (including the livelihood) of its members, it was in the interest of the *polis* to ensure that the *oikoi* remained in the possession of its own citizens,[128] and that the *oikoi* remained intact, and numerous enough to support a thriving soldier-citizen-body.

As ultimate arbiter of the ownership of land, the *polis*, like the aristocratic nobles it succeeded, made two principal demands on the *oikoi*: one that they should support the defenders of the community, its soldiers as well as its rulers, and—no less important— that they should provide the next generation of citizens and soldiers. Pericles early in the year 430 could even tell the assembled parents of the slain that it was their duty to breed new children to replace those lost.[129] On the other hand, a *polis* did not want more citizens than the *oikoi* could support; this was often one motive for colonizing, and among later writers Plato had a fixed number of *oikoi* in his Republic.[130] Aristotle too accepted the idea of a limited number in principle, and in practice, as he informs us, 'states with abundant citizens become more exclusive, and as they do so, they strike off the rolls children with one (usually female) slave parent, then children of citizen-women (and free but noncitizen father) and finally admit only children of citizens on both sides' (*i.e.* strike off children of citizen-father and free, but noncitizen mother).[131] The other was that the *oikoi* should sustain the economic foundations upon which alone the *polis* itself could exist—that is, a sufficient livelihood for the citizen-soldiers to have the strength, and the time, to fight, and sufficient over for some at least of them to contribute towards the support of the needs of the *polis* itself as a governmental institution, and to pay for its wars. These demands the *oikoi* (the family households) were vitally concerned to fulfil.

At what point the *polis* claimed the right to take over land we do not know; the first certain judicial confiscations in Athens belong to the late fifth century, though we are told that almost two centuries before this Solon had faced demands for land-division.[132] Earlier than this, Cypselus had (perhaps) divided up the lands of the Bacchiadae in Corinth, and the poet Theognis, in exile from Megara, thinks of his lands in the ploughing season in the possession of another,[133] to quote two examples. The Spartan settlement of Lycurgus traditionally involved dividing up the land, though this may have been only the newly-acquired lands of Messenia and not the old family lands of the Eurotas valley.[134] In the fourth century it frequently happened that when there was a political upheaval it was accompanied by a redivision of the land;[135] such divisions, however, were not judicial acts, but the result of revolution, and tell us nothing of the legal claims of the *polis*. They do tell us however that the idea that land could not be alienated from a family was dead.

It seems likely that the actual governmental systems of most ancient *poleis* were very cheap; few paid their officials, little or no provision was made for public services like water supplies, sewage or police, and, apart from state-salaried physicians of whom we hear from time to time,[136] social-security schemes were quite unknown.[137] In democratic Athens the jurors in the law-courts were paid a small fee when they actually sat, and those who sat on the council for policy-making and legislation were also paid from the time of Pericles, but in having these arrangements Athens was the exception, not the rule, and the idea of establishing such payments was almost certainly due to the existence of revenues arising from the tribute from the Athenian empire.[138] Defence, or war, was the other main activity for which the *polis* wanted its constituent families to provide the resources. War however has always tended to become more expensive for the state; in early times, when the citizen-soldier equipped himself and fought for short summer campaigns, with only an allowance for rations,[139] and relying on the country he invaded for his food-supplies, or on his own resources if the war was in defence of his own country, war was relatively inexpensive, and in general each *oikos* provided for the wants of its own members. In this period too it is probable that only the soldiers had any political rights, and this would certainly serve as an incentive to stimulate men's desire to serve the *polis* in person as a soldier.[140]

But when the Persians came (480–79), and the Athenians felt first the need to maintain a standing navy to ward off the Persian threat, and later the desire to do so in order to defend their empire,[141] any other *polis* which wanted to challenge Athens by sea, or indeed to avoid being coerced by Athens, was forced to do the same. Service in the fleet gave the poorer citizens a much more valid claim to a share in political power, which in Athens they attained during the long supremacy of Pericles.[142] But naval forces were also much more expensive than citizen armies; the sailors seem always to have been recruited largely from paid professionals,[143] and even when these were the poor Athenians serving their own city, it is obvious that they could not serve without payment, since their families had to have some income in order to live.[144] Before the Peloponnesian War (431–404) the Athenian subject-allies could be made to pay for the fleet, but that war brought an increase in the numbers of mercenaries, soldiers as well as sailors and marines,[145] (who were employed by both sides, and later by the Persians); the allies could not be made to pay for the whole, and (as Thucydides says) in 428 the Athenians themselves had to start paying the levies (*eisphorai*)[146] which became such regular imposts in the fourth century. These were levied on the rich, and may have been an important factor in stimulating the political struggles between the rich and the poor, and the antagonism between the upper- and middle-class army and the proletarian navy which marked the end of the Peloponnesian War.[147]

This war also both deprived the Athenians of their source of revenue from the allies and inculcated in them a dislike of service abroad in person.[148] In consequence, during the fourth century we find a situation in which the restored democracy expected their diminished supplies of money to finance not only their very extravagant governmental system, but also a navy and the most expensive form of army—mercenary forces.[149] Athenian finances could not stand the strain, and the result was that a chronic paralysis enveloped Athenian overseas enterprises owing to lack of funds, despite repeated levies.[150] Since the wealth of a *polis* was directly and exclusively the wealth of its component members, the *oikoi* of a *polis*—even of Athens—had not the resources to run their sort of democracy and a vigorous foreign policy.

THE AGRARIAN BASIS OF OIKOI

Agriculture was the main economic activity of all families in early times,[151] and of the majority even in classical Athens. We know (from Thucydides) that before the Peloponnesian War the family home of most of the Athenians was in the country,[151a] but that war, at least after the occupation of Decelea in 413, drove them off the land for a decade,[152] and the democratic constitution with its easily-earned, if very low, pay for public service provided an attraction to remain in the city,[153] where other occupations were available too. Wealthy men had small factories, like Demosthenes' father, or Comon;[154] poorer men had workshops at home, with one or two hands (*Pl. 20*); one poor man, said to have had a very busy life, was a crier in the Peiraeus;[155] among other more profitable, but more risky ways of life were mercenary service, shipping, and money-lending (including banking and marine insurance).[156] But despite such opportunities, a high proportion of Athenians depended on the land, even in the fourth century; and it is remarkable how high a proportion of those who were wealthy enough to employ the orators whose works have survived obtained some of their income from land, even if they neither lived on it, nor worked it for themselves.[157] Partly, no doubt, this can be explained by the fact that, as we are told, it was obligatory at the end of the democratic period for orators and generals to own land within the bounds of Attica[158] but farming was also thought the most honourable way of making a living and (probably) the safest investment.[159] It was also partly due to sheer innate conservative instincts, and it is quite certain that strong family attachments to the land existed, especially to land containing the family burial-places,[160] which helped to maintain a strong sentimental objection to alienating land.

The city also stimulated this concern; at the preliminary scrutiny of would-be magistrates (*dokimasia*), the candidates had to declare where their ancestral shrines were,[161] and there is clear evidence that the state was as much concerned to prevent the loss of family cults as it was to prevent the loss of *oikoi*, the family economic units of the state.

THE FAMILY IN THE POLIS, PATRIOTISM

The creation of *poleis* by no means destroyed the close association between the individual and his family. Oaths of all sorts implicated a man's family as well as himself, whether they were taken as a magistrate or in some other public capacity,[162] or as a private individual, particularly in the course of litigation;[163] in the same way curses, public and private, implicated a man's family as well as himself.[164] Utter destruction of his family, root and branch, is the general theme, though sterility of women and extinction of the hearth are also found,[165] and associated with this latter idea was the symbolic demolition of the house of one whose whole family was expelled from the state for treason or other grave cause.[166]

Family motives also inspired patriotic endeavours and service to the state, as with Callinus of Ephesus (*c.* 650), whose patriotism was motivated by the desire to save the women and children;[167] the Phocians, it was said, planned a mass suicide in the event of a defeat, the women choosing to be immolated with their children, rather than surrender.[168] To Tyrtaeus in Sparta the coward's exile was the more shameful for its effect on parents, children and wife, whereas the brave warrior's children and children's children will be famous.[169] The probably apocryphal tale told by Herodotus about Solon and Croesus, while revealing the idea of moderation which marks the sixth century out from the seventh, shows no less the deep involvement of the family and the state. Those men were the happiest (ὀλβιώτατοι), said Solon, who combined favourable family circumstances with civic distinction and a glorious death. Tellus, the happiest man, was a native of Athens, which was then prosperous, he had sons, and all his sons had children, and all survived childhood; he died gloriously in battle and received a civic funeral and a great reputation. Cleobis and Biton were Argives (it was not necessary to state that Argos was a great city); they had sufficient means to live on, distinguished themselves in the games, brought great honour to their mother, died in the hour of their glory and were commemorated by the Argives at Delphi. The city, the family, and a name that did not die all contributed a part.[170]

To Pindar in the early fifth century the family of the aristocrats for whom he wrote his epinician odes was still much more important than the city; the victor's ancestors are often mentioned and his pedigree traced back to gods or heroes; his relatives' victories in the games also receive mention.[171] But even Pindar was conscious that these families lived in a city-state, and the political conditions of the city cannot be ignored; *eunomia*, government by the rich, is seen as one of the advantages attaching to victors from Aegina;[172] dark hints reveal Pindar's embarrassment over the disgrace brought on themselves by the Thebans as a result of their medism.[173] When commissioned to write for the Alcmaeonid Megacles, the victor and the city of Athens are closely associated in what is one of Pindar's most perfunctory odes; clearly even to Pindar it did matter what sort of city his patrons lived in.[174]

To Aeschylus, too, in the mid-fifth century, city and family are closely linked in the patriotic call which the poet describes before the battle of Salamis began: 'Free your native land, free your children, wives, the shrines of your ancestral gods, and the tombs of your ancestors'.[175] The city's claim is simple, all-embracing; the family's is detailed; as always in Greek thought children are mentioned before women, and the ancestors' memorials are part of the family. Tradition also told in this age how Cyrsilus, who advised surrender to Persia, was stoned to death, and how his wife was stoned by the women.[176]

It is well enough known how much patriotic devotion to the state is extolled by Thucydides in Pericles' funeral speech; what is less emphasized as a rule is the fact that this address was made primarily to the families bereaved by the war; 'it would not be inappropriate to the moment' that the greatness of the city be expounded to show that it was in a good cause that their menfolk had fallen.[177] Moreover, on this occasion, the families had already had an opportunity to pay their tribute to the slain in the three days before the public ceremony, and the speech itself includes some words to the different classes of relatives, parents, children, brothers and widows.[178] The funeral speech is followed by the plague; Thucydides is careful to point out that the demoralization caused by this disaster was emphasized by the neglect of the family duty to procure a proper burial for the dead.[179] So too in the disaster in Sicily, it was the sight of their unburied acquaintances and relations (along with the pleas of the disabled and sick) which distressed the Athenians most as they retreated from their camp in the year 413.[180]

THE FAMILY IN POLITICAL PRAISE AND ABUSE

In the political arguments of this age, too, it appears that the acts of a man's ancestors could be used to attack or defend his position. This appears to have had particular reference to the attitude of men's ancestors to the tyranny of Peisistratus and his sons: Andocides for example, in demanding his recall from exile claims,[181] 'These acts of mine . . . . are in tune with my character and with the traditions of my family; my great-grandfather— though kin by marriage to the tyrant's family—preferred to see himself expelled with the democratic party, and to be an exile and suffer its misery, rather than to be a traitor to the people. And so I for my part, on account of my ancestors' achievements, am inevitably a natural democrat'.

Accusations of being a tyrant had been part of the stock-in-trade of the enemies of Pericles[182] (who died in 429), and are represented by Aristophanes in 422 as being a normal piece of abuse upon any occasion;[183] they were revived in attacks on Alcibiades [184] (c. 416), who was himself one of the Alcmaeonidae, so that there was contemporary relevance in Aristophanes' old men's quite unhistorical association of anti-Spartan actions with the campaigns against the tyrants,[185] and in Thucydides' polemical digression on the expulsion of the Peisistratidae with its attempt to vindicate the validity of the Alcmaeonid claims.[186]

In the political struggles following the Athenian defeat in Sicily in 413, democratic propagandists alleged that the oligarchic party in the city were molesting the womenfolk and children of the (democratic) sailors in the fleet at Samos,[187] and, later in the war, injury to the religious sentiment of the families of those who perished at Arginusae in 406 was allowed to override the law, since it was the failure to pick up the dead for burial as much as the failure to save the living which caused the terrible punishment of the generals.[188] This was because denial of burial remained one of the worst punishments which could be inflicted on a man, as it was in Homer; it classed the person who suffered this fate with those convicted of sacrilege, treason or tyranny, whose bodies were ceremonially cast out of their native land unburied.[189] Denial of burial in one's homeland was one of the consequences of exile for life, a sentence commonly inflicted on murderers, traitors and similar people.[190] Exile was thought a more serious penalty by the ancients than by us, because one consequence of such an exile was that the person so punished was unable to maintain the worship of his ancestors, and to be tended in turn by his descendants in the family burial-place. In the case of Themistocles we are told that, despite the fact that he had a fine tomb in the market-square at Magnesia, where due honour was paid, and the Magnesians thought so highly of him that his descendants were honoured by them till Plutarch's day (second century AD), as early as Thucydides' day it was rumoured that his bones had been secretly brought back at his own request by his relatives and re-interred in Attic soil.[191] In Athens we are told that by law anyone who saw a corpse was obliged to put earth upon it, even if he was not a relation of the deceased.[192] The religious Nicias, we are told, was so anxious to pick up the corpses of two men who had fallen in a successful battle, but had been missed in the first count, that he was ready to surrender the prestige of victory to the enemy.[193] Thus to deny burial to the victorious heroes of the battle of Arginusae was an appalling affront to popular sentiment. Popular resentment was also kept alive against the memory of the Thirty Tyrants (set up by Lysander in 404) by Lysias, for example, who, speaking in 403 or 402, stresses in his account of their crimes their disregard for the proper burial of their victims, and the injuries inflicted on their families in this way.[194]

In Aristophanes' plays, moreover, though the democracy and its leaders and institutions are attacked, and there are jokes about Zeus, and almost all the Olympian gods and heroes and about Dionysus, there are none about the Athenians' family cults; they were taken too seriously for jesting. Other contemporaries were Socrates and Xenophon; Socrates was the philosopher who above all directed men's minds to the relationships of men in city and family, as is very clear from Xenophon's *Memorabilia* (an interest reflected also in his *Oeconomicus*); it is no less clear from Plato's works, whatever their relation to Socrates' own conversations.

From the fourth century, apart from the many private law-suits on family inheritances, four funeral orations survive.[195] Many common elements persist: the achievements of the ancestors against the Amazons, the burial of the Seven against Thebes, the defence of the Heracleidae, the victories against Darius and Xerxes,[196] praise of democracy as making men brave and self-controlled,[197] the autochthonous character of the Athenians,[198] a word of welcome to the non-Athenians who are present;[199] but all include, especially in their perorations, sentiments addressed to the families—sympathy for the parents of the dead, a promise that the children will be cared for by the state (an element also present in Pericles' speech); the widows of the fallen are promised the support of the survivors, and their sisters will gain marriages befitting to them;[200] three of the speeches conclude with a bidding to perform the customary burial ceremonies[201]—which of course belonged peculiarly to the families.

Many similar sentiments also reappear in the political attacks at the end of Demosthenes' career. Thus Dinarchus prays the gods to save 'his native land in its perilous struggle for survival, for its children, its women, its good reputation, for all other good things it enjoys'.[202] Lycurgus' prosecution of Leocrates for treachery to Athens in that he left the city secretly after the battle of Chaeronea (in 338) is full of emotional, patriotic appeals, many of them based on the family.[203] Aeschines, in putting the responsibility for Alexander's sack of Thebes upon Demosthenes' shoulders, invites his audience to picture the scene: 'their city being taken, demolition of walls, burning of houses, women and children being hauled off into slavery, elderly men, elderly women learning late in life to forget the name of freedom, wailing, uttering supplications to you . . .'.[204]

The language of insult in this age is concentrated on three main themes, bribery, maladministration of office, and family circumstances which disqualify the opponent from public office, speaking in the assembly and even citizenship. In the speech against Androtion, Demosthenes tells how Androtion had made enemies: 'he said in public of one man that he was a slave, born of slave parents, and ought to pay taxes as a metic, of another that the mother of his children was a whore, of another that his father had been a catamite, and that another's mother had sold her body, and of another that he would publish his malversations from office'.[205] 'I will not incur enemies', says Aeschines, 'by naming the man whose father married a Scythian foreigner'.[206] He was not so squeamish about Demosthenes' family circumstances, nor was Demosthenes about those of Aeschines,[207] and we find reappearing again accusations of hostility to the democracy as inherited from ancestors.[208]

Earlier in his career Demosthenes had sued Meidias for punching him in the face; amongst Meidias' alleged offences were the bursting into Demosthenes' house and using foul language in front of his sister who was still a young virgin living at home. Symbolizing his arrogant and ostentatious wealth was the fact that Meidias drove his wife everywhere in a smart carriage, with a pair of Sicyonian greys.[209] It was such exhibitions of wealth, and the dominance of rich women over their husbands, which was at least partly responsible for the philosophers' attitudes, and specifically for Plato's attempt in the *Republic* to exclude from his Guardians any feelings of possessiveness, and hence of desire for family life, an attempt which he tried to make effective through the marriage-regulations of the *Laws*.[210] This question clearly worried Aristotle as well, for, though he rejected Plato's attempted communal ownership of property on the grounds that private ownership is valuable in making men look after that which is their own, he decided that absolute equality in property (meaning landed property) is not a particularly important end for a state to achieve; therefore, since he regarded the aggregate of a city's inhabitants' possessions (or specifically their land and its products) as the total of the wealth owned by the city, he thought that this total was best treated as a sum of individual families' properties, which should be owned by generous individuals, and not as the possessions of the community.[211] He therefore based his state on the family.

CHAPTER IV

FAMILY OIKOI AND
ATHENIAN DEMOCRACY

DEMOCRACY AND CLEISTHENES

SINCE THE ESTABLISHMENT of a written code of laws was perhaps the most important single step in creating a *polis* out of a collection of families, many states looked back to their lawgiver as the founder of their polity. Among these was Athens. In democratic Athens orators described the law as the means whereby the weaker could defend themselves against the stronger,[1] and Athenians regarded their democracy as founded by the legislation of Solon[2] (594, trad.).

Although from the political point of view this thesis can hardly stand examination, as the creator of a law code which imposed checks on the ancient families and made the law accessible to all, the claim has a sounder basis.[3] In 508, however, the aristocrat Cleisthenes headed a revolution which truly changed Athens into a democratic state. The choice of Cleisthenes' reforms as marking the start of the democratic era in Athens is justified partly by the fact that some fifth century Athenians thought it the appropriate date,[4] but mainly because (as is now generally agreed) Cleisthenes effectively ended the power of the old aristocratic families to control admission to citizenship.

CITIZENSHIP BEFORE CLEISTHENES

Before this revolution full membership of the state—citizenship that is to say—was confined to those who belonged to the family-based nexus of household (*oikos*), clan (*genos*), phratry and tribe (the four Ionic tribes); after Cleisthenes' reforms full citizenship was established on the basis of the household, the deme and the tribe (ten new tribes created by Cleisthenes on a local basis). Cleisthenes, however, left the clans and phratries undisturbed;

they therefore continued in existence for the purpose of determining kinship, and consequently for establishing succession-rights in disputes over inheritance, and for maintaining in existence the religious duties and privileges which belonged to the family groups. By Cleisthenes' settlement, therefore, the political affiliations of the citizen were, at least for the moment, sundered from his kinship and religious connexions. This, however, as will be shown later, did not last long.

The precise definition of the family group which determined citizenship before Cleisthenes' reform is uncertain; some scholars believe the citizen-roll to have comprised the members of the *genē*[5] (the clans), some the members of the phratries.[6]

The members of the *genē* claimed descent from a common ancestor, the members of the phratries were descended perhaps from military blood-brotherhoods or neighbours who had combined in defence of their lands, and whose children had often intermarried and thus become kin.[7] In democratic Athens each phratry had a communal religious life and cult based on common shrines associated with their lands, and some *genē* certainly did likewise.[8] It is highly unlikely that these cults were invented by the democracy; it is much more probable that they are pre-Cleisthenic, and indeed pre-Solonian.

EVIDENCE FOR FAMILY CONTROL

The evidence for a family basis for the political organization of the pre-Cleisthenic state is fragmentary, and inferential. Plutarch says clearly that Solon allowed foreigners to come to Athens and have citizenship, provided that they practised a trade and brought their whole families, or were permanently exiled from their native city, and not otherwise.[9] *Prima facie* this is incompatible with a family-based political structure, but Plutarch stresses that the offer was only for those who really wanted to make Athens their home—his words imply the necessity for a total removal, family possessions, cult and all, into Athens; the effect of their immigration must have been seen as an addition to the Athenian citizen-body of what was not just an itinerant worker, but a whole family with their own religious festivals and gods. They were thus, as it were, adopted by the Athenian state, since they had cut off their ties with any other community. Moreover, between Solon's time and that of Cleisthenes we hear of those whose citizenship was questioned; such people supported Peisistratus—and, by implication, were those expelled from the lists after the fall of the tyrants;[10] many of those whom Cleisthenes enrolled had dubious claims to citizenship. These may well have been the immigrant Athenians who had perhaps not been able to prove membership of any of the (family-based) bodies whose rolls made up the citizen-body, so that they could not exercise their citizenship, and they were liable to be challenged if they tried to do so. *De jure* perhaps they had obtained citizenship by Solon's law, *de facto*, however, they were treated as foreign residents, the name they are given by Aristotle.[11] Their situation, it may be suggested, was comparable to that of the negroes in the southern states of the U.S.A. in the earlier years of this century; they had citizenship, but could not exercise it because they could not get enrolled in any body which enabled them to make it effective. If these suppositions are correct, they conclusively demonstrate that political control of the pre-Cleisthenic state lay in the hands of the family-based organizations.

ARISTOCRATIC FAMILIES' POWER

Whatever the truth of the above, it is certain that the members of the leading families ran the state, enjoying before Solon's time, with the support of the law, a monopoly of public office,[12] which, in the absence of any attested court of appeal,[13] also included control of the state's judicature. Their monopoly of power is reflected in the economic malaise of the state in the early sixth century, as described by *Ath. Pol.* and Plutarch, and which provoked the reforms of Solon. They more or less monopolized the state's resources; whether or not they owned most of the land, they controlled its produce: 'the whole land', says *Ath. Pol.*, 'was under the control of a few men'.[14] Their wealth and ostentation, which extended to every aspect of life—or death—are illustrated by the magnificence of the memorials set up in memory of their dead. These are of various kinds:

1 From the ninth–seventh centuries, large, painted Geometric pots whose function was not only to act as grave markers, but also to receive libations (drink-offerings).

2 Chest-like structures of sun-dried brick, coated with stucco, surmounted with flat roofs and decorated with terracotta plaques; these latter, some of which reveal very elaborate funerals, are dated on stylistic grounds to *c.* 725–620, and are a form of art peculiar to Attica.[15] (*Pls. 21, 22*)

3 Stone (occasionally bronze) statues of youths, maidens, lions, horsemen and so on, common during the later seventh century and the sixth.

4 Stone *stelai*; the Attic *stelai* first appear in the late seventh century; they are magnificent pieces of funerary art crowned with sphinxes, the symbolic protectors of the dead, and portraying the deceased sculptured in relief, incised or merely painted on the shaft, and with a dedication inscribed usually upon the base (*Pl. 23*). They reveal clearly a society dominated by a few wealthy nobles who alone could afford costly tomb memorials, since it was only rich clients who could have afforded the importation of large blocks of marble into Athens from the islands.[16] We must note also the measures in social legislation taken by Solon to curb ostentation, measures which included the banning of elaborate trousseaux[17] and personal ornaments for women, as well as displays on family occasions such as funerals. The necessity for such legislation indicates that excessive expenditure on these occasions was quite normal.

These families' inter-relationships were also governed by private feuds such as that between the Alcmaeonidae and the descendants of the Cylonian conspirators, which must have been at least partly responsible for the observable fact that the Alcmaeonidae were always opposed to the main body of aristocratic (or oligarchic) opinion in political quarrels where the parties are detectable.[18] Even after Solon's legislation we can see in the marriage of Peisistratus and Megacles' daughter an arrangement possible only in a society whose political links were those of its aristocratic families.[19]

INDEPENDENCE OF OIKOI

Solon's Laws on Wills

Some of Solon's most far-reaching acts, if we may assume that Plutarch is correct in assigning them to Solon, were concerned with the family and its property. Their principal effect was to liberate the conjugal family (the *oikos* of husband, wife, children and dependants) to some extent from the wider kinship-groups in the matter of property-ownership. The principal element in this was the introduction of the will.[20] Wills made it necessary to make regulations for the marriage of *epikleroi* (girls, that is, without brothers) whose fathers had not adopted an heir, and to define the limits of the kinship-group entitled to make a claim against a will, and the right to intestate succession, and similar legal claims, as these limits were already defined for religious purposes, such as the avenging of homicide.[21]

Before Solon's time the *genos* (or clan) ultimately controlled the property of individual *oikoi*, since there were no wills, and therefore at a man's death his property passed automatically to his next of kin in the *genos*, whoever these were.[22] The natural, and first, successors were of course sons, and these will undoubtedly have succeeded their fathers, since in Athens a son always had an almost inalienable right to his father's estate, and, if there were more than one son, to an equal share.[23] But some men grew old or went into battle without having procreated sons; before Solon's time the only method they had of preventing their estate being inherited by their perhaps distant kin was to adopt a son in their lifetime;[24] there is good evidence that adoption with such an end in view was possible,[25] but we have no idea how frequently it was done.

At first the right to make a will was limited to those who lacked sons;[26] this limitation reveals the purpose of the law, which was to enable a man to prevent the disappearance of his *oikos* by adopting an heir to it in the event of his death, whether this was immediately imminent or not. Later the right was extended, but the feeling that men with adult sons did not make wills was so strong that as late as the fourth century orators can still claim that a man who has sons cannot make a will.[27]

In his economic legislation Solon had tried to prevent a disproportionate amount of the state's wealth and lands falling into a few people's hands;[28] his social legislation did not run counter to this. A son adopted by will (like a son adopted by a man in his lifetime) had no claim whatever to anything at all from his natural family, and testamentary freedom therefore did not make it any easier to accumulate large properties.

Solon's Laws on Epikleroi

Solon also legislated to prevent the amalgamation of estates by a man taking in marriage an *epikleros*.[29] We do not know if there were any laws about the *epikleros* before Solon's time, but Solon's laws about adoption discouraged a wealthy man from allowing himself to be adopted in order to obtain an estate with a wealthy *epikleros* to wife, and if he married one without being adopted, by Solon's laws he was liable to lose her to the next of kin who would claim her at her father's death. Solon also legislated[30] to discourage old men from claiming an *epikleros* in order to enjoy her wealth without providing an heir to her family; he is said to have laid it down by law that the husband of an *epikleros* must have intercourse with her not less than three times a month without fail (πάντως), and that if he was unable to have intercourse with her, she was permitted to have intercourse with her husband's next of kin (presumably without marriage) in order to get children to her father's *oikos*. Plutarch remarks that this was an extraordinary and absurd law, but does not doubt its genuineness, nor, it would seem, did the other commentators whose views Plutarch cites.[31] Extraordinary the law may have been, but its existence shows how strong was Solon's determination not to allow *oikoi* to be lost to the state unavoidably, or families extinguished. The greater measure of freedom conferred on the *kyrios* of an *oikos* in disposing of his property was thus designed to enable him to perpetuate his *oikos* as a living unit of the state, and to resist any claims by his *genos* to amalgamate it with the rest of the property owned by members of the *genos*, not to enable him to amalgamate it with another *oikos* in accordance with his own whims.[31a] In the interests of the whole community the legislator was anxious to maintain the highest possible number of *oikoi* in the state capable of maintaining a citizen able to serve the state in person and in purse.

THE ARCHONSHIP AFTER SOLON

Solon's legislation produced bitter *stasis*; we are told that the opposed parties were locally-based,[32] with the implication that the economic interests of the leaders of the parties varied in accordance with where their lands lay,[33] but we are also told very specifically that the object of their strife was the Archonship—not one of the archonships, but the Eponymous Archonship.[34] Solon had made the Archon responsible for administering the whole of the law affecting the family and its property;[35] perhaps this was the root-cause of the political *stasis*; the old noble families were determined to control this field of law, which might affect themselves and their families very deeply, by controlling the magistracy which administered it. The new intrusions of the state into this field, especially that of ownership, inheritance and succession, if it did not create it, must have added to this determination.

Peisistratus in his tyranny controlled the office of Archon;[36] he did not tamper with the aristocratic constitution, and neither he nor his sons succeeded in effectually integrating the non-citizens into the citizen-body. Among these was Themistocles; one of the persisting streams of information we have about him calls him a bastard; his mother was, we are told, a Thracian courtesan and hence a slave, yet he was a citizen, the leader of a popular movement and a well-known figure by 484–3, the date when he persuaded the Athenians to employ their financial surplus in building a fleet. If the tradition about his bastard birth is true, his enfranchisement as a full Athenian citizen can only belong to the Cleisthenic reforms.[37]

OIKOI AND OTHER GROUPS AFTER CLEISTHENES

Demes

By Cleisthenes' reforms, the demes, which in the country districts at least already existed, were converted into the units upon which the political structure rested, but this act was little more than a redistribution of the citizen-body into new groupings based on the location of a citizen's *oikos* instead of the kinship-group to which he had previously belonged.[37a] The redistribution itself was a once-for-all act, and the deme to which a citizen belonged was (throughout the classical period) the deme to which the *oikos* to which his ancestors belonged had been allocated at the time of Cleisthenes' reform.[38] 'A man's *oikos*', therefore, came to have two meanings: it meant his place of residence, the house and land which (usually) he had inherited, and where he lived; it also meant the group in the deme-register to which he belonged, which had descended to him from his ancestor in Cleisthenes' day. Neither *oikos* nor deme therefore were, in a political sense, comparable with a twentieth-century 'place of residence' or parliamentary constituency, neither of which is heritable, and both of which a man retains only so long as he does not change his place of residence. The Athenians' strong sense of family continuity, however, caused them to make their demes heritable, with the result that, in time, as the deme-registers came to resemble less and less the lists of those actually living in the demes, the demes came more and more closely to resemble the previously-existing family units, the phratries and *genē*.

The demes also provided no exception to the general rule that all Greek associations are religious associations as well. This is most clearly demonstrated by the fourth century inscription known as the Greater Demarchia,[39] in which the deme Erchia set out in an elaborate calendar the festivals of the deme, month by month, carefully apportioning both the cost of the sacrifices and the number and species of the victims equally among four of its citizens, and prescribing in many instances how the sacrificial meat and the additional perquisites, such as the hides, were to be disposed of. This deme, it has been suggested, had by the fourth century taken over the festivals of some at least of its constituent families in order to ensure that they were preserved, and there is no particular reason why Erchia should have been different from other demes. Demes, we know, also owned lands corporately— perhaps lands containing shrines—and since these lands could be leased, the demes had a revenue at their disposal.[40] They kept written records of their members, and of their *oikoi*, in which legitimately begotten sons were registered on attaining their majority and adopted sons as having been adopted into the *oikos* of their new parent.[41]

Demes thus acquired in time a sense of corporate solidarity; in the fourth century orators refer to demesmen in the same breath as they refer to the members of their kinship-groups,[42] and in the country-demes at least there must have been a great measure of common membership between the groups; attachment to ancestral property—especially to lands and burial-grounds—also involved attachment to the deme in which these were sited, if their initial ownership was pre-Cleisthenic, as it must have been in many cases.

Phratries

The exact relationship between the (locally-based) demes and the (family-based) *genē* and phratries is far from clear. If the phratries had had *oikoi* associated with them before Cleisthenes' day, there must have been in some parts of Attica a high degree of common membership between demes and phratries. It is clear from another inscription of the early fourth century, that containing the laws of the Demotionidae, that *oikoi* could be said to belong to a phratry; it speaks of 'those who belong to the *oikos* of the Deceleans', who appear to have been the phratry's hereditary priests.[43] Clearly this *oikos* was not an *oikos* in the sense of one conjugal family and its lands, but it does show that the subdivision of the phratries into family-groups called *oikoi* was ancient, and therefore almost certainly pre-Cleisthenic. This phratry is of particular interest, too, in that its principal sub-groups seem not to have been based on any *genos*, but were all *thiasoi*,[44] which were groups whose membership included persons who did not even claim to have a hereditary right to belong;[45] and the Deceleans were among those who claimed to be the most ancient inhabitants of Attica.[46]

Orators also speak of *oikoi* as being bodies, or groups, within phratries: 'I introduced this boy here', says Sositheus, 'to the *phrateres* of Hagnias in the interest of Euboulides, he being his daughter's son, in order that his *oikos* should not be left without an heir.'[47] Similarly, when an *oikos* lacked an heir by direct descent and a son was adopted, the son who was to inherit the *oikos* of the adopting parent passed into his phratry as well as into his deme, thus on the one hand maintaining the *oikos* in the adopter's phratry as well as his deme, and on the other severing the adopted son's religious and legal ties of kinship with his natural kinship-groups as well as his political affiliation.[48] The adopted son, however, it seems, did not appear as *kyrios* of the *oikos* in the register till he had registered a son of his own in it;[49] in the interval he was registered only provisionally, as son of his adoptive father, even if he had succeeded to the property, and was the legal *kyrios* of the *oikos*.

RURAL AND URBAN OIKOI

If *gene* owned lands, as is almost certain, then there must often have also been a close connexion between the *gene* and the demes. Before Cleisthenes' time we need not doubt that in rural Attica the lands of *gene* were already subdivided into family land-holdings which it would be reasonable to assume were known, if only informally, as *oikoi* as well as *kleroi*; it is fair to assume that when Cleisthenes created city-demes he defined them as consisting of areas which comprised numbers of *oikoi*, though these city *oikoi* may in many cases have comprised no more than a single house or a tenement. As close to Athens, however, as the Hippodrome we hear of a man who had, if not a farm, at least a garden which required several men to work it,[50] so that the number of demes consisting wholly of urban *oikoi* may not have been very large.

OIKOS–MEMBERSHIP AND THE STATE

What we cannot conclusively demonstrate, however, is that individual citizens had to be registered as belonging to an *oikos*; in this sense[50a] the fact that the Demotionidae did not have to belong to any of the *thiasoi* of which the phratry was composed makes it unlikely that all citizens always did, though their ancestors must originally have had some local affiliation in order to be registered by Cleisthenes in a deme. Poorer citizens, for example, who were mere residents in a tenement, would not be so likely to belong to this sort of *oikos*, nor would other citizens who owned no real-estate. The relationship between citizen, *oikos*, and the larger units of the state will therefore have been one in which deme and phratry (and perhaps *genos* and *thiasos*) were all equally anxious to preserve intact the *oikoi* of which they were composed, the deme for political and financial reasons, the phratry (and *genos* and *thiasos*) for social and religious reasons also, which by the fourth century were influencing the demes too; on the other hand the *oikoi* need not have comprised all the citizens, only those of means, who owned real-estate, who were the principal contributors to the funds which all of the constituent units of the state appear to have had.

DEME-MEMBERSHIP AND THE STATE

The exact relationship between the deme on the one hand and the clan and phratry on the other in regard to the individual citizen's personal rights is also not clear; it is generally agreed that citizens could belong to a deme without belonging to a phratry, since membership of a deme was compulsory for citizenship, but membership of a phratry was perhaps not.[51] A candidate's demesmen were responsible for inscribing his name on their roll of citizens,[52] and when they had done so, it seems that even the council, before whom the candidate then appeared, had the duty of determining only whether he appeared to be old enough to undergo military training. *Ath. Pol.* suggests that in Aristotle's day all boys of eighteen did military training, whether they belonged to the hoplite class or not.[53] Some modern scholars have doubted whether this can ever have been true, and almost all believe that it was not the case before the reorganization of the *ephebia* (the organization for training the young citizens) in the fourth century.[53a] There is, however, nothing in *Ath. Pol.* to support the view that those of the lowest class (*thetes*) were exempt, while the pay and allowances and the free issue of equipment by the state would not make it impossible for them to take part for reasons of poverty; their pay (four obols a day) was higher than that for a citizen attending the assembly. The fact that not all those trained subsequently became hoplites does not mean that all did not do basic training.[54]

A candidate rejected by his demesmen could proceed against them in the courts, and if he were successful compel them to enrol him. It was a risky thing to attempt, however, since the penalty for failing to win his case against the demesmen was enslavement,[55] and it would therefore only be undertaken by those who believed that they had an unimpeachable case. The law courts were also called in if there was a dispute between a deme and the council as to whether a candidate was old enough. A dispute was almost certain to arise if the council tried to fine a deme for presenting too young a candidate, and since the appearance of the candidate was the only material piece of evidence available, the jury in the law court had to inspect him—a task which Aristophanes says the jurors relished particularly.[56]

PHRATRY-MEMBERSHIP AND THE STATE

The phratry appears to have played no part in the admission process as described in *Ath. Pol.*; it is true that honorary citizens were granted a phratry as well as a deme,[57] but there is no evidence that the citizens of Plataea, whom the Athenians admitted to Athenian citizenship when they decided not to attempt to defend Plataea against the joint attack of the Thebans and Spartan alliance in 431[58] (and who of course owned no land), were given phratries—nor has our version of the decree about them any mention of a grant of phratries.

The relationship of the smaller sub-groups within the phratries to the phratries and *oikoi* is less certain, and the evidence comes from the fourth century or later. Membership of a *thiasos* was apparently not determined solely by descent; we can quote the case of Astyphilus, whose stepfather introduced him to his own *thiasos*, though (naturally) not to his phratry or deme, since he already belonged to his own father's.[59] It therefore follows that not all fellow-members of a *thiasos* were also fellow-demesmen. *Genos*-membership was traditionally transmitted solely by birth, but we know one instance when seven fellow-*gennētai* belonged to six different demes,[60] though they might have belonged to the same phratry.[61] Although some phratries comprised only *thiasoi*, some included a mixture of *thiasoi* and *genē*, like that of Aeschines, whose father, a member of a *thiasos*, belonged to the same phratry as the famous *genos* of the Eteoboutadae.[62] We should probably conclude that the phratries differed from one another in many ways and customs.

OIKOI AND PUBLIC DUTIES

Individual citizens of means were *kyrioi* of *oikoi*, which belonged to the larger units of the state, the phratries and the demes. These were equally anxious not to lose any of their constituent *oikoi*; the demes were concerned because they were responsible for a variety of civic duties; they appear to have taken over from the earlier *naukrariai* the financial responsibilities which they had previously discharged;[63] they carried out civic duties of various kinds such as electing candidates who would draw lots for certain priest-hoods,[64] and providing lists of those citizens from whom a stated number of council-members and garrison-troops would be drawn by lot.[65] The demesmen on the council and the demarch (the head of the deme for the time being) also kept the rolls of those citizens of their demes who were eligible for military and naval service,[66] and were perhaps required to produce a stated quota when a levy from the roll was called out. Each of the demes was also supposed to maintain a fair share of the burdens known as liturgies: the trierarchies, which involved the equipping and manning of a trireme, and the *choregiai* and other services associated with the state religion.[67] These, if successfully carried out, brought honour to the deme as well as to the individual and his tribe.

OIKOI AND RELIGIOUS DUTIES

The phratries were also anxious about their religious life. The inscription of the Demotionidae details the procedures for admission, and the two sacrifices, the lesser and the youth's (μεῖον and κουρεῖον) which accompanied admission to the phratry at the great family festival of the Apatouria.[68] The members of the phratries, the *phrateres*, also had the power of scrutiny over the candidates for admission, and fined those who tried to procure the admission of ineligible candidates;[69] they kept a written record of their members (at least in the fourth century),[70] of which it may be suggested that the prime purpose was to record who had the succession-rights to the various *oikoi* appertaining to the phratry. Consequently sons, as natural successors, were always enrolled, also adopted sons at their adoption,[71] and daughters who were *epikleroi*;[72] sacrifices were also offered by husbands at their marriage presumably to enrol their wives.[73] *Phrateres*, however, in the democratic period, could not overrule the city's law courts; we know at least one occasion on which a father was compelled to enrol two men in his phratry when a court decided that they were his legitimate sons; in another case it seems that a man registered in a deme as the adopted son of a deme-member, and hence a member of his *oikos*, was accepted without further difficulty into the phratry.[74] The converse appears also to be true; men whose citizenship is challenged take great pains to prove that they are *phrateres*,[75] since this will provide a strong basis for their claim to be demesmen, and therefore citizens; Boeotus and Pamphilus were apparently enrolled without difficulty as demesmen, having, after a struggle, been enrolled as *phrateres* first.[76]

PRESERVATION OF THE OIKOI

Deme and phratry were thus both constituted out of an agglomeration of *oikoi*; the *oikoi* were based on real-estate, whether landed property or houses and tenements, and the deme and the phratry were equally anxious to prevent the disappearance of any of their *oikoi*, the phratry mainly for religious reasons (and because it would diminish the numbers of those who would offer sacrifices), and the deme for financial and political reasons as well.

LOSS OF OIKOI

Oikoi could be lost to a phratry and deme if a family became extinct, and their *oikos* was amalgamated with another *oikos*; the members of the phratry and deme were therefore hardly less anxious than the family itself to prevent its extinction, especially if it had substantial means. For the deme the loss could be compensated if the acquisition of the land belonging to an *oikos* in a deme resulted in the acquirer incurring a liability to the deme in which the land was situated. It is well attested that this occurred; Apollodorus owned land in three different demes, and when in a crisis an assessment of taxes was made to raise money quickly he received demands from all three to pay up.[77] A normal tax on non-members appears from an inscription of the Peiraeeis to be well-established.[78] A third piece of evidence suggests that the purchase of the land belonging to an *oikos* in a deme made a man eligible to be enrolled in that deme; Teisias had bought some land which had clearly at one time belonged to a different family, since it had their family tombs upon it; these are described as being 'old and already built before we purchased the property'; his son claims in his peroration that his opponents 'are seeking absolutely to drive us out of the deme with their hounding of me and laying false accusations'.[79] 'How,' we may ask, 'had Teisias joined the deme, except by buying the property of one of the *oikoi* in the deme? And how, if deme-membership was not associated with the land of the *oikos*, would being forced to sell it make his son leave the deme?' On the other hand, one must always treat orators' statements with caution, and add that we know of no other clear evidence that deme-membership was obtainable by purchases of land, and regard it as possible that the orator was using the word 'deme' in a purely topographical sense in order to mislead the jurors. The phratry, however, had no comparable means of compensating itself for the loss of an *oikos*. *Phrateres* therefore were obviously no less anxious than demesmen to prevent *oikoi* from disappearing by amalgamation, or from being alienated by inheritance by a non-member.

A family might also become impoverished, and be forced to sell the lands of the *oikos*, perhaps even the whole of the real-estate, to an outsider belonging to a different phratry and deme; the family would then still exist, but the *oikos* would be unable to perform the duties it had previously performed, and when this happened a man's personal honour and esteem were affected; the spendthrift was not a man of good reputation;

extravagance is an insult aimed at opponents by orators,[80] and obviously a man who was unable to serve his *phrateres* and demesmen as his forebears had done could not expect to be thought a man of equal repute with them, and would lose face.

THE STATE'S INTEREST

Such improvidence, however, affected the whole state; it required liturgies from the wealthy citizens and was naturally affected if an *oikos* which had supported a trierarchy or other liturgies became unable to do so; the deme and phratry were similarly affected, and this will explain why wasting one's property constituted an offence which came under the jurisdiction of the Archon,[81] the magistrate whose duty it was to guard the property of the citizens, but who, it is clear, guarded it primarily in the interests of the *oikoi* and the larger units of the state rather than in the interests of the individual and his private whims and tastes.

The state's interest in the preservation of numerous flourishing *oikoi* makes it easy to see why ancient orators are so fond of attacking opponents by charging them with being, or trying to be, in possession of more than one *oikos* or *kleros*,[82] or with maltreating an *oikos* which has in the past performed public services,[83] with the object of prejudicing the court against an opponent. Modern critics are fond of castigating Athenian orators for producing such arguments, and Athenian juries for taking account of them, but such criticism is often off the target, as when it fails to acknowledge the sphere of the public interest upon which these lawsuits impinged. No modern state hesitates to claim the right to control its residents' ability to dispose of their property to foreigners or to remove property outside its own sphere of jurisdiction; many claim the right to take property away from individuals altogether and nationalize it in the public interest. Ancient Athens, although it did not exactly nationalize the *oikoi*, claimed to ensure that, within limits, priority in the deployment of the resources of the city was given to serving the interest of the city, deme and phratry before that of the individual citizens. Preventing the accumulation of *oikoi* by an individual, and striving to maintain a full quota of *oikoi* in every deme was one of the means.

CHAPTER V

MARRIAGE AND THE FAMILY IN ATHENS

PERICLES' CITIZENSHIP LAW

IF CLEISTHENES ALTERED the laws concerning the family, except for those affecting the entitlement to citizenship which have been already discussed, we have no record of it. In 451 Pericles persuaded the assembly to modify the rules for entitlement to citizenship by a law which decreed that a man's parents must both be citizens for him to be a citizen. It is not clear whether it was at this moment that a formal marriage became necessary also, or whether it had always been necessary (as Wolff for example[1] believes), or whether it only became necessary later (see below). The motives for Pericles' law have been much discussed; selfishness—*i.e.* not wanting to share the profits of empire; race-consciousness—*i.e.* fear of diluting the Athenian autochthonous stock; other motives have also been adduced, but, from the point of view of the family, much the most convincing reason was the desire of Athenian fathers to secure husbands for their daughters. In his speech against Neaira (written about 100 years later it is true) Apollodorus demands that she be condemned for usurpation of citizenship on the grounds that she is a courtesan of unknown parentage, whose picturesque career took her all over Greece, from Corinth where she was trained, in the company of various men. After saying that her acquittal will set the seal of approval on such careers he urges the jurors:[2] 'Take thought also for women of citizen birth, to see that the daughters of the poor do not become old maids. For as things are now, even if a girl be quite without means, the law sees to the provision of a sufficient dowry for her, if nature has endowed her with an appearance which is even passably moderate; but if you acquit Neaira, and the law has been dragged through the mud by you and made of

21, 22 On the decorated plaques attached to brick tombs appear various scenes of mourning. Three elderly men and one youth pay their respects to the dead (above), and a woman tears her hair and lacerates her face while a bearded man clutches his head in a gesture of sorrow (below); their parted lips show that they are wailing. The pillar indicates that the scene is indoors.

23 Amongst the most splendid marble monuments of the sixth century found in Athens is the sphinx-crowned monument to the children of Megacles. As restored it stands nearly 14 ft. high. The sphinx was regarded as the protector of the dead; the figures on the *stele* show that they both died as young children. The excellent state of preservation of the *stele* may be due to the fact that it was deliberately broken up when Megacles was driven into exile by Peisistratus, and therefore it illustrates the operation of the idea of the expulsion from the state of an entire family, the dead as well as the living.

no effect, there is no possible doubt that because of poverty the harlot's trade will come upon the daughters of the citizens, as many as are not able to have marriages procured for them, and the high regard we have for free women will be transferred to courtesans if they gain leave with impunity to breed children as they please and have a share in the religious life of the state and its honours.' The desire to ensure that all girls were found husbands was most important, as we shall also see below, and must certainly have carried much weight in influencing the decision in 451, though the other motives are likely to have been important for its timing.

BASTARDS

Prior to the law Athenians had always been able to contract legal marriages with non-Athenian women: we know that Cimon's mother was a Thracian princess named Hegesipyle,[3] and that Alcibiades had ancestral connections with one Spartan family at least; Thucydides alleges that even his name was Spartan,[4] which suggests a Spartan ancestor.

That is not to say that there were no such people as illegitimate children before Pericles' day; bastards are known in the Homeric poems, mostly the children of slave girls or concubines begotten by the great heroes[5] (the results of the seduction of noble girls by gods seem not to be called bastards), but their status and rights depended upon the decision of their father about them while he lived, or of their kinsmen when he had died.[6] When a man had no son by his recognized wife he might adopt a bastard as his heir, as Menelaus is said to have done in the *Odyssey*.[7]

In the aristocratic age we know only of the bastard sons of tyrants, who were sometimes employed, as by the Cypselids,[8] to forward their imperialistic schemes; of the poet Archilochus, if he were indeed a bastard, and rejected as a suitor for that reason;[9] and (in Athens) of Themistocles, son of Neocles and a Thracian woman who was perhaps either a concubine or an *hetaira*.[10] However, the Solonian legislation provided redress for sexual assaults on a concubine 'kept for the purpose of breeding free children',[11] and this implies recognition of the status of concubine at least as far as the personal freedom of the woman and of her children was concerned. It seems to the present writer unlikely that children of this class had any substantial claim on the *oikos* of their father in the pre-Solonian period, when the next of kin automatically succeeded to it, nor in the post-Solonian period when a man had sons (though in this case he would not be likely to keep a concubine for the procreation of children), but we cannot be sure whether they could have had unimpeachable claims to citizenship.

Solon's legislation about *epikleroi* certainly makes it clear that legitimate offspring for *oikoi* without a male heir could be obtained without a formal marriage;[12] if *epikleroi* had the right to give birth to legitimate children by intercourse without marriage with stated relatives, it seems probable that men had a similar right to procure the continuity of their *oikos* by means of a concubine's children, though this might not bind their *phrateres* or *gennētai* to accept the child into their ranks as a citizen; some of those whose citizenship was disputable in the period between Solon and Cleisthenes may have belonged to this class.

Slave girls' children, and the children of common prostitutes, must always have been classed as bastards, and so, presumably, were the offspring of parents who did not live together, such as the children of the victims of rape or seduction. What the status of children born to an Athenian man and woman who merely lived together without a formal wedding ceremony was, we do not know, but it seems unlikely that they would have a less privileged status than a concubine's children, and may well have enjoyed citizenship *de facto*, especially if their parents were inconspicuous.

Pericles' law, however, added a new class of persons to the illegitimate, by declaring the offspring of unions with non-citizen mothers non-citizens—*xenoi*[13]—however formal the marriage agreement had been, and thus the procreation of legitimate children became impossible except from the legitimate daughter of an Athenian,[14] though it is not certain that a formal marriage was necessary till the archonship of Eucleides, when the democracy was restored in 403/2, under 'the laws of Solon'.[15]

From Pericles' law till after the battle of Chaeroneia in 338 this law remained in force, apart from a few individual grants to named persons,[16] and a few concessions during the Peloponnesian War period, such as the grant of the right of intermarriage to the Euboeans,[17] the incorporation of the Plataeans and Samians and all those who manned the ships at Arginusae in 406[18] and a general dispensation, made not earlier than 413, to Athenian men to beget legitimate children from more than one wife, and perhaps from non-Athenians as well.[19]

BETROTHAL

The law required that an Athenian's marriage should be preceded by either a betrothal agreement (*engye*)[20] or a court judgment (*epidikasia*). This latter was the legal process whereby a man's claim to be the legitimate husband of an *epikleros* was established. Otherwise the normal process (through *engye*) was for a girl's *kyrios* to pledge her to a prospective bridegroom.[21] The pledge was a formal one,[22] and witnesses were present on both sides;[23] it also stated what her dowry was to be as one of its conditions.[24] It is uncertain at what age this agreement was normally made for girls; the case of Demosthenes' sister, who was an orphan, may be exceptional; she was engaged to Demophon at the age of five, and her dowry was paid over at once.[25] But it is quite certain that betrothal, though obligatory, did not itself make a marriage, since we can attest at least two cases in which a bride was pledged, but no marriage took place.[26] We do not know how far back the custom of betrothal went; the marriage of Agariste to Megacles the Alcmaeonid (circa 575) was formally contracted by her father's pledging her to Megacles 'in accordance with the Athenians' laws' and his accepting the pledge.[27] In Athens of the orators' day the rule was well established. Great care was taken to obtain witnesses of the betrothal,[28] and lack of witnesses can be said to show that the transaction was either shady or never legally conducted; as Isaeus puts it:[29] 'When he was going to betroth his daughter to a man worth three talents (his so-called daughter that is) he pretended that he had one witness present, Pyretides . . . and this is striking proof that this evidence that my opponents have adduced is patently false, for you are all aware that when we enter upon acts we have foreseen[30] which must be done before witnesses we always summon those who are closest to us (τοὺς οἰκειοτάτους), and those with whom we habitually associate . . . and we obtain evidence from those not in court who are of the highest reputation . . . written not in the presence of one or two people, but of as many men as possible. . . .' This was because, if a child's mother was not properly married, the child was a bastard, and suffered severe disabilities in respect of the capacity to succeed to property, and exclusion thereby from the full privileges of citizenship.

CHOICE OF A BRIDE

Marriages within the *anchisteia* or wider family were extremely common; they were prescribed by the law for *epikleroi*; we hear of half-brothers marrying their half-sisters,[31] and uncles often married their nieces;[32] the mother of Hagnias was also his second cousin;[33] Isaeus could also argue that it was a sign of ill-will that a father of two daughters married neither to a first cousin;[34] It is claimed that Meidylides had offered his daughter (Cleitomache) to his brother, and only married her outside his family when his brother refused her.[35] Two known exceptions to the general rule that marriage following *engye* was arranged by a girl's *kyrios* seem to prove it sound; one instance is of a father who went out to find a bride for his son, but the case is an unusual one, since the son was an adopted son,[36] and the law required adopted sons to have children of the body if they were to pass on their adoptive father's estate within their family. Another son, the only son of his mother, also found it necessary to explain that it was his father's anxiety to see grandchildren which made him marry unusually early in life—at the age of eighteen.[37]

AGE OF MARRIAGE

The normal age for men to marry seems to have been about thirty, an age approved by the philosophers as suitable,[38] but there were sound family reasons as well as those of imaginary eugenics. These lay in the Athenian custom of old men retiring from the headship of (or at least from economic responsibility for) their families in favour of their sons, and the son's marriage was an appropriate moment for this to occur; the adopted son mentioned above says he took a bride to help look after his adoptive father in his old age.[39] A man who married at about thirty would be about sixty when his son reached thirty; fifty-nine was the age at which a man's military service ended and he was therefore considered an old man.[40]

Girls were married much younger; philosophers and other writers recommended about eighteen or nineteen as suitable (Pl. 24);[41] Plutarch relates that Spartan girls were married when they were ripe for it, not when they were small and unready for it.[42] In Athens, girls were presented to the phratry on the koureotis day (the third day) of the Apatouria, when a sacrifice was made by their (new) husband; this is associated with the boys' sacrifice on the same day, made on the occasion of their cutting their hair as indicating the end of their childhood.[43] Therefore it will have been not later than about sixteen, and the Greeks' fanatical emphasis on premarital virginity will have made it tend to be earlier than this rather than later.[44]

FREEDOM OF CHOICE

A few instances are known in which a woman is said to have chosen her own husband, but in every case it is clear that it was most unusual; in the instance he cites, Herodotus says so specifically and clearly;[45] Plutarch regards it as one of the remarkable things about Elpinice, sister of Cimon, that her marriage was in accordance with her own free will;[46] Peisistratus' daughter is said to have married for love.[47] It is important to stress that all these women belonged to the highest social class, in which the women have always had markedly more independence than among the bulk of the population.

Society demanded that a man procure marriages for his daughters, and, if necessary, sisters; it was regarded as a slight on his excellence if he did not do so.[48] Nature, however, ordained (always until the twentieth century) that more girl-babies than boys should survive infancy, and battle casualties were at least as numerous as deaths in childbirth; the excess of brides seeking husbands therefore created a competitive situation for the fathers of girls, which ensured that a dowry was an invariable accompaniment (though by no means a legal requirement) of a marriage. Girls who had no dowry could not get married, and therefore to marry a girl without a dowry, or with only a very small one, was to do her a very great honour, and was a matter for self-congratulation by orators, especially when the girl was an *epikleros*.[49] Unmarried girls had either to remain at home, or enter the world of the demimondaines if they were destitute orphans.[50] After marriage, however, a girl seems to have had more ability to determine her lot. The only evidence that there was any special cachet attached to a first, or lifelong, marriage is in the religious sphere; we are told that from the earliest times it had been necessary for the wife of the King Archon (the Basileus) to be a citizen, and a virgin at her marriage;[51] she had the duty of being 'married' to the god Dionysus and spending the night with him in his temple. But for most married couples divorce was easy, and widows were often remarried.

In the choice of their second husband widows were certainly sometimes able to exercise some element of choice; Demosthenes' mother did not marry Aphobus, despite her betrothal; Demosthenes speaks of her disputing with him, and his retaliating by refusing to supply her with food, and in another speech declares that 'she inflicted on herself a life of widowhood for the sake of her children'.[52] The prosecutors of Lycophron had alleged that a widow had promised herself to her (alleged) lover and had sworn that she would refuse to have intercourse with her husband when her brother gave her to another man.[53] There can be little doubt, however, that young widows, even if they had children, were expected to remarry.[54]

Moreover, Athenian women had as much right to divorce their husbands[55] as their husbands had to divorce them,[56] and we even hear of a father taking his daughter away when he quarrelled with his son-in-law;[57] divorce by consent was also possible, especially in connection with a suit for an *epikleros*.[58] In all cases, however, the woman's dowry had to be repaid to her *kyrios*, and a large dowry is said to be something which protects a woman and prevents her being divorced. It is therefore alleged[59] that a woman whose citizenship was doubtful would necessarily have a large dowry so that her husband would not easily get rid of her.

THE DOWRY

The dowry was a field in which it is accepted that a man would express his self-esteem: 'nobody', says Isaeus, 'would give a dowry of twenty minae to a man of property'; in another speech[60] he asks if ten minae is a dowry suitable for a free-born girl being given in marriage to a man worth three talents. Demosthenes argues[61] that dowries of two talents and eighty minae must have come from a large estate, since nobody would leave his son's estate destitute. Nobody failed to give a dowry if he could help it; an uncle, it is said, guardian to four nieces and one nephew, would be sure to see that the girls were given dowries; friends gave dowries to the daughters of the poor; the daughters of *thetes*, the lowest financial class, who lacked brothers had by law to be given dowries by their relatives in accordance with their means;[62] even the state stepped in very occasionally (in return for outstanding public services) to dower a man's daughters; examples include those of Aristeides in the fifth century and, in the late third century, those of Timosthenes.[63] Dowries consisted of cash, or real-estate valued in cash; apart from sums of cash we hear of a tenement house in Cerameicus valued at forty minae, and of thirty minae in cash and ten minae promised on the bride's father's death—a sum later secured by attachment to a claim on a house.[64] Widows on their remarriage received dowries in exactly the same way as unmarried girls, and this is only natural since a woman's dowry was deemed to be her share of her paternal estate, a share set apart for her maintenance, and it is an unfailing principle of Athenian law that the head of the family who had a woman's dowry in his possession had to maintain her.[65]

Household furniture is stated in one passage to belong to a dowry,[66] but it must be assumed that this had been bought with the dowry, since there is evidence that a law of Solon's prevented dowries being constituted of elaborate personal effects.[67] It was in these, given to the bride, over and above the dowry, that Athenians showed goodwill towards their sons-in-law, since these were not valued, and could not be recovered if the marriage broke up in rancour.[68] As in our day, friends also appear to have made wedding gifts to a bride (Pl. 25). It is possible that quite large sums of money may have passed undeclared as well—since Athenians also concealed their wealth in order to avoid taxation—because Aphobus was able to allege that Demosthenes' father had four talents of silver buried in the floor of the house, of which his mother had control[69]—a charge which the orator refutes, but which must have been at least credible.

As remarked above, a dowry was intended primarily for a woman's maintenance. It remained in her husband's control while he lived; if he predeceased her and there were no children, it returned with her to her own family; if there were children, it was part of the children's inheritance provided that they supported their mother if adult, or their guardian did if they were infants.[70] Hence in one speech we hear that a widow's assets and liabilities were formally examined when her husband died, and that he had counted among his assets a debt to her. But, in this family at least, the wife had *de facto* made arrangements for her daughters' benefit, and had spent half a mina on a funeral;[71] clearly there were occasions on which a wife could dispose of property, though doubtless her husband's assent was obtained.

CHILDREN

After the betrothal (*engye*) came the wedding (*gamos*), at which the bride was brought to the bridegroom's house and the marriage really began (Pl. 24), so that the various songs of the wedding were then appropriate.[72] It was living together which made a marriage a marriage; its existence was therefore essentially a question of fact. Living together[73] (συνοικεῖν) is the Greek for being married, and the procreation of children was its explicit object. Xenophon's Socrates says: 'Surely you do not suppose that it is for sexual satisfaction that men and women breed children, since the streets are full of people who will satisfy that appetite, as are the brothels? No, it is clear that we enquire into which women we may beget the best children from, and we come together with them and breed children';[74] Neaira's accuser says: 'This is what cohabitation is; it is when a person breeds children, and presents his sons to the *phrateres* and demesmen, and gives in marriage his daughters to husbands as legimately begotten by himself'.[75]

The view that girls had a right not merely to marriage but also to children is clearly implied in what one speaker says of Menecles: 'Menecles said that he viewed with anxiety the passing of his vigour and his wife's childlessness; it was not right that she should be rewarded for her virtues by being made to grow old with him in childlessness'.[76] Support comes from another passage,[77] where it is clearly implied that a wife who was still of an age to have children could have, and should have, been given a new husband, but avoided this by repeatedly pretending she was pregnant.

The Athenians were even a bit sentimental about children, if about anything; weeping children were a stock-in-trade of the defendant at a trial—Socrates refused to countenance such behaviour at his trial;[78] the emotional appeals of Sositheus in his peroration[79] were obviously accompanied by the boy pleading in person before the court. 'Even when people's estates are confiscated by the court for some offence', says Demosthenes,[80] 'you, the people, do not confiscate all they have, but out of pity either for their womenfolk, or for their little children, you always leave something even to them' (*i.e.* criminal offenders). 'When we are dying,' says Xenophon's Socrates,[81] 'if we want to commit to someone the duty of educating our sons, guarding our virgin daughters and preserving our money, shall we think the intemperate man worthy of our trust?' Xenophon was clearly thinking of a man's most important responsibilities.

Formal marriage and the birth of children from it also had a public side; this was due to the importance of asserting the child's legitimacy. With this in view a marriage was registered with the *phrateres*, the husband's *phrateres* in most cases, but also, when the girl was an *epikleros*, with her family's.[82] Similarly, when a child was born, it was exhibited at least to relatives on the tenth day festival, at what seems to have been a big celebration; and on this occasion the father named him.[83] It was possibly on this occasion that the child was introduced to the *phrateres*, but this seems usually to have happened later; the father swore 'that he knew that the child had citizen-status, being born to him from a citizen mother, properly (*i.e.* formally) married'.[84]

Children who could not substantiate their claim to legitimacy were bastards; they not only lacked rights of succession after 403—their maximum inheritance was a thousand drachmae—they were also excluded from the family religious observances, and did not enjoy full citizen-rights.[85] This did not mean that they had no rights; our legal sources, being, as they are, mainly disputes about inheritances, give a distorted view. Bastards resembled outsiders (*xenoi*) in that they lacked the right to claim citizens' estates,[86] but they must have had rights at law, as did *xenoi*, in whose interests one of the state's chief magistrates, the Polemarchos, was responsible for the administration of justice.[87] *Xenoi* had duties too; metics certainly served in the army and there is no reason to suppose that bastards (if they were rich enough) did not do so likewise.[88] Metics paid extra taxes too;[89] having the duties but not the rewards of citizenship, it is not surprising that they sometimes tried to usurp it—we hear in the orators of 'the tricks of those who try to claim citizenship'.[90] The state was therefore very severe on attempts to obtain citizenship clandestinely.[91]

WIVES AND CONCUBINES

In his speech against Neaira, Apollodorus cites a law[92] forbidding a foreigner to live with a citizen woman as his wife (συνοικεῖν), and a foreign woman to live with a citizen, on pain of enslavement or a heavy fine; clearly this did not mean a prohibition of sexual intercourse across these boundaries, nor a prohibition on keeping a concubine, or, in the case of a woman, a lover, but it prohibited such people from pretending that they were formally married, and from claiming to breed citizen children. Similar prohibitions barred attempts to marry a daughter born of one citizen-parent to an Athenian as if she were free-born.[93] Thus Apollodorus can maintain that his opponent Stephanus must either claim that Neaira (the woman in question) is a citizen, and his wife in conformity with the laws, or admit that Neaira is a concubine in his house and not his wife, in which case the children claimed to be citizens must be the offspring of another woman, a relative of his own, whom he had earlier married. This is the context of the often misquoted dictum[94] on the courtesan, the concubine and the wife: 'we have courtesans for pleasure, concubines to look after the day-to-day needs of the body, wives that we may breed legitimate children and have a trusty warden of what we have in the house'; it does not state that we cannot have either pleasure or care of our persons from our wives—quite the reverse; the services to a man of the three classes of woman are intended cumulatively, and it is the purpose of the argument merely to stress that you can beget legitimate children only from a properly married wife.

During the Peloponnesian War, after the Sicilian disaster in 413, we are told[95] that the Athenians temporarily abandoned their rules about requiring a child's father and mother to be formally married because of the shortage of men, and citizens were allowed to marry one wife, and breed children (that is, legitimate children) from another. This has shocked commentators, especially those of the Victorian age, but it accords fully with the Athenian view of marriage—as an arrangement for maintaining the *oikoi*, and (in the case of the city) for replenishing the supply of citizen-soldiers. After the battle of Chaeroneia (338) foreigners also were enrolled, and those who had been deprived of citizenship were restored; the orator Lycurgus does not say how many were involved.[96]

<h2 style="text-align:center">ADULTERY</h2>

The importance of being able to prove legitimacy had two principal results; it made adultery a public as well as a private offence, and it made the Athenians excessively preoccupied with the chastity of their womenfolk, with the result that they were guarded in a manner nowadays thought to be intolerable.[97]

Adultery in Athens (it is sometimes said) meant 'the sins of a wife'. The evidence is not quite so unequivocal; in the first place, the punishment of death is prescribed for the adulterer and not the adulteress—she was punished, naturally, but it is odd that, if the offence was only hers, her lover should be put to death, not she.

Secondly, in the version of the law which we have, it is stated[98] that a man may with impunity kill an adulterer caught in the act with any of the women in his *kyrieia*—his mother, sister and daughter are mentioned as well as his wife. If the law is correctly reported, and there are no good grounds for believing it is not, this must disprove the idea that the right to kill was to protect a man's own marriage, and that it was because a woman was married that her paramour was able to be punished by her *kyrios*; the man concerned therefore committed an offence as well as the woman.

The punishment of death for adultery is said by Euphiletus to be universally demanded by all states; Lycurgus the orator declares that the adulterer is 'one who betrays nature's instincts', and Xenophon compares the man who cannot control his lust to a silly bird, pointing out that the needs of nature can be satisfied without committing adultery.[99] Plato's laws on sexual matters are revealing. They were intended to be as severe for men as for women, but, as he admitted, he had to compromise; though he wished to brand all sexual intercourse with anyone other than a wife as adultery, and claimed that the law of nature was to preserve virginity until the age of procreation, then to remain faithful to one's mate, he admitted that most men, both Greeks and non-Greeks, did not do this; he therefore fell back on 'the possible', which was to prohibit all sexual intercourse with freeborn or citizen women other than a man's wedded wife, to forbid sodomy, and impose secrecy on intercourse with any other (*i.e.* non-free) woman on pain of disfranchisement.[100] Obviously Plato was reacting against contemporary attitudes, which did allow men extra-marital sexual relations provided that they were not with women in the *kyrieia* of other citizens. This is to say that adultery was not *solely* an offence by a female; a man was punishable as an adulterer if he seduced a woman he was forbidden to seduce, and his punishment was apt to be more severe, as his liberty of action was greater.

Athenian women had no sexual liberty, but the explanation of the Athenians' attitude was primarily civic, not moral. Euphiletus says that 'the lawgiver prescribed death for adultery' (though not for rape)[101] '. . . because he who achieves his ends by persuasion thereby corrupts the mind as well as the body of the woman . . . gains access to all a man's possessions, and casts doubt on his children's parentage'. This was the point; if an Athenian had an affair with a citizen-woman not his wife, a baby would not have any claim on his property or family or religious associations, nor impose on them a bogus claim for citizenship; but the woman would be compelled to claim that her husband was the father, and his kinship-group and its cult was therefore deeply implicated, since it would be having a non-member foisted upon it, and if she were detected, all her husband's children would have difficulty in proving their rights to citizenship if they were challenged. An unmarried Athenian girl who had been seduced could be sold into slavery according to Solon's laws; Hypereides implies that it was more usual 250 years later merely to keep her at home unmarried —when he hints that neither she nor a widow who had been seduced would be able to get a husband.[102]

Death for an adulterer, even if caught in the act, was quite certainly not always demanded; comedy speaks of payment, depilation and other humiliating, vulgar but comical indignities being inflicted on an adulterer, which would prevent him appearing in public, certainly from appearing in the wrestling-school, for some time.[103] Divorce for a woman taken in adultery was compulsory,[104] but we may be pretty certain that the demand was not always complied with; a woman with a large dowry would have to have it repaid, and this might be impossible for her husband, or be something he was unwilling to do. Hypereides declares[105] that an adulterer causes many women to live with those with whom legally they ought not to be living, but there is no certainty that the orator is speaking of those known to be adulteresses.

An interesting compromised case of adultery is revealed in the speech against Neaira.[106] A man who had slept with Neaira's daughter was accused of adultery with her, and was allowed to buy himself out by giving security of thirty minae, being kept under constraint until he paid; he subsequently sued for wrongful imprisonment (because the girl, he said, was an *hetaira*, not a citizen-girl), the condition being that if he were to be convicted of adultery he could be abused before the court as the accuser wished, save that weapons were barred. In fact the case was settled out of court for a payment of ten minae, 'because he had slept with the girl and owed her a good turn'. In return he was to have access to her whenever he was in Athens; she became in fact a concubine with the maximum endowment permitted by law for one who was not a legitimate wife. Other cases of concubinage are rare; one is mentioned by Isaeus, when the orator says, 'even those who give their womenfolk for the purposes of concubinage make in every case an arrangement in advance about the endowment which will be given to the concubines';[107] this 'concubine', claimed by the orator to be an illegitimate daughter of a citizen, had, like Neaira's daughter, the maximum bastard's portion from her father's estate.

Non-citizens could contract legally valid marriages and dower their daughters to non-citizens,[108] and the Athenian law upheld their contracts;[109] what the Athenian law was concerned to prevent was non-citizens claiming to be citizens, and making claims on the property of citizens, the *oikoi* which comprised the demes.

OLD AGE

The attitude of the Athenians to old age was somewhat unusual. On the one hand they hated old age with its loss of the youthful beauty which they so much admired, and they dreaded the time when they would no longer have the strength to earn their daily bread.[110] Senility moreover was one of the causes which made an Athenian's acts invalid at law in that it was deemed that he was out of his mind if senile.[111] Nothing could be more tasteless to our minds than what Pericles has to say to the old who had lost their sons in the first year of the Peloponnesian War.[112] On the other hand the city laid it on children as a legal obligation, not merely a moral duty, to ensure that their parents were looked after when they were old. Maltreatment of parents[113] ranks with maltreatment of orphans and *epikleroi* as a prosecution in which a prosecutor ran no risk of punishment, and 'do you treat your parents well?' was a question asked at the examination not merely of aspiring archons, but of all public officers, including orators.[114] From other phrases, too, we may gather that expectations did not stop at refraining from maltreatment; positive services were required, especially the provision of food-supplies.[115] This indeed seems to have been an obligation laid on everyone, as is clearly implied in the exceptions allowed by Solon not to do so, a version of which (how much amended we do not know) survived until the fourth century.[116] Hence getting children in order to have someone to tend their old age is a frequently-mentioned motive for parenthood, and equally for adoption.[117]

The state also made provision for looking after old women; here the law was explicit; the person who had charge of her dowry had the obligation to maintain her. A failure to do so properly rendered the negligent party liable to an accusation.[118] The class of people most obviously concerned are widows, whose situation at the death of their husbands was possibly that they could remain in their husband's *oikos* and be maintained by its new *kyrios*, who was sometimes a son, sometimes the guardian of an infant, or (if she were childless) a relative; alternatively the widow could return to her own family, if she had no children, and get her dowry back, or interest on it at a prescribed rate;[119] or, if she were young enough, she could be remarried with an appropriate dowry (and we can cite at least two cases when a widow took the children of her first marriage with her), or she could be adjudicated as *epikleros* if her situation warranted it.[120] But whatever happened, the person who was *kyrios* of her dowry had to support her.

On the other hand, one effect of the law about senility was that fathers of adult sons often handed over the management of their *oikos* to their sons, and virtually stepped down from the management of the house; it is evident that when old Menecles had adopted a son and got him to marry, he retired and left his adopted son in charge of the *oikos*; his daughter-in-law helped to look after him.[121] It is obvious from Lycurgus' famous description of the plight of the city on the morrow of the disaster at Chaer-oneia[122] that the old men who scurried about the city with their cloaks pinned double around them had retired from public life and were not normally to be seen away from their firesides. As an example from comedy it is fairly plain in the *Wasps* that Bdelycleon is the effective head of the family.[123] The balance of such a father/son relationship was obviously delicate, and must have varied from family to family; it was one of the subjects on which Socrates as well as Aristophanes had stimulated discussion—it is evident from Xenophon that his accusers had made his views a target for their attack.[124]

Throughout his life an Athenian was essentially a part of his *oikos*; as a baby his birth had to be accepted by the *kyrios* of his *oikos* (his father) and registered by the *phrateres* of the phratry to which his *oikos* belonged—the city was not interested in him directly until he was ready to be trained to serve it in war; as a man he married usually at an age at which his father was ready to retire from economic responsibility for the *oikos*, and his *phrateres* took note of his marriage, so that his son in turn would readily be accepted as a member of the *oikos*; when he retired in his turn, his *oikos* continued to support him under its new *kyrios*, his son. An Athenian woman was equally a part of her *oikos* until she married, at which time she removed into her husband's *oikos* taking with her a portion out of the possessions of her own *oikos*; this was designated for her support until her dying day whether she was wife or mother or widow or even divorcée. All the Athenian law was framed with this membership of the *oikos* in view; a man's *oikos* provided both his place in the citizen body and what measure of social security there was, and this helps to account for that passionate determination to defend the *oikoi* alike against foreigners and against grasping individual Athenians which is characteristic of the democratic period.

24, 25 Brides were escorted to their new homes by torchlight (the ancient Greeks did not go away on honeymoon); the moment caught here is when the bridal pair are about to enter their home. The bride is crowned, her long veil hangs down her back, and her heavy robe is girt only by a loosely-knotted cord, her virgin's girdle having been dedicated to Artemis. She carries in her hand what is probably a pomegranate, symbol of fertility and given to her by the bridegroom on entering the house. Note the youthful bridegroom (right) and the fully mature bride. Below, on an *epinetron*, worn on the thigh while seated, is a bride, perhaps Alcestis, and her friends. The graceful vases shown were often wedding-presents, brought the morning after the marriage was consummated.

26, 27 Jars like the graceful *loutrophoros* on the right were used to bring water for a bridal bath; they were also used to mark the tombs of those who had died unmarried. In a detail from such a jar (above), a girl, crowned as if for her marriage (*cf. Pl. 24*), is mourned by a relative tearing her dishevelled hair, and a haggard slave. On the centre frieze (right) a youth is mourned by women who tear their hair; the lower frieze shows a cavalry procession, whether merely as an ornament or because the deceased was a knight, is uncertain.

28, 29 From the middle of the fifth century, marble memorials, many of great beauty, were erected in Athens. Ampharete (left) proclaims 'Here I hold my daughter's child, my darling, whom once I held on my knee when we both lived and saw the sunlight; now I am dead, and hold her, dead too'. Above, Damasistrate, Polycleides' wife, bids her husband farewell. Both monuments are about three feet high, and date from *c.* 400.

30　This little oil-jar shows a tomb, where offerings of similar jars and wreaths were made by relatives. The figure on the panel probably represents the dead man keeping watch, reflecting the Greek belief in their ancestors' continuing desire for cult-worship.

CHAPTER VI

PROPERTY AND THE FAMILY
IN ATHENS

SUCCESSION AND DIVISION

IN ITS DETERMINATION to maintain the numbers of the *oikoi* the Athenian state interfered extensively in men's private property; there was complex legislation designed to protect the persons and property of *epikleroi,* orphans, and *oikoi* without an heir.[1] Also, a man could be prosecuted before the Archon for madness, as being one who is 'out of his mind and wasting his property',[2] and if so convicted he would be disbarred from disposing of his property, or from any valid legal act, such as making a will, since no man could perform a legal act if he were out of his mind. A law quoted once, and referred to many times, lists the causes of a man's being incompetent at law: 'lunacy, or being out of his mind by reason of old age, drugs or disease, or by reason of a woman's (perhaps wife's) persuasion, or if he is held under constraint or imprisoned'.[3] We can quote no certain case in which this was actually done in a man's lifetime, but it was often enough invoked to impugn wills, as by the opposition to the speaker of Isaeus II,[4] and no doubt it was when men died leaving no adult son that the property of an *oikos* was most liable to suffer wastage.

Both before and after it was legally possible to make a will, however, Athenian law provided that sons succeeded their fathers without question or possibility of argument about shares; all sons had an unassailable right to an equal share in the *oikos* unless they had been adopted out of the family or formally disinherited.[5] Adoption was freely practised, and recognized as entirely creditable; formal disinherison seems to have been rare, and highly discreditable.[6] Since Themistocles' enemies accused him of having been disinherited, it must have been possible in the sixth century;

Demosthenes, Plato and Aristotle all knew of its existence two centuries later, Demosthenes regarding it as the merited fate of his opponent, Plato stating that disinherison, like suits for madness, was the act of men whose moral code is utterly gone in baseness, but adding that in other states (*i.e.* other than his own Republic) a boy who was repudiated would not necessarily lose his citizenship;[7] whether this rule applied in Athens or not, we do not know.

The rule about sons having a right to equal shares does not mean that *oikoi* were of necessity split up; a certain Aristodemus claimed that his grandfather's brother 'did not choose to marry, but for this reason even agreed to allow the property to be undivided and lived on his own in Salamis.'[8] The fact that he did not marry—in fact he declined the offer of a bride—was sufficient motive for his not wishing to divide his father's *oikos*; the speaker later informs us that both brothers had enough to live on.

Such a failure to divide an estate is by no means unique. A certain Menecles (who for many years had no heir) and his brother were clearly in joint ownership of a piece of land. Despite our speaker's protestations, it is very likely that the land in question was land which had been inherited from their father, and it was only Menecles' attempt to sell it which caused his brother to assert his legal rights; since the brother alone had procreated an heir he had the more reason to resent its alienation from the family.[9] For some time after the heirs of Pasion the banker had divided up the other property, they kept undivided those assets in their father's estate which were leased to produce a revenue,[10] indeed it was subsequently maintained that even this property was only divided because the elder son, Apollodorus, was so extravagant that the guardians of his brother, who was still a minor, procured a division in their ward's interest; the leased assets, a bank and a shield-factory, were divided when the minor came of age. An appeal to prevent fragmentation of an *oikos* also appears in a speech of Isaeus, in which the claimants to an estate maintain that their grandfather had instructed his only son, Cleonymus, if he died childless, to bequeath his estate to his only sister's sons, of whom there were at least two. He had in fact bequeathed it to other people whose names we know, but not their relationships, by a will made long before his death, so that the claim in law was a weak one, but the appeal to the jurors to prevent the fragment-ation of the *oikos* was calculated to enlist their sympathy, as was the fact that the litigants had lived with the testator, Cleonymus, their mother's brother, when their guardian, who had been their father's brother, had died.[11]

A number of other cases show how *oikoi* and families were felt to be peculiarly closely linked. Euergus and Theophemus for example had divided their common property in the lifetime of their father; this the speaker discovered by asking Euergus.[12] Euergus lived with his father in the family house while Theo-phemus lived as a bachelor on his own elsewhere; Euergus was married (since he had a brother-in-law), and hence (by implication) had assumed the responsibility for continuing the family into the next generation.

How new *oikoi* could be established appears from the family of Bouselus, 'who had five sons, and they all grew to manhood, and their father divided up his property for them, and after they had divided it up each of them took a wife in accordance with the laws of Athens, and all of them had children and grandchildren born to them; five *oikoi* came into being out of the one *oikos* of Bouselus; they each lived separately in possession of his own property begetting his own descendants.' It was the fact that they married and begot children which brought the five *oikoi* into existence.[13]

Euctemon may also have tried to establish several *oikoi* for his descendants, though he was frustrated by deaths. During his lifetime he settled property (including real-estate) on Philoc-temon his son, perhaps when he married, for we know that he did marry, though he obtained no children; this property was moreover in a real sense Philoctemon's, since he not only served as a cavalryman and as a trierarch (both of which imply consider-able wealth), and performed other liturgies, but he also made a will and bequeathed his property to one of his sister's two sons whom he adopted, 'lest he leave his *oikos* without an heir'. An attempt was later made to introduce a son into Philoctemon's *oikos* and another into that of a brother after their deaths, while Euctemon their father still lived, and to obtain from the Archon leases of the *oikoi* as belonging to boys who were orphans (*i.e.* orphan minors), despite the fact that their grandfather still lived.[14] How it came about that sons could possess *oikoi* of their own outside the *oikos* of their father while he was still alive we do not know, and we cannot discover from this speech, since the son adopted by Philoctemon's will appears not to have claimed his estate at his death.[15]

Euctemon, however, was 96 years old at his death and had been over 80 when his last surviving son Philoctemon died.[16] As is clear from Aristophanes' *Wasps*, for example, sons sometimes took over their *oikos* in the lifetime of their father in so real a sense and to such an extent that the father can represent himself as being a child not yet of age to perform legal acts.[17] So long as he had a son (Philoctemon), Euctemon appears to have assumed that he would succeed him, and made an agreement with him as his heir about the allocation of one piece of estate to a child whom our speaker maintains was a prostitute's bastard, but who was probably in fact son of Euctemon, and a destitute orphan *epikleros* called Callippe.[18] When Philoctemon died, however, Euctemon cancelled the agreement and turned his own real-property into cash with the purpose (says our speaker) of conveying it surreptitiously to the 'bastard' and his brother, but made no attempt to dispose by sale of the property in the *oikoi* of his deceased sons;[19] the property in question must therefore have been formally registered as in the *oikoi* of these latter sons.

Generalizations based on this speech are particularly dangerous, because our speaker seems an unusually egregious liar;[20] it does seem to suggest, however, that there was a link between a man's *oikos* in the sense of his *kleros*, his estate, everything he inherited from his father, and his *oikos* in the sense of his place of registration in the deme as a citizen that is, the *oikos* in the deme in which his ancestor had been registered in Cleisthenes' day, or in which he had been registered if, like Pasion, he was a metic granted Athenian citizenship. The situation may have been that, when a man underwent his *dokimasia* and was approved, he was enrolled in his deme as a citizen in the *oikos* of so-and-so, and this gave him his status as a citizen, and the financial standing enjoyed by his *oikos* at the same time.[21] When a man like Bouselus had several sons, they were all enrolled as 'Bouselus' son', but their sons were enrolled as 'son of the appropriate father, son of Bouselus', so that in this way new *oikoi* were created, as Isaeus says (above). Euctemon had several sons too; all had been enrolled in the deme as 'son of Euctemon', and each had had a presumably equal portion of Euctemon's property allocated to him. None of them had procreated heirs, however, so that none of their *oikoi* had ever been registered in the deme as a fully separate *oikos* by having a son registered in it; only Philoctemon had made a formal adoption in his lifetime, so that, on Euctemon's death, the only *oikos* registered in the deme as having an heir was that of Philoctemon. His brothers' *oikoi*, having no heirs, remained unestablished.

Secondly, this speech suggests that when division of an estate took place in a man's lifetime the sons actually gained control (as *kyrioi*) of the portion which they were allotted. How much (as a proportion of the whole estate) this was we do not know; the very wealthy may have kept back most of their estate,[22] making their sons *kyrioi* of only enough to satisfy their *philotimia*,[23] but in the case of poorer men, it may have involved virtually (or even actually) the whole estate, to enable them to qualify in the property-class to which their father belonged. No Greek would have regarded less as acceptable.

Some such supposition is supported by the statement of Pollux, that when a man was enrolled on the citizens' roll, he then used to assume control of his patrimony, and that property inherited from one's father was also called one's allotted portion;[24] the word Pollux uses for this ($\lambda\tilde{\eta}\xi\iota\varsigma$) is used elsewhere of holdings of land. This must indicate that when a man passed his *dokimasia* he was enrolled in the property-class to which the amount of his father's *oikos* entitled him, and that in this *oikos* the most characistic element was land, by which agricultural land was meant, especially an ancestral estate—and it is characteristic of Attic law that it should have prohibited men from cutting down their own olive-trees in any number as well as trees which had been designated as sacred, even when these latter were dead and nothing but a stump.[25]

It is also possible that a man's marriage may have marked the time when he assumed *kyrieia* of his *oikos*;[26] Plato in a number of passages seems to think that the age of thirty was one of the landmarks in a man's life; this was also the age at which men became eligible to serve as members of the council, and as jurymen, and the age at which most men seem to have married[27]—and their fathers will often therefore have become above military age. In the *Republic* Plato speaks of those who engage in philosophy as 'those newly fledged from the status of children, in the interval between (then and) the time they take to managing their *oikos*, and earning their living', but it is impossible in the context to say whether he was thinking of their entering on initial military training or the age of entering on marriage.[28]

RETIREMENT

Since senility invalidated a man's acts by rendering him 'out of his mind' (note, for example, how the speaker of Isaeus VI harps on Euctemon's senile incompetence)[29] the law may have provided an incentive to men to divest themselves of their property to their adult sons, and they may also have been encouraged to do so by the fact that their sons were legally obliged to support them in their old age. Aristotle, in discussing how to define a citizen, says that it is neither residence nor liability to action under the law and going to law, because some foreign residents have those rights, some in full, some with reservations, but 'as in the case of children who are not yet enrolled because of their youth, and of old men who have been discharged, one must say they are citizens in a sense, but not without reservations, adding "still under age" for the former and "retired" for the latter or some such reservation'.[30] The people Aristotle had in mind will have been men whose sons had taken their place in their deme and phratry as *kyrios* of their *oikos*, and who were therefore not able to sue or be sued for property which was not theirs to claim or defend.

This does not imply retirement from public life. Aristotle says that a citizen is a man who has the right to attend assembly and sit as a juror upon his fellow-men. From these activities he gives no hint that men retired, and it is clear that, at least in the fifth century, the old did not retire from being jurors or from the assembly, as Philocleon clearly had no intention of retiring as a juror, nor had those formidable Acharnians whom Dicaeopolis had to deal with.[31] In the more serious atmosphere of Pericles' funeral speech too, the fathers of the fallen will continue to attend the assembly and vote on public policy,[32] though the implications of the hint that the citizen who has sons in the army will be more worthy of attention may be important. Socrates, as we know, did not retire, being a member of the council in 406, when about 65,[33] but his sons were still not adult at the date of his death in 399.

Plato, however, did want his state officials to retire. In the *Laws* 'the Guardians of the Laws shall retire at seventy years of age, being elected not before fifty for however many years will bring them to seventy'. In the *Republic* he was less precise: 'when the citizens' vigour begins to fail and becomes unable to cope with military and political duties, then we should turn them loose to feed on philosophy', though this would appear from later in the book not to exempt fully-trained Guardians 'from each taking their turn at ordering the city and private individuals and themselves for the rest of their lives . . . labouring at political duties and holding office for the city's sake' from the age of 50.[34]

WILLS

The law about wills as reported[35] seems to say that a man may dispose of his property by will as he wishes if he has procreated no legitimate sons (and by inference, if he has sons, he may not dispose of his property); it was not so simple as this, however. In the first place, if he had daughters they would have to be given their rights as *epikleroi* or the will would be invalidated.[36] Secondly, a man with one or more sons who were still minors could certainly make a will, as Demosthenes' father did.[37] He was a wealthy man, his fortune at his death amounting to nearly fourteen talents, and his motive in making an extremely detailed will was no doubt to establish the value of the estate which was to be administered for his son by trustees till he attained the age at which he could claim its *kyrieia*,[38] and the will was to preserve the estate for the minor, not to strip it of its assets—which Demosthenes does not claim that his father could not have done, only that he would not have done so.[39]

Even men with adult sons did in fact on occasion make wills; Pasion had two sons, one adult, but left a magnificent dowry to his widow, and some property as a gift; Conon not only dedicated half his huge fortune to Athene and Apollo but left gifts to his nephew and his brother.[40]

These dispositions seem to defy Solon's law, but in fact they probably did not do so. In Conon's case it is argued that Conon would be likely to have provided his son Timotheus with 'sufficient' in Athens, and kept the rest in his own hands in Cyprus, so that before Conon's death his son was worth 'not as much as four talents'. Cyprus was, Lysias says, as safe a place as Athens in which to have money, and support a family. Therefore Conon's will did not defy Solon's law, because the money which was in Cyprus, and left to persons other than his son Timotheus, was not under Athenian jurisdiction, and the Archon's court therefore had no power to make decisions about its disposition; what was in Athens—Timotheus' *oikos* in the city, seventeen talents—was quite large enough to bear the liturgies and other charges which the Athenian state wanted to levy, and in respect of that Solon's law was not defied.

In Pasion's case the situation is highly complicated, in that he had two sons, one adult, aged twenty-four, one a minor, aged ten.[41] Pasion was very rich; he had twenty talents in real property and more than fifty talents in loans, of which eleven talents were in loans made by his bank, but in Pasion's own name, this being necessary because Phormion, the lessee of the bank, could not distrain on the security provided since it was in land, and he was at the time only a metic. Pasion's right to make a will on his death-bed rested on the fact that he had a minor son to whom he wanted to appoint guardians (wisely, if there is any truth in Demosthenes' allegations), and he did appoint them.[42] One of them was Phormion, the freedman metic who had been Pasion's manager before the latter's death, and to whom Pasion had evidently

31 In this scene, from democratic Athens, a reveller comes roaring home.
It is clear that he has been at a drinking party, as he is wreathed. His sole
garment, a cloak, hangs loosely over one shoulder, a reminder that partial
nakedness was customary in Athens and total nakedness not unknown. He
batters drunkenly at the door with the butt-end of his torch, while his appre-
hensive wife, carrying a lamp, hurries to admit him. Her dress, attitude and
hairstyle indicate that she is the mistress of the house and not an *hetaira* or a slave.
The roof suggests a vestigial verandah, intended to protect the door from the
summer sun and winter rain.

32, 33 Two school-scenes, painted on a cup; above, the boys are learning to play the lyre and to sing and recite Homer and the other traditional poets; the tablet says 'O muse, I begin to sing of broad Scamander', the opening lines of a poem, now lost, by Stesichorus. Below, the flute-lesson, and some practice in reading. This was an essentially aristocratic, and an almost wholly oral, education. In both scenes the *paidagogos* sits and watches.

34 It is not certain whether swinging was merely a pastime, or whether it had, or was even restricted to, ritual significance. It may have been associated with courtship, and the inscription on this cup (not shown) reads 'you are lovely, Antheia'; certainly only girls appear on swings in art, and some examples show what looks like a circle of admirers. In this scene, from a cup of *c.* 480, the action is particularly vigorous, as the girl's clothes and hair fly behind her in her rapid motion. The swing is made from a stool suspended from ropes which she clutches in her hands, and is pushed by a satyr of the 'gentlemanly' type which appeared in vase-painting about this time. His presence, and the girl's flowing hair and bare feet, indicate that she may be a maenad, and that the scene is therefore allegorical, illustrating perhaps the festival of the Anthesteria in the spring, when the broaching of the new wine was the occasion for games and merrymaking of all kinds; there were also ceremonies in honour of the ancestors and prayers for fertility and growth, all of which are associated with swinging in several cultures.

35   This Roman bronze copy
of a Greek marble statue of
about 400 was made before
AD 79, when it was buried in
Herculaneum. This figure, a
young girl pinning up her robe,
stands about 4 ft. 6 in. high, and
is one of a group known as the
'dancing maidens'. Like the
bride, the dead girl, and the
swinging girl (*Pls. 24, 26* and
34) she is clearly a maiden past
the age of puberty, and almost
fully grown up; this suggests
that the literary evidence on the
extreme youth of brides may
be exaggerated.

instructed the minor son's guardians to let his two businesses until the younger son was adult. Phormion was also given Pasion's widow in marriage; it is clear that Phormion lived in the house with Pasion's family, and that the marriage took place soon after Pasion's death.[43] Thus Pasion used his will to try to secure the position of his minor son, which was perhaps especially difficult to ensure when his adult son—and heir—was not in Athens at the time. This will therefore did not breach Solon's law either, though it showed a fundamental weakness in it, since one son was adult (and thus prevented his father from making a will), one was a minor (and thus enabled him to do so); the fact that the elder son was away from Athens at the time of Pasion's death, and the consequent need to guarantee—as far as possible—the integrity of the *oikos* may have been the factor which validated the will.

SLAVES AS PROPERTY

Slaves formed another and rather special kind of property; the slave was himself saleable and could thus be valued, but he (or she) also produced wealth, so that he was valuable from that point of view as well; as Demosthenes expressed it: 'my father left two factories, both on no mean scale of business; one had thirty-two or thirty-three cutlers, worth up to five or six minae each, none worth less than three minae, from which he got an annual revenue of not less than thirty minae clear profit'.[44] Male slaves worked in such factories, which might be in a part of the house or elsewhere, or in farm-work; the female slaves of a family were productive workers in their capacity as spinners and weavers, and also performed household tasks. Others were brought up, or bought, and trained as entertainers, courtesans etc. and hired out by their owners. In a family there seem always to have been female slaves, but in a lower-middle-class family like Euphiletus' there is no sign of any male slaves. In wealthier houses, like that of Xenophon, there were numbers of slaves whose training and management were in the hands of the master of the house.[45] In this passage Xenophon also explains why the women's and men's quarters were separated by a locked door— to prevent pilfering and unauthorized sexual intercourse by the slaves—though he regarded permission to beget children a valuable incentive for good slaves.[46] Xenophon in fact regards the women's quarters as being separated from the men's in order to keep the males out rather than the females in. In another comparatively well-to-do household, intruders found the male slaves working on the land outside the house, the mistress with her children and an elderly freedwoman lunching in an enclosed garden and the female slaves at work in what the orator calls 'a tower' which they were able to shut off, and where they are said to spend their time;[47] they were making clothes.

The management of the slaves was an important part of household economy and the tending of sick slaves is said to be one of the important duties of a wife.[48] The economic importance of slaves was such that 'Socrates' lists them with houses and lands and farm animals and equipment as being things that are both acquired and looked after with care, and he criticizes his contemporaries for caring for their slaves more than for their friends, remarking that men purchase household slaves in order to have fellow-workers and allies on the ground that they need assistants.[49]

Being an economic asset, a slave could be disposed of by will as well as by sale, and this included the gift of freedom, or the remission of part of the price with which he might have bought it. Demosthenes' father we know liberated a slave called Milyas by his will, and the wills of the philosophers which have survived in the pages of Diogenes Laertius all contain provisions for the liberation of slaves, on various conditions.[50] Slaves were liberated by living masters too, the best known examples being among the bankers, of whom both Pasion and Phormion obtained first their liberty, then the much more inaccessible privilege—the Athenian citizenship; a certain Socrates, himself a freedman, freed his slave Satyrus; other examples can be quoted from Athens and Aegina, and we are told that many others could be mentioned.[51]

WOMEN'S PROPERTY

A woman's property always remained separate from her husband's *oikos*. Her husband had control of it while he lived, and control passed to their children (if adult) or their guardians when he died, but while he lived he was always responsible for it to his wife's family, being obliged to repay it if for any reason she ceased to be his wife without leaving him any children. If a man had two wives, both of whom had children, the children inherited their mother's property separately from their father's estate;[52] thus, although she never owned it in the sense of being able to dispose of it, it could never be alienated from her at all, or from her paternal family except through her children; so far as we can see it was always able to return to her family unless she had adult descendants. In this connexion it should be noted that before the Solonian economic reforms, though we hear that men had to sell themselves and their children into slavery for debt, we are never told that they had to sell their wives;[53] presumably they could not, since the wives belonged (in the property sense) to their own families.

Athenian law, however, tried to ensure that women could not easily accumulate large estates; the women's entitlement to claim against a collateral relative's estate was limited to sisters. The point is fully illustrated in Eupolis' family; he had had two daughters; when he died, he left one living without children, the other deceased, leaving a grown-up son. The surviving daughter and her nephew succeeded equally; but when her first cousin died the surviving daughter could (our speaker argues) make no claim; the estate would have passed wholly to her deceased sister's son had not the cousin, Apollodorus by name, adopted a son.[54]

EPIKLEROI

Daughters, however, had an absolute right to inherit their father's *oikos* if they had no brothers: girls of this class, known as *epikleroi*, were in the democratic period the subjects of a whole complex of legislation designed to ensure that families or *oikoi* did not die out through lack of descendants, and that *oikoi* which had only female descendants did not disappear unless it was inevitable, as it must sometimes have been. The rule of the legislation was, in brief, that the *epikleros* was to marry her next of kin on the male side, who was obliged by the law to obtain a court-judgement in his favour; the couple were then regarded as lawfully married by the court's verdict, the process being known as *epidikasia*.[55] These suits were held in the Archon's court, and measures were taken to see that everyone who might have a claim to the estate had the opportunity to be informed about it.[56] It is clear, however, that the *oikos* was more important than the *epikleros*, since the law forbade taking the estate without the girl, and provided exactly the same rules for inheritance to estates without an *epikleros* attached.[57] The fact that these estates were known to the law as *kleroi* strongly suggests that the real-estate, that is the land, was the essential property.

The next of kin was not absolutely obliged to marry her; a law quoted by Sositheus for the marriage of daughters of *thetes* (the poorest class) who became *epikleroi* lays the responsibility for providing a dowry on the relatives on a set scale if they do not wish to marry the *epikleros* themselves. The same rule is implied in the hypothetical proposition of the orator who declares: 'if our uncle had died leaving daughters without means of support, we would have been compelled by reason of our closeness of kin either to take them to wife ourselves or endow them with a dowry and give them in marriage to other men; that is what our kinship and the laws and our self-respect before you would have compelled us to do, or else to become liable to incur the severest punishments and the most bitter criticism.' In another case we do not, unfortunately, know the proportion of the estate which Leagrus handed over when he gave his *epikleros* to Callias or his son; presumably, from the fact that he is said to have been paid for his services, he handed it over intact, and obtained his profit from the payment, not by reducing the estate.[58]

The great number of different suits which could be undertaken on behalf of *epikleroi*, orphans, minors, and even unborn children[59] reveals the great importance attached by the Athenian state to the protection of families without an adult male heir. In this, consideration for the interests of the citizen body as an army was certainly involved; the soldiers of the state wanted to know that the state had the determination and the means to protect their dependants if they fell in battle; as Thucydides says in Pericles' Funeral Speech, 'in regard to the children of the slain, the city will support them at public expense from now until they come of age, thus proffering a mark of honour which is of service to the fallen as a reward, and showing to those who are left that there is a reward for struggles such as these.'[60] Consideration for the corporate religious life of the community was also involved, no doubt, but the main purpose was the maintenance of the *oikoi*, the economic and political primary units of the state.

Among these suits are found suits for wrongful behaviour; all belong to the class which any citizen could bring without incurring liability to the usual sanctions imposed upon those who failed to obtain one-fifth of the jurors' votes.[61] Other suits provided for the appointment of the guardian who was responsible for the care of their *oikos* for all minors, and for deciding between rival claimants. The Archon was also responsible for the welfare of (ἐπιμελεῖσθαι) orphans, *epikleroi* and widows who claimed to be pregnant,[62] and to look after the leases of the property of orphans, and of *epikleroi* up to an age usually restored in the text of *Ath. Pol.* as fourteen,[63] including taking security for them, and ensuring that guardians maintained their wards.[64] Suits to claim *epikleroi* and estates were also the only actions a young citizen undergoing his military training could undertake[65] in Aristotle's day.

The obligation to marry an *epikleros* laid upon her next of kin through males (her nearest agnate), or to give her in marriage like a daughter with a dowry, obviously involved complications if either the *epikleros* or her next of kin was already married. Isaeus in a well known passage[66] states categorically that married women who become *epikleroi* are liable to be adjudicated by the court (ἐπίδικοι), and that many men have lost their wives for this reason. This statement has caused much argument; it is hard to believe that this was the automatic result of a woman losing her father or only brother—for example in battle or shipwreck—as we should have to assume if it were literally true at all times and in all places, and indeed there is evidence that there were ways out, although it is of a somewhat indirect sort, since the truth is obscured by the misrepresentations of the orators.

One situation in which an *epikleros* would not be likely to be claimed was when she had already got an adult son, because in

him his grandfather's estate would be vested, and the *epikleros*
would be merely the channel through which the grandson became
possessed of it, and her new husband could not acquire her
wealth. Isaeus once seems to suggest[67] that though her father's
next of kin could have claimed an *epikleros*, he could not obtain
the estate, to which her son (the speaker) had succeeded. The same
might also apply (though less clearly) if the *epikleros* had an infant
son; a new husband's children could not oust this son from his
share, though a claimant might still think a share of her estate
made it worth making a claim. An *epikleros* in such a situation
might, however, decline to make a claim to the estate, and thus be
enabled to remain with her previous husband; this is said to have
happened in one of Isaeus' speeches,[68] and it is not impossible that
this is the truth in the case pleaded by the opponents of the speaker
of Isaeus III, which our speaker naturally declines to countenance.[69]

It is not quite certain whether a man already married could
acquire an *epikleros* as well without divorcing his wife. As the
Greeks were monogamous this seems *prima facie* unlikely; the
divorce of Euxitheus' mother by Protomachus when he became
eligible to marry a rich *epikleros* provides an example of a divorce
taking place on these grounds. But a very interesting feature of
this divorce is the speaker's description of how it came about:
'Protomachus was a poor man; when he became entitled to the
hand and estates (κληρονομήσας) of a rich *epikleros*, as he wanted
to give my mother away in marriage, he persuaded my father
Thoucritus (who was an acquaintance of his) to take her. And
my father engaged himself to marry my mother at the hand of
her brother Timocrates of Melite in the presence of both his
uncles and other witnesses.'[70] It is to be noted that it was the
divorcing husband who found his wife a new husband, and not
his wife's brother, although it was her brother who actually gave
her away in marriage, being, as he was, her *kyrios* once her husband divorced her and found her a new husband. A second feature
of great interest is the expression used by Euxitheus to describe
Protomachus' matrimonial status—he is described as 'having
become entitled to the estate of the *epikleros*' before he initiated

his divorce. This implies that he had already successfully obtained an adjudication of the *epikleros* before seeking divorce, which means that an Athenian court had adjudicated an *epikleros* to a married man, and a married man could acquire an *epikleros* without divorcing his wife. Such an inference could hardly be drawn from the use of one verb in one tense in one speech, but this is not the only evidence for the fact that Athenians could and did have more than one legal wife at certain times and under certain conditions.

Much the simplest explanation of the background to the cases pleaded by the opposition to Mantitheus in the two Demosthenic speeches numbered 39 and 40, and to Chaerestratus' friend in Isaeus' speech Number 6 is that the two fathers Mantias and Euctemon had both a wife obtained by the normal process of betrothal agreement (*engye*) and another spouse whose children had a claim to citizenship and at least to their mother's possessions. In Euctemon's case we know that Callippe was the orphan daughter of an Athenian who died in the Sicilian expedition and whose *kleros* of land, being in Lemnos, was lost as a result of the Peloponnesian War; hence she was an *epikleros* of the poorest possible class, one literally without means of any sort. Naturally our speaker does not admit that Euctemon obtained an *epidikasia*, so we cannot say whether or not he did, but the action of Philoctemon in agreeing under pressure to admit her son to his phratry, and (as heir) to a small portion of his landed estate would be fully in accordance with a situation in which a fully legitimate only surviving son would find it hard to rebut the claims of impoverished half-brothers, offspring of an orphan *epikleros*, possibly even despite the fact that she had not been formally adjudicated, and hence he decided to come to terms with them.[71] In the case of Mantias, it appears that Plangon's children were decreed by an Athenian court to be legitimate when their mother swore an oath as to their paternity; we know that Plangon was not an *epikleros* since she had three brothers; we also know that her father Pamphilus was an Athenian and was a state-debtor, and our speaker alleges that her son will argue that Mantias received from the magistrates the sum which was over and above Pamphilus' indebtedness to the state when his property was sold—as a sort of dowry for Plangon presumably. This arrangement could have been legally undertaken, perhaps, if Mantias was Plangon's next of kin apart from her brothers, and took her as if she were a portionless *epikleros*, though again there may have been no formal adjudication because the daughter of a deceased state-debtor would not be the object of much competition, even if she was a handsome woman.[72]

Certainty cannot be attained; on the one hand modern prejudices as to what the Greeks ought to have done has certainly induced some scholars to seek for any ingenious excuse not to believe the plain meaning of texts; on the other, since we only have the opponent's story in both these cases, it is particularly difficult to be sure of the facts, and no Athenian orator would hesitate to omit the fact that there had in fact been an *epidikasia*. What is very improbable however is that a man of means would have succeeded in a claim for a rich *epikleros* if he were already married; the fact that one party was rich and the other poor was undoubtedly important in influencing Athenian juries, and so was the assertion that a man was in possession, or seeking to be in possession, of two *oikoi*.[73]

It was thought to be creditable for an unmarried man to take an *epikleros* to wife if it was his duty to do so, and especially creditable if she were not well-endowed. The claimant to Cleonymus' estate makes much of his supposed duties, and a more striking instance is provided by Andocides; although he is probably lying about the poverty of the estate of the *epikleros* whom he married (since he was most anxious to obtain control of the whole estate when his *epikleros* died and her sister became possessed of both halves and was still available for *epidikasia*), nevertheless he can only have intended to impress the jury, and gain credit in their eyes, when he claimed: 'it is not right,' I said, 'for us to choose either another man's money or his exalted station and thus to despise the daughters of Epilycus. Because, if Epilycus had lived, or had died leaving a rich estate, we would have claimed the right as next of kin to have the girls to wife. Well, that would have happened either out of regard for Epilycus himself or for the money—but as things are we shall do it because of our honour. So do you claim one of the girls before the court and I will claim the other'.[74]

ADOPTION

For a father with a daughter and no sons, the simplest method of preventing her becoming claimable as *epikleros* was to obtain her a husband, and adopt either him or one of their sons; as the father at his death would then have a son, his daughter would not become an *epikleros*. Polyeuctus did this;[75] what is interesting for us to note is that in this case there is no right of primogeniture visible: it was his younger daughter whom he married to his brother-in-law, whom he then adopted; a number of examples can also be cited of men adopting their grandsons and nephews.[76]

Adoption was not difficult; it could be done either *inter vivos* or by will. In the former case the adoptive son was presented to the *phrateres* and to the demesmen of the adopting parent; in the latter case the adopted son had to establish his claim by action (*epidikasia*) in the Archon's court in the same way as a claimant to an *epikleros*, and when successful he became son and heir simultaneously.[77] It is clear that the court was also concerned to see that the daughters of the family were properly provided for.[78]

Adopted sons were usually chosen from within the family. The adopted son of Menecles (who was not a kinsman) goes to some length to explain why Menecles did not adopt one of his blood-relatives. 'He saw that my opponent' (who was Menecles' brother) 'had only one son, and so it seemed to him that it was a discreditable thing to make his brother a man without male heirs by making him give him his son to adopt; he therefore discovered nobody who was closer to him than we are'[79]—in fact the speaker was brother to Menecles' second wife from whom he had separated on friendly terms. It can be alleged to be a sign of ill-will to your kinsmen to adopt a son from outside the circle of your relatives, and Apollodorus even alleges that Phrastor made an attempt to legitimize a bastard son in order to deprive his relatives, whom he hated, of his estate; this was a working man too,[80] and not a rich one. It can also be alleged that nobody would adopt a son who has legitimate sons of his own, but if a son was adopted and a legitimate son was subsequently begotten, the adopted son was entitled to share equally in his father's estate.[81]

Adopted sons differed from other sons in the respect that they could not make a will, and hence could perpetuate the *oikos* of their adoptive father only through direct descendants. If they had procreated a son, however, they were allowed to return to their own family themselves, provided that they left him (or one son if there were several) in the family of their adoptive father; the son so left then became registered as the adopted son of the original adoptive father, and became in turn responsible for providing him with descendants. According to Aristodemus' son this process was once continued through three generations, and Leocrates, his son and grandson were in turn enrolled as adopted son of Archiades, who was Leocrates' great-uncle; it was only when Leocrates' grandson died without a legitimate heir that the kinsmen of Archiades took action to acquire the estate which our speaker still calls the *oikos* of Archiades. Adopted sons also differed in that they could be more easily repudiated, as another Leocrates was repudiated by Polyeuctus though he was brother-in-law, son-in-law and adopted son.[82]

Only citizens could be adopted by private individuals;[83] the reasons for this may have been sentimental in part, but the practical needs of the *oikoi* for successors were probably predominant. Only citizens could own, and hence inherit, the *oikoi* of the Athenian state; thus, if a non-Athenian were able to be adopted, not only would an outsider be introduced to the worship of the family's shrines and ancestors, but at the adopting parent's death the *oikos* itself would pass to the next of kin by birth, and the purpose of the adoption thus be frustrated. It may be taken as certain that foreigners were from time to time illegally adopted, both from the expulsions from the rolls at times of revision, and from references to the corrupt practice of admitting them as adopted sons in return for money.[84] As, however, the main object of the rule was to prevent the amalgamation of *oikoi* as a result of adoptions, it provides yet another example of the Athenians' determination to keep their *oikoi* intact, and in their own hands.

THE PROPERTY OF NON-CITIZENS

This is not to say that metics and other non-Athenians had no rights; they had full rights over movable property which was not part of the Athenians' *oikoi*, sums of money in cash and loaned, slaves, articles of property, etc., and we know that the Polemarchos acted for them in the same way that the Archon did for the citizens in cases of inheritance and *epikleroi*.[85] They could also sue and be sued in the city's courts, where they were represented by the patron under whom they were obliged to register, and our sources reveal one such successful plea.[86]

MAINTENANCE OF THE OIKOI

The Athenians' determination to maintain the number of *oikoi* in the *polis* had, for adoption, the result that the separation of an adopted son from his original family was total, and, unless he had a son of his own, irrevocable; as one speaker puts it: 'Cyronides . . . was adopted into another *oikos*, so that none of the property belonged to him any longer', and another speaker declares that 'when his father returned to the deme of the Eleusinians he no longer retained any legal kinship to his son'.[87] No citizen, if the Athenian state could prevent it, should be the possessor of two *oikoi*.

Emotional appeals to juries point to the same policy: 'Think, men of the jury, that this lad here is set before you as a suppliant's wand on behalf of the deceased Hagnias and Euboulides and the others of Hagnias' descendants, and that he implores you jurors not to allow their *oikos* to suffer obliteration at the hands of these dreadful creatures who are of the *oikos* of Stratius and have never at any time been in the *oikos* of Hagnias . . . and do not allow his ancestors to be even more despised than they are now despised if these fellows carry out what they want to.'[88]

RELIGIOUS DUTIES

Another similar appeal lays more stress on the family's religious duties: 'This fellow now wants to make me bereft of my father's inheritance (*kleros*), . . . and to cause him to lie dead without a son and without a name, that nobody may honour the family's cults on his behalf nor make the annual sacrifices on his behalf year by year, and that he may be robbed of the honours which are his due.'[89] These religious duties towards the deceased members of the family were most important; for the family, tending the ancestors' tombs was quite as important as worshipping the city's gods, and the city itself showed its concern for the families' cults in that 'where are your ancestors' tombs?' was one of the questions asked at the *dokimasia* (preliminary scrutiny) of aspiring magistrates.[90] Part of this concern may have been to ensure the validity of the candidate's claim to citizenship, but the major part was with the cult of the dead, based on the feeling that the dead were not wholly gone, a feeling also apparent in the festival of the Anthesteria,[91] when the dead were thought to walk abroad, and in the measures taken to assuage the anger of a man who had died by violence, whose spirit's demand for revenge on his killer was regarded as a motive quite as important as the anger of the gods in seeking to avenge blood-guilt.[92]

Amongst the religious duties of kinsmen (οἱ προσήκοντες) are listed those of burying any member of the family who died, and performing the funeral rites[93] (*Pls. 26, 27*). The right to do these duties was jealously guarded; and, since no unfriendly person should be in charge,[94] the duty and privilege devolved upon the heir; and to have carried out the burial formed part of his claim to be heir if he were an adopted son, so that we find in one case that there was a quarrel over who should conduct the burial, and even a scuffle at the graveside.[95] At a funeral the men walked in front of the bier, the women followed, and only those female relatives who were within the recognized degree of kinship were allowed to take part if they were under sixty years old.[96] Families had their own burying-places marked by monuments of various types (*Pls. 23, 28–30*); burial within the family burial-ground is argued to be a ground for proving kinship, and burial elsewhere for denying it.[97]

At least from the mid-fifth century it was customary to bring home the bones or ashes of Athenians who had died abroad, so that individuals could be buried in their family burying ground, the state's dead (who had all been cremated together) in a communal grave.[98] Burial however was only the first duty to the dead; there followed the third and ninth day ceremonies,[99] at the end of thirty days a feast called Kathedra in the dead man's honour, and thereafter annual commemorations.[100] These last included worship at the tombs of the ancestors, which provided a focus for them (*Pl. 30*) so that we find their upkeep an obligation, and the due performance of the ceremonies a virtue, and the opposite an opportunity for abusing an opponent.[101]

The state encouraged these worships with the state festival of the Genesia, and part of the Apatouria was also devoted to the deceased members of the phratries,[102] but it is highly probable that their private festivals had a more immediate hold on the consciousness of individuals, and it is worth remembering that while legislators from Solon to Demetrius Poliorcetes thought it necessary to diminish extravagance on private religious observances, no legislator ever had to intervene to limit a man's contributions to civic festivals.[103]

Festivals designed to promote fertility and prosperity were also held alike by both city and family. The great festivals of Dionysus took place in the city, when tragedies and comedies were performed, but the families of the demes celebrated the rustic Dionysia on their own lands in the country-districts; of these we know little except for the scene in Aristophanes' *Acharnians* which depicts its performance.[104] However, we also hear that in the fourth century some people left the city for their country-properties, taking their children with them, and that the *Demarchos* of the deme Myrrhinous had to manage the business connected with the festival.[105]

Another family festival was that of Zeus Ktesios, the god of the store-chamber, associated by Dionysius of Halicarnassus with the Roman Di Penates, whose sacrifices were in some families restricted to members of the family, in some families open to outsiders also. Zeus Ktesios also had his public rite,[106] but the worship of the family's Zeus Ktesios was certainly more vital, since the very existence, let alone the prosperity, of a family was dependent on the economic survival of its *oikos*. Menophanes, the subject of a satirical epigram of the first century AD, makes the point:

'Menophanes bought a property, and through starvation hanged himself on someone else's oak-tree; there was not enough earth on his property to cover his corpse, so he was buried, for a fee, in a neighbour's land. Had Democritus known of Menophanes' land he'd have said the world was made not out of atoms, but out of properties.'[107] Menophanes' lands were too small to maintain an *oikos*; other men's crops might fail, and then they too would starve; it is small wonder, then, that the spirits of the ancestors and their land had a power which long outlasted the Olympian gods' ability to retain the ordinary man's devotion and, as the *pagani*, to provide Christianity with its most stubborn opposition.

CHAPTER VII

WOMEN IN DEMOCRATIC ATHENS

THE WOMEN'S PLACE

THE SOCIAL LIFE of the family in Athens—or as it is usually expressed, the position of the women—is a subject which has provoked much controversy.[1] One cause has probably been a failure to consider whether it may not have varied considerably between different social classes and historical periods, but a more important failure has been that the subject has usually been treated in isolation without attempting to put the subject into the context of the position of the whole family in the state.

Even among socially comparable families, however, the pages of the orators should warn us that simple generalizations will mislead us; containing, as they do, both hostile and sympathetic pictures of family life, these speeches provide as wide a spectrum as could well be imagined. The important thing for a student to consider is not whether any of these pictures is true or not (for this had little relevance to a Greek orator), but what feelings they were intended to evoke in the jurors—whether, in fact, they were intended to arouse sympathy or the reverse, and, to do either, we must remember that they must have seemed credible.

On one side we hear of a certain Polyeuctus and his wife (who had only two daughters and no son) managing their property in their daughters' interests.[2] Spoudias, the opponent, and our speaker were the husbands of the girls. Our speaker declares that he and Spoudias received or purchased numerous items of property from their wives' parents: Spoudias received a loan of money from his mother-in-law, also a shallow cup (φιάλη) and some jewellery which he and his wife pawned; some awnings and other similar objects are also mentioned, and at her death his mother-in-law left papers enumerating all her gifts and loans.

The daughters also took part in administering the family property: they were present at the making of Polyeuctus' will; our speaker maintains that both daughters knew its contents, and claims that Spoudias' wife would have reported to her husband if she had not received a fair share, and that Spoudias himself had declined to attend the will-making, being busy, saying that his wife's presence was enough. We are also told that Spoudias' wife never raised any objections then or later, and that the two sisters both acted as witnesses to the genuineness of Polyeuctus' sealed papers. Later the speaker's wife is said to have paid a mina of silver out of her own share, advancing the money, for the remembrance-ceremonies for her father.

The picture here is one in which the women of the family are fully apprised of its financial affairs, being present at many, if not all, the important legal transactions, taking part as witnesses and even disposing of property without apparently being subordinated to their husbands, although legally they had no unfettered right to make such dispositions. It must be remembered, of course, that these two ladies had no brother and hence were doubtless more independent than many, but the picture of the family council settling collectively its members' financial relationships is one which would not seem at all out of place in the modern world.

On the other hand, in Aeschines' roughly contemporary portrait of Timarchus,[3] we are told of how he helped a certain Hegesandrus to squander the estate of an *epikleros* whom Hegesandrus took in marriage; he then proceeded to squander his own patrimony, selling his inheritance piece by piece—a house, some slaves, a suburban property, and a country property in which (we are told) he refused to leave unsold even enough for his mother to be buried there, despite the fact that she pleaded and begged him to leave a part of it unsold. An equally unpleasant picture emerges at the end of the fifth century in the picture of Callias provided by Andocides;[4] he married a girl, but after less than a year took her mother also as his wife, and kept both mother and daughter in the same house, at which the daughter was so filled with shame that she tried to hang herself, and subsequently ran away. Callias then got tired of the mother, put her out of the house though she was pregnant (she claimed by him), and repudiated her son when it was presented by her relatives at the Apatouria for enrolment; however, he subsequently felt a desire to have her back again, brought her back to his house along with the boy, and got him enrolled in his own *genos*, the aristocratic, priestly Kerykes. Clearly no generalization will cover all three of these cases, which indicate such differing attitudes of mind, and many more; all that we can say is that there were, as we ought to expect anyway, families with responsible and considerate menfolk, and their opposites.

RELEVANT COMPARISONS

Scholars have also tended to put Homer's women beside those of classical Athens to the detriment of the latter; one might as well compare the lady of a medieval manor with a Victorian lower-middle-class housewife—or a modern factory-worker; the qualities of the patterns of life are utterly different. The heroic woman enjoyed great social freedom within her husband's house and the domain of his power, but her position depended entirely on his success as a warrior and his ability to maintain his family's independence in a jealously competitive world in which failure brought slavery or starvation, or both; her position in respect to her husband was also wholly dependent on his pleasure, or the ability and willingness of her relations to bring pressure to bear on him. In Athens, in the aristocratic period, the upper classes retained some features of the heroic pattern; the great families enjoyed a comparable freedom of social intercourse, which lasted at least as far as the time of Cimon and Elpinice in the mid-fifth century. But the Homeric élite, the upper strata of society, were supported by a nameless, forgotten population of serfs and other semi-free poor folk, who lived on the borders of starvation, and who appear but rarely in literature,[5] and in history only on occasions when, as in pre-Solonian Athens, the élite had monopolized such an excessive share of the community's wealth that the small, independent, fighting man who was, after all, the backbone of the state, began to be affected.

THE IMPACT OF DEMOCRACY

By the mid-fifth century the Athenian democracy had under-mined the way of life of this élite. The laws, and the courts which enforced them, imposed controls upon their freedom of action in many fields, for example in augmenting their possessions, or in acquiring wives and concubines at will and regarding whom they would as their heirs. Later, the Peloponnesian War caused immense losses to the older, landed, families because of its de-mands on the citizens' pockets, its cutting off of their income from their lands for a decade, and the wastage which customarily followed the death of the father of a family on military service.[6]

After the end of this war, too, the reign of the Thirty Tyrants and the revolutions which accompanied it impoverished a further number of families, while the expansionist ambitions of the re-stored democracy provoked constant demands for taxes and service as trierarchs,[7] and this, with the customary liturgies of all sorts, made further inroads not merely into the income, but also into the capital of the wealthier citizens.[8] The attitude of the democracy's jurors too, with their preference for the poorer liti-gant over the one with the better case, and their determination to prevent the amalgamation of *oikoi* if at all possible, all combined to promote an economic levelling-down among the citizens.[9] Other features hastened the process; heavy fines and confiscation of property seem to have been the punishment for innumerable offences, some of which seem to us to be of the most trivial nature;[10] men who undertook important military and naval commands were liable to become impoverished for failing to carry out the missions for which the democracy had failed to equip them adequately;[11] even trierarchs were apt to find them-selves involved in litigation to recover excessive expenditures in which they had been involved,[12] while the state totally failed to secure the execution of the judgements of its courts, as it did in purely private cases also, as for example in the case of Demos-thenes' successful action against his guardians.[13]

This does not mean that there were no rich men in democratic Athens; there undoubtedly were, both in the fifth century and in the fourth, but by then they were not, in general, the old landed nobility, since their incomes will have failed to keep pace with inflation[13a] because they had not the means (or probably the ability and inclination) to introduce better farming techniques, and a supply of abundant, and hence relatively cheap, grain was a cornerstone of the state's policy. We meet soldiers of fortune like Conon, whose wealth was enormous, and we hear that wealth could be quickly made by similar successful adventurers.[14] Demosthenes' father, who had inherited considerable wealth from his mother, increased it by his successful direction of two factories manned by slaves,[15] a certain Comon also made money by factory-owning, employing slave-workmen, and so did several people quoted in one of Xenophon's tales.[16] Bankers and money-lenders may have had fluctuating fortunes, as did the family of Cephalus, Lysanias, Protomachus and Lysias,[17] but some seem to have done well, as Phormion and Pasion did; their status as metics may in fact have been an advantage in this rather than a dis-advantage.[18] But money made in business was often later capital-ized into farms; land, indeed, was the best as well as the most honourable form of investment.[19] Even if having one's money in land produced the result that concealment was less easy, and made the owner liable to be chosen for liturgies or service as trierarch,[20] the Athenians' desire to make a show[21] (*philotimia*) and at the same time to have the best security tended to overcome their reluctance to pay taxes.

SELF-HELP

The Athenian democracy also expected its citizens to practise a great deal of self-help; the law asserted the rights of search and of seizure, which had sometimes to be forcibly carried out, as in one instance cited by Isocrates, when a litigant sought to obtain a vital piece of evidence;[22] judgments given in court had to be executed in person;[23] private citizens had to obtain witnesses when involved in situations which were likely to lead to action in the courts (one case we know of was to witness a quarrel following the serving of a demand on a reluctant trierarch,[24] another to witness the surprising of an adulterer in the act);[25] all these involved raising a posse of friends to act as allies if force were needed. Some of

Aristophanes' comic choruses provide examples of such posses,[26] and there are enough references in the orators to breaking into houses,[27] drunken revellers roaming the streets (Pl.31),[28] and men being beaten up,[29] apparently without the slightest interference from police or other guardians of the peace, for us to conclude that the democracy was at least somewhat lax in maintaining law and order.

A citizen's interests were therefore best served by maintaining friendly relations with a wide circle of men, including friends as well as neighbours and relations,[30] and this necessarily involved him in associations and social gatherings with these friends rather than with his family; in consequence, the family normally did not provide the central focus of a citizen's social life. The behaviour of these social gatherings was sometimes civilized, sometimes less so, as is very clear from Plato's *Symposium*, and some of the associations (especially among the wealthier classes) are known to have had political aims as well, as was the case with the *hetaireiai* which were the mainstay of the oligarchic attacks on the democracy, but which had also the object of combining for the defence of their members against judicial and other attacks.[31]

CONFORMISM

The slogan of the Athenian democracy was 'to live as you please', but it was not so liberalizing as it sounds, and in practice the democracy, through its courts, imposed a considerable measure of conformity with the customs of the numerically dominant middle and lower-middle-classes,[32] and provided, in the persons of the informers, the means whereby the wealthy could be forced to toe the line. Display of all kinds was liable to provoke jealousy and malice; the career of Alcibiades illustrates the hatred and distrust engendered by a brilliant aristocrat who refused to conform.[33] Half a century later Demosthenes attacked Meidias in the words: 'Alcibiades is reputed to have been an Alcmaeonid on his father's side—and they say that they were expelled by the tyrants for taking the people's part . . . and threw out the sons of Peisistratus —and on his mother's side of the house of Hipponicus, great benefactors of the people. . . . Besides, he himself twice took up arms on the democracy's side in Samos and once here in the city, showing where his inclination lay, not by word of mouth, or by his money, but by risking his person. In addition he competed and won at Olympia with his horses, was the best commander and had the reputation apparently of being the finest speaker. But even with all this your ancestors would not tolerate any of his acts of wanton pride . . . but exiled him . . . and thought anything preferable to putting up with such behaviour.'[34] Earlier, the private life of Pericles illustrates the sort of accusation which a public man provoked if he asserted his independence of the normal social conventions,[35] and Aristophanes in 422 thought fit to deny that success brought him to pride or haunting palaestras or condoning sodomy, acts which were clearly associated with Cleon's aristocratic opponents.[36]

The trial of Socrates in 399 provides an example both of a man whose independence of mind brought suspicion on him, and of the dangers awaiting those who associated with the upper classes, who always remained an object of suspicion to the democracy, and the victims of its judicial system.[37]

Conformity, too, is claimed as a virtue; several of Lysias' clients found it necessary to claim that they lived sober lives,[38] and aspersions upon their opponent's morals are part of the stock-in-trade of Aeschines and Demosthenes and their contemporaries.[39]

HOMOSEXUALITY

We are sometimes told that the Greeks were fully bisexual, enjoying both homosexual and heterosexual intercourse, and that romantic love in Greece was associated with attachments to boys and not to girls. Whatever the truth of the latter statement, there can be no doubt that, while the Greeks had a deep admiration for the physical beauty of the young male, in Athens the practice of sodomy was strictly circumscribed by the law. Boys still at school were protected against sexual assaults by a law (said to go as far back as Dracon and Solon),[40] and we hear of strict regulations about schools with this in mind; schoolboys always had a *paidagogos* escorting them; in art the *paidagogos* is always depicted as carrying a long and heavy stick (*Pls. 32–3*); what was this for if not to protect their charges?[41] Adult citizens (those enrolled on the deme-registers) who were catamites, or had been catamites as adults, suffered some diminution of civic rights;[42] those who procured free boys for sodomy are said to have been punishable by law.[43] This evidence may give a clue to the truth of the situation, which was perhaps that free Athenians practised homosexual intercourse only for a short period of their lives—between the period when they cut their hair (about the age of sixteen) and started to frequent the gymnasium and wrestling-school as part of the process of strengthening their bodies for military training (when they were the target of lovers), during military training and for a short period thereafter (when they were the lovers). Sodomy was thought reprehensible for older men even when the catamite was not a citizen, as is clear from a speech of Lysias,[44] but it was not illegal; it may be thought that the law in this field is likely to have been similar to that about adultery; what was quite legal with slaves and other non-citizens was illegal with citizens, and the law took notice of the private morals of individuals, and punished offenders.

Paederasty was expensive; whether this was because the youths' admirers wanted to compete in generosity for favours or the youths were able to use the law virtually to blackmail their admirers no doubt varied in individual cases, but the result of the expense was to make paederasty a habit of the upper class and of those who imitated them, and hence suspect to the common people and a means of arousing prejudice in legal cases.[45] Plato's attack on sodomy, especially in the *Laws*, reveals that the practice was not unknown to him, and that it was more repugnant to his ideals than heterosexual intercourse outside marriage, since this latter (if secret) was tolerated in the *Laws* as a second-best to the ideal of virginity till marriage and sexual intercourse only within marriage for the purpose of breeding children.[46]

THE PROTECTION OF WOMEN

The citizenship law of Pericles, re-enacted in the archonship of Eucleides in 403/2 BC, combined with the Athenians' litigiousness and covetousness and with the activities of the informers in restricting the freedom of the women in social intercourse. It was of such overriding importance not to allow the least breath of suspicion to fall on young girls that they were not virgins, or on young wives that their child was not properly conceived in wedlock, that they were protected to what to our minds is a wholly unreasonable degree. Ischomachus' bride had lived 'under strict supervision in order that she might see as little as possible, hear as little as possible and find out as little as possible . . . she knew only about the working of wool herself and what could be expected of a slave, . . . but she also had had a really good training in management of the food, which seems to me to be the most important accomplishment to have, both for a man and his wife'.[47] So Xenophon writes. A speaker can claim that his sister and nieces in the women's quarters in his house had lived 'with so much concern for their modesty that they were embarrassed even to be seen by their male relatives'.[48] Other speakers claim that wives do not go out to dinner with their husbands, and do not even eat with their husbands when they are entertaining male visitors, unless they are relatives.[49]

This last was not perhaps as unreasonable as it might appear at first sight; male company was not always as orderly as a modern mixed dinner party; the orators narrate some parties at which no doubt women would not have wished to be present.[50] Other passages speak of quarrels arising 'through drunkenness, quarrelsomeness or playfulness, arising out of abuse, or fighting over a mistress' (Pl. 19),[51] and Athenaeus cites several extracts on this theme.[52] Orators also deny they had even been to their opponents' houses for such reasons; one denies that he had ever been one of the young men who go in for gaming and drink;[53] even in the circle of Plato we find that the philosophical discussion on love was agreed upon partly because all of those present at the symposium except Socrates were suffering from sore heads as a result of previous excesses.[54] It is to be remembered that since gay parties and serenadings were regarded as the mark of a kept woman,[55] this provided yet another reason for a wife not to wish to attend.

But citizen-women took part in such business activities as the making of wills; apart from the wife and daughters of Polyeuctus

mentioned above, Lysias in a memorable passage tells how
Diogeiton's daughter stood up in a family council to remonstrate
with her father over the treatment of her two sons, who were at
the same time his nephews and his grandchildren: 'The boys'
mother', says the orator, 'kept begging me and imploring me
(their sister's husband) to call a meeting consisting of her father
and their friends, saying that even if she had not been in the habit
before of speaking amongst men, the extreme degree of their ill-
fortune would compel her to reveal all the details of the wrongs
which they had suffered . . . And when we assembled she asked
him what sort of man he was to think it right to act in the way
he had acted towards the boys; he was the brother of their father,
she said, "and my father and both their uncle and their grandfather; and if you have no feeling of embarrassment towards any
man, you ought to have feared the gods; you received, when your
brother set sail, five talents from him on deposit. And in support
of this I am willing to put forward my children, both these boys
and those of my other marriage, and swear on oath upon their
heads anywhere you care to name. And you know I am not so
wretched a specimen, nor am I so covetous of money as to die a
perjured wretch who has invoked curses upon my children, and
to rob my own father of his property in defiance of justice".' Then
she proved him to have received seven talents and forty minae on
bottomry loans and showed written proof of it, for when she
moved house into the house of Phaedrus (her new husband presumably) the children happened to light on the account book,
which had been thrown out, and brought it to her. And she
showed that he had received certain other sums of money . . .
'And then', she said, 'you had the audacity to claim, though you
had all this money, that their father left two thousand drachmae
and thirty staters, the sum which was bequeathed to me, and I
handed over to you when he was dead.' Clearly here is another
Athenian woman fully apprised of the financial standing of the
house, although naturally she did not have the management of
the estate herself. Lysias then goes on to narrate her indignant
appeal to her father, at the close of which, says the orator, 'all of
those present were so affected by what this man had done and by

the things which she had said to him, when we saw the boys and the injuries inflicted upon them, and remembered the deceased and how unworthy a trustee he had left for his possessions, and when we reflected on how difficult a thing it is to find a man who could be trusted with what he ought to be trusted, none of us who were there could utter a word, gentlemen of the jury, we could only weep as sadly as the victims of these doings and depart in silence'.[56] Another account of the women's presence at their husbands' will-making is contained in Lysias' account of how the victims of the Thirty Tyrants, when condemned to death, sent for their women-folk in the prison, 'one his sister, one his mother, one his wife, one any female relative he happened to have; Dionysodorus sent for his wife and in her presence made his last will and testament as he thought fit . . . and laid the duty upon his wife, whom he believed to be pregnant by him, that if she bore a son she was to tell him that Agoratus was his father's murderer, and bid him avenge his father'.[57]

Another consequence of the feeling that women should be secluded is that it was easy to arouse prejudice against a man by alleging that he had entered the women's quarter of a house without the master's knowledge. In a number of speeches this is said to have been a material part of the injuries opponents had inflicted.[58] That it was primarily because of the effect on the women-folk is shown by the allegations in the speech against Euergus; Euergus and his brother Theophemus burst into the speaker's house and into the presence of his wife while the speaker was out; bystanders who came to witness their misdeeds would not enter the house in the absence of the master; the speaker himself would not enter the presence of Euergus' father and mother who lived with him, though he says he went into the house of Theophemus, having already informed himself that Theophemus was not married, and there he had no compunction about giving the servant girl orders, and even threatened to carry her off as security for a debt he claimed.[59] To our minds perhaps the most significant fact in the accusation against Lycophron is that when he had had leave to come and go into a friend's house, in what we should call a normal way, and to speak to his wife, he found himself in court charged with adultery.[60] This same feeling explains why burglars and thieves were liable to be killed, and, says Euphiletus, 'if you do not punish adulterers with death you will make them so bold that you will make even thieves claim to be adulterers in the knowledge that . . . if they give this as the reason for their being in a house nobody will touch them'.[61]

VIRGINITY AND MARRIAGE

The civic necessity for virginity also ensured that girls were married very young; we have no statistical information on the customary age; all that we can say is that the law on *epikleroi* appears to have made them legally possessed of their property (in so far as they ever truly possessed it) at the age of fourteen, and this must have coincided with their marriage.[62] Xenophon's Ischomachus, himself a fully mature man of about thirty, married a girl of fourteen, [63] but Xenophon, like Hesiod, Plato, Aristotle and Plutarch (or his source), thought that the customary age of marriage was too young, and that the customary age in Sparta (eighteen to twenty) was much more satisfactory[64] (*Pls. 24, 25*).

As noted in Chapter V, a girl's *kyrios* usually took the initiative in obtaining her a husband; when her future husband was one of her relatives, she was presumably already acquainted with him, however slightly, and will certainly have known of him by repute. When he was not a relative we cannot be certain that she had ever met him face to face before her betrothal. It is improbable that she did; even in modern Greece a girl may well not meet her prospective husband until he has come to terms with the head of her family.[65] Xenophon, it is true, speaks of marrying a beautiful girl as being desirable, and we have a hint that a girl who was not even moderately passable to look at (ὁπωστιοῦν μετρίαν . . . ὄψιν) might not get a husband, and of course this could only be determined by the husband-to-be if he had seen her in person, but personal descriptions of the bride might well have been part of the duty of the match-maker, as it is in India today.[66]

From the point of view of society and social life, one inevitable and evil result of the immaturity of Athenian brides, and the wide gap in age that was normal between husband and wife, lay in that they were most unlikely to have any common friends; Aristotle did not consider this aspect of friendship at all in his treatment of the subject,[67] and there is more than a hint of paternalism rather than partnership underlying the whole of Xenophon's treatment of the customary husband and wife relationship in Athens in his own day.[68]

THE EDUCATION OF GIRLS

Athenian girls were also less well educated than boys; while there is plenty of evidence that many were taught to read and write,[69] few received any higher education even when boys began to get it, from about the middle of the fifth century. Most of the more highly educated women of whom we hear were non-citizens like Aspasia, or belong to the Hellenistic age like Hipparchia, who lived as the wife of Crates the Cynic, and whose behaviour would probably provoke the intervention of the law even in twentieth century Britain.[70] Xenophon attributes wives' lack of education to their extreme youth at marriage; the often-quoted question, 'Is there anyone with whom you hold fewer discussions than with your wife?', and its answer, 'If there is anyone, there are not many at all events', is prefaced by illustrations (from sheep and horses) that it is the fault of the person in charge if what is under his care is in ill condition, and the argument that a husband must teach his wife to manage his property, since she is entrusted with more of his valuable possessions than anyone else. 'And', says his Socrates, 'did you not marry her as just a young girl who had seen and heard as little as possible? Is it then not much more to be wondered at if she understands any of the things she ought to say and do than if she fails to do so?', and goes on 'And I think that a wife who is a good partner in an *oikos* is in every way as important to its well-being as her husband.'[71] Though his treatment is patronizing in that he assumes that a bride has no education and therefore needs to be taught, he explains the need in terms of her youth, not of her capacity to learn, and therefore is, to modern ways of thought, somewhat in advance of Plato, who states unequivocally his view that a woman's capacity to learn is less than that of a man.[72]

FAMILY LIMITATION AND ECONOMICS

The economic demands of the Athenian *oikos* must also be taken into account; there is a marked contrast between the economic position of those Homeric families of whom we hear and the Athenian families. The Homeric families had an abundance of provisions; they could afford to entertain handsomely and to consume large quantities of meat (though it should be noted that all feasts had some purpose except for those in the house of Odysseus which by definition were mere wastage),[73] and did not have to consider where the next meal was coming from. Many of the citizens of democratic Athens of whom we hear had much less margin between sufficient to eat and want.[74] The loss of a day's pay is represented as a serious matter in comedy, since this trifling sum was what the family depended upon for its supper.[75] The needs of the *oikos* therefore prescribed strict limits to the family's ability to choose its way of life.

In the first place economic considerations dictated the size of the family parents could rear; there can be no doubt whatever that the exposure of surplus children was practised throughout antiquity, though too many discussions of this practice have failed to take into account the possibility that different strata in different societies in different eras may have produced differences in practice.[76] In Athens, anything like an accurate assessment of the extent to which exposure was generally practised can emerge only from a consideration of the *oikoi*, and the contrasting demands for enough children to ensure its continuance, and sufficiently few for the *oikos* to be able to support them.

There can be little doubt that the first child of a marriage (whichever its sex) was never exposed if it was healthy (or appeared to be), though it might be repudiated, as in Herodotus' story about Hippocrates, father of Peisistratus. However we can cite at least one congenitally defective man among the families whose history is given by the orators.[77] It is unlikely that the second would be exposed either in families of mixed sexes: it is also unlikely even if both were girls, since the wish for descendants was so great, and life so precarious; however, when the babies were both boys, some of the poor may have shared Hesiod's view[78] that one son is enough, and have preferred the risk of losing their only son to the danger of having to divide the *oikos* if more than one survived infancy. Certainly, when children were more numerous than two, the economic resources of the family must have been an important factor in deciding whether or not to rear additional children. Five children are not uncommon among the families who employed the orators whose works have survived[79] (whose speeches, it must be remembered, were mostly commissioned because a family lacked an heir, and their estates were therefore the subject of litigation); all except one, that of Bouselus who had five sons, had both sons and daughters. We do not know the sexes of the five children of the soldier's widow in Aristophanes' *Thesmophoriazusae*, a poor woman,[80] but before her husband's death the family had probably been more prosperous.

It has been argued that girls were more likely to be exposed than boys from evidence of two kinds, one by transference from the Hellenistic period, when this seems to have been so, the other by an argument from silence—that we hear only of the sons born to famous Athenians—however, this latter argument is worthless when we can quote the example of Cleomenes, of whom Herodotus says: 'he died childless, leaving an only daughter called Gorgo', and observe that in modern Greece a man habitually ignores his daughters when enumerating his children.[81] In Classical Athens moreover, when family ties were still very strong, it must have been on economic grounds that a decision as to whether or not to rear a baby will have been made, and here a girl might have had a stronger claim to be reared than a boy, since she might be found a husband with only a small portion, whereas a boy would be able to claim his full share in the family *oikos*, a division the *oikos* might not be able to stand. The mother's feelings might also have been a little relieved by the fact that an exposed boy might have more chance of being acquired as a supposititious child, since a father who longed for a son will have been more willingly hoodwinked than others.

So much is speculative; the families whose estates are disputed by the orators' clients give no hint of any preference either way— nor, in fact, of exposure being practised at all. In addition, if exposure was freely practised, it seems odd that the disposal of her children in this way does not form part of any of the women's tirades against men in the literary sources such as those of Euripides' *Medea*, or Aristophanes' *Lysistrata* and other female spokesmen.[82] It might indeed be the case that very few healthy legitimate citizen-children were in fact exposed, although there may have been some change in the climate of opinion in the fourth century, as there certainly was in the period after Alexander.[83]

There were other means of limiting families; natural sterility played a part, also sterility induced by ancient gynaecological methods, and by abortion, which was also practised; surplus children were probably also avoided by refraining from sexual intercourse. The evidence for this is of course indirect, but it is consistent; Xenophon's declaration that men do not get married for sexual satisfaction but to procreate children is supported by the advice to marry at about the age of thirty, an age at which the most peremptory sexual desires are over. Writers also speak of the desirability of not having over-sexed wives; if these writers were only the comic poets, such statements could be ignored as wishful thinking, or mere jesting, but they are not; Aristotle regards it as established, both in his biological writings and in his *Politics*, that girls married too young are sexually demanding.[84] It stands to reason that a wife who demands frequent sexual satisfaction from her husband is liable to become pregnant frequently; a wife who is prepared to bear a small family and then allow her husband to expend his surplus sexual appetite elsewhere does not encourage the procreation of legitimate children who have to be exposed.[85]

These, however, must be regarded as the standards of the dominant middle- and lower-middle-classes; the poor must have both lost an even greater proportion of their babies from natural causes and bad hygiene, and probably have resorted to exposure more frequently; however, the largest number, and the highest proportion, of exposed infants will have been those produced by unions formed out of wedlock, the bastards of slave girls, courtesans and prostitutes of all classes, though not even all of these were necessarily exposed; for example we know that

Neaira allegedly kept three of her children.[86] In later times, Aristotle's will reveals that his bastard children from Herpyllis had been reared;[87] the plots of many of the plays of New Comedy —to judge from the fragments and surviving Latin versions— arise from the survival of children who had either been exposed or disposed of at birth, but these seem to have been mainly the offspring of extra-legal sexual intercourse, either rape (as in Menander's *Epitrepontes*) or seduction (as in Menander's *Hero*).[88] There must have been a significant number of others too, for the law was not likely to have recognized bastard as a legal status unless there were in fact some people living who could properly be so described. Among slaves, very many must have been foundlings reared and trained by their owners, often to work as *hetairai*.[89]

Among children born to citizen-parents in wedlock the proportion, and even the number, exposed was in the classical period perhaps pretty small, but any estimate must be based on the assumption that the needs of the *oikos* were regarded as paramount in making the decision whether or not to rear an infant.

MARRIED WOMEN'S LIFE

In their rearing girls were treated less generously than boys; Xenophon tells us that they were brought up on a sparse diet, with very little protein (and we hardly need to add that this meant next to no meat) and scarcely any wine, unless it was well watered;[90] this must surely have been dictated by the economic needs of the family, from whose point of view it was more essential that the boys should be strong and able to maintain the *oikos* when they grew up. As married women too in such families we find that borrowing, mortgaging and pledging property were part of their (and their husband's) ordinary family life[91]—for this the evidence of comedy rings true. Consequently, to be a good manager, to be economical and thrifty,[92] to prevent stealing,[93] to make the family independent in the production of clothes and to have something in reserve were thought to be cardinal virtues in a wife. All these activities required her presence at home,[94] and in response to civic duty and the economic demands of their family some Athenian women remained in their houses to such an extent that it was even possible for unscrupulous orators to pretend that they did not exist. Among the law court speeches which have survived there are two in which the orator brings evidence to prove that a woman who had married and borne children had actually existed; it is clear that the opposition had cast doubts on her existence in precisely the same way as the friend of Chaerestratus in the sixth speech of Isaeus questions the existence of the daughter of Pistoxenus, and Apollodorus in his speech against Neaira challenges Stephanus about the mother of his children.[95]

This is not to say that wives never went out; comedy may complain that it is hard for a woman to get out of the house, and it appears that they did not normally do the shopping (*Pl. 36*) but we do hear of them going out for walks with their maids; they carried spinning-baskets (*Pl. 37*) and had parasols;[96] they went out to the neighbours to borrow, and to get a light if their own had gone out.[97] Elderly women also went to attend women in labour,[98] but it was at religious festivals that women were principally seen by men, not only the state festivals for which they could dress up in their best clothes, such as the great processions with their maiden participants (*Pls. 40, 41*), but also the simpler rustic Dionysia,[99] and other family occasions such as marriages[100] (*Pl. 24*) and funerals, although in the latter case at least we know that women attending had to be close relatives of the deceased or older women, over the age of 60.[101] But the Athenians assumed that a woman's life would mainly be spent at home, and in consequence often in no great comfort, since town houses were small and probably dark, if we may judge from that of Euphiletus.[102] The house of a trierarch in the suburbs, however, was much more pleasant, having as it did a courtyard garden in which the mistress of the house and her children had meals and may have played games (*Pl. 34*); the much richer Xenophon, who lived in the country, had a spacious and comfortable villa.[103]

During the day a wife would see little of her husband since he was normally away from home by day—Xenophon at least regarded it as disgraceful for a man to remain in the house during the day, and in this he seems not to have been exceptional[104]—and for company she was thus largely dependent on the slaves of the household whose work she was responsible for supervising. Often however she also had elderly relatives living in the house, and the wife of one trierarch brought an old faithful retainer, a freed-woman, to live with her while her husband was on service, to act as housekeeper.[105]

A woman also had her children in their early years; not even Plato wanted (in the *Laws*) to deprive the children of their mothers, and both he and Aristotle wanted women to be educated as being 'half of the free population'.[106] Moreover, that the women's influence over the children did not end when they went to school is illustrated by one of Xenophon's vignettes, which provides a text for Socrates to give a striking tribute to mother-hood: Lamprocles, Socrates' son, complained of how harsh his mother was to him; Socrates replied, basing his argument in typically practical fashion ultimately upon the obligation to return good to those from whom you have received it; gratitude is due to a mother 'who receives the (her husband's) seed, and carries it within her, and is weighed down with the burden of it, and risks her life for it, and gives it a share of the food by which she herself is fed; and after bringing it forth after much labour she feeds it and looks after it, an act which is not in return for any good service, and no more is the baby aware of the source of the benefits it receives, or capable of indicating what it wants, but the mother herself has in view what is appropriate and pleases her child, and tries to satisfy its wants; and she feeds it for a long time, keeping up her labours through the day and night without know-ing what gratitude she will receive in return'. And when Lam-procles declined to be convinced, Socrates pointed out that all her scoldings were designed only for his good.[107]

THE BIRTH OF CHILDREN

The high value placed on children also made a fertile wife much valued; the description of his relations with his wife given by Euphiletus speaks volumes: 'when I married, for a time my behaviour was not to bear down on her, but not to leave it to her too much to do just what she liked; I looked after her as well as I could, and paid attention to her as was reasonable. But when a child was born, I at once began to trust her entirely and handed over to her all I possessed.'[108] Clearly he expected the jury to accept as normal this change of attitude to his wife on the birth of his son. No wonder that we hear of supposititious children being smuggled in by wives who were either barren or miscarried, or whose children were still-born or died soon after birth.[109]

Euphiletus claims to have been considerate to his wife's needs also as a young mother; he allowed her the downstairs quarters so that she would not risk her neck every time she had to go to the baby, and she often slept downstairs so as to suckle the baby if it cried, and not upstairs with Euphiletus. Moreover when she left him one night after they had had supper together and the baby was crying, she shut him in the upper room telling him as a joke he'd been making a pass at the maid—a piece of horseplay Euphiletus claims to have taken in good part. This picture may not be true; Euphiletus may well not have been as kind and considerate as he claims, but the picture was intended to appeal to an Athenian jury; it must have been intended to evoke in their minds the opinion that this was a reasonable, kindly man, and is therefore important—indeed one of the most important pieces of evidence we have from the world of the lower-middle-class.[110]

WORKING WOMEN

A typical virtue for this class is that of a husband who can afford to keep his wife so that she does not have to go out to work; this attitude was prevalent in Athens too, where poorer women did go out to work. The tale of Aristarchus in Xenophon's *Memorabilia* epitomizes this attitude;[111] when his sisters, nieces and cousins took refuge with him in a crisis, it never occurred to them that they might help or work, since they were brought up 'as befits free people'. Since there were fourteen of them, the economic drain on his resources was severe, and Aristarchus was driven to desperation. Socrates reminded him of how profitable men found it to have slaves working for them, and, arguing that free men and women are better than slaves, told him to get his relatives to work. They all knew how to work wool, so they worked morning and afternoon in return for their keep, and were content. This tale is as significant in illustrating the solidarity of the family, in that Aristarchus accepted all these women-folk into his house, as it is for showing the women's lack of independence in that they sought a male relative to shelter them in the civil war situation prevailing in 404–3. The story further contrasts other men's slaves who worked as a matter of course, and the gentlefolk who did not think to work until they were asked. Xenophon moreover criticizes the Athenians for making girls sit still all the time working wool, and bids his young wife not to sit still at home herself all day, but to take part in the housework and keep her youthful beauty by getting some exercise, mixing flour, kneading dough (*Pl. 43*), shaking the blankets, and standing at the loom demonstrating (*Pls. 38, 39*), and learning herself from other slaves who do something better than she; it improves the appetite he says, and makes her more attractive (than the slave girls) to her husband—a most revealing sentence.[112]

Poor women went out to work;[113] citizen-women were engaged mainly in retail trade, and seem to have had, if not a monopoly, at least a privileged position in the market-place; the soldier's widow plaited and sold garlands; the mother of Euxitheus (speaker of Demosthenes LVII) sold ribbons at one time, and worked as a wet-nurse (*Pl. 44*) at another; Euxitheus stresses her poverty.[114] All kinds of comestibles were sold by women, both retail and as café or inn-keepers;[115] these were generally less well thought of than workers of wool, most of whom were thought to be poor but honest. One woman vase-painter is known (*Pl. 42*) but, as with the market-women, we cannot be sure that she was a citizen.[116] It used to be argued that trade was not possible for citizen-women, since the limit of their contractual competence was the value of one *medimnos* of barley; it has however now been shown that this was not a paltry sum, but equivalent in value to more than a poor petty-trader's stock-in-trade, and enough to provide food for a family for several days.[117] In the country, obviously, peasant women helped in the fields as they have done from Hesiod's day to our own (*Pl. 45*).

Non-citizens, both foreigners and slaves, worked as entertainers such as flute-girls and courtesans, who provided the female company at men's dinners and riotous parties[118] (*Pls. 16, 18, 19*), also as kept women of various kinds, from regular concubines down to prostitutes of the lowest sort. The successful were able to obtain their freedom, retire and keep brothels or schools to train other courtesans, and we hear of one such who acted as a go-between in business deals of men.[119] An impoverished freedwoman, a widow, was taken in by her old master's family when her husband died because the son whom she had nursed felt himself obliged (or so he says) not to allow her to be in want;[120] other freed-women in the fourth century are attested by inscriptions; these consist mainly of wool workers, nurses and retailers, though there is surprisingly one cobbler among them.[121]

WOMEN'S INFLUENCE

Many wives doubtless were dominated by their husbands, many no doubt were neglected, and others were discontented with their lot; some reacted by taking to drink, some took lovers,[122] some became scolds, as Socrates is said to have been nagged by his wife, though, to judge by the ages of their children, she must have been very much younger than he;[123] old Euctemon's wife complained—perhaps not too unreasonably—of his behaviour in going off to stay with his children from Callippe and the old freed-woman ex-prostitute who looked after them.[124] Alcibiades' wife, we know, walked out on him because he brought courtesans to the house while she was at home; on the other hand we hear that Lysias was ashamed to bring an *hetaira* to his own house because of his wife (who was also his niece) and his old mother who lived with him.[125] That Apollodorus, a married man, had bought the freedom of one *hetaira*, and procured the marriage of another is regarded as a prejudicial allegation, as is not to have married at all, but to have kept an *hetaira* in luxury.[126]

Some wives, however, had a habit of getting their own way. Aristophanes portrays Strepsiades' high-born wife as having much influence on how her son should be named, and the decisive voice in his mode of education and upbringing;[127] in the family of Macartatus, his mother's anxiety to have kinsmen to succeed in her deceased relatives' family prevailed over the family's attachment to the father's side;[128] the Athenian law found it necessary to provide that the persuasion of a woman was a cause sufficient to invalidate a man's legal acts along with senility, drugs, disease or constraint.[129] Plato and Aristotle[130] both thought that marriage was intended to promote happiness, and this is in truth also the picture of comedy despite occasional misogynistic remarks,[131] and gross distortions for comic effect. On the other hand husbands and wives did quarrel, as they do in every society; Mantitheus can argue that 'when a husband and his wife quarrel, they are much more likely to become reconciled for the children's sake than because of their mutual ill-will to hate their children also'.[132] Swearing in front of women moreover was an allegation made by orators to arouse prejudice,[133] and what we are to make of the remark made to Alcibiades when he fought with tooth and nail that he bit 'like a woman'?[134]

Married women also maintained social contacts with their neighbours; Euphiletus' wife said she went to borrow a light for the lamp at night from her neighbours;[135] Aristophanes speaks of loans of garments, jewellery, money, drinking-cups—all without witnesses too;[136] in the country we hear of the mothers of a speaker and his opponent enjoying a common social life, visiting each other and enjoying social relationships before their sons quarrelled.[137] The fact that this was in the country may account for the greater degree of social freedom enjoyed by the women, or perhaps the fact that they were, obviously, women of mature age.

By some means or other both in town and country the women knew enough about the other women of their deme to elect a president for the Thesmophoria;[138] was this through social intercourse with one another, or was it through knowing from their husbands who the most distinguished men in the deme were? We cannot say, but we can provide some evidence that the women took an interest in public affairs. 'Some women do not allow their husbands to give false evidence', says one orator.[139] 'Well then, surely your wives will be furious with you when you go home and say you have acquitted Neaira', says Apollodorus (in effect).[140] Such evidence can only mean that women did talk to their husbands about public affairs, and take an interest in them, as Aristophanes confirms.[141]

LEGAL FACTORS

In law, too, the Athenian married woman had an economic security not enjoyed even by the modern married woman; her property was securely settled on her, and if she left her matrimonial home, as she could do if she wanted, her husband had to return her property or pay interest on it; if she did not leave her home, her husband had to support her.[142] Granted, this was no guarantee against her being made penniless if her husband lost his all and died,[143] but there was protection against the wayward husband of the modern divorce-courts who could support his family but refuses to do so. Ancient Athens also tried (whether consciously or not) to cope with the problem of loneliness; the mother left to live on her own is an unknown phenomenon because of the action for maintenance (δίκη σίτου), and the spinster aunt almost unknown, unless her father had met with financial ruin. Women, other than courtesans, did not live on their own.[144]

In legal actions the Athenians allowed their womenfolk to give evidence, and such evidence was in one case at least preferred to that of a man.[145] This evidence, in a case of disputed paternity, was sworn at the Delphinium, but we can cite other cases in which women's testimony was held to be valid evidence, especially of events which took place within the family;[146] stepdaughters are once cited[147] as knowing what went on in a family, and it is wholly unreasonable to assume that when relatives are mentioned[148] as knowing the affairs of a family the women are not included, especially since even slaves are stated several times[149] to know about whether or not there was a marriage and a bride existed. The family in fact was its own record office[150] and in this field the women's evidence was apparently reckoned by an Athenian court to be as good as the men's.

OLDER WOMEN

As women grew older they became more independent, especially if they were widowed; Lycophron's accusers alleged[151]—and whether their accusations were true or not they must have sounded plausible—that a widow had sworn to marry him, and that he had urged her to refuse to have sexual intercourse with the new husband to whom she was married. This situation implies, it is true, that her wishes about her second marriage were being disregarded, but it also implies that it was not inconceivable for a woman to refuse conjugal rights. This same woman is also said at the death of her husband to have been mistress of the house and able to punish her servants.[152]

Still older women had more freedom of movement within the city;[153] their age protected them against assault,[154] and the family had lost interest in them as contributors of children to the next generation, so that they moved freely, as midwives[155] and bearers of messages, and, when above the age of sixty, they were allowed to take part in the funerals of persons not closely related to them, perhaps as professional mourners.[156]

EMOTIONAL APPEALS

Orators could make emotional appeals through wives and mothers as well as through children, and defendants brought their wives as well as their children into court to excite pity. Demosthenes pleads with the jury: 'by your children, by your wives, by all the good things you possess', and Lysias joins with them the Erinyes, the goddesses of the Areopagus.[157] Apollodorus, attacking Polycles, seeks to gain sympathy for the defenceless state of his family: 'My mother was ill and at the point of death . . . my wife too whom I treasure very highly was in a very sickly state during my absence, and my children were very small . . . how do you think I felt as I longed to see my children and my wife and my mother whom I had very little hope of ever seeing alive again? What is sweeter than these to a man? or what would a man want to go on living for if he should lose them?'[158] Others speak of their destitute mothers if the jury imposed a confiscation of estate on them, of appeals to pity through orphans and *epikleroi* and old age and lack of means with which to support a mother, and Demosthenes claims that he is liable to be worse off than even those condemned by the law since they would have something left to them by the jurors' charity.[159]

WOMEN AS PART OF THE OIKOS AND POLIS

To sum up, we may say that the middle-class standards demanded by the democracy deprived the aristocratic families of the freedom of social intercourse they had enjoyed in Homeric society and other aristocratic societies like that of Sparta, and even in Athens before the day of Pericles. Within this middle class, however, women were probably as well protected by the law as in any century before our own, and, granted a reasonable husband or father, enjoyed a life not much narrower and not much less interesting than women in comparable classes of society elsewhere. Emancipated women nowadays, naturally, have much more personal freedom but less protection against unscrupulous males.

It should also not be forgotten that in some fields Athenian men too had much less freedom in regard to their families than modern men; divorce and extra-marital love affairs were easier for the Athenians, but their choice of wife was limited to citizens' daughters, the law obliged them to support their parents, they could only with the greatest difficulty disinherit their sons, they might be obliged to marry a cousin or a niece or to endow her with an estate so that she might marry someone else, and it may be doubted whether even modern taxation, especially of the middle class, is as severe as that in Athens in times of crisis.[160] Athenian women as much as Athenian men were regarded as part of the city, so that they too were expected to subordinate their duty to themselves to their duty to the state and to the *oikos* to which at their marriage they would come, or had already come. This duty comprised bearing the next generation of warriors and wives and mothers, and being their husband's partner in maintaining the economic power of the *oikos* and perpetuating its religious life. Plato's *Republic* was not so vast an intellectual jump from the society in which he lived as it is sometimes thought to have been.

CHAPTER VIII

THE FAMILY IN PLATO'S STATE, SPARTA AND CRETE

PLATO'S STATE

THE ANCIENT WORLD knew of at least two societies and probably more[1] in which the family did not hold the central place. Of these one, Sparta, was a community which actually existed, others were the creations of speculative philosophy, such as the Republic of Plato (427–347, trad.) and the state of Diogenes the Cynic (*c.* 400–325). Of this latter so little is known that certainty cannot be achieved, but it seems very unlikely that it was based on the family in view of the fact that Plutarch remarks that it was modelled on Sparta,[2] and we know that Diogenes regarded promiscuity by mutual consent[3] as the most satisfactory sexual arrangement, and the practice of the sexual act as something not particularly private (if the habits of Crates and Hipparchia reflect the school's teaching). Most of the surviving dicta of the early Cynics reflect their dissatisfaction with the restrictions imposed on man by his membership of a *polis*, and there is no sign that their 'natural' man with his total commitment to individualism owed duty to anyone other than himself and his fellow 'wise men'.[4]

Plato, a slightly older man than Diogenes, also rejected the family in the ideal state of his *Republic*, but for diametrically opposite reasons; the family, he thought, in making men claim things for themselves—wives and children and the means for their support—created struggles between the citizens, litigation, and the worries and anxieties of mind inseparably associated with bringing up children and providing for the physical needs of the *oikos*.[5] But even in the *Republic* it is not clear (and Aristotle, who should have known Plato, did not know what Plato intended[6]) whether it was only the Guardians or all the citizens who would own all things in common, including lands and houses, and enjoy temporary sacred marriages with the women as arranged by the authorities.[7] Moreover, when in his old age Plato came to write the laws for his state, he rejected his earlier notions about marriage and the life of the family, and made the patriarchal family the basic unit of his state. It was only a partial restoration, however, which left the family far short of its position in Athens.

IMMORTALITY THROUGH THE FAMILY

At the end of Book IV of the *Laws*, when Plato describes how the lawgiver would set about his task, he compares him to a doctor who combines prescriptions to deal with specific ailments with exhortations to the patient designed to explain his disease and encourage him to accept medication; he therefore decides to preface his state's laws with commendatory discourses for the citizens, and the first law to be laid down 'following the order of nature' regulates the starting-point of procreation, 'which lies in the union and partnership of marriages'.[8] We then are given an example of the two sorts of possible marriage law, one in the form of a peremptory demand, the other by means of a hortatory regulation based on the innate human longing for immortality, 'bearing in mind that there is a way in which the human race by nature partakes in immortality, a thing for which every man has the strongest desire implanted within him; for to be renowned and not to die a forgotten nobody contains also the desire for some such thing. The human race then is a thing that is coeval with eternity . . . achieving immortality by the method of always leaving children's children, and remaining one and the same always by means of reproduction, and partaking of immortality' (721B–C), and it is wicked (οὐχ ὅσιον) for a man voluntarily to deprive himself of this heritage.[9]

After this example of legislation Plato goes on to deal with the soul; he returns to the family with his practical constitution 'for men of the education his colonists will have', which is to be as close as possible to the ideal, in which the word 'private' is entirely rooted out of every part of it by every device (the constitution outlined in the *Republic*) (*Laws* 739A–740A).

THE MAINTENANCE OF THE KLEROI

The basic unit is the family unit supporting one soldier;[10] there are to be 5040 of these, each with his own plot of land; the *kleros* is neither wholly private, since it cannot be sold or given away, nor wholly public, for the state cannot take it away, and the *kleros*-holder has the power to name which of his sons, if he has more than one, shall succeed him, or which of other men's sons he shall adopt, if he has none. The number 5040 is to be permanent and maintained by men always leaving one son as their successor, never more, giving away on a friendly basis any surplus sons they may have to men without sons, and their daughters to be other men's wives; a public list of the holders of *kleroi* is to be maintained, so that it is known who the holder of each *kleros* is (741C); a colony will have to be resorted to if the excess of population becomes uncontrollable; a series of natural disasters might force acceptance of outsiders despite their 'bastard education' (740A–741A). Plato then turns to various financial regulations designed to maintain a rough equality—or avoid an excessive inequality—in wealth, which is (he says) what generates *stasis*, or rather disruption, in the state (744D). Later (in Book VI), when Plato turns to his regulations for marriage, his first concern is to banish ignorance, both the man's of the girl and of those from whom he takes her, and the girl's *kyrios* of the man and of those to whom he gives her; this was to be achieved by playful dances for both boys and girls, each clad in no more than modesty demands (771E–772A), in order that they should both see and be seen, and make their choice as a result.

MARRIAGE AND CHILDREN IN THE 'LAWS'

Men are to become eligible for marriage at twenty-five,[11] after this manner of scrutiny, and receive ten years' grace within which they are to marry before becoming punishable by monetary penalty and loss of public esteem (772D–E, 774A–C); in his exhortation about choice Plato urges men to avoid choosing a bride on grounds of wealth or poverty, to choose a girl of a temper complementary to his own, to choose with an eye to the state's benefit rather than his own delight, but adds that this is the sort of thing about which legislation is impossible (773A–E). Plato then turns to dowries; these he had already outlawed (742C), and here he repeats the regulation, adding rules about trousseaux; a significant remark is that dowries are not necessary because all the inhabitants of his city have their necessities already provided,[12] and their abolition will diminish the wanton insolence of wives and the humble and illiberal servitude arising from money inflicted on those who have married them (774C).

A girl's *kyrios* is enjoined to engage her by *engye*, the order of priority in doing so approximating to that used in Athens (774E–775A), and a limit is set on the cost of the wedding (especially the feast), and 'nobody is to spend more than he can afford'—surely a significant remark (775A–B). The bride and bridegroom are urged to remain sober since they should be fully in control of themselves when they are embarking upon a 'not insignificant change in their lives', and since Plato believed that a child would be affected by the over-indulgence of its parents at the time of begetting (775B–E). Young couples should, moreover, not live with the parents of either, but on their own in the other part of the *kleros* (each of which had two houses,[13] 745E) since too close proximity leads to quarrels (776A), though it is clear from his perfunctory treatment that Plato had little interest in the houses themselves (778B–779D), adding it as a postscript to his discussion of slaves, who are to be treated 'aright' (ὀρθῶς)—for 'it is in a man's treatment of those whom it is easy for him to injure that it is evident whether he is genuinely just, or a hypocrite' (777D).

Married life till the birth of children is then to be regulated by the rule that the men and women should continue to attend the public messes as before marriage; how long this was to go on Plato never states, being taken up with the difficulty of the idea of common messes for women (779D–781C).[14] From food and drink he then proceeds to regulating sexual conduct, the 'last of the threefold desires of men to emerge, and the greatest need and the most violent in the desire it inspires' (782Ef.). The procreation of children is said to be like everything else done in partnership— only when people pay attention to what they are doing do they

36 Toilet articles came in small phials like the one illustrated on this jar. The girl is either a slave sent out by her mistress to buy ointment or perfume, or else she is an *hetaira* preparing for an assignment. Her hair and dress suggest that she is not a free woman.

37-39 Making clothes occupied much of the time of all Greek women; suspended spindle spinning as practised on the wine-jug of *c.* 490 (left) may still be seen in country districts today. The weavers on the warp-weighted loom on the tiny oilflask (6¾ in. high) above, had to walk to and fro as they passed their bobbins through the threads of the warp. Shaking blankets, and folding them (below, from the same flask) was then, as now, a vigorous task. On the edges of the scenes, other women spin and prepare yarn.

40, 41   The centre of the East frieze of the Parthenon (above) shows the priest and his attendant folding the new robe for Athene; a priestess receives the first of two stools from a maiden. Maidens also walked at the head of the processions making their way towards the ceremony; those shown in the section of the frieze below carry the instruments of sacrifice, an incense-burner, jugs and shallow bowls.

42–44 A detail from a mixing bowl shows a scene in a potter's shop; a girl paints a vase in the company of four men (not shown here); her hair suggests that she is a free woman earning her living. Two terracotta figurines show other occupations, a baker, kneading dough vigorously (4¾ in. high, from Rhodes), a nurse (1 ft. 2 in. high, from Boeotia). All three works are of the fifth century, the figurines about 450, the bowl earlier.

45, 46 The rich and the poor. Above, a peasant ploughs with a bull, while a woman sows. Both appear to be naked, but this may be due to the artist's crudity. Below, sales of property confiscated from aristocrats condemned for impiety in 415/4 were recorded. On the left, line 3 we read '. . . in the land in . . .'; lines 11–2 'slaves of . . . of Alcibiades'; the first three named are all called 'Thracian', two female, one male. On the right, furniture is listed, 'kli[ne]', = bed occurs five times.

47, 48   The bronze figurine (4½ in. high) has one breast bare and holds her short skirt up above her knees as she runs. Though found in Albania, she is usually called a Spartan. The cup below, illustrating a military funeral, was certainly made in Laconia. The soldiers have the long hair always worn by Spartans, and the bearded corpses and the more youthful bearers confirm that youths did not form the front line. The bearers wear greaves and carry their spears but not their shields or helmets. Their helot attendants will have carried these, and their cloaks.

49 The Locrians of South Italy had a shrine of Persephone, where offerings
of the sort shown above were made. The leading worshipper is leaning down
and offering cakes, either at an altar or into a pit. The woman behind carries a
cock for sacrifice, and a basket of other offerings. The plaque is 10 in. high,
and dates from *c.* 470–460.

produce what is excellent and good—so the bridegroom is urged to turn his attention to his bride and to begetting children, and the bride likewise, especially for as long as they have no children; they are to be supervised by women supervisors who are to report men and women of the age of reproduction who have their minds on other things;[15] this age of reproduction and supervision is to be ten years—no more, when children are abundant—and if they have no children after ten years, couples are to be divorced (783B–784B).

When children are born, they are to be recorded in the ancestral shrines and on the lists of the phratry from birth (785A). Parents who are detected breaking the rules suffer punishments amounting to partial disfranchisement. After the age of procreation men and women will be punished for adultery with a person who is still of the age of procreation, but men and women who restrain themselves are commended, and Plato declines to lay down the law so long as most people behave in a reasonable way, though he envisages laws being enacted if disorderly conduct occurs (784E–785A).

EDUCATION AND SEXUAL BEHAVIOUR

In Plato's educational system, the only thing which prevents him from legislating for children from the earliest years, and legislating to curb what is customarily practised in the privacy of the home, is that it would make the law ridiculous (788A–B), though he wants children to start to attend the state's religious celebrations at the age of three (794A); the sexes are to be separated at the age of six (794C). Education is to be compulsory because children 'belong to the city even more than to their parents' (804D), and to be the same for boys and girls (805C–D etc.), because women are half of the population.

After a full account of education he returns to sexual behaviour, observing (sensibly enough) that if you put young men and women together with nothing to do but dance and feast they will be inclined to sexual desires (835D–E). 'Other desires', says Plato, 'can be brought under control; cutting off extremes of wealth would be of considerable use in promoting self-control (because

subduing the acquisitive instinct); so is education and the supervision of the young effective in keeping the other human desires
(*i.e.* for food and drink) under control, but not the desires engendered by sexual instincts' (835E–836B abridged). He advised
educating the young in the belief that they were in training to
obtain self-control by victory over pleasure, comparing themselves to athletes who voluntarily abstain from sexual pleasures to
obtain the physical fitness which will enable them to win victory
in the games (839E–840C). For those unable to attain his ideal—of
abstention from all sexual acts not intended to procreate children
(which he regarded as the 'law of nature', 840D–E)—he commended the exact opposite of the ideas of Diogenes; the strictest
privacy, and punishment by disfranchisement not merely for
sodomy and incest (as being unnatural), and for adultery and
fornication with citizen women, but also for sexual acts with
slave concubines, whether detected by man or woman (841C–E).

These educational laws, and those affecting sexual conduct,
make it very clear that the reinstatement of the family was not
primarily in the interest of the family. Plato's families were mere
units within the state; the *kyrios* of each family was in a sense only
an agent of the state with the responsibility of using his family to
secure the ends of the state; even his *kleros* of land was 'the common property of the whole state' (740A). A citizen's marriage,
his procreation of children, and his other sexual acts were planned
purely in the interests of the state, and its need for the next generation of citizens. The laws of succession also restricted very severely
his ability to choose his heir, and no succession through the female
line was possible, since there were no *epikleroi* without adopted
sons to marry them.

ECONOMIC FOUNDATIONS OF THE 'LAWS'

In the economic field, according to Plato, the citizen's inalienable
kleros will guarantee him a supply of food, and the common
messes for men and women support that guarantee; the strict
controls on his ability to acquire additional (movable) property
above a certain amount would seem to eliminate much of the
grasping acquisitiveness of contemporary Athens. However, even

in the management of his *kleros* the citizen was strictly controlled; forbidding the removal of boundary marks and encroachment, preventing men acquiring other men's swarms of bees, prohibiting encroachment by tree-planting and damage by failing to control fires, banning the interception of water supplies or denying the use of a well to a man whose land had not an adequate water supply, or access to market, are all natural and not surprising (842E–844D), but prohibitions on picking his own grapes when a man pleases (844D) seem unnecessarily interfering, especially when stealing apples, pears and pomegranates involved no disgrace if undetected, and only a retribution in blows (not wounds) if detected, and when a man over thirty may help himself to what he eats on the spot (845B–D).

No citizen is to be a craftsman, since serving and maintaining the state demands his whole attention, and no craftsman is to practise more than one trade, nor to try to supervise any other than his own (846D–847B). Similarly, a man's marketing and disposal of his property is strictly controlled (847E ff.), and citizens are prohibited from retail trade under any sort of device; he who engages in retail trade is accused of 'disgracing his *genos*' and, if convicted, of 'sullying his ancestral hearth'; he is imprisoned to stop him from continuing to do so (919E).

SUCCESSION RULES IN THE 'LAWS'

Here, in Book XI, Plato came near to considering the family as having more claims than as a mere unit in the state. The context is his dealing with wills and the succession to men who die without leaving an adult son (922A ff.). Maintaining that those who make wills at the point of death are not, as a rule, fully in control of their faculties, Plato delivers an exhortation to remember that 'you yourselves, my friends, and this your property are not your own, but belong to your whole *genos*, past and future, and even more is your whole *genos* and its property the possession of the state' (923A), and therefore last-minute recognition of recent favours should not outweigh 'what is best'. A will may decree which one of a man's sons is to succeed to his *kleros* and its equipment; a man may not name more than one, to prevent division of the *kleros*, but he may give the rest of his property to his other sons; he may also give sons to other men for adoption. He may not give anything to a son who already has a *kleros* (having been adopted), or to a daughter engaged to be married, or who became so after the will was made. If he has no sons he may adopt one and marry his daughter to him if he has one, or one of his daughters if he has more than one. If he has lost his heir he is to adopt an heir to take his place; if he is wholly childless he is to adopt an heir and has freedom to give away up to one-tenth of his property over and above his *kleros* and its equipment. He may name a guardian to an infant heir. If he fails to do this, the next of kin on father's and mother's sides are statutory guardians, two on each side, with one friend of the deceased (924B).

If a man dies wholly intestate, leaving only daughters, the state will secure an heir (and husband for one of the daughters) 'looking to two of the three things a father would consider—nearness in kinship, preservation of the *kleros* and suitability in character and behaviour'—and attending to the first two of these. An order of succession is laid down, starting with half-brothers, and providing by physical inspection (males naked and females stripped to the waist) that the ages are suitable, and ensuring that only those who have not got a *kleros* are considered. If there are no kinsmen eligible, the girl and her guardians are to choose someone outside the kinship-group who is willing to marry her and be heir. Repatriation of those who have gone out to colonies through not having a *kleros* is allowed as a last resort, kinsmen receiving preference (924C–925C). Similarly, if a man dies intestate and wholly without issue, a man and a woman are brought into the *oikos* and the *kleros* and are married, the members of the kinship-group taking precedence (925C–D). Appeals are allowed by those who would be compelled by the law to marry someone utterly repugnant to them through defect of mind or body (925D ff.).

Yet despite all this legislation the family is only partly reinstated, since, as has been noted, 'the whole *genos* and its property is the possession of the state' (923A). Besides, the integrity of the *kleros* takes top priority; the family is the means to achieve this end—the *kleros* is not the means to preserve the family.

It is in the religious sphere that the ineradicable preconceptions of Plato's Athenian upbringing may be seen most clearly to clash with his philosophical ideas, and the family steals in as it were through the back door, undermining his aim to get as near as possible to 'rooting out entirely the word "private"'. In dealing with homicide, both intentional and accidental, the family was to take responsibilities similar to those undertaken by Athenian families (865A–874D), and Plato accepted as natural the peculiar repugnance felt for killings within the family, and the view that a man was justified in killing in defence of his family against thieves and footpads, and of its members' honour against rape or sexual assault on women and children, or assault on parents, wife or children (874B–D). In the context of assaults Zeus Patroös actually appears once[16] (881D).

Plato of course provides a place for the gods of the family, which include the dead ancestors, but this is hardly surprising when we take into consideration the multitude of gods with whom Plato's state is concerned. There is no indication that the tribe named after each of the twelve Olympian gods will enjoy any special place in the worship of its eponymous god,[17] and the daily sacrifices to be made by the officer responsible are on behalf of the city, not for any of its smaller units.[18] The possibility of hereditary priesthoods is dismissed very cursorily: 'priests and priestesses of shrines should not be disturbed if any (of the colonists) have hereditary priesthoods, but—as is likely to be the case with those who are being established in a community for the first time—if there are either none or very few people who have them already, we must establish (*sc.* in our city) those that already exist' (759A–B). In the priesthoods of Plato's state, however, there is no kind of hereditary succession; all appointments are to be by lot for short periods of not more than a year and subject to a kind of *dokimasia*, which concerns itself with the holder's family only to the extent of his own and his parents' purity. The importance of Hestia,[19] the goddess of the dwelling-place, reveals the same pre-occupation with the *kleros* rather than with the linear descent, real or imaginary, of the owner, as does the non-appearance of the gods of the phratry and *genos*, the absence of the worship of Zeus Ktesios, and of the Attic Apatouria, Genesia[20] and Anthesteria, and the strict limitations on funerals, burial-grounds and memorials (958D–960B).

The gods of the family appear among the last (and the least)[21] of the gods whom the self-controlled ($\sigma\acute{\omega}\phi\rho\omega\nu$) colonist is exhorted to honour, ranking with those ancestors who are still alive (717B–718A), and, when Plato comes to divide out the land, the holder of the *kleros* is responsible for the family cult only in the same way that he is responsible for cultivating ($\theta\epsilon\rho\alpha\pi\epsilon\acute{\nu}\epsilon\iota\nu$) his land, 'which is a goddess' ($\delta\acute{\epsilon}\sigma\pi o\iota\nu\alpha$), and the native ($\grave{\epsilon}\gamma\chi\acute{\omega}\rho\iota o\iota$) gods and spirits (*daimones*), and for handing on a successor to the cult of all of them (740A–C).[22] The reason the holder of the *kleros* was always to be a son, or an adopted son of his predecessor in the *kleros*, is (presumably) because Plato was anxious not to have any daimones or spirits angry because of a lack of cult; and the reason the citizen's worship of them was believed to increase his own chances of fertility is because it was assumed that they too would want to aid the citizen to procreate those who would worship them.[23] Plato was in fact really only concerned with these family cults because they were the manifestation for each individual of the means by which by its nature the human race has been given the capacity to participate in immortality (721B).

THE SPARTAN MYTH

There are many points at which Plato's ideas seem to reflect Spartan society. It is usual to say that Plato was influenced by Sparta; this is attested by Plutarch[24] and may well be true, but it may be truer that Plato was influenced by an idealized rather than an actual Sparta, and that the account we have of Sparta, especially of 'Lycurgan' Sparta, is of an idealized society rather than one which ever actually existed.

Admiration of Sparta went back at least to the fifth century among the upper classes;[25] the victory at Plataea as much as that at Salamis had saved Greece from the Persians, and Spartan fashions among the upper classes are satirized by Aristophanes.[26] Critias, who became one of the Thirty Tyrants, was a member of

Socrates' circle and wrote a eulogy of Sparta;[27] so did numerous others including Xenophon, though he was aware of failings as well.[28] Yet these failures—even when noticed—were seen as personal,[29] and not to detract fundamentally from the Spartans' supreme achievement, *eunomia*, the system of laws and training associated with Lycurgus, which enabled them to overcome for centuries the besetting sins of Greek *poleis*, military weakness and internal strife,[30] *stasis*, the perennial class-struggle between oligarch and democrat, that is, stated in more simple terms, between rich and poor.[31]

In the late fifth century in Athens, dissatisfaction with their democracy also played a part in this admiration; for example Thucydides, in two of the judgements which have most vexed modern critics, states that the Athenians' most ghastly mistake, the Sicilian expedition's failure, was due to political rivalry at home, and that their ultimate failure in the Peloponnesian War was attributable to self-interest, and a breakdown in internal harmony;[32] these Spartan *eunomia* would have avoided. Pericles was accused by his critics of having made the Athenians talkative and idle;[33] the Spartans were notoriously laconic. In Athens this dissatisfaction had led to demands for the restoration of the 'ancestors' constitution'; what this was is of little relevance, but what is important is the fact that it resulted in a copious flow of propagandist pamphleteering as democrat and oligarch sought alike to claim the stamp of the ancestors' approval for the constitution they wanted to establish;[34] looking abroad it led Athenians to admire Sparta, and literary activity to justify this admiration.[35]

In the early fourth century Sparta appeared outstandingly successful; the Spartans had overthrown the Athenian empire which had appeared to be (and Thucydides was convinced that it was) incomparably the stronger power in the Peloponnesian War,[36] and no Spartan knew of any political upheaval in the state ever having taken place since the establishment of the Lycurgan system, apart from attempts by the helots and Messenians to revolt[37] (Cinadon seems to have been conveniently forgotten[38]); for all this time, as Demaratus had told the Persian King, their master had been the laws.[39]

In 371, however, occurred the battle of Leuctra, at which the Theban general Epameinondas inflicted on the Spartans a crushing and decisive military defeat, and followed this up by dismembering the Spartan system; he broke up the Spartan League, which had overawed the smaller inland states of the Peloponnese, by organizing an Arcadian League, and he confiscated the lands of Messenia and liberated the inhabitants who had for three centuries been kept in the semi-free status of helots, and had by their labour enabled the Spartans to devote their entire attention to the art of war. The Greek world was stunned, and, inevitably, men began to ask how and why the Spartan system had failed. The answer they found is of particular interest from the point of view of the family; they argued that the strength of Lycurgan Sparta had lain in the exclusion of the family from its central position in society, and its relegation to the status of a state-controlled apparatus for breeding and bringing to adulthood the next generation of soldiers and their mates. How far this was encouraged by the Spartans themselves, and more especially by the poorer Spartans, we do not know, but in this age criticisms of Sparta certainly began to mount, Plato in the *Laws*, and Aristotle in the *Politics* being two of the severest critics.[40] Thus, condemnation of the 'present degeneracy' conspired with admiration of the previously successful system to adorn the Lycurgan system with a variety of features which disinterested historical enquiry might have failed to discover, and we must at least suspect that Plutarch's sources for the *Lycurgus* drew more on quasi-philosophical theorizing than on attempts at genuine research.

'LYCURGAN' REGULATONS AND FAMILY STRUCTURE

According to Plutarch, though his accuracy is highly doubtful, Lycurgus had divided up the whole of Laconia into nine thousand equal *kleroi*[41] for Spartiate citizens known as *homoioi*, or equals, and thirty thousand for the so-called *perioikoi*, the free, non-Spartiate inhabitants of Laconia, who enjoyed personal freedom and autonomous local self-government but lacked an independent foreign policy. When a child was born, it was presented by the father to the elders of the tribe who had the right to decide whether it should be allowed to live or not, and, if it was, allotted it to one of the *kleroi*;[42] presumably (though Plutarch does not say so) this was as heir-apparent,[43] and this scrutiny applied only to male children, since it appears from Plutarch's account of Lycurgus' regency[44] that girl babies were merely handed over to the women of the house to attend to. Boys were reared at home till their seventh year, from which time until they were thirty years old they underwent continuous surveillance and training for war, eating in the common messes (or *syssitia*), and sleeping in barracks in age-classes, while their education and up-bringing[45] at every stage was supervised by the elder citizens who were married, by young 'lovers', by their own leaders and by those who belonged to their own *syssition*, who had to approve them at the time of their admission. This approval was important, since membership of a *syssition* was obligatory for full citizen rights.[46] The *syssition* was also important as an instrument in equalizing the wealth of the citizens; it was compulsory to attend, and to provide a contribution to the common table, which naturally affected a citizen's power to dispose of the produce of his *kleros*.[47] Obligation to attend the *syssition* unless he had not returned from hunting also meant that it was impossible for a Spartan to live on his estate; this fact may account for the establishment of the *krypteia*, the secret police, a body formed out of the young men undergoing military training, whose duty it was from time to time to conduct a campaign of terrorism against the helots, slaying without trial any who appeared to be potential ringleaders of a revolt.[48] This, and hunting, were the means whereby the Spartans in the city found out the state of opinion, and the extent of loyalty, in the countryside they ruled.

MARRIAGE AT SPARTA

Marriage for Spartans was compulsory, and to a Spartan girl;[49] persistent bachelors were punished by partial loss of rights (*atimia*).[50] How Spartan marriages were arranged is quite uncertain; the theory was of marriage by capture, and there survives a picturesque story of how boys and girls were all shut up together in a dark room and each married what he caught,[53] but as early as Herodotus' day we hear of engagements (though in one case in point someone else managed to steal the bride);[54] Plutarch merely says that girls were carried off (presumably to the bridegroom's parents' house, though Plutarch does not say so); the bride was disguised as a boy by having her hair cut by her bridesmaid, and putting on a man's clothes; she was then left alone, and was visited by her husband after he had dined at his mess; he had intercourse with her and returned to his mess-mates for the night; the married couple were able only to snatch such brief interludes of intimacy, by arrangement on each occasion, until the bridegroom was thirty years old.[55]

This account, if true, reveals an instance of the trial marriage, which is known in other societies,[56] whose object is to secure that if a girl fails to become pregnant both families can pretend there never was a marriage, and neither party can be thought to suffer any disesteem. 'Some men', says Plutarch, 'are fathers before they ever see their wife by light of day'—the story is probably apocryphal, but it indicates clearly that the companionship of marriage was not the reason why the Spartans gave their girls the same education as they gave the boys, and married them when they were fully grown[57] to young men of similar age. This latter we must assume from the story that the Spartans encouraged young men's sexual instincts by permitting them to watch the maidens dancing and walking in processions in scanty clothing (Pl. 47), and vice versa, performances confirmed bachelors were not allowed to watch.[58] The state's concern in promoting marriage was to obtain children to replenish the citizen body; in Sparta perhaps more than anywhere else the children were 'not the individual possession of fathers, but the common possession of the state'.[59]

This is particularly clear in the case of the kings (of whom Sparta always had two). Anaxandridas, king of Sparta in the late sixth century, had no children; the ephors (magistrates) urged him to divorce his wife, arguing: 'If you have no forethought for yourself, you know we must still not overlook the fact of the race of Eurystheus becoming extinct'. Anaxandridas refused to do so because he loved his wife. The ephors and council then threatened to take action against him unless he married another wife who would prove fertile: 'We do not ask you to divorce your wife,' they said, 'but do you for your part continue to treat the wife you have as you have always treated her and take another wife besides to bear you children'. This he accepted, says Herodotus, and 'had two wives and lived in two houses, in a thoroughly un-Spartan fashion';[60] both wives subsequently conceived, and bore sons. A contemporary king, Ariston, had no children by his first two wives; it seems clear that he had divorced his first wife, and it is to be presumed that he divorced the second also when he fraudulently obtained a third from her husband;[61] though Herodotus does not say so, this may be an instance of wife-sharing, and, besides her exceeding beauty, the lady may also have had the merit of having borne her first husband a son.

Evidence for the custom of wife-sharing, which of course reflects a community rather than a private attitude to marriage, is so unequivocal that it is impossible to disbelieve it altogether. Plutarch[62] mentions both old men with young wives selecting a young man to provide them with an heir, and a man whose wife was barren, or perhaps deceased, obtaining permission from a father of sons to procure himself a son from the fecund wife; the latter seems more probable than the former, unless the young wife were a second wife, possibly an *epikleros*,[63] since, as we have noted, the Spartans (unlike the Athenians) married girls of much the same age as themselves. In a later age Polybius even states that it was a Spartan custom during wartime to send home those in the peak of condition from campaigns in order to beget children; he implies that this does not mean only from their own wives.[64]

Spartan women were said to be libidinous;[65] certainly the custom of the bride lying alone in the dark waiting for her husband gave unusual opportunities to a cuckoo to enter the nest, and Herodotus' story[66] about the birth of Demaratus shows that adultery was not as difficult as it was when young women were sheltered in a women's quarter, though we should note that the alleged god deceived Ariston's wife into believing that he was her husband. How girls lived for the first few months after their marriage we do not know; obviously their shorn hair would betray their marriage if they appeared in public, and their husband's identity if they appeared in his household; they may have lived alone for a month or so till they knew that they were pregnant, or have lived in their parents' home and gone out only in the evenings to their rendezvous with their husband[67] (secrecy would be facilitated by the fact that the months for marriage in Greece were the winter months), and have appeared in public only when pregnant. When, however, a baby was born they must surely have taken up residence in their husband's *oikos*, though it appears from Plutarch that Spartan women employed nurses (presumably helots or slaves) to look after young babies.[68]

PROPERTY AND THE SPARTAN FAMILIES

Plutarch's account of the property-arrangements is full of problems and omissions; despite his theory of exactly equal *kleroi* of land and the theory of succession given in the *Lycurgus*, in this same work he notes that Lycurgus was unable to effect an equal distribution of movable property[69] (we may think he possibly did not try), and says that for this reason he banished all gold and silver from the state, forbidding the Spartiates to own any, and thus discouraged foreigners wishing to trade from coming to the state, such as 'sophists, soothsayers, keepers of harlots, goldsmiths and silversmiths'. The prejudice evident in the list is obvious, and so is its irrelevance to the seventh century or earlier,[70] but that the Spartans were unfriendly to strangers who wanted to live in Sparta is well attested.[71] Spartan austerity was also reflected in their houses, which were designed to be uncomfortable, and in the strict control established by the state on funerals, which were of extreme simplicity and unusual brevity (*Pl. 48*). The family was excluded from these to an unusual degree in that all burials were in the city, not on private estates.[72]

KLEROI AND CITIZEN-NUMBERS

On two occasions we hear hints of a possible excess number of citizens; after the end of the Messenian War (trad. 708) Taras (Tarentum), Sparta's only acknowledged colony, was founded by sending out a force reputed to be bastards, but the suggestion that they were in fact supernumerary citizens for whom there was not a *kleros* available in Messenia is attractive.[73] In the late sixth century, when Cleomenes was made king, and not Dorieus, the latter 'asked for people and led Spartans off for a colony';[74] Dorieus would of course be dependent on his half-brother for support, and may well not have had a *kleros*. However, it appears that he had a son, whose claim to the kingship must have been extinguished since this son was superseded by his two cousins, sons of Leonidas and Cleombrotus, after the death of the latter.[75] Plutarch also states that Lycurgus did not legislate for contracts; he presumes to know Lycurgus' thoughts on this subject—which were that those who were rightly educated would know what to do in changing circumstances.[76] This might mean that there was an enactment which said no more than that they were not to have written laws, or it might mean that the Lycurgan legislation, which was designed entirely with a view to maintaining the army, merely ignored such things, as it appears to have ignored the question of women's rights to own property and to succeed to *kleroi*, a failure which Aristotle believed to have been the basic cause of subverting the Spartan system.[77]

It is clear from Herodotus that the system of allocating *kleroi* by tribe at birth, if it ever existed, did not last; the kings, he tells us, presided over the adoption of sons—presumably by men who lacked, or had lost, their own.[78] The right to adopt a son is obviously natural in a military society—no man can be sure of returning on his feet from a campaign—and Rome can be quoted as a parallel,[79] but it is also characteristic of a family-based society, a society which thinks in terms of inheritance through the family, and associates a man's place in society with his family and his descent.[80] The allocation of this task to the kings is also significant, because the king's prime function was as commander-in-chief, and he was therefore concerned to maintain the number of *kleroi* supporting soldiers at its maximum.[81] In the Persian Wars, when a Spartan force was picked to go to defend Thermopylae, although it was led by Leonidas, who was king, he had a twin brother and both had sons, so that the king's line would not become extinct if Leonidas died, and his force was composed of three hundred hoplites, who were all men who had procreated sons.[82] These regulations mark the dangerous character of the expedition as the Spartans saw it; they took precautions to see that even if the whole force perished, they would not lose their royal line, nor leave any *kleros* without an owner.

CLASSES IN SPARTA

The hereditary nature of the kingship too, and the great anxiety that the royal houses should not die out in this period also reflects a family-oriented society.[83] The fact that the kings frequently married within their own kinship-group[84] strongly suggests that there always was a Spartan aristocracy, whose existence is clearly attested in Thucydides' day,[85] and in later times is even more convincingly shown by the system whereby *Mothakes* or *Kasens* were adlected into Spartan society as the followers of a noble, and the system of *Boagoi* and *Synepheboi*, within the *syssitia*. These practices, though known only in later ages, may in fact derive from very primitive times. An aristocracy of wealth is known from at least the sixth century, and through the fifth,[86] and other aristocratic features are found in all ages.

Hereditary trades are also known in Sparta; heralds and flautists were fully appropriate to the military caste, as the Spartans marched into battle to the sound of the flute, but cooks were customarily held in less esteem in the ancient world, even if they served on campaign;[87] other craftsmen, potters for example, may have belonged to the class of *perioikoi*,[88] so may the makers of Spartan furniture, whose simplicity and excellence is praised by Plutarch,[89] and a military state must also have required smiths to make weapons and armour, and leather-workers to make shoes, horse-harness and other necessary equipment. All these must have been *perioikoi* if Agesilaus' claim is a true one, that war was the only trade the Spartans knew.[90]

EPIKLEROI AND SUCCESSION IN SPARTA

Women were able to claim estates in Sparta at least as early as Herodotus' day, since the kings were charged with regulating the marriage of virgin *epikleroi* whose fathers had not engaged them;[91]

these girls must have been orphans. Whether a father who promised his only child in marriage had any choice in the husband he selected we do not know; in Aristotle's time he did.[92] We also note that it was only unmarried girls, and must conclude that marriage extinguished a girl's claim. However, the existence of *epikleroi* undermined the Lycurgan *kleros*-system as described by Plutarch, since there could be no young Spartan without a *kleros* able to marry an *epikleros* in the normal way without causing an amalgamation of *kleroi* not rectified till she had borne two sons, one to be allotted to the *kleros* of each parent; the only cure would be to marry her to an older man who had already begotten a son to his own *kleros* in the hope that he might now procreate one for hers, or at least obtain one with the aid of a young man he admired. This may have been what Lycurgus intended, and it might account for the 'old man with a young wife' in the stories of wife-sharing, though *epikleroi* are not mentioned by Plutarch in this context.[93]

SPARTAN WOMEN

The exclusively military life of the Spartan men, and the liberation of Spartan women from the main tasks of women elsewhere in Greece (making clothes and nursing children),[94] suggests that Spartan women may in fact always have managed their husbands' affairs, as Aristotle says,[95] and it is certain that by his day women were wealthy;[96] he tells us that two-fifths of all the land was in their hands, and that men were in the habit of giving their daughters dowries.[97] Plutarch tells us that in the next century King Agis was frustrated by the women in his attempt to 'restore the Lycurgan system' and that his own womenfolk were the wealthiest in the state; he also speaks of mortgage-papers.[98] Dowries clearly envisage marriage following engagement, not marriage by capture, and they indicate that a certain amount of choice could be exercised by both parties to the match; marriage by choice is also implied in the early fourth century in Xenophon's story of the indignities inflicted on those convicted of cowardice[99] —that they could not secure marriages for their daughters, nor obtain a wife for themselves.

SPARTA'S FAILURE AND THE FAMILY

The Lycurgan system, Spartan tradition asserted, had made Sparta great and powerful by channelling their citizens' interests into public life, and making the force of public opinion the principal sanction governing the citizen's behaviour; Plutarch's *Lycurgus* repeatedly stresses[100] that in Sparta all a citizen's aspirations were directed to gaining a good reputation among his fellows, and he states that Lycurgus thought that such questions as the laws of contract were best decided when they arose, and refused to legislate about them.[101] Plutarch did not invent this view; it was clearly familiar to Aeschines' audience in 345,[102] and to Aristotle who says, approvingly, that Lycurgus made it disgraceful to buy or sell land (or perhaps property) a man had inherited[103]—that is, both the vendor and the purchaser suffered a measure of damage to their reputation. As long as public opinion inhibited purchasers from attempting to buy land, obviously would-be vendors could not easily sell, nor was there any need to set a limit on what a man might acquire; and there was no such limit.

By the end of the fifth century, however, time had made some of the Spartan *homoioi*, or equals, less equal than others. The disastrous earthquake in 464, and the heavy casualties suffered in the major wars of the sixth and fifth centuries, must have diminished the number of *homoioi*; there is clear evidence for a shortage of manpower from the Spartans' deep concern about the loss of an insignificant number of *homoioi* on Sphacteria in 425, and from their failure to disgrace permanently the survivors, perhaps because to do so would cause an undesirable further diminution in the manpower available to the state.[104]

Casualties could have been replaced by requiring survivors to procreate children for the families without a successor, but this the Spartans had failed to do. The Lycurgan regulations, according to Aristotle, had allowed those who wished to do so to give away or to bequeath their lands,[105] and the ending of the king's power to approve of adoptions, and to arrange for the marriage of *epikleroi* whom their father had not betrothed, removed any check on the power of fathers of daughters to marry them to whom they pleased, and adopt their son-in-law, a process which would convey the succession to their *kleros* with their daughter. Some families had thus acquired very large estates by marriage, and when such families had only female children, the girls were the sole successors to them.

One feature which seems common to all societies is that rich men want to marry their daughters (especially only daughters) to the sons of rich men, and the Spartans seem to have been no exception. A shortage of eligible men leads to a competition for husbands; girls who were *epikleroi* were more desirable brides than those without estates to bring with them, and therefore found it easier to obtain husbands. Fathers of sons therefore had to provide dowries for their daughters, and, as Aristotle says, by his day men did endow their daughters with large dowries.[106] Such a social structure encourages the limitation of families, and, as family limitation becomes more and more practised, the process of reducing the size of the citizen-body is cumulative, and accelerating. Rich women, moreover, commonly do not bear large families, especially when, as in Sparta, they are independent and not subordinated to their husbands, and, whatever the situation in the fourth century, we hear that before Cicero's day Spartan women were unwilling to bear children.[107]

The provision of dowries involved the acquisition of gold and silver. Spartans abroad had always been susceptible to bribes, according to Herodotus;[108] Plato regarded the Spartan system of education as defective, in that it taught only the virtue of courage, and failed to inculcate the (more important) virtue of self-control,[109] and Aristotle criticizes the system for engendering only military skill and toughness.[110] The Spartans of the fourth century were characterized by Isocrates, for example, as being given to 'injustice, indolence, lawlessness and love of money';[111] the Spartan state attempted to nationalize all gold and silver early in the fourth century, but public opinion did not support the measure and it failed.[112]

It was this influx of gold and silver in private hands to which Plutarch attributed the failure of the Spartan system, along with a law of Epitadeus, which is said to have allowed a man to dispose by will of his *oikos* and *kleros* as he wished.[113]

This latter law may well have been no more than an affirmation of the legality of an already existing situation, but Plutarch makes a point not made elsewhere (*e.g.* by Aristotle),[114] that Epitadeus was a man who had a son—and the tale implies that it was an adult son—and that his object was to disinherit his son. Plutarch adds that his example was followed by others who wanted to prevent their kinsmen from inheriting their estates. If Plutarch's story and its implications are reliable (which is doubtful), the law was an important innovation, and must belong to the early fourth century. However, it is evident that a law (of whatever date) empowering a man to give away his land opened the way for sales of land under an agreement whereby the purchaser receives the land under the guise of a gift, or on the vendor's death, as a bequest; such an arrangement would, however, have little point until the ownership of real money enabled the purchaser to offer something which the vendor found attractive enough to take in return for his land.

Aristotle blamed the failure of the Spartan system on the lawgiver's failure to control the women; they comprise half of the free population, he says, and in the time of the Spartan empire (404–371) they controlled many things, including their husbands, and it was their independence in managing their money which contributed to the Spartans' acquisitiveness in that age. It was the fact that the women owned two-fifths of the whole of Laconia which brought it about that though the country was capable of supporting 1500 cavalry and 30,000 hoplites, the Spartiate *homoioi* numbered less than 1000.[115] In the next century the number is said to have fallen to 700, many of whom had encumbered their lands with debts.[116]

It was the loss of their manpower which prevented the Spartans from playing an important role in the Greek world after the battle of Leuctra in 371, and which perhaps in fact contributed materially to that defeat. It is generally assumed that the Spartans' shrinking manpower involved a shrinking in the total population of Laconia, but this is by no means certain. Even as early in the fourth century as the revolt of Cinadon the full Spartiate *homoioi* were only a minority even in the Spartan market place, since

Xenophon says there was but one Spartan to one hundred of the other inferior classes.[117]

The next year King Agesilaus raised a force of two thousand *neodamodeis*[118] without any difficulty, which proves that they must have been numerous, and it is clear that non-citizens were trained in Spartan military methods, since they were able to fight in the Spartan phalanx. Aristotle claims that at one time (he does not say when) such volunteers were able to become full Spartan citizens.[119] What seems to have happened in the fourth century was that the Spartiates deliberately became an exclusive caste and admitted to full citizenship only those who were qualified by birth and ability to contribute to the *syssitia*, this latter qualification becoming much more significant after the disaster at Leuctra and the loss of Messenia, which must have increased very much the number of impoverished citizens. Indeed, the obligation to contribute may belong to this period, since Xenophon, writing early in the fourth century, declares that those who do the training, regardless of wealth or physical strength, can become *homoioi*,[120] whereas Aristotle, writing later than Leuctra, declares that those are disfranchised who cannot contribute to their *syssition*.[121]

The obligation to belong to a *syssition* made it possible for the Spartiates to limit their numbers if they wanted to do so; if the system of election was as described by Plutarch,[122] it was easy for rich men to reject candidates, and if it was as practised in Crete, and in Sparta in Roman times, it was equally easy for the rich to refuse to 'adopt', or adlect, youths into the ranks of the *syssition*.[123]

For the study of the family in Sparta, however, it is clear that the consensus of opinion among ancient writers is that the Spartans' success had depended on their being willing to suppress the family in the interests of the state, and that the decisive factor in destroying the way of life that had brought success was a change in popular sentiment which allowed the family interests of the citizens to override those of the state, and led to accumulations of private property, often in the hands of women. Yet perhaps the most interesting feature of this consensus of opinion is that in all probability it is wrong; the family in the great period of Spartan power was always strong. If the law of Epitadeus is a reality, family succession was guaranteed prior to its passage, and the *epikleros*-system and facilities for adoption show a similar desire to maintain family continuity. The Spartan family was weak only in the field of religion; the Spartans seem to have lacked the sedulous family religious cult of their ancestors which characterized the Athenians, and religion contributed to Sparta's decline in so far that if it had been strong it might have provided a stimulus to the preservation of the separate identity of the families.

It seems more likely that the real cause of the crumbling of the Spartan system was political; it was danger to the state which had made the Spartans impose on themselves and maintain their rigid discipline, and caused them to be anxious to keep up an abundant supply of hoplite soldiers. The victory over Athens in 404, and the accommodation with Persia which accompanied it, persuaded the Spartans that they could relax their discipline. But once they had relaxed it they found themselves unable to restore it when their policy of empire failed, and great sacrifices would have been needed to restore the state to its old position of leadership in Greece.

CRETE AND THE GORTYN CODE

Closely associated with Sparta in Greek thought, and especially in that of Plato and Aristotle, was Crete;[123a] the Cretans, like the Spartans, were the descendants of a Dorian conquering élite, who held down a subject semi-free population;[124] they were hostile to strangers;[125] their education was designed to produce military efficiency and power, and not to train the mind, although Cretan soldiers specialized in archery and in fighting as light-armed infantry rather than in fighting in the Spartans' solid hoplite phalanx.[126] In political life they were renowned for their law-abiding character, and their laws were reputed—at least in later times—to have inspired many of the Greek lawgivers.[127] Regulations from one Cretan law code have survived, in the remarkable series of inscriptions from Gortyn, the Cretan town reputed to be the home of Thaletas, and which Plato declares to be the

Cretan community with the highest reputation.[128] The inscriptions themselves belong to the fifth century, but since the regulations are sufficiently sophisticated to show that those who drafted the laws were not inexperienced draftsmen, and a number of them provide clear internal evidence that the whole is a revision of a previous set of laws, the 'code' provides some ground for the belief that the tradition of lawmaking was deeply rooted in Crete.[129]

This Gortyn code (a rather misleading description, but a convenient label) comprises a series of laws to deal with unusual, or exceptional, circumstances; these are, disputes over slaves, sexual assaults, divorce, division of property, payment of ransom, children of mixed marriages, marriage and property of an *epikleros*, loans, limitation of gifts (presumably death-bed gifts), adoption, and some supplementary regulations probably added later. It is therefore important to remember that it has little or nothing to say about what was normal in matters affecting the family; the normal can only be deduced by arguing from the abnormal, and certainty is not always possible.

KLAROI AND ANDREIA

The society is clearly based on the ownership of lands which were divided into *klaroi* (i.e. *kleroi*); the size of these *klaroi* is quite unknown, and it is very clear from the code that there must have been—whether written or not—an entirely separate series of regulations to deal with *klaroi*; literary authors also speak of public lands and their produce, and of flocks, of which the code knows nothing.[130] The means whereby the family and the state were linked is also very obscure; we do not know how the family was linked to the *klaros*—for example, when property was to be divided between sons, all that was to be divided is defined, but never the *klaros*; provision is even made for a lack of money, but never for the lack of a *klaros*.[131] Nor are we certain how wide the kinship-group was; 'those entitled to succeed' (*epiballontes*) appear regularly as successors,[132] but we have no certainty whether they derived their title from a common great-grandparent to the deceased (thus limiting the kinship-group to second cousins once or twice removed), or to a remoter ancestor, but it is likely that, after sisters and their offspring, succession was limited to the male side, and, by presumption, to males.[133]

The most helpful piece of evidence, though not Gortynian, is the so-called Testament of Epicteta, which comes from a Dorian city, probably on the island of Thera, and dates from the second century.[134] This inscription, whose primary ostensible purpose is religious—the perpetual commemoration of Epicteta, her husband and her sons (all of whom had predeceased her)—nevertheless reveals that the society to execute this purpose, 'the *koinon* of the *andreion* of the kinsmen',[135] was in existence before her death, since she summoned it; the members of the *koinon* (an inner circle) were those who were in enjoyment of certain possessions by hereditary right, either males in their own right, or the husbands of *epikleroi* by virtue of their wife's right. Outside the *koinon* were the 'kinsmen' of the *andreion*; these are sometimes adult males (which proves that mere adult male status was not enough for membership of the *koinon*), sometimes sisters, wives and children of members (which proves that not all members of a family belonged to the *koinon*), sometimes the husbands of *epikleroi* who have not yet entered upon their inheritance because their father still lived. But nobody belongs to both *koinon* and 'kinsmen': when brothers appear, they are either all in the *koinon* or all among the 'kinsmen'; and since fathers and sons can all be in the *koinon*, clearly the *koinon* was not restricted to those who were heads of families.

These regulations conform to the implications of the law as established at Gortyn, which provides that sons had a right to succeed to the appropriate share of family property in their father's lifetime—though division was not obligatory—and that a widowed *epikleros* had the right to succeed to, and dispose of, her property[136] under certain conditions. From the inscription it has been concluded that the *koinon* was an aristocratic kinship-group of adult males enjoying the usufruct of common property; outside the *koinon* lay a larger group of 'kinsmen', who were, however, within the *andreion*, and this group included women. What the property was which they enjoyed in common we do not know, but it is very difficult to believe it was not land;[137] if it was land, and if there are genuine parallels in institutions between Dorian states, the land was probably a *klaros*, and if this is so, then a *klaros* was a family allotment of land in the wider sense of the word 'family', not in the narrow sense in which it is usually used in modern British society, and this may be true not merely in Epicteta's state, but also in Sparta and Crete and elsewhere.

HETAIROI AND ANDREIA

The society at Gortyn was essentially aristocratic, admission being based on public esteem; the family home was, as at Sparta, not the centre of a man's life, since the full citizen (known as a companion—*hetairos*) had to belong to a *hetaireia* or *andreion* (plural *andreia*), the Gortynian name for a *syssition*, having come through the ranks of the boys' troops (or *agelai*), into which we are told boys were gathered by the sons of the most distinguished and influential of the citizens.[138] The function of the *agelai* must have been that of military training, since the *agelai* fought against one another on specified days.[139] The minimum age of admission appears to have been sixteen.[140] Prior to that, from the age of puberty—nominally perhaps twelve—boys were known as youths;[141] during this period all that we are told is that 'they learned to write, and the lays which were the laws and certain forms of music'; we must presume that they lived and slept together like the members of *agelai* and *hetaireiai*. Boys while still younger attended their father's *andreion*, where they sat on the floor under the charge of an overseer (παιδόνομος), and served at the men's tables; this may have begun at about the age of six, the age at which the Spartan training began. Before that they lived in the women's quarters, and were, it seems, known as '*skotioi*'[142] because, presumably, they were not even seen.

The young men in the *agelai*, known as *apodromoi*,[143] were kept separate from the fully adult *hetairoi* for most of the time (since we are told that *apodromos* means one who is not yet allowed into the men's exercising grounds), but they were recruited from the *agelai* by adult *hetairoi* who were known as 'lovers'. The 'lover' gave notice to an *agele* that he proposed to capture a named youth;

if the youth was approved by the *agele*, the members made only token resistance, the youth was carried off to the 'lover's' *andreion*, whose members then all went hunting together with him and feasting for a maximum of two months; the youth was presented with a military cloak and other gifts (unspecified but said to be very substantial), and an ox which he sacrificed at the feast at the end of the expedition. All noble youths were expected to find a 'lover' in this way (Strabo says), and thereafter they became 'comrades in arms' of their 'lovers', and were distinguished by their special clothing at public gatherings.[144] When they left the *agelai*, the young warriors became *hetairoi*, and members of a *syssition*, or *andreion*, and full citizens, as at Sparta.

'The *syssitia* each had two adjacent buildings, one in which the members ate, called *andreion*, and one in which they gave *xenoi* a bed', says Athenaeus; this would imply (by silence) that members of the *andreion* went home after their dinner, but this is unlikely; it is much more probable that the whole of the *andreion* slept together (as did the Spartan messes up to the age of thirty), up to an unknown age.[145] This may gain support from Aristotle's statement about the Cretan system, that it was 'to secure the separation of the women from the men, in order that they shall not bear a great many children'.[146]

MARRIAGE

The Gortyn code was, however, very anxious to ensure that *epikleroi*, known in the code as *patrōïōkoi*, were married; the age of marriage is laid down as twelve,[147] but whether this means merely 'puberty' or the actual age of twelve we do not know. Pressure, in terms of loss of property or income, is imposed on the *epikleros* and on her statutory husband if, being of age, they decline to consummate.[148] Marriage of girls who were not *epikleroi* was presumably not quite so early; we have no evidence on this point, although it should be noted that the Cretan marriage-system, like the Spartan, caused the men to marry much younger than they did at Athens, since, according to Ephorus, Cretans were compelled to marry when they were selected out of the *agelai* and joined their *andreion* (men's mess). Marriage, however, did not

involve living together; Ephorus says that 'they do not immediately take the girls they have married to their own houses', and
the Gortyn code apportions penalties for a man who commits
adultery 'in the house of a woman's father or brother or husband',
a rule which clearly envisages the possibility that a wife may live
elsewhere than in her husband's house.[149] Ephorus adds that the
girls go to their husband's house 'only when they are capable of
managing the business of their *oikos*'; this must suggest that the
normal age, if greater than twelve, cannot have been very much
greater. It also implies that the women had a large share in the
management of the *oikos*, as they did in Sparta.[150]

EPIKLEROI AND SUCCESSION

It is clear from the rules determining the succession to the right
to marry *epikleroi* (who were of course the means whereby a
family without male heirs could be provided with an heir in the
next generation) that the unit beyond the statutory husband and
the successors-at-law (*epiballontes*) was the tribe; she was to marry
'any she likes of the tribe from among those who apply' in several
circumstances.[151] It is interesting to note that she did not marry
outside the tribe unless no one within it applied; in this event she
was proclaimed to be marriageable for thirty days by her relatives
by marriage, *i.e.* her mother's kin (she lacked father's relatives by
birth *ex hypothesi*), and then married 'anyone she can'. On the
other hand, property could not be inherited outside the successors-
at-law (*epiballontes*); 'those of the *oikia* who compose the *klaros*'
succeeded to the money of a man who had no *epiballontes*; that is
to say, his serfs, known variously 'as servants of the *oikos*' and
aphamiotai,[152] a word not known elsewhere. The *klaros* naturally
did not pass to them, since they were serfs; we do not know to
whom it passed: it may have been added to the public land, of
which we hear nothing in the code.

ADOPTION

The code contains no provision for wills, but it does admit the
practice of adoption by *hetairoi*; the body receiving the adopted
son is the *hetaireia*.[153] The code makes it clear that the purpose was

not solely to provide a successor to an otherwise vacant inheritance, since it is envisaged that adopted sons may have brothers and sisters as a result of the adoption.[154] We may wonder perhaps if it was another means by which rich and noble men could augment their following for war, and, since there is no evidence that adoption was restricted in any way at all,[155] possibly it was a method of recruiting into the citizen-body those who were outsiders, or perhaps Cretans unqualified by birth.[156] R. F. Willetts has pointed out that if an adopted son was subsequently repudiated, the formal repudiation took place before the Xsenios Kosmos, the Cretan magistrate who dealt with non-citizens;[157] the act therefore must have involved the disinherited son in expulsion from the citizen body. Since it will have involved his exclusion from the *hetaireia*, this view must be correct.

HETAIREIA AND ANDREION

Herein we may detect the link between the *hetaireia* and the *andreion* in a property-owning sense; the *hetaireia* comprised the *andreion* (in the sense of the noble kinship-group) plus the members added to it by adoption, by gathering an *agele*, and by recruiting 'comrades in arms'; the members were all *hetairoi*, and full citizens, and since they all ate together in the *andreion*, the *hetairoi* were corporately known as an *andreion*. *Andreion* therefore has two meanings, and this may be the explanation of some of the *prima facie* confusing and contradictory statements we hear about the women; that they belonged to an *andreion* (which in a kinship sense they did), and that they were supported by the *syssitia* (which they were, because they too were fed from the produce of the land),[158] but they were kept separate from the men (which they were, since they did not belong to the *andreion* in the sense of an *hetaireia*).

WOMEN'S POSITION

In their conduct Cretan women had little more freedom than Athenian women; assaults on their honour could not be avenged by death; rapists and adulterers who paid their fine were punished only by monetary penalty;[159] a woman's word that an attempt at sexual intercourse had been made was not valid without witnesses[160]—and in all this field a woman is treated by the code no differently from a boy. If a divorced woman gave birth to a child, she had to present her baby to her ex-husband, who had the power to accept or reject it; the power to decide its fate then—and only then—passed to her; if she suppressed the child without consulting her ex-husband she was punished.[161] The location of these rules after those about adultery and preceding those about children whose status is in question, and bastards, strongly suggests that adultery was regarded as the principal reason for a husband to divorce his wife.[162] The causes of divorce of a husband are nowhere stated, but the code says that if a husband was responsible for the divorce he must pay his wife over and above her property the (relatively derisory) sum of five staters—half the sum demanded in compensation for rape by a free man upon the son or daughter of an *apetairos* (a free non-citizen).[163]

WOMEN'S PROPERTY

The code is also much concerned to preserve the property of women; it has been usual to argue that these provisions show that women at Gortyn enjoyed a more privileged status than they did in Athens, and it is true that they had a greater range of powers in respect of their property. An *epikleros* for example had the power to buy off a statutory husband by surrendering a part of her inheritance (whereas an Athenian *epikleros* would have to abstain from making a claim at all); a girl also had a claim to a statutory part of her father's estate, but no more,[164] whereas in Athens a girl's dowry remained in her father's discretion; her share could moreover be in the usufruct of land or flocks, or in money let out at interest perhaps, since the code envisages that it may bring in income or produce[165] (καρπός, the Greek word is the same). Her property was, moreover, her own, and always so called in the code;[166] it remained hers as long as she lived, and was separated from her husband's if he died in debt, or if either of them were fined.[167] But a woman had no power of disposal: there were, it seems, no wills, and she was not allowed to adopt;[168] if she had children, they succeeded to her property, if she had none, her successors-at-law in her father's family inherited it.[169] Moreover there appears to be no statutory provision for the maintenance of a widow; if she left her late husband's house she received her property back, the only admissible addition being what her husband had given her in front of three witnesses.[170] Even this was severely limited in amount to twelve staters, later amended to one hundred staters or objects to that value.[171]

In short, a woman's position in society was no higher than it was in Athens; it may indeed have been less honoured if membership of the *andreion* went on throughout a man's life, with the result that there was very little of that mutual association in marriage from which strong attachments could, and no doubt did, grow. The property-regulations of the code are uncompromising in the view that the woman's place was to be the means for a man to procreate heirs to his family;[172] once she had given birth to a child, her own family's claim in her property was extinguished as long as the child lived.[173]

RELIGION

Little is known of family religion; that there were festivals which it was the heir's duty to perform is clear from the laws on adoption,[174] and is suggested also by the Testament of Epicteta; it would be surprising if these were other than the commemoration of ancestors which we have met in Athens and in Plato's idealized society.

So, in Gortyn too, the family underlay the organization by *andreion* and *hetaireia*, despite the fact that the latter two were ostensibly inimical to the former; besides, the close correspondences between Sparta, Gortyn and the unknown home of Epicteta suggest that this may have been a standard pattern in those Dorian societies in which the Dorian aristocrats maintained their grasp—that of a class society in which the families of the aristocratic leaders provided the entire basis of the social, political, legal[175] and economic structure.

CHAPTER IX

THE FAMILY IN OTHER STATES

A COMMON PATTERN

THERE IS NOT enough available evidence to allow us to attempt a systematic account of any other Greek state before Alexander; this is partly through lack of literary output, partly because, as Aristotle appears to have thought, other states may all have fallen into a standard pattern, except those which he discussed in Book II of the *Politics*, that is, the actual constitutions of Sparta, Crete and Carthage, and the theoretical constitutions of Plato, Hippodamus of Miletus and Phaleas of Chalcedon. At the end of the book Aristotle gives a quick résumé of unusual features, and of innovations made by various lawgivers—Charondas, lawgiver of the colonies of Chalcis in Italy and Sicily, who first made perjury a statutory offence, and Androdamas of Rhegium who legislated for the colonies of Chalcis in the north-west corner of the Aegean (Chalcidice), and who was author of the laws on murder and *epikleroi*—Aristotle's suggestion is that he first drafted the laws which came into general use, but he is not clear on the point.

The 'unusual' features mentioned are the savageness of the penalties established by Dracon in Athens, the laws of Pittacus of Mytilene on Lesbos who made drunkenness a cause for increasing and not modifying penalties, and of Philolaus, lawgiver of Thebes, whose laws about the getting of children, which they call 'placing' laws, were in order to preserve the number of *kleroi*.[1]

The laws of Dracon—and here Aristotle cannot have meant only the Athenian laws on homicide—'had no unusual features', nor are any peculiarities mentioned in Solon's; Demosthenes declares that many Greek states had adopted the Athenians' laws,[2] and this may be the reason for Aristotle's silence; we should therefore expect that most *poleis* had a pattern of law similar to

ns, as described in Chapters I and IV, because they
on the occupation of land by families, kinship-groups
intermarriage among neighbours, and *poleis* built on a
kinship-groups which constituted the *polis*.

FAMILIES, LANDS AND CULTS

Poleis were exclusive units and not open societies, and were ultimately, in economic terms, the sum total of their constituent
families' possessions (that is, principally, of their lands and their
produce), in social terms, the sum total of the members of the
families (that is, those who shared in the common worship of
hearth and ancestral cult). Since the family and its land, hearth and
cult were inseparable, the economic and social units coincided
exactly, and their defence was the responsibility of every man,
woman and child, because the defence of the city was the defence
of the whole community.[3]

Two consequences followed from the existence of this standard
pattern; the first was a common attitude towards family customs,
monogamy for example, and the refusal to adopt the oriental
custom of the harem.[4] 'Hellene' and 'barbarian' (non-Greek, that
is) are frequently contrasted by Herodotus, when he pinpoints
the strangeness of such things as the marriage or funeral customs
of some of the Greeks' neighbours,[5] and in casual remarks such as
that 'the Persian attitude to women is more contemptuous than
the Greek', or that 'it was the Persian custom not to bring a child
to his father till he was five years old lest the father be sorry if he
lost him'.[6] On the other hand, we also find in Herodotus stories
like that about the birth and upbringing of Cyrus, in which
Harpagus, Astyages and Mandane all behaved in a thoroughly
Greek way, or the tales about Croesus, whose attitude to his
children was Greek, and whose son in turn showed true '*philotimia*' when he refused to be deterred from taking part in hunting
a savage boar which was ravaging the kingdom, asking, 'what
sort of a man would his wife think him if he did not go out to
deal with the boar?'[7]

The second common attitude was a fanatical devotion to land,
hearth and home; this was partly because citizenship was in early

times related to ownership of land—as Aristotle declares that in some communities those who had no land had no citizen-rights, and in Thebes political life was permitted to craftsmen only when they had given up their trade.[8] But to be settled agriculturists was also to Herodotus a sign of Greek behaviour, as for example when he speaks of the Gelonoi, who live among the Boudinoi: the latter 'are autochthonous and nomadic . . . whereas the Gelonoi are workers of the soil, eaters of bread and owners of gardens'; they were descendants of Greeks who had fled inland from the coastal settlements of the Black Sea.[9] Moreover, this fanatical devotion had a religious basis in the intimate connexion between the cult of the ancestors and the ownership of land. This connexion was overstressed by Fustel de Coulanges for example, but has probably been understressed in some more recent work; it seems to be well expressed by Burckhardt when he says: 'The right to own land was causally related to veneration of hearth and graves . . . and the duties deriving from ancestor-worship carried with them the right of inheritance'. In consequence 'to be removed from his ancestral graves must have spelled a misfortune for the Greek',[10] and on at least one occasion we are told that those who had not the right to be born or to be buried in a place had no claim to call it their native land though they might live all their lives there.[11]

At first sight this devotion may seem paradoxical in a people so vigorous in their colonization as the Greeks were, but there were other factors to be brought into consideration. Firstly, not all Greeks were landowners, and those who were not landowners could not have had the same opportunity, or motive, for worship of their family graves; craftsmen, for example, were mobile as early as the Homeric age; secondly, conquest by a stronger enemy might have involved loss of ownership of lands, and emigration appeared an alternative preferable to trying to hang on as a landless labourer; thirdly, excess of population sometimes meant a choice between emigration or starvation, or near-starvation; emigration must then normally have seemed preferable, although even in these conditions the islanders of Thera had to compel some of their citizens to go to their new colony (*c.* 630),[12] despite the fact that there would still be some members of each family left in Thera to continue the ancestors' cult.

Colonies were therefore sent abroad, and they normally took with them the cults of their mother-city, and this is true to such an extent that modern scholars have been able to establish from their cults the origins of some colonies whose mother-city used to be unknown to us.[13] In at least one instance, that of the Locrians' colony at Naupactus, early in the fifth century,[14] the two communities continued to enjoy mutual succession rights, and a colonist was allowed to return to his Locrian town if he left a grown-up son or brother for his household in the colony,[15] a regulation which, as A. J. Graham temperately remarks, 'may imply that the Greeks were less clear and definite that the colonist ceased completely to be a citizen of his mother-city than some modern scholars have been'.[16] Within the colonies, too, scholars have noted different racial units remaining separate for long periods,[17] a separation which their family cults will have made easy if not inevitable. Aristotle moreover states it as a general rule that people not of the same nation (*phyle*) quarrel when settled in the same *polis*, and we note in two colonies at least that tribal divisions were established on a racial basis for organizing or re-organizing the citizen body;[18] this too will have been encouraged by the existence of common cults brought by the settlers from their home lands.

THE INDESTRUCTIBILITY OF CLAIMS

Conquered Greek peoples were almost unbelievably tenacious of their claims to land—and nationality; after the battle of Leuctra in 371 Epameinondas had merely to appeal to the descendants of Messenians to return and build a new capital, for them to flock back to their ancestral land, though some of them had for more than three centuries been scattered throughout the Greek world. Other examples abound: the Plataeans, expelled in 427, settled by the Athenians in the lands of Scione in 421/0, expelled from there after 404 by the Spartans and resettled in their own land in 386, and expelled again by the Thebans in 373, returned to claim their lands at Philip's invitation after the Thebans' overthrow at the battle of Chaeroneia in 338; when the Sybarites, whose town was blotted out by the men of Croton in 510, returned in 446/5, two years before Thurii was founded in 444/3, they attempted to claim precedence in religious observances and land allocations.[19] Greeks, it is fair to say, never relinquished claims to land, even border lands disputed with their neighbours; when the Argives lost Thyrea they swore not to wear their hair long like warrior-nobles, nor to allow their women to wear gold, until they recovered it.[20]

Victorious Greeks knew this; that is one reason why victors sometimes slew the men and enslaved the children along with the women, and, if the city was to be inhabited again, brought in new inhabitants, as the Athenians did at Scione in 420 for example; if it was not to be resettled, the land was often dedicated to some god, as the plain of Crisa was to Delphian Apollo after the first 'Sacred' War (c. 582). This fact may also explain why victors who did not massacre the whole of an enemy population retained undying enmity to survivors who tried to keep up a corporate identity, as the Athenians did towards the Aeginetans, whom they had expelled in 431, when they captured their place of refuge in Thyrea in 424.[21] The same undying demand for restoration, and for vengeance upon a successful adversary, ruled in disputes between families and within cities: 'A fool is he who kills the father, leaving the son alive' was a Greek maxim, for nothing was more certain than that the son would die rather than fail to seek vengeance.[22] After political struggles, Isocrates in the fourth century assures Timotheus of Heraclea that a humane prince 'brings exiles back, restores their property and compensates those who had bought it'.[23] This was the only way by which enmity could be assuaged, and we can quote occasions when it happened.[24]

CITY LAWS AND FAMILY LANDS

All Greek states therefore had laws about land, and most had laws to prevent undue accumulations of land; Sparta may have been almost unique in not having any.[25] The Thebans had laws to prevent the number of *oikoi* from falling, as has been noted, and supported them with laws about the getting and adopting of children; their lawgiver was a Corinthian, whose native city was said to have been given similar laws by its first lawgiver, Pheidon. There was a law to prevent the disposal of ancient *kleroi* at Leucas, and another to make sales of land difficult among the Locrians.[26] Besides Plato, both the authors of theoretical *poleis* mentioned by Aristotle laid down laws about the tenure of land, Hippodamus of Miletus dividing it up between the sacred—to provide offerings; public—to feed the warriors; and private, for the farmers; and Phaleas of Chalcedon prescribing that when men married, the rich should give but not receive dowries (presumably in land), while the poor should receive but not give them.[27] The Athenian law about wasting property may also be seen at Abdera if the story is true that Democritus the philosopher was accused of wasting his patrimony.[28] Such legal texts as survive confirm the picture; at Halicarnassus before 454/3 disputes over land are regulated in a much-discussed inscription; in the next century, two neighbouring cities confirm the sales of land and property confiscated from political opponents of Mausolus of Caria: they are exiled for ever; the purchasers and the prices are recorded, and the validity of the transactions is asserted.[29]

Two centuries earlier, in Argos, it appears that when a defaulter went into exile and his goods were sold, the purchasers with the first right to bid were the magistrates, and the exile's kindred; the citizens in general were only eligible if there were neither magistrates nor kinsmen prepared to acquire the property.[30]

The public character of the land caused grants of citizenship and the right to own land in a city (*enktesis*) to go hand in hand; all over the Greek world grants of citizenship and the status of *proxenos* are accompanied by the privilege of *enktesis*; most of the examples found are post-classical, but there are enough in the period before Alexander for us to be sure that it was not an innovation of Hellenistic times.[31]

ENROLMENT OF OUTSIDERS

Cities varied greatly in their attitude to grants of citizenship to outsiders; Herodotus comments on Spartan exclusiveness, and on generosity at Delphi;[32] this latter was perhaps natural at the Greek national shrines. In criticizing the Athenians for their generosity in this matter, Demosthenes contrasts them unfavourably with the much smaller cities, Megara, Aegina and Oreus in Euboea, all of whom, he declares, were much more exclusive, and with less reason. By the fourth century, however, it seems there had been a considerable lessening of exclusiveness, when, for example, Isocrates declared that some cities had conferred citizenship upon famous artists.[33]

A more usual reason for enrolling new citizens was defence, the need to strengthen the army. This happened frequently in the Sicilian cities, from the time of Gelon of Syracuse, who incorporated into Syracuse the military classes of Gela, Camarina, Megara Hyblaea and Sicilian Euboea to meet the Carthaginian threat in 480,[34] to that of Timoleon in the fourth century, who recruited settlers for the devastated cities of Sicily from all over Greece, Italy and Sicily,[35] and again later, but it also happened in the Greek homelands; in Corcyra, for example, fourteen years after the bloody revolutions described by Thucydides, slaves were freed and foreign residents (*xenoi*) made citizens for fear of the revenge of the massacred nobles' families.[36] In Argos, after the appalling loss of manpower suffered at the dreadful defeat at Sepeia (*c.* 494), we hear that the city was handed over for a time to non-citizens;[37] Herodotus calls them slaves, but they may have been serfs.[38] The aftermath of this débâcle is of particular interest: Plutarch says that the newly-enfranchised were given the wives of those who had been killed; Herodotus says that when the sons of those who had fallen were grown up (ἤβησαν), they expelled their stepfathers, who captured Tiryns, and the end of the affair was that some time later the Argives defeated their 'slaves' in battle, perhaps in the war which resulted in the destruction of Tiryns and Mycenae, about thirty years later.[39] There is no clear evidence that these incorporated outsiders were ultimately more than temporary guardians of the Argive children, nor that any children whom they procreated were given Argive citizenship, nor in fact that their expulsion by their citizen-born stepsons was more than an enforced retirement to the country part of the Argive nobles' estates.

When cities were refounded, naturally, new settlers were summoned, as at Sybaris, where new citizens came to join the descendants of the survivors at the founding of Thurii; new citizens must also have joined the old at the resettlement of cities destroyed by enemies, Miletus, Melos and Aegina for example, and we know that colonies were often reinforced by new parties of settlers from the mother-city.[40]

SIMILARITY OF LAWS

In many other fields of civil law, the overall picture seems to be one in which there was a general similarity in Greek institutions, but many local differences. A lack of evidence makes it impossible to prove positively that any feature was universally applicable, and the lack of proof positive must always make doubt a reasonable alternative view. Caution is particularly justifiable when we can point to one piece of incontrovertible evidence that there were differing rules about succession to estates within a group of cities as small as the Locrians who founded the colony of Naupactus.[41] Further, though less reliable, support comes from a speech written to be delivered in Aegina in which Isocrates declares unequivocally that there are many points of difference in the laws of various cities.[42]

Some laws, however, had more than local application; some cities used the laws of others; Demosthenes' statement, already noted, that many cities used the Athenian laws cannot be fully substantiated anywhere, but the island of Amorgos has been shown to have used a number of Athenian legal and commercial institutions which are also found in places which came at some period or other under direct Athenian government.[43] The laws of Ceos, Isocrates informs us, were also used on the island of Siphnos.[44] The laws of Charondas were in use in a number of cities of the western Greeks; whatever the validity of the two surviving accounts—and the preface in Stobaeus XLIV, 24, is almost certainly a late forgery—it is perverse to assume that the laws never existed in something like the form given by Diodorus for example, though we must be careful not to be too confident that details antedate the Hellenistic era.[45]

MARRIAGE LAWS

For laws on marriage, the evidence seems to show that marriage following betrothal was the common form in all states; for example, Polycrates of Samos, when trying to silence his daughter's fears for his safety, threatened to make her stay a maiden for a long time if she did not desist; at Epidamnus on one occasion a magistrate found it his duty to fine the father of his son's fiancée, on another, in Delphi, a bridegroom refused to go through with his marriage because of a bad omen at the wedding; a banker in Aegina is said to have 'given' first his wife then his daughter to his trusted slave (presumably when his wife had died).[46] All these stories presuppose that the weddings had been preceded by betrothals.

The practice of giving dowries also reveals that marriages resulted from an arrangement made in advance between two families; the rich and prosperous Acragantines like the philosopher Empedocles are said to have regularly given dowries to poor men's daughters in the fifth century, and Charondas' laws are said to have commanded that a dowry be given to a poor *epikleros* whose next of kin did not want to marry her.[47] Dowries are also attested by the discovery on the islands Amorgos, Lemnos, Naxos and Scyros of the stones known as *horoi*, which are found otherwise only in Attica;[48] these *horoi* are inscribed stones set up as evidence that a given piece of land or other real property is pledged as security for a sum of money, or that a part of it is so pledged, and the sum of money in question is very often a dowry, or part of one.[49] Two other islands, Myconos and Tenos, have produced dowry-inscriptions from the age following Alexander, and Ephesus one from the third century;[50] among the theoretical writers, Phaleas proposed that dowries be used as a means of equalizing the citizens' wealth—which implies that he believed that dowries were normally provided in his day.[51] Even today a recent litigant has argued in court that universal Greek practice entitled him to receive a dowry with his wife.[52]

Dowries were not invariable, however; Herodotus tells us that King Darius' Greek doctor Democedes (a Crotoniate) was so anxious to marry the daughter of the famous Milon of Croton that he gave her father a handsome gift of money for her, an arrangement which may show the survival of the double pattern met in Homeric society.[53]

In the fourth century at least, intermarriage between members of different cities seems not too uncommon: Isocrates claims[54] that marriages between Cypriot Salaminians and Greek women were 'nowadays' widely practised; in his speech delivered in Aegina Isocrates' client said that when a Siphnian aristocrat married for the third time, he took to wife a woman from Seriphos, 'of more standing than you would expect of a Seriphian'[55] (an island whose barrenness was a joke, hence a shrunken old maid was 'a woman of Seriphos'); he also had friends and *xenoi* on Paros. It was a mark of the bitterness of the party struggle in Samos that the exiled nobles, whose lands were confiscated, were even forbidden to intermarry with the victorious commons.[56] How many states had strict laws about the legitimacy of children we do not know; but it is clear also that in some places temporary liaisons must have had some claim to be marriages. Isocrates' client makes no attempt to deny that Thrasyllus, a travelling seer ($\mu\acute{\alpha}\nu\tau\iota\varsigma$), begot a number of children by the women (perhaps wives) he had in many cities, though none, says Isocrates, did he consider legitimate; however, the suggestion certainly is that the last of these believed that she was a legitimate wife, as she must have done for her daughter to have thought fit to put in a claim to his estate.[57] The marriages of Thargelia of Miletus, who had fourteen husbands, were perhaps mostly of an informal and temporary character.[58]

The laws of Charondas are said to have disfranchised men who had legitimate children and subsequently remarried; Diodorus says his object was to prevent the troubles caused by stepmothers, but this seems unlikely. If the law is correctly reported, which may be doubted, the main consideration is likely to have been a desire to safeguard the *oikos* of the first wife's children; this may be thought the more likely when we note that these same laws also contained ingenious regulations for protecting orphans, under which the person of an orphan was entrusted to its mother's family, its property to its father's, and the latter alone would succeed should the orphan fail to survive to adult age.[59]

Under these laws, too, divorce was permitted both to women appellants and to men, but Diodorus adds that the laws were later changed in such a way that their intention was frustrated, when the initiator of the divorce was not allowed to remarry a new partner younger than the previous one.

LAWS ON ADULTERY

Adultery was an offence which was generally regarded as a public offence, and not merely a private injury; this was, as has been remarked above (Chapter V), because the ancestors' cult was grievously injured by having an outsider introduced into the patrilinear group, and hence the wife's unchastity was serious in a way that the husband's was not, so long as he confined his amours to non-citizen women. Hence public, and ceremonial, dishonour was probably a normal penalty, and divorce presumably accompanied it; men were also punished by ceremonial dishonour, and in some places even more savagely, as at Italian Locri where the laws of Zaleucus caused adulterers' eyes to be put out.[60] Adultery is said by Aristotle to have been one of the sources of personal enmity which led to civil wars, as at Syracuse, when a young man whose rival had won away his boy-love revenged himself by seducing the other's wife; also at Thebes, and at Heraclea in Boeotia, where two men were justly punished for adultery, but 'in a spirit of party'. Marriage-suits are also named as a general cause of civil strife,[61] and tyrants' inability to keep their hands off citizen-women provided a cause for their expulsion. One of the causes of hatred between Thebes and Sparta was the suicide of a number of girls who had been ravished by some Spartans, and that between Dionysius I of Syracuse and the Locrians arose from his insulting behaviour to young girls.[62]

WOMEN IN SOCIETY

In some places universal education extended to the girls, and we are told by Diodorus of one woman who succeeded in playing a part in politics by speaking in the assembly; this was at Thurii.[63] The Western Greeks seem to have given their women more freedom than most; in prosperous Acragas rich Acragantine girls

kept pet birds, and built them charming memorials.[64] They were
not soft, however; when Acragas was evacuated under the threat
of Carthaginian assault in 406, the women braved the march to
Gela. Other Sicilian women actually fought in this desperate,
bloody war, either supporting the troops on the walls by bringing
supplies of food and ammunition, or rebuilding walls which had
been breached, and joining in the fighting, as when at Selinus they
joined in hurling roofing-tiles at the Carthaginian force which broke
into the city. Their bravery compared favourably with the Spartan
women's demoralization in Epameinondas' invasion in 369.[65]

It is difficult to know how independent women were generally;
Aristotle several times speaks of 'superintendents of women' as
an office which actually existed in states 'which had more prosperity and leisure and were concerned with propriety': they were not
found, he explains, in democratic states, since you cannot stop
the women of the poor from going out of doors, nor in oligarchic,
since you cannot stop the womenfolk of oligarchic rulers from
being luxurious;[66] they were therefore presumably not very
common, and intended to ensure conformity with some sort of
sumptuary legislation. This may perhaps also be seen in the
laws of Zaleucus, which are said to have attempted by ridicule to
stop ostentation and immorality—a free woman may not have
more than one girl escorting her unless she is drunk, may not
leave the city at night except for adultery, may not wear gold nor
costly garments unless she is an *hetaira*.[67]

The regard men had for their women and children also seems
to have varied. In Thebes, Plutarch's *Life of Pelopidas* (who died
in 364), for what it is worth, gives a number of vignettes of family
life reminiscent of Athens; of Charon whose young son lived in
the women's quarter, thus showing that these were known in
Thebes (IX, 5); of a violent quarrel between a husband and his
wife, who had lent his horse's bridle without telling him (VIII,
4–5)—a quarrel which 'lasted most of the day'; of the scandalous
conduct of the oligarchic rulers who planned to have other men's
wives brought to their revel (IX, 2, X, 2, XI, 2). Xenophon also
gives a picture of a leading citizen at home, after dinner, re-
laxing while his wife sat by him working wool.[67a] In Thebes too

the Sacred Band, the pick of the hoplite troops, were clearly in a *syssition* or several *syssitia*, and here the system of adlection by 'lovers' was also employed; it was generally believed that sodomy was freely practised in Thebes, but whether this was true or a false interpretation of the institution of 'lovers' we do not know.

The Sacred Band was evidently maintained at public expense, and we hear that the system of *syssitia* was in use also at Thurii and Miletus; Plato adds that *syssitia* were known in Boeotia, but there is little sign of their use outside Thebes and the Sacred Band.[68] How far the resemblances to Crete and Sparta went we cannot say, since Plato does not explain, but *syssitia* were in general thought to be inimical to family life. However, the idea of *syssitia* was popular among theoreticians and commended several times by Aristotle, twice in connection with land-distribution and the army, once as a political device hostile to tyranny as 'inculcating self-confidence and mutual trust'. He also says that they were adopted by the native tribes of Italy when they turned from a nomadic to an agricultural life.[69]

On the other hand, Polycrates of Samos, when besieged in c. 524, successfully prevented his troops from being disloyal by using their womenfolk and children as hostages, and Pelopidas tried to get into his hands the wives and children of some mercenaries who had deserted him, in order to punish them.

Eubotas the athlete, we are told, had too much respect for his wife to bring home to Cyrene Laïs, a lovely courtesan who had fallen in love with him, but at Troezen at one time the girls were married so young that an appalling number died in childbirth; in Ceos too the young girls at one festival were obliged to do the most menial tasks for their own and other girls' parents and brothers.[70]

KYRIOI OF FAMILIES AND EPIKLEROI

Women's legal acts in all parts of the Greek world seem to have required the consent of a *kyrios* except for manumissions of slaves, and gifts to religious bodies;[71] the dates of the inscriptions indicating this are various, and mostly late, but it is very unlikely that the rules became more severe in Hellenistic and Roman times than they were in classical, and it is fair to assume that the rule was general, and of some antiquity. Rules about the rights of *epikleroi* and their next of kin may have been invented in Chalcidice, as has been suggested above, but they must have existed everywhere, and are attested in many parts of the Greek world; in Mytilene, Aristotle reports that the revolt from Athens in 428, narrated also by Thucydides, had its origin in a quarrel over *epikleroi*, and almost a century later the Sacred War which led to the humiliation of the Phocians (356–46) began by rivalry over *epikleroi*; the laws of Charondas also dealt with *epikleroi*.[72]

One Greek society appears to have employed matrilinear succession as the normal method; this was Italian Locri (also known as Western or Epizephyrian Locri). There the inhabitants traced their descent back to the 'Hundred Houses' of Opuntian Locri, in a matrilinear succession. The background of this most unusual tradition is far from clear, but, as has already been remarked, it is clear that the Locrian cities had no uniform rules on succession. The subject was already one of controversy in antiquity,[73] though, since it was apparently unknown to Herodotus, its ancient origins may be doubted. The Locrians also had a famous shrine of Persephone, a leading female deity (*Pl. 49*).

ORPHANS AND GUARDIANS

Apart from the guardianships of orphans under the laws of Charondas, already noted, we hear of orphans' estates on *horoi* from Amorgos and Naxos,[74] and of guardians in Ephesus at two moments about three hundred years apart; in the mid-sixth century, Pindarus was compelled by Croesus of Lydia to submit, exile himself and leave his son and property in the hands of a guardian; in the third century, during a new emergency, guardians and trustees were put under pressure by a surviving decree to fulfil their obligations, and were not given the concessions granted to debtors and others in a financial crisis.[75] It is hard not to assume that the legal tradition was unbroken.

SUCCESSION

Rules for succession must also have been universal; this does not mean that there were never quarrels—Aristotle mentions one as a cause of a civil war[76]—and the rules were certainly not uniform. The decree from Naupactus and Isocrates' speech in Aegina both make it clear that rules for succession and inheritance varied from place to place, but both show some non-varying features: the Locrian cities, it appears, like Athens and Gortyn, all allowed a man to divide his property between his sons in his lifetime without their necessarily becoming fully possessed of it. Isocrates' Siphnian client declared that every state acknowledged a man's right to adopt a son. Such external evidence as we have supports his statement, although in Aegina, according to this speaker, a local variation was that the adopted son had to be of equal rank to his parent. In Thebes the law about 'placing' may even have compelled a man to adopt a son if he had not one of his own, if Aristotle is right in saying that the law's purpose was to prevent any fall in the number of *kleroi*.[77] Thebes is also said to have been the only Greek community in which infanticide was unknown.[78]

RITES FOR THE DECEASED

It seems clear that the duties to the dead were universally regarded. In this respect, the whole atmosphere of Isocrates' speech in Aegina could have been that of Athens: Thrasyllus, (father of Thrasylochus) 'began to long for his native Siphnos when he grew older and rich'; the opponents are accused of 'wanting to make the *oikos* of Thrasylochus desolate',[79] they had failed to come to the funeral, and ignored the death of Thrasylochus' brother Sopolis when he died after attempting a *coup d'état*—they had sacrificed and held festival, whereas the speaker had mourned for him (though he had died in Lycia);[80] Thrasylochus and the speaker used to go to all the religious festivals together, and had the same friends and *xenoi*; the speaker looked after Thrasylochus on his deathbed, where Thrasylochus betrothed his young sister to him; in his devotion to Thrasylochus, it is implied, the speaker lost his own mother and young sister when Thrasylochus persuaded them to go to Troezen, with the result that they perished 'in a foreign land and amongst strangers'.[81] This last was in general a disaster, since it made it all but certain that the deceased would not receive the proper cult offerings unless his remains could later be removed to his native land. It was not a disaster only if the citizens of the land in which a *xenos* was buried thought fit to give him cult-worship. This was not too uncommon; the Plataeans tended the communal graves of those who fell in the great victory of 479, at least until 431; in the case of individuals, the person commemorated by cult-worship was often enrolled as a local 'hero', as Brasidas was at Amphipolis, or Timoleon at Syracuse.[82] Herodotus quotes an interesting example at Samos, where a Spartan called Archias in the sixth century was given a public funeral for conspicuous gallantry; his son was renamed Samius, and his grandson, says Herodotus, was also called Archias, 'who honoured the Samians most of all *xenoi*' for what they done for his grandfather.[83]

On two occasions the Plataeans used their care for the graves of those who fell in 479 to appeal for consideration; to the Spartans, when the city fell in 427, and to the Athenians when appealing for its restoration in 373–1.[84] On the first of these occasions the Thebans, says Thucydides, countered with references to the sons of the dead at Coroneia in 446, and to the fathers grieving for those who died in the unsuccessful attempted *coup* in 431.[85] In Corcyra, the exiled oligarchs from Epidamnus, we are told, backed their pleas for help by appeals to the tombs of their ancestors in the city. On the other hand, the Locrians, we are told, revenged themselves on Dionysius I of Syracuse by ensuring that his children, whom they murdered, could not have a proper burial.[86]

Prohibitions on extravagance at funerals are also attested by laws; at Iulis on Ceos the garments adorning the corpse were to be worth not more than 100 drachmae, the bier was to be simple, the procession to the tomb was to be in silence, only traditional victims were to be sacrificed.[87] At Delphi, too (*c.* 400), costs were to be limited, and silence maintained; no long pauses on the way to the cemetery, no lamentations for former dead, nor wailings and dirges at the annual commemorations.[88] Several of the philosophers commanded that there be no elaborate ceremonies at their funeral;[89] Aristotle commanded only that he should have the bones of Pythias (his wife presumably) laid with his own.[90]

Annual commemorations were a major feature in Epicurus' will, and these were still being conducted in Pliny's day more than three hundred years later.[91]

ALEXANDER AND THE DIVORCE OF FAMILY AND STATE

Alexander the Great's career of world-conquest ended the age in which the wholly independent city-state was the only political institution considered acceptable to Greek political practice and thought. Thereafter, in the Greek homeland, even the 'autonomous' cities had always to formulate their policies with one eye on the monarch who had, for the time being, achieved dominance by land or sea. Abroad, in Egypt and Asia for example, the Greeks who were given lands and settled as colonists were émigrés, who had left their native city not as a result of any corporate civic decision to found a colony, but as a result of their own individual initiative. The cities which they formed therefore lacked the family traditions and cults which were the unifying bonds of the civic colonies of an earlier date, and since the majority of the settlers were soldiers of fortune, they are most unlikely to have brought wives with them from their native city. If they married therefore, they are likely to have married non-Greek women, and their children will have lost contact with the family traditions of earlier generations. After Alexander's campaigns, therefore, the position of the family in relation to the state changed; no longer was it true to say that a Greek city-state consisted of the sum of the *oikoi* (human and material) belonging to its citizens and their *xenoi* and nothing else.

The family, however, continued uninterruptedly as the fundamental social unit of the Greeks, and at the centre of the civil law, through centuries of foreign occupation, till it emerged as firmly entrenched as ever in the Greek Civil Code of 1946, which is the law in force today.[92]

ABBREVIATIONS AND BIBLIOGRAPHY

ABBREVIATIONS

The abbreviations used for ancient authors are in general those used in Liddell and Scott's Lexicon (*LSJ*), whose reference-system has been used except in references to Aristotle, *Politics* and *Ethics*, Plutarch's *Lives* and Strabo, for which authors I have used the Loeb numeration. Sundry authors' names have been abbreviated, as Herodotus to Hdt., Thucydides to Thuc., Demosthenes to Dem., Diodorus Siculus to Diod., Dionysius of Halicarnassus to Dion. Hal., Diogenes Laertius to Diog. La. Others, and their works, where abbreviated, are as in *LSJ* or as noted on their first introduction. References to Pauly-Wissowa's *Real Encyclopädie der Classischen Altertums-Wissenschaft* are given as author, *RE* volume, date and column. For the fragments of the historians I have used either F. Jacoby's *Fragmente der Griechischen Historiker* abbreviated as F. Jacoby *FGH* and fragment number (*e.g.* 90, 61) or volume and page number (*e.g.* IIA, 387), or else C. Müller's *Fragmenta Historicorum Graecorum* abbreviated as Müller *FHG*, fragment and page number. References to Dittenberger's *Sylloge Inscriptionum Graecarum* 3rd ed. are given as to *SIG*, those to Schwyzer's *Dialectorum Graecarum Exempla epigraphica potiora* as to Schwyzer.

BIBLIOGRAPHY

The following short list of books is intended to indicate those works which I have used most, and which students may find useful for exploring further in various fields. The abbreviations indicated are those used in the notes in this book.

BONNER, R. J. and SMITH, G., *The Administration of Justice from Homer to Aristotle* (1930–8) [*Justice*]

BURCKHARDT, J., *History of Greek Culture* (Eng. trans. 1964) [*HGC*]

BURN, A. R., *The Lyric Age of Greece* (1960) [*LA*]

CHRIMES, K. M. T., *Ancient Sparta* (1949) [*AS*]

DEUBNER, L., *Attische Feste* (1932) [*AF*]

EHRENBERG, V., *People of Aristophanes* (2nd ed., 1956) [*People*]

— *The Greek State* (Eng. trans. 1960)

FARNELL, L. R., *Cults of the Greek City-States* (1896–1904) [*Cults*]

FLACELIÈRE, R., *Daily Life in Greece at the time of Pericles* (Eng. Trans. 1964)

FINLEY, M. I., *The World of Odysseus* (1959)

— *Studies in Land and Credit in Ancient Athens* (1952) [*SLC*]

FORREST, W. G., *The Emergence of Greek Democracy* (1966)   [*EGD*]

FRANCOTTE, H., *La Polis Grecque* (1907)

GERNET, L., *Droit et Société dans la Grèce Ancienne* (1955) (a collection of earlier papers, revised and republished)   [*D. et S.*]

GLOTZ, G., *La Solidarité de la Famille dans le droit criminel en Grèce* (1904)
          [*Solidarité*]

— *The Greek City* (Eng. trans. 1929)

GOMME, A. W., *Commentary on Thucydides* (1945–56)   [*Comm. Thuc.*]

GRAHAM, A. J., *Colony and Mother City in Ancient Greece* (1964)

HIGNETT, C., *A History of the Athenian Constitution* (1952)   [*HAC*]

JONES, A. H. M., *Athenian Democracy* (1957) (a collection of papers, mainly published earlier and revised)   [*AD*]

KANELLI, S., *Earth and Water* (1965) (a study of a modern Greek family from the inside)

'LICHT, H.' (Brandt, P.), *Sexual Life in Ancient Greece* (Eng. trans. 1932)   [*SL*]

LIPSIUS, J., *Das Attische Recht* (1915)

MACDOWELL, D. M., *Athenian Homicide Law* (1963)   [*Homicide*]

NILSSON, M. P., *History of Greek Religion* (1925)

SAVAGE, C. A., *The Athenian Family* (1907)

TOD, M. N., *A Selection of Greek Historical Inscriptions* (1933–48)   [*GHI*]

VAN EFFENTERRE, H., *La Crète et le Monde de Platon à Polybe* (1948)   [*Crète*]

VINOGRADOFF, P., *Outlines of Historical Jurisprudence*, II (1922)

WILAMOWITZ-MOELLENDORFF, V. VON, *Aristoteles und Athen* (1893)

WILLETTS, R. F., *Aristocratic Society in Ancient Crete* (1955)   [*ASC*]

WOLFF, H. J., *Marriage Law and Family Organization in Ancient Athens* (Traditio II) (1944)   [*MLAA*]

WYSE, W., *The Speeches of Isaeus* (1904)   [*SI*]

ZIMMERN, A., *Greek Commonwealth* (5th ed., 1931)

ANDREWS, A., *The Greeks* (1967)

This work, the first History of Greece to acknowledge the importance of the family, and of the legal structures of the Greeks, appeared only when this book was already in proof. Had it appeared earlier, it would have been used extensively, and cited many times in the Notes. For one issue on which I disagree with the author, see the Appendix at the end of the Notes.

NOTES

CHAPTER I

THE FAMILY IN THE CITY-STATE

1 *Politics* I, 1, 3–6 (1252A–B); I have cited the *Politics* throughout by the reference system used by H. Rackham in his Loeb edition (1959 reprint). I use the word οἶκος throughout this discussion in the belief that Aristotle did not see any difference between οἶκος and οἰκία for his purposes; see *Pol. loc. cit.* Fustel de Coulanges in *La Cité Antique* (2nd ed. 1866), the original, fundamental work, used the simile of a series of concentric circles to describe Greek society, with the family in the centre; for a criticism, G. Glotz, *The Greek City* (English translation 1929), 1–5

2 Quoting earlier writers, Charondas who called them ὁμοσίπυοι, Epimenides the Cretan ὁμόκαποι—or possibly ὁμόκαπνοι—which has reference not to the meal table, but to the family hearth, the centre of the household worship. For a discussion see F. Susemihl and R. D. Hicks' edition of Aristotle's *Politics* (1894), note *ad loc.* (p. 143)

3 Arist., *Pol.* I, 2, 2 (1253B): ἔστι δέ τι μέρος ὃ δοκεῖ τοῖς μὲν εἶναι οἰκονομία τοῖς δὲ μέγιστον μέρος αὐτῆς . . . λέγω δὲ περὶ τῆς καλουμένης χρηματιστικῆς. Oikos is equivalent to Latin *familia*, a totality of the family's human members and goods, M. I. Finley, *Studies in Land and Credit* [*SLC*], 40f

4 Arist., *Pol.* I, 2, 1 (1253B). A complete (τελεῖος) oikos consists of free persons and slaves . . . and among its parts are master and slave, husband and wife and father and children. *Cf.* Stobaeus LXVII, 25 (quoting Antipater, περὶ γάμου, second century BC): a fully successful life for the family (τελεῖος οἶκος καὶ βίος) cannot be achieved except with a wife and children, and *id.* 21 ff. taken from Hierocles, on marriage (περὶ γάμου, first–second century AD). W. L. Newman, *Politics of Aristotle* (1887) II, 131 f. The idea is as old as Homer; *Iliad* II, 701 speaks of the 'incomplete household' of Protesilaus (δόμος ἡμιτελής), who died without having procreated a son

5 On colonization as a means of coping with surplus population, (*e.g.*) A. Zimmern, *Greek Commonwealth* (5th ed. 1931), 319 ff. Greek mercenaries appear in Egypt in the mid-seventh century, Hdt. II, 152, 4; *cf.* M. N. Tod, *GHI* I (1946), 4 (early sixth century), also from Egypt; Alcaeus fr. 350 (E. Lobel & D. L. Page, 1955) as reconstructed by C. M. Bowra, *Greek*

Lyric Poetry (1961), 139, for Greek mercenaries in Babylon in the same age. Seafaring and colonization were a product of the settlement of city-states, N. G. L. Hammond, *History of Greece* (1959), Chapter 2. It cannot be without significance that the cities with the least land and best harbours and coastal positions were amongst the earliest and most vigorous colonizers; *cf.* Thuc. I, 15, 1. Colonists were not all volunteers; for pressure on each family to contribute to a colony see *SEG* IX, 3 (Cyrene), and Hdt. IV, 153: that famine was the basic cause here, A. J. Graham, *Colony and Mother-City* (1964), 41, note 3. For the refusal of a mother-city to receive back colonists, note the conditions of *SEG* IX, 3 (above), and the story in Plutarch, *Moralia*, 293A = *Greek Questions* 11. For the provision that colonists should be drawn from the two poorest classes only, Tod, *GHI* I, 44, lines, 40–42 (fifth century Athens). For Archilochus' decision to embark for Thasos through poverty, fr. 105 (F. Lassère and A. Bonnard 1958), Critias, fr. 165 (*id. Introduction*, cviii), but see also note 12 below

6 For the Homeric world, Chapter II below

7 Thuc. VI, 17, 2–3; they neither invest in equipping their land, nor engage in patriotic expenditures (on arms), and for new citizens' unwillingness to fight, Plutarch, *Timoleon* XXV, 4. The Parian colonists at Thasos were 'hommes déracinés, livrés à leur seule force, livrés à leurs passions, à leurs haines et à leurs deceptions'. J. Pouilloux, *Fondation Hardt Entretiens* X (1964), 23. For attempts within colonies to attach the colonists to the soil by making their allotments inalienable, Arist. *Pol.* II, 4, 4 (1266B); *cf. id.* VI, 2, 5 (1319A). Perhaps it was to counter this that colonists set great store on their links with their mother-city, Graham, *op. cit.*, 14ff, 17ff (evidence from Rhegium); *cf.* an appeal to their ancestors' tombs in their mother-city, Thuc. I, 26, 3

For continuing relations between colony and mother-city, see the Naupactus decree (Tod, *GHI* I, 24) which allows colonists to continue to enjoy succession-rights at home, and the families of colonists to succeed to them; Graham, *op. cit.*, Chapter IV. For a religious link, the Athenian colony at Brea, Tod, *GHI*, 44, Graham, *op. cit.*, 62; for other examples, and the Corcyreans' failure to maintain this as part of their disloyalty, *ibid.*, 159ff

8 For a recent account of Syracuse in this period see A. G. Woodhead, *The Greeks in the West* (1962), 87ff. These struggles, and transplantations of population at Syracuse had made it particularly hard to establish strong roots in the soil; *cf.* note 7 above

9 T. J. Dunbabin, *The Western Greeks* (1948), 68 ff, for an analytical account of the lawgivers in this area

10 T. J. Dunbabin, *op. cit.*, 359 ff

11 Alcaeus provides an example of a poet writing in a tradition of popular poetry in a local dialect (*i.e.* poetry in short and comparatively simple metrical patterns), C. M. Bowra, *Greek Lyric Poetry* (1961), Chapter IV.

Importance of parentage, fr. 72 E. Lobel & D. L. Page (=D14), line 11, whether Page's interpretation (*Sappho and Alcaeus* (1955), 171–9) or Bowra's (*op. cit.*, 148–9) be correct; ancestral possessions—'what my father and my father's father have grown old possessing'—and his 'rightful' place in the assembly (ἀγορά) and council (βόλλα) come to his mind in exile, fr. 130 Lobel & Page (=G2); for drinking and boys, Bowra *loc. cit.* Sappho also used a pre-existing tradition—colloquial language in wedding-songs (fr. 111 and 110 Lobel & Page)—but aristocratic attitudes include scorn for the countrified peasant-girl (fr. 57 Lobel & Page), and praise of her brother as holding the post of wine-pourer at the *prytaneion* (town hall) of Mytilene (Athenaeus X, 425A), whose holders were chosen for beauty of looks and nobility of birth. Bowra, *op. cit.* Chapter V, Page, *Sappho and Alcaeus*, 140 ff, A. R. Burn, *LA*, Chapter XII for recent discussions of Sappho and her society

12 M. I. Finley, *The Ancient Greeks* (1963), 92; individualistic poetry indicates a weakness (or absence) of *polis* (*i.e.* city-state) life. Archilochus provides evidence for an intermediate stage between the Homeric attitude to bastardy (pp. 42–3 below), and that of the classical *poleis* (pp. 103–4 below). G. Tarditti, 'La nuova epigraphe archilochea', *Parola del Passato* 1956, 124ff, has argued that Archilochus was not a bastard; N. M. Kontoleon and others in *Entretiens Hardt* X (1964), 77–8, 81–2, though as παῖς he may have been less than υἱός, M. Scherer, *loc. cit.* K. J. Dover (*ibid.*, 199–210) has pointed out the dangers of assuming too readily that fragmentary lyric poets are always speaking in their own person

13 Burn, *LA*, Chapter XIII. The tradition of elegiac poetry for political advocacy was well-founded, perhaps by Tyrtaeus in Sparta (late seventh century), K. J. Dover, *op. cit.*, 192–4; *cf.* also Solon in Athens (early sixth century); the genre is closely associated with that of wise sayings (or *gnomai*), which must also have been traditional, as was the whole vocabulary of epic hexameter poetry, in mainland Greece as well as the Aegean world; see J. A. Notopoulos, *Hesperia* 1960, 177 ff., and references there cited; *cf.* also D. L. Page's paper in *Entretiens Hardt* X and the discussion (pp. 119 ff)

14 For Athens in Solon's day, and his legislation, Chapter III below

15 Plut., *Themistocles* I–III; his mother was certainly not an Athenian. If the version that her name was Abrotonon is true, she may well have been a slave; this would make Themistocles the bastard (νόθος) which he is always described as being. He rejected the aristocrats' social accomplishments of music and singing in favour of the public (aristocratic) activities of speaking and public affairs. If his family belonged to the *genos* of Lycomidae (as is probable) it may have been a subordinate branch, excluded from leadership. See also below, p. 90

16 *E.g. Laws* 923A, where Plato claims that 'neither the members (of his ideal state) nor their possessions belong to themselves, but to the whole of

their *genos*, past and future (σύμπαντος δὲ τοῦ γένους ὑμῶν τοῦ τε ἔμπροσθεν καὶ τοῦ ἔπειτα ἐσομένου); and even more does the whole genos belong to the city, with all its possessions' (καὶ ἔτι μᾶλλον τῆς πόλεως εἶναι τό τε γένος πᾶν καὶ τὴν οὐσίαν)

17 *Pol.* I, 5, 3 (1259B): οἰκονομία is more concerned with the humans than with the inanimate, and with the free rather than with the slaves: πλείων ἡ σπουδὴ . . . περὶ τοὺς ἀνθρώπους ἢ περὶ τὴν τῶν ἀψύχων κτῆσιν, καὶ περὶ τὴν ἀρετὴν τούτων . . . καὶ τῶν ἐλευθέρων μᾶλλον ἢ δούλων

18 *Pol.* I, 5, 1–2 (1259A–B)

19 Many of the speeches which have come down to us under the name of Demosthenes were quite certainly not written by him, but for their use as evidence, see preface, p. 10

20 Dem. XXVII, 53–5, *id.* XLV, 74; Hypereides, Budé edn. 138, Loeb edn. (*Minor Attic Orators* II) Lycophron II, frag. 1 (=Pap. Oxy. XIII, 1607). Athenian women were *kyriai* of up to one medimnos of barley, for whose value, L. J. Th. Janssens, *Mnemosyne* 1941 (series III, 9), 199–214

21 At Gortyn this right has been asserted, but, though the produce of the land (ἐπικαρπία or καρπός), the movable possessions (κρήματα) and what a woman has woven (κότι ἐνύπανε) are disposable by a woman, the house (στέγα) seems to be disposable only with her; see also Chapter VIII below

22 V. Ehrenberg, *The Greek State* (1960), 30. A. H. M. Jones, *Athenian Democracy* (1957) (*AD* hereafter) Chapter IV, especially 79–81; *cf.* Dem. XXII, 65=XXIV, 172 for the more prosperous

23 For the earliest (*i.e.* Homeric) times, Chapter II below. For land-division at the Athenian colony of Brea, Tod, *GHI* I, 44, 6–11; 'as dividers of the land there are to be elected ten men, one from each tribe; they are to divide up the land . . . and the portion of land that has been set apart for the use of the Gods (*temenē*) is to be kept as it is, but new *temenē* are not to be made'

24 As at Corinth, Arist. *Pol.* II, 3, 7 (1265B). Spartan *klaroi* (Doric for *kleroi*) do not seem to have been identical in size either. For equal *kleroi*, Plato, *Laws* 744B (as an unattainable ideal); *cf.* Phaleas of Chalcedon, Arist. *Pol.* II, 4, 1–2 (1266A)

25 *Pol.* VI, 2, 5 (1319A), *q.v.* also for a prohibition on lending money on the security of land; for conditional sales at Locri *id.* II, 4, 4 (1266B)

26 *Id.* II, 3, 7 (1265B), Corinth; II, 9, 7 (1274B), Thebes

27 For Solon, W. J. Woodhouse, *Solon the Liberator* (1938), 74ff, 199; Naphthali Lewis, *AJP* 1941, 144ff, criticized by J. V. A. Fine, *Hesperia Suppl.* IX, 1951, 179ff; for Cleisthenes, J. H. Oliver, *Historia* 1960, 505; for the Peloponnesian War, N. G. L. Hammond, *JHS* 1961, 98, and Fine *loc. cit.* For the evidence provided by the *horoi*, *cf.* M. I. Finley, *Studies in Land and Credit* (1951), 7, 200, note 26, *et al.* H. Swoboda, *Zeitschr. d.*

Savigny-Stiftung 1905, 236–45, argued for alienability before Solon; so W. G. Forrest, *EGD* 148–9, A. Andrewes, *The Greeks* (1967); see Appendix

28 Prohibition of the sale or mortgage of particular pieces of land (*e.g.* those owned by religious and other associations) is also found later, Hammond, *op. cit.*, 87. Plato proposed that the *kleroi* in his Republic should be inalienable, *Laws* 740A–B, 741A–B, 923C ff

29 *Op. cit.*, 84–5; *q.v.* also (87) for the earliest recorded examples of confiscation and permission to acquire land in Attica. *Cf. Pl. 46*

30 For ostracism, O. W. Reinmuth, E. Seewald, *RE* XVIII.2 (1942), 1674–85. R. J. Bonner and G. Smith, *The Administration of Justice from Homer to Aristotle* (*Justice* hereafter) (1930), 193–5. For other references, *RE loc. cit.*

31 Plato, *Laws* 923A, cited note 16 above

32 Diog. La. III, 41–2; 'The following is the property left by Plato and his disposition: the land in the deme Iphistiadae . . . nobody is to have the right to sell it or to alienate it, but it is to be the property of the boy Adeimantus to all intents and purposes; also the land in the deme Eiresidae, which I bought from Callimachus . . . three minae of silver, etc.' τὸ ἐν Ἰφιστιαδῶν χωρίον. . . . μὴ ἐξέστω τοῦτο μηδενὶ μήτε ἀποδόσθαι μήτε ἀλλάξασθαι ἀλλ᾽ ἔστω Ἀδειμάντου τοῦ παιδίου εἰς τὸ δυνατόν, καὶ τὸ ἐν Εἰρεσιδῶν χωρίον ὃ παρὰ Καλλιμάχου ἐπριάμην . . . . Adeimantus was Plato's nephew; the disposition of the estate which he bought is not clearly stated in Diogenes' version— probably it should be understood that it was to go to Adeimantus without the specific prohibitions against sale or alienation: I have translated the sentence in this sense

33 *E.g.* Dinarchus, *in Demosthenem*, 71

34 *E.g.* Aeschines I, 96–101

35 One exception has been quoted: in Crete in the mid-fifth century, but the inscription distinguishes between property (χρήματα) and land (χώρα) in the relevant sections (V and VI); Tod, *GHI*, I, 33, 23–6. In ownership we must include the right of disposal; for this reason only adults of military age can be counted as citizens for this purpose. Neither a woman nor a minor could dispose of land

36 J. H. Lipsius, *Das Attische Recht* (1915), 482, 'steht die Frau in allen rechtlichen Beziehungen lebenslänglich unter Geschlechtsvormundschaft'; before marriage it goes without saying that girls were in parental *kyrieia*

37 Nor, specifically, in Plato's ideal state. For Sparta see also Chapter VIII below

38 *Epikleros* (ἐπίκληρος) is the Attic word; in Gortyn she was called πατρωϊῶκος (code VII, 15–16 et al.), in Sparta πατροῦχος if the text of Hdt. VI, 57 is correct. For the various regulations at Athens and Gortyn see Chapters VI, VIII below

39 Aeschines I, 95; on such accusations, Chapter III below, and for ἐπικλήρου κάκωσις p. 141 below

40 *Iliad* IX, 493–5 is sometimes quoted in this sense; there is no suggestion of succession to property however; the childless Phoenix is shown as concerned with obtaining protection in old age. His ancestral property was at his father's house, whence he had exiled himself, *id.* 446–80. A more likely-looking case is that of Iphidamas; see p. 40 below. In Athens, adoption *inter vivos* was possible before Solon; Dem. XLVI, 14, see p. 88 below. *Cf.* L. Gernet, *La Loi de Solon sur le testament, Rev. Ét. Gr.* 1920, revised and reprinted in *Pub. de l'Inst. de droit romain de l'Univ. de Paris* 1955, *Droit et Société dans la Grèce Ancienne, (D. et S.* hereafter)

41 Dem. XLIV, 36–42. It must be remembered that it was in the speaker's interest in this case to assume that this was so; the speaker's veracity must therefore be doubted. See also below, Chapter VI

42 Except for brothels and similar establishments, but women of this class were, in Athens, not normally of citizen-families; even they would therefore have to have a male protector (προστάτης)—Zobia in Dem. XXV, 56–8, for example, or Neaira's protectors, *id.* LIX, 37ff

43 Dem. XXIV, 107, Diog. La. I, 55 etc. See also pp. 116–8 below

44 Plato, *Laws*, 775E–776B

45 Harpocration s.v. γεννῆται: οἱ τοῦ αὐτοῦ γένους κοινωνοῦντες . . . οὐχ οἱ συγγενεῖς μέντοι ἁπλῶς καὶ οἱ ἐξ αἵματος γεννῆταί τε καὶ ἐκ τοῦ αὐτοῦ γένους ἐκαλοῦντο, ἀλλ' οἱ ἐξ ἀρχῆς εἰς τὰ καλούμενα γένη κατανεμηθέντες

Cf. Pollux VIII, 111, quoted note 50 below. For a *genos* which had become a mere religious association, W. S. Ferguson, *Hesperia* 1938, 1 ff, on the Salaminioi of Heptaphylae and Sounium. For *genē* artificially created by revolution in Samos, G. Busolt, *Gr. Staatskunde* (1920), 260, note 3, *q.v.* for references

46 V. Ehrenberg, *The Greek State*, (1960), 13; 'The *genos* . . . as a product of settled conditions, . . . the means by which the nobles exercised themselves politically.' It was, however, in my view more fundamental and more important than this; *cf.* Forrest, *EGD* 50ff

47 N. G. L. Hammond, *JHS* 1961, 77f, *q.v.* also for the view that the term came to be used more loosely. For a different view of Eupatridae, H. T. Wade-Gery, *CQ* 1931, 1ff

48 For the view that this reflects an originally matriarchal society, M. Miller, *JHS* 1953, 46–52

49 *Odyssey*, 21, 214–16; in return for their help in defeating the suitors of Penelope in battle Eumaeus and Philoitius are promised by Odysseus that they will be called the 'brothers and comrades' of Telemachus (ἑτάρω τε κασιγνήτω τε ἔσεσθον)

50 Pollux, VIII, 111; some γεννῆται were γένει μὲν οὐ προσήκοντες ἐκ δὲ τῆς συνόδου οὕτω προσαγορευόμενοι. There can be no doubt that even the slaves were fully part of the *oikos* by association; see pp. 30–1 below.

51 For Homeric times, note 49; that these were not real *gennētai*, Hammond,

op. cit., 79, though even he seems to agree that ultimately they were called *gennētai*. Poor men put themselves under the protection of a powerful noble for safety, giving labour or services in return, Forrest, *EGD* 150

52 *Athenaion Politeia*, frag. 5 [hereafter quoted as *Ath. Pol.*]. This work was attributed in ancient times to Aristotle, and belongs without reasonable doubt to the collection of constitutions assembled in Aristotle's lifetime in his school. For the view that it is by a pupil, C. Hignett, *A History of the Athenian Constitution* (1952) (*HAC* hereafter), 28-30. A recent bibliography in J. Day and M. Chambers, *Aristotle's History of Athenian Democracy* (1962). The fragment survives in the schol. to Plato, *Axiochus* 371E, Harpocration, s.v. γεννῆται etc. *Cf.* Hammond, *JHS* 1961, 77; this view on the text of *Ath. Pol.*, frag. 5 and Harpocration must be right

53 οἱ ἐγγυτάτω γένους; also οἱ ἐγγυτάτω γένει, and other variants. W. Wyse, *Speeches of Isaeus* (1904) (*SI* hereafter), 612 (note on VIII, 33, 3, 4)

54 Further support comes from the (admittedly late) phrase 'the *gennētai* of Apollo Patroös and Zeus Herkeios', Dem. LVII, 67, where the two cults of kin and locality are associated. For the meaning of this phrase, A. Andrewes, *JHS* 1961, 3 ff, especially 7 f

55 *Iliad* II, 362-3 in the form φρήτρη, as the subdivisions of the tribe (φῦλον). It is usually assumed that Homeric φῦλον and φρήτρη may be identified with the Attic φυλή and φρατρία, though this has not been undisputed; in Athens, even after the Cleisthenic reorganization, the φυλαί were the basis of the army organization

56 Note 52 above. For the use of ἀφρήτωρ (the man without phratry, *Iliad* IX, 63-4) of the outcast, Hignett, *HAC*, 55, *q.v.* for a discussion of the Athenian phratries' origins and functions

57 Hignett, *HAC*, 58-9

58 Ehrenberg, *op. cit.*, 13; a group of *genē*, Forrest, *EGD* 50-51; a group of 'patrai', Schwyzer 323 (Delphi)

59 A. Andrewes, *JHS* 1961, 14

60 Note that in the scenes from everyday life in Homer as depicted on Achilles' shield, the one really civic activity was a homicide trial, *Iliad* XVIII, 497-508; wedding-celebrations formed the other part of the scene, but the public were spectators, not participants, *id.* 491-6

61 Tod, *GHI* I, 87, restored from Dem. XLIII, 57 *et al.* For the phratry's part in homicide proceedings, D. M. MacDowell, *Athenian Homicide Law* (1963), 18, 27, 124 (*Homicide* hereafter)

62 Ehrenberg, *loc. cit.* In Classical times, and from the earlier period too, *hetaireiai* were associated with political action—G. M. Calhoun, *Athenian Clubs in Politics and Litigation* (1913). The political aspects of these clubs have been more stressed than the military, but the wish to have trusty friends as neighbours in the battle-line must have been as strong an incentive as political aspirations. It must not be forgotten that the poorest class did not serve in the army

63 Thuc. VII, 75,4; Xen. *Anabasis* V, 8, 5 and 6 etc., and see Liddell and Scott (9th edition, *LSJ* hereafter) for other examples and inscriptional evidence. Xenophon also uses similar words for the Spartan common life, *Lacedaimoniorum Politeia* (*Lac. Pol.*) V, 2 and XIII, 1; *cf. Hellenica* (*H.G.*) III, 2, 8; V, 3, 20. A pariah to whom nobody would be σύσκηνος, Lysias XIII, 79

64 The organization of the ἐφηβία in Athens is not known before the fourth century, Thalheim, *RE* V, (1905), 2737–41, *s.v.* ἐφηβία ; it was instituted after Chaeroneia, perhaps in 336/5, A. Brenot, *Recherches sur L'Éphébie Attique*, 1910, 41. For the performance of their duties as περίπολοι in the fifth century, A. W. Gomme, *Commentary on Thucydides* (1956), (*Comm. Thuc.* hereafter) note on IV, 67, 2. There is no information on the organization of training for 'the youngest', who fought with Myronides in 458–7 (Thuc. I, 105, 4), but it must be taken that there existed some organization for this purpose

65 Ehrenberg, *op. cit.*, 16; *cf.* M. P. Nilsson, *History of Greek Religion* (1925), 202 ff, 'No such unity as we find in Greece between state and religion has ever existed elsewhere . . . State and religion were one.'

66 For Zeus Herkeios, Nilsson, *op. cit.*, 125, O. Jessen, *RE* VIII (1913), 686 ff. A. B. Cook, *Zeus* III (1940), 243. Nilsson, *op. cit.*, 123 ff for the importance of Zeus in the worship of the family and its means of subsistence as Zeus Ktesios. *Cf.* Cook, *Zeus* II, II, Appx. H. and Nilsson, *op. cit.*, 35 and *Ath. Mitt.* XXXIII, 1908, 279 ff. For Zeus Meilichios, Cook, *id.*, Appx. M; note the presence of the whole family at worship in the two sculptures illustrated by Cook (p. 1106) reproduced in *Pls. 2–3*

67 Apollo was above all the deity of the organized *polis*, but only in Athens among Ionic communities; he has connexions there with phratries (*CIA* 2, 1652) and with *genē* (*CIA* 4, 1074e), having respectively a shrine (ἵερον) and a *temenos*. L. R. Farnell, *Cults of the Greek States* (1907) IV, 152–61

68 Zeus Phratrios, Plato, *Euthydemus* 302C: 'to all Athenians whether at home or emigrant Zeus is not called Patroös, but Herkeios and Phratrios'. Farnell *op. cit.* I, 55. He was closely associated with Athene in the worship of the phratries, schol. on Aristophanes, *Acharnians* 146; associated with Zeus Herkeios, Cratinus Jun., frag. 9 (Edmonds) = Meinecke, *Frag. Com. Gr.* III, 377. The editors' differing accentuations of ἐστὶ prove that they interpret the sense differently. Zeus was Patroös and Poseidon Phratrios at Delphi, Schwyzer 323, B12–6

69 *Ath. Pol.* LV is not specific that this form of *dokimasia* was only for candidates for the archonships, though its introduction at this point in the work would suggest it. It is clear that all office-bearers had to undergo some form of *dokimasia*

70 Plato, *Euthydemus* 302C–D, *q.v.* for the belief in the common descent of all Athenians from the gods, so that they can be called 'ancestors and lords' (πρόγονοι καὶ δεσπόται).

71 Though many modern scholars believe that it was in fact necessary.

Ehrenberg (e.g.), op. cit., 23, remarks that the most important duty of the phratries was to watch over admittance to citizenship; M. P. Nilsson, op. cit., 245, assumes that phratries were necessary. For another view, A. Andrewes, JHS 1961, 1 ff

72 Arist. Pol. VI, 2, 11 (1319B); Nilsson, op. cit., 246. 'Other tribes (φυλαί) must be created larger in number than the old ones (πλείους), and phratries (φρατρίαι), and the rites of the private cults (τὰ τῶν ἰδίων ἱερῶν) must be amalgamated into a few common to all' (εἰς ὀλίγα καὶ κοινά). This is the origin of the Attic Genesia, F. Jacoby, CQ 1944, 65–75

73 Philochorus, Jacoby, FGH 328, 67, Homer A. Thompson, Hesperia 1937, 110. Note the association of this altar with a complex of buildings associated with Zeus Phratrios and Athene Phratria, Thompson op. cit., 104 ff, and the association of the three divinities in the literary sources noted

74 E.g. those of Elasiadae, IG ii², 2602, Gephyraioi, id. 3629–30

75 Harpocration, s.v. ἑρκεῖος Zeus, Photius, s.v. ἑρκείου Διός, schol. on Plato, Euthydemus 302D. Nilsson believed that one effect of city-life was to supersede Zeus Herkeios by the gods of the street, op. cit., 125

76 IG ii², 1237 (= W. Dittenberger, SIG³ (SIG hereafter), 921). Whether they were a phratry or a genos is fully discussed by Andrewes, loc. cit.; it makes no difference to this argument. If they were a genos, not a phratry, the unifying power of Zeus Phratrios is even more signally stressed

77 This must be assumed from the regulations about 'where the Deceleans gather', lines 61–64, 115 ff; cf. Lysias XXIII, 3. It is also by no means certain that the lesser sacrifice (τὸ μεῖον) had to be made at the Apatouria; cf. Isaeus VII, 15 for the presentation of an adopted son at the Thargelia. Schwyzer 323, 23–28 for the rules at Delphi

78 Nilsson, op. cit., 244–8, especially 247; cf. Sterling Dow BCH 1965, 197 ff for this process in operation in the deme Erkhia, q.v. also for the process at Eleusis

79 Gortyn code V, 10–29. Collaterals are 'those to whom succession falls in regard to the source of the money—'οἷς ἂν ἐπιβάλλῃ ὅποθεν ἂν ᾖ τὰ χρήματα. The final category reads (Atticized) εἰ δὲ μὴ εἶεν ἐπιβάλλοντες τῆς οἰκίας οἵτινες ἂν ὦσι ὁ κλῆρος τούτους ἔχειν τὰ χρήματα. It is clear that there could not be a failure of these latter, since someone must compose the klaros (Attic kleros); unfortunately the rules for succession to klaroi are quite unknown from the code, including the degree to which 'those who compose the klaros' were free or semi-free persons, though they are generally assumed by scholars to have been serfs; see Chapter VIII below. They are obviously not the same as 'any member of the tribe (φυλή) who asks', who is the husband appointed for the girl who has no heirs at law (ἐπιβάλλοντες), code VII, 50–2

80 ἀνεψίων παῖδες, known also as ἀνεψιαδοῖ/αῖ; these latter words first appear at the end of the fifth century in the comedians (LSJ, s.v.)

81 For burial, Dem. XLIII, 57–8. For homicide, Dem. *loc. cit.*, XLVII, 72, etc., see D. M. MacDowell, *Homicide*, 12–18 etc. For Plato's choice, *Laws* 865A ff

82 The estate of Hagnias (Isaeus XI, Dem. XLIII) was certainly awarded to a second cousin (a son of the deceased's father's first cousin) who constantly talks about himself as if he were within the *anchisteia*, Isaeus XI, 10–11. Whether this was due to the orator's skilful misrepresentations, or confusion of mind and inattentiveness among the jurors, or a genuine doubt about the strict meaning of the law is unascertainable. Most commentators assume the first

83 Thuc. II, 16–7 for the forced migration of the country-dwellers to the city in 431; it is clear that many had no *pied-à-terre* in the city

84 For the plague, Thuc. II, 47–54, especially 51 for the losses; Gomme, *Comm. Thuc. II* (1956), notes *ad loc.*, especially pp. 150 ff, for a recent discussion. On Athenian citizen-numbers, A. W. Gomme, *The Population of Athens in the Fifth and Fourth Centuries* (1933), A. H. M. Jones, *AD*, Chapter IV, the Social Structure

85 As in the *Iliad*, for example, Agamemnon was both commander in chief and conducted sacrifices on behalf of the army as its priest, *Il.* II, 402–418; contrast the individuals' sacrifices for themselves, *id.* 400–1; see also *id.* III, 245–313, where Agamemnon and Priam, the two kings, make sacrifices and take oaths

86 Bonner and Smith, *Justice* I, 67 ff for a summary of their activities. That the laws were the basis of society is a favourite platitude of the orators of the fourth century

87 Ehrenberg *op. cit.*, 79; γραφαί (public suits) are quite clearly distinct from δίκαι (private suits)

88 Aeschylus, *Agamemnon* 1035–8. Cassandra is called within the palace to take a part in the family libation, 'standing near the altar of Zeus Ktesios with many (other) slaves', J. D. Denniston and D. L. Page, *Aeschylus, Agamemnon* (1957), note *ad loc.*; cf. Aristophanes, *Lys.* 1129–30; those who sacrifice together are 'kinsmen' by reason of the sacrifice. Since all Greeks are included, the sense of kinsmen (συγγενεῖς) cannot be literal. For the libation as being the family-rite *par excellence*, Sophocles, *Oedipus Tyrannus* 240–2, Dem. XX, 158

89 Dem. XLV, 74, Aristophanes, *Plutus* 768 and scholiast *ad loc.*, Harpocration s.v. καταχύσματα

90 Even that of Zeus Ktesios, Antiphon I, 16–18, and the clear implication of Isaeus VIII, 16. For an introduction to the religion of the family, M. P. Nilsson, *Greek Popular Religion* (1940), 65 ff, though A. B. Cook, *Zeus* II, II (1925), 1127, denies that the guardian spirit of the family, the Agathos Daimon, was thought of as a snake until Hellenistic times

91 Arist. *Pol.* I, 1, 6 (1252B). *Cf. Exodus* XX, 17: 'thou shalt not covet thy neighbour's house . . . (nor his) wife, nor his manservant nor his

maid-servant nor his ox nor his ass nor any thing that is thy neighbour's.' The named things are, with the land, what most especially constitute the *oikos*

92 γεωργὸς καὶ τῶν ἐν ἀνθρώποις καμάτων κοινωνός, Aelian, *Varia Historia* V, 14

93 Aristophanes, *Acharn.* 1018-36

94 Ehrenberg, *op. cit.*, 68. For the 'divine guests', the Dioskouroi, the sons of Zeus, supposed to attend every family meal, Nilsson, *op. cit.*, 124

95 Aeschines III, 224; II, 22 etc. For the man with whom 'nobody will share fire or light or food or drink', Dem. XXV, 61

For the interpretation of Helen as the betrayer of ξενία, the rights and duty of a *xenos*—Alcaeus fr. 283 Lobel & Page (= N1) and the roughly contemporary Stesichorus, on whom C. M. Bowra, *Greek Lyric Poetry* (1961), Chapter III. *Cf.*, in the seventh century, an oath 'by the salt', Archilochus fr. 95 Diehl

96 Zeus Hikesios A. B. Cook, *Zeus II, III*, 1093ff; for an interpretation in tragedy, Aeschylus, *Supplices*. For harbouring a goddess in disguise, Homer, *Od.* 17, 483-7; *cf.* Homeric *Hymn to Demeter*, H. J. Rose, *Handbook of Greek Mythology* (1928), 92, and, for later treatments, *id.* 99, note 57. For benefits derived from harbouring a hero, Sophocles, *Oedipus Coloneus* etc.

CHAPTER II

THE FAMILY IN HOMERIC SOCIETY

1 In this book it is assumed that the Homeric poems portray a society which the Greeks of the classical period believed to have been that of their ancestors, and that this society is generally consistent in the values it held, and the customs it practised which affect the family, and its property. Such differences as appear (*e.g.* pp. 42-3, below) may be explicable by a change in viewpoint, the family being in general viewed from the inside in the *Odyssey*, from the outside in the *Iliad*. Modern specialist literature on the Homeric poems is so vast that I have decided to omit virtually all references to it, believing that students should approach Homer for themselves

2 *Od.* 13, 42-6; *cf. ib.* 61-2 (to Arete); for the sake of clarity books of the *Iliad* will be designated by Roman numerals, books of the *Odyssey* by Arabic

3 *Il.* III, 299-301

4 Phoenix, *Il.* IX, 453-6; for his attempt to obtain a warrior to protect his old age, *ib.* 493-5. *Cf.* Cisses and Iphidamas, *Il.* XI, 221-6, below p. 40;

Elpenor, *Od.* 11, 66–8; *cf.* Odysseus' oath, *Il.* II, 259–60 'May my head no longer remain on my shoulders, and may I no longer be called the father of Telemachus'—*i.e.* may he die, too

5 *Od.* 4, 207–11; *cf.* Nestor's prayer (*Od.* 3, 380–1) for himself, his children and his wife; Odysseus' prayer, *Od.* 19, 367–8

6 *Il.* XXIV, 534–40; *cf.* Priam, *ib.* 543–551 with 493–501, destined to lose all his wealth, and his sons in battle. *Cf.* his fears for all his family, in XXII, 60–5

7 *Il.* XIX, 321–33; *cf. Od.* 4, 224–6, death of mother or father, or the sight of brother or son slain in battle—contrast Achilles' shade's joy even in Hades at the account of his son's prowess, *Od.* 11, 505–40

8 *Od.* 11, 489–91

9 *Il.* XV, 494–9; note the inclusion of houses and lands. *Cf. Il.* VIII, 55–8, XXI, 586–9 and IX, 325–7, men defending their own women-folk and children are proverbial for stout resistance; the same idea is clearly implied in Sarpedon's criticism of the Trojans in *Il.* V, 472–92; *cf.* his appeal for help, *ib.* 684–8

10 *Il.* IX, 590–4; *cf.* Andromache's lament for Hector (*Il.* XXIV, 725–38), or his fears for her should Troy fall (*Il.* VI, 447–465); also Hyperenor, who 'did not return home to delight his wife and parents', *Il.* XVII, 28

10a *Il.* XIV, 484–5 and p. 48 with note 89 below. *Il.* V, 152–8 shows the succession of χηρωσταί; see p. 46 with note 73 below. Above (Chapter I, n. 46) for the view that the *genos* is a product of the life of a settled community

11 Diomedes for example appears under his own name 87 times in the *Iliad*, he is called son of Tydeus 98 times (Tydeides 69, son of Tydeus 29); on the other hand Achilles appears over 350 times, son of Peleus about 110 times. The argument must not be pressed too far, since metrical considerations will always have affected the poet's choice also

12 The proportion varies very widely in different parts of the *Iliad*. In the opening battle (IV, 457–V, 84), 14 warriors are killed; of these only 2, one Greek, one Trojan, lack patronymic, but both are described (Leucus was 'comrade of Odysseus', Odius was 'chief of the Alizones'); of the 12 with patronymics, we know of 11 fathers, 1 grandfather as well, and the loss to their families of two is vividly stressed. In the battle over Patroclus' body (*Il.* XVII, 288–355), all 5 heroes who fell in the first clash have patronymic, of whom the first is said not to have repaid his parents for his upbringing. In Achilles' opening battle, 3 of the 4 heroes whom he slew before the abortive duel with Hector have patronymic, after the duel 6 out of 10. In two battles, Diomedes' first sally (V, 144–165), and Agamemnon's first sally (XI, 91–144), the first two victims lack patronymic, the others (6 for Diomedes, 4 for Agamemnon) are described; in both accounts they are pairs of brothers and reference is made to the parents when the second pair fell. In Patroclus' sally (XVI, 284–350), in the first list only 3 out of 10

have any biographical details, two of whom (brothers) fell to Nestor's sons; their father is named as the man who kept the Chimaera; Patroclus' victim was merely 'leader of the Paeonians; in the second list, before Patroclus met Sarpedon, the figures are 2 patronymics out of 9. In these lists there seems an unusual lack of interest both in the victims slain and in the ways they died

13 Glaucus, *Il.* VI, 145–211; Aeneas, *Il.* XX, 200–41

14 Isaeus VIII, 32 for these limits of kin

15 Achilles, *Il.* XXI, 188–9; Idomeneus, XIII, 448–53; *cf.* Crethon and Orsilochus (victims of Aeneas), two generations from the River Alpheius, V, 541–9

16 Diomedes, *Il.* XIV, 113–27; Telemachus, *Od.* 16, 117–20, *cf.* 14, 180–2; Theoclymenus, *Od.* 15, 225–56

17 On Catalogue Poetry as one of the streams in the traditions of oral poetry, G. S. Kirk, *Songs of Homer* (1962), 162 f, 223–6 etc.

18 Telemachus, *Od.* 24, 506–9; Glaucus, *Il.* VI, 207–10

19 On the *agathos* (ἀγαθός) and his standards of conduct and achievement, A. W. H. Adkins, *Merit and Responsibility* (1960), especially Chapter III

20 *Il.* VI, 441–6; *cf.* VIII, 146–50 (Diomedes), XI, 408–10 (Odysseus), XII, 310–21 (Sarpedon), XIII, 260–73 (Idomeneus and Meriones)

21 *Il.* XV, 661–6; αἰδώς (aidos) is the sentiment which prevents a man from doing a thing of which he would afterwards be ashamed or embarrassed. *Cf. Il.* V, 529–32 (=XV, 561–4)

22 This applies not merely to the *Iliad*, where it might be expected (*e.g.* IX, 328–67, especially 364–7, XVIII, 28 etc.), but Odysseus' possessions also are said to have been acquired by plunder, *Od.* 1, 397–8; *cf.* 23, 355–8, where it is said that Odysseus will recover his wealth by plunder

23 For the irrelevance of this to the story of the Iliad, D. L. Page, *History and the Homeric Iliad* (1959), Chapter IV

24 Telemachus' mastership, *Od.* 1, 396–8, 402–3 etc.; the assembly, *Od.* 2, 26–9 with 1, 372–5 and 384–7; the kingship and Odysseus' *oikos*, *Od.* 1, 389–404, *JHS* 1966, 61 ff

25 *Od.* 2, 252–6, and 318–20 for the fact that they had refused him, *id.* 382–7 for the personal character of the following; *id.* 253–6 for the supposition that it might be Mentor or Halitherses who might raise it, if anyone, and *id.* 306–8 for Antenor's patronizing, probably sarcastic, assurance

26 *Od.* 4, 642–72

27 But in *Il.* XVII, 220–6 Hector claims that he and the Trojans provide their allies with gifts and food supplies 'in order that they may defend the Trojans' wives and children from the Achaeans'. In *Od.* 4, 171–80, Menelaus tells how he had urged Odysseus to migrate to his domains with his family and possessions; the vital importance of the means of subsistence is very noticeable

28 Priam's sons-in-law, *Il.* VI, 247–50; Hector's claim, V, 473–4. Amongst

Priam's recruits for the defence of Troy are Imbrius, husband of Medicaste, a bastard daughter, XIII, 170–6, and Melanippus, XV, 545–54; Democoön was a bastard son of Priam's own, IV, 499

29 Othryoneus, *Il.* XIII, 365–6; Achilles, *Il.* IX, 283–9; cf. Neoptolemos *Od.* 4, 5–7; Bellerophon, *Il.* VI, 191–3; Tydeus *Il.* XIV, 119–25; the Cretan, *Od.* 14, 211–13; Odysseus, *Od.* 7, 311–16, *JHS* 1966, 59–61

30 *Il.* XI, 221–6 and 241–5, *JHS, ibid.*

31 Megapenthes, *Od.* 4, 10–12; Achilles, *Il.* IX, 393–400. The bard assumes that heroes' sons, especially only sons, will marry, and thus ensure the continuation of the family; cf. Helen's assumption that the 21-year-old Telemachus will marry, *Od.* 15, 125–9. In the *Odyssey*, princesses (*e.g.* Nausicaa) are in fact represented as having some say in their choice of husband; *Od.* 6, 280–4 implies this, though it is only what a base fellow (κακώτερος) might say (*id.* 275); *id.* 27–30 imply that she will in fact soon marry

32 *Il.* XXI, 82–9 and XXII, 49–51; Altes came from Pedasus, which does not appear at all in the Trojan catalogue. Page (*op. cit.*, 143 f) has argued that it was quite an important place, but very peripheral to the world of the *Iliad. Cf.* Castianeira, *Il.* VIII, 304–5

33 *Od.* 11, 287–91 and 15, 235–8

34 A plot, *Od.* 24, 164–9; a challenge, *Od.* 19, 572–81; for consciousness of waste, *Od. passim*

35 W. K. Lacey, *JHS*, 1966, 55 ff. Hephaestus obtained Aphrodite from Zeus her father by the *hedna* (ἔδνα and ἔεδνα are the same) which he gave (*Od.* 8, 318–20), and Neleus obtained Chloris from Amphion by 'countless *hedna*' (*Od.* 11, 281–4)

36 M. I. Finley, *Marriage, Sale and Gift in the Homeric World* (*Rev. Int. des droits de l'antiquité*), 3, vol. 2 (1955), 167ff

37 It was a mark of Odysseus' rank that Laertes obtained μύρια ἔδνα for Ctimene (*Od.* 15, 367), and πόλλα would have to be paid back to Icarius if Penelope were sent back to him against her will (*Od.* 2, 132–3), and of Hector's that he gave μύρια ἔδνα for Andromache (*Il.* XXII, 472). The marriage of Hippodameia and Alcathous is interesting (*Il.* XIII, 427–33) in that the bard states it as a matter of course that the 'best' man in Troy should marry the girl who was 'outstanding in her circle for her beauty and skill and intelligence'. In the simile in *Il.* XXII, 126–8 the sort of flirtation described between the boy and the girl was not necessarily a prelude to marriage

38 The fact that the offers to Achilles and Othryoneus were ἀνάεδνον—without *hedna*—in circumstances in which *hedna* would have been expected, since the brides were to go to their husbands' houses, shows that *hedna* belong only to marriages into the husband's *oikos*

39 Also for 'other girls', *Od.* 21, 159–62; for Nausicaa, *Od.* 6, 158–9

40 This is not to deny that there may have been a time when to do this was

the suitors' intention; it is probable that there was, but there would have been no *hedna* offered, and in any case such a situation antedates the *Odyssey*

41 Laertes, *Od.* I, 429–33; Chryseis, *Il.* I, 111–15; Phoenix, *Il.* IX, 448–52

42 Menelaus, *Od.* 4, 10–14; *Cf.* Odysseus' tale of the bastard Cretan, *Od.* 14 199–213

43 *Il.* IX, 336, 663–5 and 340–3

44 Before Agamemnon took her away Briseis was Achilles' wife (ἄλοχος) in the sense of his 'bed-mate' already. Her lament, *Il.* XIX, 295–9

45 *Il..* XVI, 179–92 and 175–8 for Polymele and Polydora, mothers of captains of the Myrmidons; other bastard warriors are Boucolion (*Il.* VI, 23–4), Medon, bastard son of Oileus (*Il..* XV, 333–6), and Pedaeus (*Il.* V, 70–1), all of whom were spearmen. Telamon's bastard son Teucrus was only a bowman (*Il.* VIII, 283–4), unlike Ajax his great brother; Isus was his legitimate brother's charioteer (*Il.* XI, 101–4), as Cebriones was Hector's (*Il.* XVI, 737–9)

46 That these were real marriages, Finley, *op. cit.*, 170–1 for Helen: for Clytemnestra, *Od.* I, 36, W. K. Lacey, *JHS* 1966, 62–3, where the situation is discussed and it is pointed out that the poet says 'he wed her' of both husbands (ἔγημε) and Aegisthus 'took her (Clytemnestra) to his house' (ἀνήγαγε ὅνδε δόμονδε), *Od.* 3, 272

47 Helen, *Il.* III, 39–57 and 403–12, etc.; Clytemnestra, *Od.* 3, 261–75, especially 265–6 *et al.*

48 *Od.* 8, 321–58: the goddesses were shocked, the assertion that compensation was due was not disputed

49 Note the specific and quite unnecessary statement that Eurycleia was never Laertes' mistress, *Od.* I, 429–33

50 *Od.* 15, 417–81; *cf.* 18, 321–5 etc. for Melantho

51 *Od.* 19, 498 (=22, 418); 22, 463–4; 20, 14–21

52 *Od.* 22, 431–45 ff; *Od.* 16, 106–9 (=20, 316–19), and *cf.* 22, 35–41. For what was expected of a man, note how Odysseus' adultery with the two goddesses Calypso and Circe is very carefully obscured; Calypso took the lead in wanting him (*Od.* 1, 13–15, 5, 118–29, 155), was compelling him to stay with her (1, 13–15), and he owed her a debt of gratitude (5, 130–65); Hermes warned him that he must accept Circe's seduction of him in order to achieve his object (*Od.* 10, 296–301)

53 *Od.* 16, 73–7; 23, 149–51 etc.; *Od.* 18, 143–6 and 22, 35–41

54 *Od.* 18, 269–70; *cf.* 11, 177–9, where Odysseus asks if she has remarried

55 The absent husband appears in the ancient cuneiform law-codes. 'The principle is that a wife may remarry if her husband has left her without support, or can be presumed to be dead, but that she may not do this so long as there is a presumption that he will or may return to her' G. R. Driver and J. C. Miles, *The Assyrian Laws* (1935), 215–16

56 See p. 21–2 above

57 This cannot seriously be doubted; even in Classical times women could leave their husband's houses and divorce them by so doing

58 W. K. Lacey, *JHS* 1966, 61ff

59 *Il.* VI, 425–8; Bellerophon, *Il.* VI, 174–80; Meleager, *Il.* IX, 566–7; *cf.* Autolycus' interest in his daughter Anticleia after Odysseus' birth, *Od.* 19, 399–409

60 *Od.* 14, 96–108; *cf.* Achilles' ghost's implied statement that the most miserable existence on earth is to serve as a labourer to a man of small substance, *Od.* 11, 489–91

61 *E.g.* Achilles (*Il.* XIX, 328–33), Sarpedon (*Il.* V, 472–92); *cf.* Hector's encouragement (*Il.* XV, 494–9), and Achilles' thoughts for his father (*Il.* XXIV, 534–40), and for Priam (*id.* 543–51)

62 Achilles, *Il.* XXIV, 488–9, and *cf. Od.* 11, 494–7; Andromache, *Il.* XXII, 489–506; *cf.* the simile of the men quarrelling over lands, *Il.* XII, 421–4, and *Od.* 17, 470–2, a man does not mind a blow or two in defence of his possessions and animals

63 On the contempt felt for a mean man, *Od.* 19, 329–34; *cf.* the insult in *Od.* 17, 454–7

64 *Il.* VI, 234–6, *Od.* 1, 316–18

65 *Il.* II, 226–33; *cf.* Achilles' claim to have given all his spoils to Agamemnon (*Il..* IX, 330–3); Odysseus could be said to be gathering gifts from the neighbouring peoples on his way home (*Od.* 14, 321–6, =(in part) 19, 282–95). See also *Il.* VII, 470–1 for gifts of wine to Agamemnon—which made it his duty to entertain the leaders, IX, 71ff

66 The exception is Arete's gift of a box to contain Odysseus' gifts of clothes, *Od.* 8, 438–9; all Homeric women spin, weave and make clothes, including Helen (*Il.* III, 125–8, VI, 323–4 etc. and *Od.* 4, 125–36), Andromache (*Il.* VI, 490–2), Penelope (*Od.* 17, 96–7, 19, 138–56, 24, 129–46, *cf.* 21, 350–2, 22, 421–3 etc.), and even the goddesses Circe (*Od.* 10, 221–3) and Calypso (5, 61–2), and making things (ἔργα) was one of a woman's accomplishments—*e.g.* Hippodameia (*Il.* XIII, 428–33). Cloth was however also bought (*Il.* VI, 289), unless the Sidonian women who wove it were bought as slaves like Eumaeus' nurse (*Od.* 15, 425–9), who was herself a skilled worker (*id.* 417–18). It was also possible for a poor woman who had no husband to make a poor living by spinning for others (*Il.* XII, 433–5)

67 Helen, *Od.* 15, 125–9; Arete, *Od.* 8, 441; the bride, *Od.* 6, 26–30

68 Eumaeus, *Od.* 15, 368–70; the beggar, *Od.* 17, 549–50 and 21, 338–41; Telemachus' rebuke, *id.* 344–53

69 *Od.* 4, 756–7. 'There will always be a man of the race of Arcesias who will possess the hall with its high roof and the rich fields'. Contrast *Od.* 1, 115–17, 1, 163–15, 2, 55–61 etc., where only Odysseus' power could maintain his movables and flocks

70 *Od.* 2, 335–6 and 16, 384–6

71 Mentor, *Od.* 22, 216-23; Odysseus' oath, *Od.* 22, 61-4; note that in the *Odyssey* it is assumed that all men can work in the fields; in the beggar's brush with Eurymachus (*Od.* 18, 357-80) both speakers assume the other is competent at farm-work. Laertes devoted his whole time to it (*Od.* 1, 189-93), though there is considerable stress on the wretchedness of his status; on the other hand Odysseus' imaginary Cretan did not like it, preferring to be a soldier (*Od.* 14, 222-6)

72 Iphidamas is perhaps the clearest case in the Iliad (*Il.* XI, 223-6), but Alcinous' marriage to Arete clearly was the basis of his royal status in *Od.* 7, 63-8. Bellerophon, Tydeus and the imaginary Cretan all became possessed of what their father-in-law had given them (see pp. 39-40 above)

73 *Il.* XX, 179-83 and V, 152-8

74 *E.g.* Ilioneus (*Il.* XIV, 489-505), or the loss to the mother of Lycaon and Polydorus (*Il.* XXI, 123-4)

75 *Il.* IV, 477-9 (=XVII, 301-3); Dolon, *Il.* X, 317, 378-81

76 Kirk, *op. cit.*, 382 ff

77 *Od.* 5, 394-7, *Il.* V, 406-9; cf. *Od.* 12, 41-5, and the two similes, *Il.* IX, 481-2, a great love is 'that of a father for his only son', and *Il.* II, 291-4 impatience is 'that of a sailor who has been storm-bound for a month in winter and longs for his wife.'

78 *Od.* 15, 363-70 and 374-9—cf. what the poet tells us of Melantho (*Od.* 18, 322-3)

79 Andromache, *Il.* VI, 383-4; the flirtation, *Il.* XXII, 126-8; the housewives, *Il.* XX, 252-5; the shield, *Il.* XVIII, 495-6 and 514-15

80 *Cf.* P. Demargne, *Aegean Art* (1964), Pls. 181, 191ff. *Cf.* in Attic sixth-century art, *Pls. 14, 22*

81 *Od.* 1, 356-9: for the bow 21, 350-3; the lines are identical except where τόξον (the bow) replaces μῦθος (discussion). *Cf. Il.* VI, 490-3 with war (πόλεμος), and a slightly different ending

82 *Il.* XXIV, 35-8; cf. *Od.* 24, 292-6; parents alone (especially the divine mothers) of either Aeneas or Achilles, *Il.* XX, 206-11; mother and wife (*i.e.* Hecuba and Andromache) for Hector, *Il.* XXII, 86-9; father and mother will not close Socus' eyes (*Il.* XI, 452-3); if Diomedes is slain, his wife will wail (*Il.* V, 412-15); in the case of Ilioneus, an only son, his father and mother are stressed more than his wife (*Il.* XIV, 501-5); Achilles and the captive women will lament for Patroclus (*Il.* XVIII, 339-42), Sarpedon was to be buried by brothers and retainers (*Il.* XVI, 456-7), cowards will not be buried by their kin (γνωτοί τε γνωταί τε) (*Il.* XV, 348-51)

83 *Il.* XXIII and *Od.* 24, 36-94

84 *E.g.* Andromache's father (*Il.* VI, 416-22), the Greek dead (*Il.* VII, 333-5, cf. 408-10); cf. Elpenor, who was most anxious to secure proper burial (*Od.* 11, 52-78)

85 *Od.* 1, 291-2; cf. *id.* 234-40, Odysseus would have had a proper burial had he been killed in battle

86 For a kinsman, *Il.* V, 20–1—the criticism is implicit; *Il.* XIII, 463–7 for Aeneas' brother-in-law who brought him up, and *Il.* XVI, 495–501, *id.* 544–7 for Sarpedon, *Il.* XVII, 120–2, 556–9, XVIII, 176–80 for Patroclus etc.

87 In and after *Iliad* XI talk of leaving corpses to dogs and vultures is frequent; as a punishment for cowardice (XV, 348–51), or due to defeat (XI, 816–18, *cf.* XVIII, 270–2), or malice, XIII, 831–2, and *passim* in XVII (Patroclus) and XXII etc. (Hector). Achilles insulted Lycaon by feeding him to the fish, XXI, 122–7; *cf. id.* 280–3 for drowning as a shameful death

88 *Il.* XXIV, 46–9; *cf. id.* 610–13, even Niobe took food after nine days

89 *Il.* XIV, 484–5; *Il.* XXIV, 725–38 for Andromache. In *Il.* XIII, 658–9 it is noted that Harpalion's father failed to avenge him; Ares' fury at his son's death, *Il.* XV, 115–18, and Euphorbus' attempt to avenge his brother, XVII, 34–7. The *Iliad* however contains many stock phrases for emotion at deaths of warriors other than near relatives, *e.g. Il.* IV, 491–4, V, 669–70, XIII, 202–3, XIII, 660–1. Brothers are distressed in XI, 249–50 (Coön), XVI, 319–20 (Maris), XX, 419–22 (Hector)

90 *Od.* 3, 195–8

91 *Il.* XVIII, 497–500; *cf.* 'A man receives a price ($\pi o \iota \nu \acute{\eta} \nu$) for the killing of a brother or for his son when he is dead'. *Il.* IX, 632–3; for Odysseus, *Od.* 20, 42–3; *cf.* 23, 133–9, where the mock marriage is said to be designed to conceal the fact that the suitors are dead

92 They had a duty to do so, *Od.* 24, 433–5; *cf.* the repeated praise for Orestes for having avenged his father, *Od.* 3, 195–8 etc.

93 *Od.* 16, 376–82 and 23, 118–22, and the suitors would kill the beggar for killing Antinous, *Od.* 22, 27–30.

94 *Il.* XXIV, 480–3, a suppliant who suddenly appears at a house is likely to be a homicide; *cf. Od.* 15, 223–5 and 272–4, Theoclymenus fled, having killed a man with many kinsmen; *Il.* XV, 333–6, Medon killed his step-mother's kinsman; *id.* 430–2, Lycophron killed a man; XVI, 573–4, Epeigeus killed a cousin; XXIII, 85–8, Patroclus killed another boy in a quarrel; *Od.* 14, 379–81, a lying Aetolian, who deceived Penelope, killed a man

95 For a parallel from classical times, Xenophon, *Mem.* II, 1, 14–15

96 $\delta \eta \mu \iota o \varepsilon \rho \gamma o \acute{\iota}$—*Od.* 17, 382–7

97 Irus, *Od.* 18, 6–7; the beggar, *Od.* 19, 27–8; 17, 20–1; 18, 357–80; Trojan allies, note 27 above

98 *Od.* 19, 314–19 and 20, 129–30; *cf.* 6, 303–15 and 7, 14–17 etc.

99 *Od.* 17, 549–50; *cf.* 16, 78–84; for class distinction, *Od.* 21, 314–17

100 Lycaon, *Il.* XXI, 40–4; Axylus, VI, 14–17; Diomedes, VI, 215–33

101 *Od.* 8, 204–11. The fact that Achilles slew Lycaon who had 'eaten his bread as a prisoner' (*Il.* XXI, 76–7) showed his savagery

102 *Od.* 1, 175–7; Telemachus at Pylos, 3, 346–55; Mentes, 1, 187–9; the Cretan, 19, 194–202, 241–3; Laertes, 24, 269–79; Menelaus, *Od.* 4, 31–5

103 *Od.* 19, 134–5; *cf. id.* 314 ff, whatever precisely $\sigma \eta \mu \acute{\alpha} \nu \tau o \rho \varepsilon \varsigma$ may mean

104 *Od.* 15, 513–17 and 540–3; *cf.* 17, 78–83

105 *Od.* 14, 257–86; *cf.* Nestor's question in *Od.* 3, 71–4; piracy was not a disreputable trade; the Homeric bards were well aware that hunger was its main cause, and fully in sympathy with the beggar's views on the needs of the body (*Od.* 17, 286–9; *cf. id.* 473–4), probably from personal experience

106 *Od.* 1, 398, 23, 357; *cf. Il.* IX, 406

107 Paris, *Il.* XIII, 626–7; the Phoenician, *Od.* 15, 459–70; saying farewell, *Od.* 15, 49–55

108 *Il.* I, 280–1, Agamemnon is a better man (φέρτερος) than Achilles since he rules more people; *cf.* IX, 37–9. Troy's wealth had been proverbial, *Il.* XVIII, 288–92

109 *Il.* IX, 412–16, etc.

CHAPTER III

THE FAMILY AND THE EVOLUTION OF STATES

1 M. I. Finley, *The World of Odysseus* (1964), especially Chapter II; Thuc. I, 12, marks it as beginning 'after the Trojan War', Gomme, *Comm. Thuc.* *ad loc.*

2 H. Francotte, *La Polis Grecque* (1907), 95 ff, with stress on the many variations in synoecism (συνοικισμός), and the view that a political organization was the most fundamental element; A. Zimmern, *Greek Commonwealth* (5th edn., 1931), Part II, still one of the most valuable books in English. If colonists took their mother-city's customs with them, the mother-city must have had some for them to take, which puts the start of the process back to the eighth century and the age of colonization, but these customs were not at first written

3 For early attitudes towards judgement by 'Kings' (βασιλεῖς), Hesiod, *Theogony* 81–97, the ideal; *Works and Days* 33–41, the reality. For later attitudes to the laws, Hdt III, 80, tyranny (arbitrary rule) was the denial of law; *id.* VII, 104: 'the Spartans are not absolutely free; they are under an overlord, the laws' (ἐλεύθεροι γὰρ ἐόντες οὐ πάντα ἐλεύθεροί εἰσι. ἔπεστι γὰρ σφι δεσπότης νόμος); Euripides, *Supplices* 429–37 etc.; Plato, *Crito* 50A ff; Xen., *Memorabilia* (*Mem*) 1, 2, 40–6; Arist. *Ethics* (*EN*) X, 9, 9 (1180A) etc. Stress on law as creating the spirit of the *polis*, Forrest, *EGD*, 143ff

4 The village (κώμη) was the unit beyond the household, of some size but united enough by ties of blood to be ruled by a single chief man, βασιλεύς or 'king', Arist. *Pol.* I, 1, 7 (1252B); Thucydides describes early Greeks as living in '*poleis* which lacked walls and were settled in villages', I, 5: πόλεσιν ἀτειχίστοις καὶ κατὰ κώμας οἰκουμέναις

5 G. Glotz, *The Greek City* (1929), 18 ff, Burn, *LA*, 25–6, to whom I owe many of the references in this Chapter. Cf. Thuc. I, 7–8, piracy explained why the Greeks built *poleis* near but not on the coast. Threats of massive invasion however may have prevented fragmentation into *poleis*, as in Macedonia (the suggestion of G. T. Griffith)

6 H. D. Westlake, *Thessaly in the Fourth Century B.C.* (1935), especially Chapter II

7 Burn, *LA*, 26

8 Thuc. I, 5, 3–6, 3. Cf. *id.* III, 94, 4, on the Aetolians who have no *poleis*, living in villages; rumour even alleged that they ate their meat raw, *ibid.* 5

9 *Odyssey* 17, 470–2; Lysias IV, 5–7, different sorts of assault; *id.* III, 40–3, premeditation as a cause for punishment; Plato, *Laws* 845 B–D, distinguishes a thrashing from an assault

10 Glotz, *op. cit.*, 105–7, attested by the first appearance of written codes in colonial settlements; Plato, *Laws* 679A ff, Arist. *Pol.* I, 1, 9–12 (1253A), for theories on the emergence of laws in *poleis*

11 'No city has no plain'—that is, where there were no agricultural lands there was no *polis*, Burn, *LA*, 15. 'Deep soiled'; $\dot{\epsilon}\rho\iota\beta\hat{\omega}\lambda\alpha\xi$ is the Homeric word: the King's demesne is also $\beta\alpha\theta\upsilon\lambda\dot{\eta}\ddot{\iota}os$—'with thick tall crops', *Il.* XVIII, 550; *cf.* Dunbar's *Concordance to the Iliad* (1962 revised), *s.v.* $\beta\alpha\theta\epsilon\dot{\iota}\eta s$ etc. $\beta\alpha\theta\upsilon\lambda\dot{\eta}\ddot{\iota}os$ is a variant reading, rejected by *OCT*

12 Thuc. I, 2, 3–6 with Gomme, *Comm. Thuc.* note *ad loc.*

13 Charcoal burners (*c.* 600) Diog. La. I, 104. The men of Acharnae are said to have been hoplites as well as charcoal-burners, but they also owned vineyards; Aristophanes, *Acharn.* 179–83, 214–5, 230–2, 325ff etc.: *cf. ibid.* 271–6 for fetching in wood from the hills; Andocides, frag. 4: 'may we never again see the charcoal-burners from the hills coming into the city' . . . (*i.e.* as during the occupation of Attica 413–404). In Aesop's fable 29 (Hausrath, = 59 Halm) the charcoal-burner tried unsuccessfully to share a house with the fuller

14 Thuc. I, 2, 5–6, 'As for Attica . . . the same folk always inhabited it.' For the validity of this view see (*e.g.*) Gomme *Comm. Thuc. ad loc., q.v.* for aristocratic families who claimed to have found refuge in Attica; *cf.* Hdt. V, 65 etc. The claim to be autochthonous is democratic propaganda of the late fifth and fourth centuries; it was however very popular, Euripides, frag. of Erechtheus (from Lycurgus, *in Leocratem* 100), *Ion* 29, 589 etc., Aristophanes, *Wasps* 1076, *Lysistrata* 1082. In earlier times, aristocratic families traced their autochthonous claims by descent rather than locale, Ed. Meyer, *Geschichte des Altertums* III, 284, n. 2 (1937, Stuttgart edn.), who quotes the Spartae at Thebes, Eteoboutadae (from Erechtheus) and Titakidae (in Attica), called autochthonous by Herodotus (IX, 73). For the Athenians' tenacious adhesion to their lands till the Peloponnesian War, Thuc. II, 16; contrast the nobles of Leontini, *id.* V, 4, 3

15 Francotte, *op. cit.*, 119 f, argues that Athens differed from other *poleis* by

being an amalgamation of pre-existing *poleis*, not of tribes. He fails to note however that all the parallels he cites are colonial, or late creations, or both: Elis (471), Diodorus XI, 54; Rhodes (408–7), Diod. XIII, 75; Stiris and Medeon (second century), *SIG* 647; Teos and Lebedos (*c.* 303) *ibid.* 344. Aristotle, in *Pol.* II, 9, however, does not remark on Athens as having many peculiar features in its legislation; see Chapter IX below

16 Dorians and non-Dorians at Sicyon, Hdt. V, 67–8; in Boeotia the Thebans claimed to have 'settled Plataea . . . and other places . . . after expelling people of mixed races' (ἡμῶν κτισάντων Πλάταιαν καὶ ἀλλὰ χωρία μετ᾽ αὐτῆς ἃ ξυμμείκτους ἀνθρώπους ἐξελάσαντες ἔσχομεν), Thuc. III, 61, 2; *cf.* Strabo IX, 2, 3 (C 401) (Loeb numeration). Ephorus, F. Jacoby, *FGH* 70, 21, explains the retention of the distinction between Thebans and Thebageneis (Θηβαγενεῖς). The Boeotians also had their special cults at Onchestus and Chaeroneia, F. Cauer, *RE* III (1899), 643 ff (*s.v.* Boeotia). In the Dorian (Cnidian) colony at Corcyra Nigra the settlers are still listed in their Dorian tribes in the fourth century, *SIG* 141; on Calymna, where the three Dorian tribes continued for religious purposes after the local tribes had superseded them for other purposes, *GDI* 3593 with *id.* 3565, A. J. Graham, *Colony and Mother City in Ancient Greece* (1964), 14 ff; at Rhegium the settlers from Messenia long remained distinct from the Chalcidian (from Chalcis), *id.* 17–19

17 On Sparta and Gortyn, Chapter VIII below

18 (Aristotle) *Oeconomica* I, 2, 1, (1343A) (Susemihl) citing Hesiod

19 Before the introduction of the possibility of making a will, the family-group must be unlimited in width, since it must be possible to establish an heir, however distant, to a childless man. In Athens, for example, it was only in Solon's day (594 trad.) that wills were introduced

20 For a theory of primitive communism, George Thomson, *Studies in Ancient Greek Society* I (1949), 302–3 and note 15, 313 ff; Francotte, *op. cit.*, 101, very early abandonment of common family ownership of land. In some colonial settlements the village played a part, and neighbours had to witness land-sales, Stobaeus XLIV, 20 (from Theophrastus), at Thurii; oaths to Apollo κωμαῖος and before three inhabitants of the village (κώμη) by vendor and purchaser at Ainos in Thrace; G. Glotz, *La Solidarité de la famille dans le droit criminel en Grèce* (1904) (*Solidarité* hereafter), 195 f, for another view and for the repunctuation of Hesiod, *W. and D.* 340–5 in this sense. See also Appendix

21 'Crime' in this context means an action detrimental to the survival of the *genos*, Glotz, *Solidarité*, 22 ff

22 νηποινεὶ τεθνάτω; this exact form of words appears only relatively late, *SIG* 194, 10 (Amphipolis, fourth century), laws cited in the orators (Andocides I, 9ς, Dem. XXIII, 60). The kindred νήποινος ('off scot-free') appears in the *Odyssey* of a killer only in curses (1, 380; 2, 145); elsewhere it is always of a plunderer of property. Neither word appears

in the *Iliad*, which may suggest that the idea is associated with the development of law, and the idea that some homicides may be justifiable

23 The meaning of ἀτιμία—the *genos* no longer sets value (τιμή) on his life. Superstitions about werewolves were common (*e.g.* Pausanias VIII, 2, 6, Plato, *Republic* 415 E, 565 D; as an exile Alcaeus (frag. G2 Lobel & Page, line 25) says 'like Onomacles, . . . solitary I settled among wolf-thickets'— D. L. Page, *Sappho and Alcaeus* (1955), 198ff, (especially 205, note *ad loc.*); L. Gernet, *Dolon le loup*, in *Mélanges Cumont* I, (1936) 200, Glotz, *Solidarité*, 23

24 Examples of accidental homicide include Peleus (Apollodorus III, 163), Heracles (Diod. IV, 36, 2–3), Oxylus (Pausanias V, 3, 7), Perseus (Pausanias II, 16, 2–3); *cf.* also Chapter II above for Homeric attitudes, and note 22 above for the un-Homeric character of νήποινος, νηποινεί, in connection with homicide. Hyettus was the first man to punish adultery with death; he too fled, Pausanias IX, 36, 6–8. Ares, we are told, murdered his daughter's seducer, and was the first to be tried for this sort of homicide (ἐπὶ τούτῳ τῷ φόνῳ), Pausanias I, 21, 4

25 Nicolaus of Damascus (Nic. Dam.), Jacoby, *FGH* 90, 61; here the murder was a family one, since the paramour was Isodemus' brother; *cf.* Adrastus who accidentally killed his brother and fled, and 'lost all', Hdt. I, 35, Plut. *Mor.* 244 E–F

26 Hdt. V, 71, Thuc. I, 126, Plut. *Solon* XII, 3. For sacrilege and the divine wrath, Glotz, *Solidarité*, 560ff *et al.*

27 Aeschylus, *Eumenides* 483–4. Burn (*LA*, 23) believes it was to stop vendettas. 'Vengeance', says Glotz (*Solidarité*, 57), 'was always a pleasure as well as a duty'; for examples of vendettas as illustrating the family's solidarity, *op. cit.*, 56, 76 ff. Pausanias IV, 4, 4 ff, describes the Areopagus as well-established by *c.* 740

28 *Ath. Pol.* LVII, 2

29 On the shield of Achilles a primitive homicide-trial is the only real community-activity, *Il.* XVIII, 497–508, Chapter II above

30 *Ath. Pol.* III, 2–3. The names of the archons were traditionally known from 683, when the archons started to give their name to the year. *Ath. Pol.* LVI, 2 (the Archon's oath) proves that his function was to be guardian of property. *Cf.* P. Vinogradoff, *Outlines of Historical Jurisprudence* II (1922), 203

31 *Ath. Pol.* III, 4, 'many years later'

32 *Ath. Pol.* LIX, 2

33 Hignett, *HAC*, 307 ff

34 Arist. *Pol.* II, 9, 9 (1274B)

35 Glotz, *Solidarité*, 28f; for debt, Solon, ap. *Ath. Pol.* XII, 4; for unchastity, Plut. *Solon* XXIII, 2

36 Glotz, *Solidarité*, 248ff, *q.v.* for varying views. The text reads 'The *patria* (*i.e. genos*) and *genea* (*i.e.* family) and his property (τὰ αὑτοῦ) are secure

(from seizure); if any person accuses a male Eleian, if the supreme magistrate and the Basileis (Kings) do not apply the means of securing justice ... If anyone bind (or perhaps flog) an accused before he has been convicted ... For 'a male Eleian' C. D. Buck, *Greek Dialects*, 259, would read 'a man as if he were an Eleian'

37 Apart from securing the accused's family and property, and himself from physical abuse, the Eleian *rhetra* is much concerned to coerce the officers into action. For the view that tribal Kings (Basileis) were apt to neglect their duty, Hesiod *et al.*, notes 108 ff below

38 W. J. Woodhouse, *Solon the Liberator* (1938), the standard histories; more recently, Forrest, *EGD*, 147 f, a new view

39 Periander was not Corinth's first lawgiver, if Arist. *Pol.* II, 3, 7 (1265B), is correct; Pheidon's laws, as reported, would suit a restricted citizen-body very well. Periander's father Cypselus had modified the previous system of punishments, Nic. Dam., Jacoby, *FGH* 90, 57–9, Aristotle, frag. 611.20 (V. Rose); Periander himself both suppressed the oligarchy and curbed their displays of wealth. For Cypselus as doing in Corinth what Solon did at Athens, E. Will, *Korinthiaka* (1955), 477 ff, 622 *et al.*

40 The date of the origin of the Spartan *eunomia* is still disputed; compare the account of N. G. L. Hammond in his *History of Greece* (1959), 102 ff with (*e.g.*) *CAH* III, 558 ff and the works cited. Forrest, *EGD*, 128, dates the reform *c.* 675. For Pittacus, Diog. La. I, 74–81

41 Chapter I above, p. 19 with note 9. Note however at Massilia the attempt to keep new citizens out of the highest office, Strabo IV, 1, 5 (C 179); Aristotle (*Pol.* IV, 3, 8 (1290 B)) reports that at Teos and Apollonia the first colonists formed an oligarchy, which monopolized the state's offices

42 'In ancient times there were oligarchies in all those states whose strength lay in their cavalry', Arist. *Pol.* IV, 3, 2 (1289B), quoting as examples Eretria, Chalcis, Magnesia on the Meander, and many others in Asia (Minor); *cf. ibid.* 8 (1290B) for Colophon, *id.* IV, 10, 10 (1297B), VI, 4, 3 (1321A) as being generally true in early times, and always true in lands suited to cavalry warfare, Heracleides Ponticus, *Kym. Pol.*, 6 (Müller, *FHG* II, 216) for Cyme

43 Assuming (*e.g.* with Hignett, *HAC*, 101–2 *et al.*) that the *hippeis*, if duly qualified by birth, had access to office and to the council even before Solon's day. The third class (*zeugitai*) were eligible for the archonship only from 457/6, *Ath. Pol.* XXVI, 2

44 Strabo X, 4, 18 (C 481–2)

45 *Id.* X, 1, 10 (C 448): 3,000 hoplites, 600 *hippeis* and 60 chariots recorded their procession; *cf. SIG* 123, where Eretrian *strategoi*, *boule* and *hippeis* exchanged oaths with their Athenian counterparts in 394/3

46 *Cf.* the *geomoroi* at Samos, whose influence lasted till 412, and the revolution. Thuc. VIII, 21; Boerner, *RE* VII, 1 (1912), 1219

47 Strabo XIV, 1, 3 (C 632–3), F. Cauer, *RE* III, 1 (1899), 909, *s.v.* Branchidai

48 M. P. Nilsson, *Greek Religion* (1925), 205–212 for a brief, coherent account of Dionysus and the Eleusinian mysteries; on the admission of slaves to the latter, L. R. Farnell, *Cults of the Greek States* III (1907), 155, note 173; yet even in this festival, in which emphasis was laid on the individual rather than the family, in the fourth century some representatives of the Milesians prayed for 'the Athenians, their children and their wives' along with their own children and wives, *ibid.*, 157. Cleisthenes of Sicyon also encouraged Dionysus' worship in place of a Dorian cult of Adrastus, Hdt. V, 67, 5

49 Burn, *LA*, 33

50 The Geometric period extends from *c.* 900 to *c.* 725 in Corinth, 700 in Athens, 650 in the Aegean world, R. M. Cook, *Greek Painted Pottery* (1960), 16, *q.v.* (p. 20), 'funerals, processions of chariots, fighting by land and sea' as favourite subjects of Geometric artists; *ibid.*, 22–3, horses on Argive Geometric ware

51 Burn *LA*, 53; C. T. Seltman, *Greek Coins* (1955), 46–8, Cook, *op. cit.*, plate 9c(*c.* 650). Léon Lacroix, *Études d'archéologie classique* I (1955–6), 89 ff, argued against any certain identification of heraldic emblems with specific families; they were, as in Aeschylus, *Septem* 377 ff, intended to frighten or insult. But note line 398, taken from Alcaeus (so schol.), that blazonry does not wound and lines 590 ff. See further note 53 below

52 Spartan phalanx, Burn, *LA* 282, Photius, *s.v. Λ*; M for Messenians, *Σ* for Sicyonians, Xen. *H.G.* IV, 4, 10, *Ψ* (= X) for Chalcis, Seltman, *op. cit.*, 57; Mantinea's trident-badge, Lacroix, *op. cit.*, 104

53 Seltman, *op. cit.*, 46–8, 52–3; the view has been controversial, and is rejected by many. Seltman's choice of evidence was defective, but his critics have never got around the fact of city blazonry (note 52), or the fact that blazons could be called hereditary (οἰκεῖον, Euripides, *Phoenissae* 1107), or that Alcibiades could be expected to use a blazon on his shield that was πάτριος, Plut. *Alcib.* XVI, 1–2. That the badges were recognized as belonging to individual nobles, if not to their families by hereditary right, J. H. Jongkees, *Mnemosyne* 1952, 47ff. For similar Milesian coins, Seltman, *op. cit.*, 26–8, K. Freeman, *Greek City-States* (1950), 133

54 For the helmeted Athene, Jongkees, *op. cit.*, for the owl, (*e.g.*) Seltman, *op. cit.*, and *Plates 8, 9*, p. 58 above

55 Hdt. II, 160; J. Burckhardt, *History of Greek Culture* (*HGC* hereafter), 1964, 54: *kalokagathia*, the ideal of aristocrats, was expressed in part in athletics. H. A. Harris, *Greek Athletes* (1964), 37–8, 42 ff, there was a social contrast between the predominantly wealthy and aristocratic entrants of the pre-Classical age and the growing professionalism of later ages; but Socrates implies that athletes are at least comfortably off in Plato, *Apology* 36D. J. K. Anderson, *Ancient Greek Horsemanship* (1961), 100f, has noted that hunting-scenes disappear from Athenian art after Cleisthenes' reforms; his explanation of the reason is unconvincing. Hunting was essentially

aristocratic, and certainly continued, as is evident from Xenophon, *Cynegeticus* and other references

56 V. Ehrenberg, *Society and Civilization* (1964), 50–1, *q.v.* (fig. 23) for an illustration

57 Tyrtaeus, fr. 9 (Diehl), athletic prowess, good looks, wealth, famous ancestry, eloquence—all are inferior to courage. Xenophanes, fr. 2 (Diehl), athletes are second best; later, Euripides, *Autolycus* fr. 284 (Nauck), on the uselessness of athletes and athletics; both from Athenaeus X, 413C–414C; Phocylides, fr. 3 (Diehl), from Stobaeus LXXXVII, 28, on nobles who lack good qualities

58 Hdt. III, 142–3, a noble's snub prevented the restoration of constitutional government in Samos; Theognis, 183ff, dislike of *nouveaux riches* who marry into noble families

59 Xenophanes, fr. 3 (Diehl), from Athenaeus XII, 526 A–B

60 Adolescent and lover a subject for Attic black figure pottery from *c.* 570, Cook, *op. cit.*, 72; from the start of red figure pottery, from *c.* 530, scenes from the wrestling-school (*palaestra*) are shown, like Pl. *17*, *id.*, 169. For drinking, Xenophanes, fr. 1 (Diehl), from Athenaeus X, 462C; the praise of moderation implies that excess was not unknown. On Alcaeus, Page, *Sappho and Alcaeus*, 299ff, but Pittacus' legislation, which increased penalties for drunken offenders (Arist. *Pol.* II, 9, 9 (1274B)), suggests that drunkenness was rather common in Lesbos; *cf.* Theognis 467–510, 627–8, 939–42 *et al.* Note the appearance of drinking-scenes (naturally) on drinking vessels of the 'Ripe Corinthian' style (*c.* 625–550) and Attic black figure style (*c.* 570–550), Cook, *op. cit.*, 58, 72 *et al.* Drunken riots are recorded; Burn, *LA*, 83 and note 85, a riot at Corinth which led to a homicide and the banishment of the perpetrators as colonists; at Naxos, Athenaeus VIII, 348 A–C, said to derive from Aristotle

61 Legislated against extravagant display generally (τρυφὴν ὅλως περιαιρῶν), Aristotle, frag. 611.20 (V. Rose).

62 Plut. *Solon* XXI, 4; Charondas, Stobaeus XLIV, 24. For other examples, including Delphi, see *Proc. Cambridge Philological Society*, 1964, 49, and note 3

63 Plut. *Lycurgus* XXVII, 1–2

64 Hdt. VI, 126–30; *cf.* the fragmentary Wooing of Helen (Hesiod, frags. 94 and 96). The suitors were ὅσοι σφίσι τε αὐτοῖσι ἦσαν καὶ πάτρη ἐξωγκώμενοι; 'descent', the Pindaric sense of πάτρη, seems more likely than that given in *LSJ* ('native-land'). Hippocleides disgraced himself at the betrothal feast and lost his bride to Megacles the Alcmaeonid

65 Diod. XIII, 84 (dated 406); the chariot-procession is reminiscent of Geometric vases such as the dipylon crater of the last half of the eighth century, illustrated by Ehrenberg, *op. cit.*, fig. 8

66 They handed on their political power within the *genos* (κατ᾽ ἀγχίστειαν), not from father to son (Burn, *LA*, 20–21), a procedure which evolved

into an annual chief magistracy appointed by election by the Bacchiadae from out of their own number, Diod. VII, fr. 9. In Athens the Medontiadae may have done the same (Burn, *LA*, 23–4). Other ruling families were Penthilidae at Mytilene on Lesbos, Arist. *Pol.* V, 8, 13 (1311B), Alcaeus, fr. 48 (Diehl) (perhaps), Basilidae who ruled at Ephesus and Erythrae on the Asiatic mainland, Arist. *Pol.* V, 5, 4 (1305B), Suidas *s.v.* Pythagoras Strabo XIV, 1, 3 (C 633), Neleidae who ruled at Miletus, Aristotle, fr. 556 (V. Rose); for others, G. Glotz, *The Greek City* (1929), 14 f

67 Hdt. V, 92, β–δ; δοκέουσά σφεας φιλοφροσύνης τοῦ πατρὸς ἕνεκα αἰτέειν φέρουσα ἐνεχείρισε αὐτῶν ἑνί. The baby was not killed; the murderers could not endure the task when the baby smiled at them— a thoroughly Greek dénouement to the tale. For a similar tale (about Cyrus the Mede), Hdt. I, 107–18; the fact that the intended killer was a close relative is stressed. Tyrants' families tended to acquire traits of 'heroic' legend; *cf.* the omens attending Peisistratus' impending birth, Hdt. I, 59

68 Examples of small councils include 30 at Sparta (Hdt. VI, 57, 5, etc.), 80 at Argos (Thuc. V, 47, 9), 90 at Elis (Arist. *Pol.* V, 5, 8 (1306A)), 180 at Epidaurus (Plut. *G.Q.*1 = *Moralia* 291E), though this is a very small state, 60 on Cnidos (Plut. *G.Q.*4 = *Moralia* 292A–B; *cf.* Arist. *Pol.* V, 5, 3 (1305B)). All but Elis are Dorian states; Elis was probably settled at about the same period, Burn, *LA*, 25. *Cf.* Gamoroi (Geomoroi) at Syracuse and Samos, Hdt. VII, 155, and Macan's note *ad loc.*, Thuc. VIII, 21. Gamoroi were presumably those who originally divided the land in Syracuse, most of whom had come from one village in the territory of Corinth, Strabo VIII, 6, 22 (C 380), so were peculiarly closely related, presumably

69 Pollux IX, 83; her father is called King (βασιλεύς) of Cyme

70 Hdt. I, 92, 3. Melas' marriage, Aelian, *V.H.* III, 26. For Homeric marriages *JHS*, 1966, 59–60

71 Hdt. I, 146

72 Hdt. IV, 108, 'The Gelonoi are a people who were Greeks long ago, but have given up trading and settled among the Boudinoi; their language is Scythian in part and in part Greek'. Like the Greeks of the homeland they preferred to be settled agriculturalists. *Id.* IV, 78, Ariapeithes, a native, married a woman from Istria, 'not a local girl either, since she taught her son, Skyles, to read and write Greek'; at the end of the sixth century Miltiades of Athens married a Thracian princess, Hegesipyle, Hdt. VI, 39, 2, Plut. *Cimon* 4, etc.; *cf.* also Callippidae, Hdt. IV, 17, Mixhellenes, *SIG* 495, 114, (third century). Traditional tales also spoke of intermingling of Greek and native in Italy and Sicily, though most of them indicate treachery on one side or the other, Polybius XII, 6, Polyaenus V, 5, Justin XLIII, 4; at Massilia, according to Aristotle (Athenaeus XIII, 576 A–B), there was intermarriage between the chief families

73 Thuc. I, 126, 3 etc.

74 Burn, *LA*, 184–5, 188, from Diog. La. I, 94; many families claimed descent from Aristomenes the Messenian leader, Pausanias IV, 24, 1–3. Both Periander and his father used their families to forward their imperialist schemes, Burn, *LA*, 188–91

75 *Ath. Pol.* XVII, 4. She was still young enough to bear Peisistratus two sons; for the view that Peisistratus was a bigamist, and that Timonassa's sons were Argive and not Athenian citizens, L. Gernet, *Mariages de tyrans*, in *Hommage à Lucien Febvre* (1954), 42–4. Peisistratus' eldest son Hippias married twice, both Athenian girls; Hippias' daughter married the son of Hippoclus of Lampsacus at the eastern entrance to the Hellespont, probably in pursuance of Athenian ambitions in that area, Thuc. VI, 59, 3; Hegesistratus, Hippias' half-brother, had been made master of Sigeum at the southern approaches, Hdt. V, 94 etc.

76 Timaeus, in F. Jacoby, *FGH*, 566, 93, schol. on Pindar, *Isthmian* II; these marriages were also 'heroic' in concept, in that only a tyrant was sufficiently *agathos* to be allowed to marry the daughter of a tyrant, Gernet, *op. cit.*, 44 ff, *q.v.* for the importance of the disposal of the daughters, and the durability of links with a mother's family; *cf.* Homer, *Il.* VI, 425–8, IX, 566–7 *et al.*, above, Chapter II

77 Hdt. VI, 126–30; Thuc. V, 43, VI, 89, 2, VIII, 6, 3; but for another view, Xen., *H.G.* V, 4, 22, VI, 3, 4. Pericles was a *xenos* of the Spartan king Archidamus, and believed that this might result in his estate being spared from plunder in the Spartan invasion of 431, Thuc. II, 13, 1. The men of Decelea had hereditary privileges in Sparta, Hdt. IX, 73, 3

78 Pindar, *Olympian* XII (early fifth century), a Cretan immigrant at Himera in Sicily; Hommel, *R.E.* XV (1932), 1424 ff, *s.v.* Metoikoi; Mazzarino, *Athenaeum* 1943, 48–9, with stress on the importance of Zeus Xenios. For Cypselus, Burn, *LA*, 206, with refs. The family claimed heroic descent, from Aeacus and Aegina, and to have migrated to Athens in heroic times

79 Diod. VIII, 7, Pausanias IV, 4, 4 ff, a fuller account; note the absence of the idea of personal responsibility in this story. Hdt. VI, 86 for Glaucus

80 *Cf.* the daughter of Cleoboulus, who wrote poems and advocated women's education and avoidance of public demonstrations of affection between husband and wife, as they avoid quarrels in public, Diog. La. I, 89–92, also note 72 above

81 Fr. G2, 32–5, D. L. Page, *Sappho and Alcaeus* (1955), 199 ff, *Anth. Pal.* IX, 189, Athenaeus XIII, 609E–F, Elis is mentioned, and Tenedos as well as Lesbos as the scene of these; M. P. Nilsson, *RE* X, (1919), 1674

82 Fr. 7 (Diehl), 57–70

83 The earliest version of the list of the 'Seven Sages' is that of Plato, *Protagoras* 343A; Pittacus himself was a 'Sage', as was Solon, and (in most versions) Periander, Burn, *LA*, 207–9; Diog. La. I, 13; for advice to marry your own kind *id.* I, 70 (Chilon), I, 92 (Cleoboulus); marry a girl of your own age, Theognis 457–60

84 Athenaeus XIII, 589F, Periander and Melissa; Plut. *Moralia* 189C, Peisistratus' daughter; Theognis 261–6 seems to be about a frustrated love-match, not a philanderer; Semonides, *loc. cit.* (note 82), 85–7; she also bears him fine children; *cf.* Theognis 1225–6, 1253–4

85 Euripides, *Hecuba* 466–474 and schol. *ad loc.*, Suidas *s.v.* χαλκεῖα, ἐργάνη; Farnell, *Cults*, I, 296 f, Deubner, *Attische Feste* (*AF* hereafter), 31 ff. It is clear that both aristocratic women and slaves worked at the robe. In a later age thanks were voted to the workers, *Deltion Archaiologikon*, 1889, 15 (in 99/8)

86 *Hymn to Apollo*, 146 ff (of the Delian festival of Apollo); for an attack on a band of pilgrims to Delphi, Plut. G.Q.59 = *Moralia* 304E–F

87 Plut. *Solon* XII, 1; the versions of Hdt. (V, 71) and Thuc. (I, 126) omit this detail.

88 E. A. Freeman, *History of Sicily* II (1891), 190, following Pollux IX, 85, rather than Diod. XI, 26; for another story of Demarete, schol. on Pindar, *Olympian Odes* II, 29, K. Freeman, *Greek City States* (1950), 50.

89 Aeschines I, 183: Solon's aim was to make 'life not worth the name', and 'to prevent her corrupting innocent women'. Chapter V below for the law in democratic Athens

90 Examples at Cyme, Plut. *Moralia* 291F (= G.Q. 2), Lepreum, Heracleides Ponticus fr. 14 (Müller, *FHG*, II, 217); *cf.* Glotz, *Solidarité*, 26, note 2, examples from other societies, Chapter VIII below for Gortyn

91 Plut. *Lycurgus* XV, 10

92 *Ath. Pol.* XVIII, 2, Thuc. VI, 56 etc.; in *Ath. Pol.* Thessalus, the brother of Hipparchus, was Aristogeiton's rival. For ὕβρις, Arist. *Pol.* V, 8, 9–13 (1311A–B), V, 9, 13 (1314B); for other examples, Hdt. V, 92η, 3, III, 48, both at Corinth, III, 45, 2, at Samos

93 *Ath. Pol.* XIX, 6, Hdt. V, 65. Despite the use of the plural Peisistratids' (Πεισιστρατιδῶν) in both these, Thucydides (VI, 55) says that only Hippias had any children at the time

94 In Athens, free meals in the Prytaneion (Plato, *Apology* 36D; *IG* I (ed. min), 77), similarly in Ceos, Paros and elsewhere. C. M. Bowra, *Pindar* (1964), 184 ff for varying views on athletic prowess and its deserts. Solon laid down a cash gift of 500 drachmae for an Olympic victor, 100 for an Isthmian (Plut. *Solon* XXIII, 3); the former was equivalent to the annual income of the top property class. That this was a curtailment of their honours is suggested by Diod. IX, 2, 5, Diog. La. I, 55–6. For personal esteem, Pindar, *Pythian* IX, 98–103, a maiden's prayer is for a husband or son who is an Olympic victor. For a sweetheart's encouragement to a wrestler, Philostratus, *Gymn.* 22 (she sent him a message that 'she would not think him unworthy of love-play (τὰ παιδικά) with her if he won an Olympic victory'): she was however probably an *hetaira*; the date is 404

95 Herodotus (V, 71) mentions Cylon's Olympic victory; *cf.* the implication

of *id*. VI, 35–6, that Miltiades' victory inspired him with confidence; for Croton and Sybaris in this age, T. J. Dunbabin, *Western Greeks*, 360–4, for Milon, Harris, *op. cit.* (note 55), 110–3

96 Hdt. VI, 126, 2; Pindar, *Olympians* I–III, for Hieron of Syracuse and Theron of Acragas, both of whom were successful in the four-horse chariot-race between 480 and 470; *Pythians* I–VI, *Isthmian* II, *Nemeans* I and IX were also written for tyrants. For a less decorous celebration (in 373), Dem. LIX, 33, that of Chabrias for a Pythian victory

97 First, second and third according to Euripides, Plut. *Alcibiades* XI; Thuc. (VI, 16, 2) in a speech put into Alcibiades' mouth claims only that no private individual (ἰδιώτης) had ever done so much

98 Thuc. *loc. cit.*: 'By custom such things are honourable, and, from the achievement power also (δύναμις) is inferred at the same time'—*i.e.* the power of Athens which observers had thought might be enfeebled by war. A contemporary critic however (the so-called 'Old Oligarch') claims that the Athenian people were prejudiced against those who went in for athletics and music (ps–Xenophon, *Ath. Pol.* I, 13), but a famous athlete, Dorieus of Rhodes, who constantly opposed Athens, was freed even without a ransom when captured and brought to Athens in 406, Xen. *H.G.* I, 5, 19, in a period when prisoners were frequently killed out of hand

99 Hdt. VIII, 17, Plut. *Alcibiades* I; Philippus of Croton served with his own ship and crew under Dorieus in 510, Hdt. V, 47

100 *Ath. Pol.* XXIII, 1–2; *cf.* Arist. *Pol.* V, 3, 5 (1304A)

101 *Ath. Pol.* XXVII, 3–4; an exaggerated version in Plut, *Cimon* X; Athenaeus XII, 533 (from Theopompus); *cf.* Plut. *Alcibiades* XVI, 3

102 Plut. *Nicias* III, Plato, *Gorgias* 472A for a slight variation; ps–Xenophon, *Ath. Pol.* I, 13, a critic's view of the people's attitudes

103 Xen. *Oeconomicus* (*Oec.*) II, 5–6, XI, 8–9, 14–18

104 Apollodorus, Dem. L, 7 ff for example

105 Dem. LI is a claim for this prize. Note also Apollodorus' claims that his ship was chosen to convey ambassadors because it was the fastest in the fleet, *id*. L, 46. For the celebration of a victory in the tragedies, Plato, *Symposium* 173 A–174 B

106 Hesiod, *W and D* 633–40

107 *W and D* 37–9; that land could be bought in this age is proved by *W and D* 341, but this may be explained by the fact that Hesiod is not speaking of the best, deep-soiled land, but of hill-land, which may have been pasture or scrub-land when the original family *kleroi* had been allocated, with the result that (like common land) it remained outside the normal rules restricting alienation. See Appendix

108 *W and D* 240–7; contrast the righteous in *W and D* 225–37. For examples of injured parties in traditional stories obtaining revenge by suicide after laying a curse on the offending community, Glotz, *Solidarité*, 64 ff

109 *W and D* 248–64, 30–2

110 *W and D* 701; cf. 715–6, 760–4, 343–6. 'The people's talk' (δήμοιό τε φήμη) is already a deterrent in the Odyssey (Chapter II, above)

111 *W and D* 242–5, 325–6

112 *W and D* 321–32, 182–9. Cf. Theognis 271–8, to have undutiful children is a man's worst fate

113 *W and D* 376–80

114 *W and D* 695–701; 344–5 for neighbours

115 Seafaring and trading are rash (note 116 below); cf. Theognis 179–80, even seafaring is better than penury; loose women, *W and D* 373–5

116 *W and D* 646–9; cf. 236–7, 682–7, 633–4 etc.

117 *W and D* 519–21

118 δμῶες, the Homeric word, *W and D* 459, 502, 573 *et al.*

119 *W and D* 602–3; a bachelor's housekeeper follows the plough, *id.* 405; for an illustration in art, *Pl. 45*, sixth century

120 *W and D* 330

121 *W and D* 399–400; or bastard children of slave-girls perhaps, derided by Theognis, 535–8

122 *W and D* 477–8, 497, 533–5 (the old man is used as a simile), 717–8

123 For refugees, Tyrtaeus fr. 6 (Diehl); Theognis 209–10, 1211–1216, 1197–1202 (probably); Alcaeus frag. G2, Page, *op. cit.*, 198 ff; Alcaeus must be speaking of lands. Such men, being unbroken in spirit, provided recruits for mercenary-armies in later times, in earlier ones for free-lance adventurers like Dorieus the Spartan (Hdt. V, 42–6). Isocrates XIV (*Plataïcus*), 46–9, for a highly rhetorical fourth-century description of their plight, Antiphon II, IB, 9, a man exiled for murder will end up as an old beggar. Poverty also made pirates and highway robbers, and was regarded as a sort of productive trade, H. A. Ormerod, *Piracy in the Ancient World* (1924), 68ff

124 Mikkiades, his son Achermus, his two sons Athenis and Boupalus, Burn, *LA*, 223, *q.v.* for refs.

125 R. M. Cook, *op. cit.* (note 50), 81–2, the potter Ergotimus, his son and (perhaps) grandson, also Theson son of Nearchus, (mid-sixth century)

126 Pausanias X, 19, 1–2 (sixth century); Sappho, frags. 57 (she doesn't know how to dress), 104a (Lobel and Page) (perhaps)

127 Theognis 53–8, 847–50, 183–196 *et al.* But Theognis also knew the bitterness of poverty, as (*e.g.*) 173, a poor man cannot say what he thinks; 181–2, death is better than penury; a girl's parents will not look at a poor suitor despite her wishes, 261–6

128 It was an almost invariable rule that ownership of land and houses was vested solely in citizens; the violation of this principle was one of the gravest injuries to the allies imposed by the Athenian empire, reflected by the inscription recording the formation of the second league in 377, Tod *GHI*, II (1948), 123, 25–31, 35–46. Cf. Chapter I above, note 35

129 Thuc. II, 44, 3

130 For the colonizing of Cyrene from Thera, A. J. Graham, *Colony and Mother city* (1964), 224 f *et al.* for discussion. Plato, *Laws* 740A–741A, especially 740D, exactly 5040 citizen-occupiers of *kleroi*; see also Chapter VIII below

131 Arist. *Pol.* VII, 4 (1326A–B), III, 3, 4–5 (1278A). The words in brackets are mine

132 N. G. L. Hammond, *JHS* 1961, 87; for demands in Solon's day, *Ath. Pol.* XII, 3 *et al.*

133 Hdt. V, 92, ε 2 says χρημάτων ἀπεστέρησε; Nic. Dam. says that he took away τὰς οὐσίας, Jacoby, *FGH* 90, 57, 7; this usually includes lands, Theognis 1197–1202

134 Chapter VIII below for Sparta

135 Plato, *Republic* 565E–566A, Isocrates XII (*Panathenaicus*), 259; everyone opposes land-division, *Laws* 684D–E: the jurors' oath in Athens as cited by Dem. XXIV, 149, binds them to oppose it, *cf. id.* XVII, 15. Division of οὐσίαι (which must include lands) is one of the vices which subvert a democracy according to Aristotle (*Pol.* V, 4, 3 (1305A), *cf.* V, 7, 11 (1309A)). Aristophanes, *Clouds* 202 ff, mockingly speaks of geometry as being studied for land-division. *Thuc.* VIII, 21, a division of nobles' lands after a revolution in Samos; other examples, Glotz, *Solidarité*, 535

136 Hdt. III, 131, a famous physician who worked (at an ever-increasing salary) in Aegina, Athens and Samos; in Athens, *cf.* Pittalus, Aristophanes, *Acharnians* 1027–32, 1222–3, Plato, *Gorgias* 514D–E, *Politicus* 259A

137 Some tyrants, like Polycrates in Samos, executed public works like aqueducts, but these are exceptions. Athens, which was exceptional, had police, since the democracy retained the 'archers' first recruited by Peisistratus, but the Spartan secret police (κρυπτεία) were citizens doing a duty laid upon them by the state. A possible exception to the lack of social-security schemes was the διωβελία in Athens at the end of the fifth century, but this was temporary, and an emergency measure. Tod, *GHI*, I, 206 and references there cited

138 M. I. Finley, *The Ancient Greeks* (1963), 76

139 In the fourth century in Athens a soldier was still obliged to appear under arms with three days' rations, a requirement which many found difficult to fulfil, *Lysias* XVI, 14; *cf.* Aristophanes, *Acharn.* 194–8, *Peace* 312, *Knights*, 1079 (perhaps) for the fifth century. The same provision was made by the Corinthian force at Sybota, Thuc. I, 48, 1. For ration-scales in this period, Thuc. V, 47, 6, quoting the inscription in Tod, *GHI* I, 72, 22–5; 3 obols per day for hoplite, archer and light-armed trooper, 1 drachma (twice as much) for each cavalryman

140 In Athens, for example, Solon was the first to acknowledge that the *thetes* (those who were too poor to provide their own arms and armour) had any claim to be full citizens—*i.e.* to have any public rights at all. Hignett, *HAC*, 84, though he doubts whether either they or those who owned no

land at all had in fact public rights till Peisistratus' tyranny, *id.*, 79, 101, 122

141 Thuc. I, 75, 82–4, II, 63, 2, etc.

142 For a critic's view of the political power of the oarsmen, ps–Xenophon, *Ath. Pol.* I, 2, etc.

143 Plut. *Cimon* IX, 4, records the payment of a fleet as early as 478; the arrangements of the Delian League for the provision of ships and men or money clearly envisaged the hiring of sailors and marines

144 Dem. L, 12

145 H. W. Parke, *Greek Mercenary Soldiers* (1933), 16, the first war in which the Athenians had engaged mercenary soldiers; yet even in 413 the Athenians could not afford to hire 1300 Thracians at 1 drachma per man per day, Thuc. VII, 27

146 Thuc. III, 19, 1 and Gomme, *Comm. Thuc.* II, 278; more recently, G. E. M. de Ste. Croix, *Classica et Mediaevalia* XIV, 1953, 30 ff, and *CR* 1966, 90–3, in an adverse review of Rudi Thomsen, *Eisphora* (Copenhagen, 1964)

147 To Aristotle, (*Pol.* III, 5, 4–7, 1279B–1280A), 'oligarchs' are the same as 'the rich' rather than 'the noble'; they were often indistinguishable, but some nobles (like Pericles) were 'democrats'; Aristotle had more evidence at his disposal than we have; we should therefore in a matter of this sort be careful about discarding his evidence

148 Dem. IV, 24 (spoken in 351), declares that no force of Athenians had served abroad since the Corinthian war (394–87); he exaggerates, since Athenians certainly served in the Mantinea campaign of 362 (Xen., *H.G.* VII, 5, 15 ff), and in 352 at Thermopylae (Diod. XVI, 37, 3 with Dem. XIX, 84), and probably elsewhere; *cf.* note 150 below

149 Mercenaries were also unreliable, especially when (as often) unpaid, even when raised and commanded by Athenians; Dem., IV, 24, 'it is impossible to command if one does not pay', οὐ γὰρ ἔστιν ἄρχειν μὴ διδόντα μισθόν. *Id.* XXIII, 149–51, a mercenary captain's career

150 See (*e.g.*) Dem. XLIX, 13–15. Timotheus' force ran out of money; Timotheus borrowed from his personal fortune to pay his Boeotian crews; his Athenian troops merely endured privation

151 Even in Homeric times however the *demioergoi* (skilled craftsmen) may have had landed property; the poet assumes them to be itinerant, *Odyssey* 17, 382–7, and there is no sign of family in this passage, but modern peripatetic village potters from Thrapsanos in Crete are part-time agriculturalists, S. Xanthudides *Essays in Aegean Archaeology* (ed. S. Casson.) 1927, 118 f. The soldier of fortune of *Odyssey* 14, 211–13, 222–7 certainly left his family at home

151A Thuc. II, 16–17

152 Thuc. VII, 27–8 for its effects

153 For a caricature of a juryman, Aristophanes, *Wasps*, *passim*, written in 423–2; Chapter V below for the view that the juryman did not have primary responsibility for maintaining his *oikos*

154 Dem. XXVII, 9, XLVIII, 12; their employees were slaves

155 Dem. XLIV, 4; he was 'too busy to attempt litigation'; cf. Plato, *Republic* 565A, Arist. *Pol.* IV, 4, 1 (1291B). For poor men's workshops, and their part in public building as workmen, H. Francotte, *L'industrie dans la Grèce ancienne* (1900), I, 205–7 *et al.*; Jones, *AD*, Chapter I for a demonstration that the majority of Athenian citizens were workmen, and comparatively poor. Xen. *Mem.* II, 8 for a day-labourer in financial straits

156 Dem. XXXVII, 54; 'risking my life sailing,' πλέων καὶ κινδυνεύων; *id.* XXXIV, 10, a ship lost through overloading; XXXV, 10, a rate of interest of 22·5% over the duration of a voyage; XXXII, 5–6, an attempt to defraud creditors by sinking the boat; speeches XXXVI and XLV–VI are concerned with the banking firm of Pasion and Phormion

157 Examples include Aphobus, Dem. XXX, 26–8; Theopompus (and Hagnias), *id.* XLIII, 69 ff, Phaenippus, *id.* XLII, 5, Euctemon, Isaeus VI, 33, Ciron, *id.* VIII, 15–6; Lysias VII, 4–10 for land as an investment owned for letting purposes; Francotte, *op. cit.*, 213 *et al.*

158 Dinarchus, *in Demosthenem* 71; sale of his house is said to be part of Leocrates' perfidy, Lycurgus, *in Leocr.* 22–5. Dinarchus' statement about orators should be viewed sceptically, though there is other evidence for a *dokimasia* for orators (p. 117 below). In my view there must have been some deterrent to those who wanted to speak when the herald proclaimed 'Who wants to speak?' It is hard to believe that there was no such law at all, but the enforcement of it might have lain with the assembly when a new speaker tried to stand up, and notorious offenders might have been shouted down

159 Xen., *Oec.* V, 16–17 etc., cf. Plato, *Laws* 889D; *id.* 743D–E

160 *E.g.* Aeschines I, 99

161 *Ath. Pol.* LV, 4, Dinarchus, *in Aristogeitonem* 17, etc.

162 Council members at Erythrae, *SIG* 41, 14–16; jurors at Athens, Dem. XXIV, 151, Andocides I, 31 etc.; Glotz, *Solidarité*, 572–3

163 Glotz, *loc. cit.*; witnesses, Dem. LVII, 22, 53; cf. Lysias XII, 10, XXXII, 13, indicating the children (especially) who are implicated. For the parties at law, Dem. LIV, 41, Aeschines I, 114, Andocides I, 126 etc., and in cases of homicide, Dem. XXIII, 67, LIX, 10, Antiphon, V (*Herodes*), 11, ἐξωλείαν σαυτῷ καὶ γένει καὶ οἰκίᾳ.

164 He who injures the state in the Athenian assembly, Dem. XIX, 71, Aristophanes, *Thesmophor.* 349–50 etc. A tomb in Caria declares that, if anyone violate it, 'his progeny will be exterminated and no other child of his race shall be born'. For other examples Glotz, *loc. cit. q.v.* for refs.

165 Glotz, *loc. cit.*, *CIG*, 2555, 22 ff, Crete, second century; cf. Hdt. VI, 86, for this punishment

166 Glotz, *op. cit.*, 476–7

167 Fr. 1, 6 ff (Diehl), from Stobaeus LI, 12

168 Plut. *Moralia* 244 B–F

169 Fr. 6 (Diehl), from Lycurgus, *in Leocr.* 107; fr. 9 (Diehl) 23–34, from Stobaeus, LI, 6

170 Hdt. I, 30–1. He cannot have invented this tale; the world-picture which assumed without argument that Argos was a great city whereas Athens was prospering at the time Tellus lived (εὖ ἡκούσης), and by implication not always so, belongs to the early sixth century, not to the fifth. *Cf.* the tales of Chilon of Sparta and Bias of Priene who 'died well', Diog. La. I, 72, 84–5, Hdt. I, 32

171 C. M. Bowra, *Pindar* (1964), especially Chapter III; relatives' successes, 101, pedigrees, 66, Sicilian tyrants' claims, 117, Arcesilas of Cyrene, 138–9. Diagoras of Rhodes and his descendants' successes, H. A. Harris, *op. cit.*, 123

172 *Isthmian* V, 22; Bowra, *op. cit.*, 102–3 for the rich; *cf.* admiration of Sparta, fr. 189 (O.C.T.), from Plut., *Lycurgus* XXI, 4, Bowra, *op. cit.*, 151–2

173 Bowra, *op. cit.*, 115 ff. *Isthmian* IV, 16–18, four men lost in one day (at the battle of Plataea, fighting for Persia)

174 *Pythian* VII; Athens is the best prelude to an ode for the Alcmaeonidae, Athens is famed everywhere because of the restoration of Apollo's temple (at Delphi, by the Alcmaeonidae). *Cf.* Xenophon and Corinth (*Olympian* XIII), Diagoras and Rhodes (*Olympian* VII, 88–95), Theaeus and Argos (*Nemean* X); Bowra, *op. cit.*, 108, 144–9

175 *Persae* 403–5; *cf.* Thuc. VII, 69, 2

176 Dem. XVIII (*de Corona*), 202–4, Lycurgus, *in Leocr.* 122; Hdt. (IX, 5) gives his name as Lycidas, and adds that the women killed his children too

177 Thuc. II, 35–46; the address was to the families, 34 and 44–5; the good cause, 41, 5–43

178 *Ibid.* 44–45, 2. For the words to the widows (ὅσαι ἐν χηρείᾳ ἔσονται) see W. K. Lacey, *Proc. Camb. Phil. Soc.* 1964, 47–9, an attempt to disprove the conventional view that Pericles said that women should not be spoken of at any time by men; Pericles meant only that widows should be self-controlled (σωφρονεῖν)

179 *Ibid.* 52, 3–4; 'They turned to the neglect of all things, sacred and profane alike.'

180 *Id.* VII, 75, 3

181 Andocides II, 26; *cf. id.* I, 106

182 Plut. *Pericles* XVI, 1, XXXI, 5 *et al.*

183 *Wasps* 486–507

184 Thuc. VI, 15, 4

185 *Lysistrata* 665–70; R. J. Hopper, *CQ*, 1960, 245 ff for explanation, and parallel passages

186 K. J. Dover, *Thucydides VI*, (1965) 57–62, though Dover thinks that Thucydides was merely correcting error wherever he found it

187 Thuc. VIII, 74, 2

188 All were condemned to death, Lysias XII, 36; Xen. *H.G.* I, 7, 4 ff stresses the failure to save those who were still alive, *ibid.*, 11, but he also notes

(8 ff) the influence of the Apatouria, the festival of the families, at which the dead were honoured as well as the new members admitted. Diodorus (XIII, 100) speaks only of the failure to pick up the corpses as annoying the Athenians. The accounts cannot be reconciled, and it is likely in any case that both sentiments played a part

189 Glotz, *Solidarité*, 460 ff; in the case of treason, at Athens at least, the penalties became modified. For sacrilege, the Alcmaeonidae (seventh century), note 26 above; with which *cf.* Diod. XVI, 25, 2–3, 35, 6, 60, 1–2 (the Phocians) in the mid-fourth century

190 MacDowell, *Homicide*, 110 ff for murderers, though Plato thought (*Laws* 871D) 'that he who was convicted of wilful murder must not be buried in his victim's country (χώρα) because of his recklessness (ἀναιδείας) in addition to his godless act'. *Cf. id.* 873 B–D, the family murderer is un-buried, and the suicide is not allowed to be buried in the family grave. As MacDowell shows, however, Plato was more impressed by ideas of pollution than the actual law of Athens was (Chapter XIV)

191 Thuc. I, 138, 6 and Gomme, *Comm. Thuc. ad loc.*

192 Aelian, *V.H.* V, 14

193 Plut., *Nicias* VI, 5; in Thucydides' account (IV, 44) it appears that the victory was not so clear-cut. *Cf.* Pausanias' willingness to admit a Spartan defeat outside Haliartus because Lysander's body could not be recovered without a truce (395), Xen., *H.G.* III, 5, 19–25, Plut. *Lysander* XXIX

194 Lysias XII, 18 and 21; 'It is a disgrace not to be buried in your native land', Teles, from Stobaeus XL, 8; this is clearly a common maxim, attacked by this third-century quasi-philosopher

195 Lysias II (*c.* 392), that in the Platonic *Menexenus* (nominally 387/6), Dem. LX (338) and Hypereides *Epitaphios* (322). Only the Hypereides oration is generally thought to be a genuine speech; Lysias II was rejected by R. C. Jebb (*Attic Orators* I (1876), 206 ff); Dem. LX by L. Whibley, *Companion to Greek Studies* (1931) and W. Rennie's O.C.T. (1931); the *Menexenus* is now generally thought Platonic, but as an exercise, not a speech, L. Méridier, Budé edn. of Plato Vol. V (1931), 77 *et al.* Lysias II, 60 is at least earlier than Aristotle (*Rhet.* III, 10). For the genre, Dionysius of Hali-carnassus (Dion. Hal.), *Rhet.* VI, 1–4

196 Hyper. 4–5 (rejects the task), Lysias II, 4–16, 20–47, Dem. LX, 8–11, *Menex.* 239A–241C; *cf.* the very brief treatment in Thuc. II, 36, 2–4

197 Hyper. 25 (the rule of law), Lysias II, 19, Dem. LX, 26–7, *Menex.* 238B–239A; Thucydides' main theme for Pericles

198 Hyper. 7, Lysias II, 17, Dem. LX, 4, *Menex.* 237B–C; *cf.* Thuc. II, 36, 1

199 Lysias II, 66, Dem. LX, 13–4; *cf.* Thuc. II, 36, 4

200 Hyper. 27 and 42, fathers, mothers, sisters, children, 42, praises of Greeks will be their children, 36, defence of all Greek women; Lysias II, 70–76, the contrast between the city's gain (in the fruits of their valour) and the kins-men's burden of grief; Dem. LX, 32–7, kinsfolk (οἰκεῖοι), treated together

without special mention of women; *Menex.* 246B–247C, address to the children; 247C–248D, to parents (care for women and children); 248D–249C, the city will care for parents and children, and do the family's religious duties for them. *Cf.* Thuc. II, 43, 2–46

201 Hypereides' closing paragraphs are lost. For the close, *cf.* Thuc. II, 46, 2

202 Dinarchus, *in Dem.* 65; *cf. ibid.* 99, 109–10, *in Philoclem* 2

203 *In Leocratem* 2, an appeal to the jury; 8 and 141, the treachery of leaving, 22–5, selling ancestral property, 25, taking his family shrines (*ἱερὰ πατρῷα*) to Megara, 45, refusing to help bury the dead, 97, depriving the gods of traditional honours (*πάτριοι τιμαί*), *ibid.* and 144–7, abandoning parents to the enemy, depriving the dead of their due etc.

204 Aeschines III, 157: *cf. ibid.* 156; II, 15 for those taken at Olynthus

205 Dem. XXII, 61

206 Aeschines III, 172

207 Aeschines II, 93, III, 171–2—Demosthenes was not a citizen; II, 22–3, III, 255, a citizen has ancestors' tombs, free social intercourse, marriage and kinsmen; III, 52, 224, he was treacherous to those with whom he had eaten, etc. Demosthenes' replies are in kind:—XVIII, 129–31, 258–60, on Aeschines' parents, (*cf. id.* XXI, 149, against Meidias); 113–5, 256–8, 268, 312 on his own and Aeschines' public services; 288 on his own public esteem; 41 on Aeschines' profiteering from Thebes' destruction

208 Aeschines III, 171–2. Dem. XXV. 30–2

209 *In Meidiam* XXI, 79, 158: *cf.* 154 ff for Meidias' public services all having been done under compulsion

210 Plato, *Republic* 465B–E etc.; *Laws* 773A (wealth or poverty not a consideration when choosing a bride); 774C–D (the pride of a rich wife, the humiliating and slavish constraint put on her husband (*ὕβρις γυναιξί . . . καὶ δουλεία ταπεινὴ καὶ ἀνελεύθερος . . . . . . τοῖς γήμασι*). Dowries were prohibited, *Laws* 742C (on the distinction between dowry and trousseau, Wolff, *MLAA*, 54–8); limits of acquisition by any means, *Laws* 744E–745A, by will, 922B

211 *Pol.* II, 2, 1–7 (1262B–1263B); *id.* II, 1, 10 (1261B) and II, 4, 2–3 (1266B), criticism of Plato; *cf.* II, 6, 11 (1270A) on Sparta, II, 4, 6–10 (1266B–1267A) on Phaleas' ideas on dowries

CHAPTER IV

FAMILY OIKOI AND ATHENIAN DEMOCRACY

1 *E.g.* Lysias I, 1–2; *cf.* Aeschines I, 4, law as the characteristic mark of democracy; A. H. M. Jones, *Athenian Democracy* (*AD*), 53 for other examples; Euripides, *Supplices* 433 ff for a statement in tragedy; Plato,

Crito 50A ff for a statement of Socratic views. Plut. *Solon* XVIII, 5, claims that this was Solon's aim, M. I. Finley, *The Ancient Greeks* (1963), 32–3, etc.

2 Dracon, Athens' first lawgiver, was remembered only as the author of laws about homicide, Chapter III, note 33; if he established any others, as Aristotle, *Pol.* II, 9, 9 (1274B), seems to think, they were superseded by Solon's, *Ath. Pol.* VII, 1, Plut. *Solon* XVII, 1

3 In *Ath. Pol.* IX, 1, none of the elements 'most favourable to the people' (τὰ δημοτικώτατα) was political; all were concerned with the rights of the individual at law

4 *E.g.* Cleitophon, whose rider to the motion of Pythodorus refers to 'the ancestral laws which Cleisthenes laid down when he established the democracy': τοὺς πατρίους νόμους οὓς Κλεισθένης ἔθηκεν ὅτε καθίστη τὴν δημοκρατίαν, *Ath. Pol.* XXIX, 3. V. Ehrenberg's view (*Neugründer des Staates*, 1925, cited by Hignett, *HAC*, 130), that Cleitophon's motion meant no more than a return to the pre-Periclean state, and was largely propaganda, is probably right; what must be remembered, however, is that the Athenian people passed the motion. *Cf.* Hdt. V, 78; that by ἰσηγορίη Herodotus meant democracy, G. Vlastos, ἰσονομία: *Studien zur Gleichheitsvorstellung in griechischen Denken* (1964), 1 ff

5 That *genē* were essential is supported by the implications of *Ath. Pol.* XXI, 2; 'no investigating men's tribes' was a saying directed against those who were wanting to look into men's *genē*, (ἐλέχθη τὸ μὴ φυλοκρινεῖν πρὸς τοὺς ἐξετάζειν τὰ γένη βουλομένους); the investigators were those who were trying to challenge the rights of those admitted by Cleisthenes. The 'members of the *genē*' is a phrase with two meanings, however: one, actual kinsmen, the other, those who were the people originally distributed in the so-called '*genē*' (οἱ ἐξ ἀρχῆς εἰς τὰ καλούμενα γένη κατανεμηθέντες), Philochorus frag. 35 (F. Jacoby, *FGH*, 328, 35). Members of the *genē*, *gennētai* (γεννῆται) are also defined by him as *homogalaktes*, a word used by Aristotle, *Pol.* I, 1, 7 (1252B), for the members of a small settlement (κώμη) all related to one another. For *homogalaktes*, Chapter I above

6 The evidence for phratries being essential is based on Philochorus (Jacoby, *ibid.*), when he speaks of a rule compelling *phrateres* to enrol *orgeones*; *orgeones*, whatever their character, existed in Solon's time. There was no cause to compel the *phrateres* to enrol them unless their refusal to do so would affect the *orgeones* vis-à-vis the state. *Trittyes* might have been the essential unit; it is implied in *Ath. Pol.* XXI, 3, that the pre-Cleisthenic *trittyes* had kept rolls of their members, but it is odd, if *trittyes* had kept the rolls before Cleisthenes, that they were retained in politics in the vestigial form in which they did survive, and no longer kept any register. For recent accounts, N. G. L. Hammond, *History of Greece* (1959), 153 ff; that Philochorus frag. 35 is from a law established by Cleisthenes, M. P. Nilsson, *A History of Greek Religion* (1925), 245; that it concerns admissions to

phratries subsequent to Pericles' citizenship law, A. Andrewes, *JHS*, 1961,
1 ff, *q.v.* for an entirely different view (from Hammond's) about the
character of *orgeones*; more recently, Forrest, *EGD*, 53ff

7 See Chapter I above

8 See below pp. 96–7 for phratries; W. S. Ferguson, *Hesperia* VII (1938), 1ff
for the *genos* Salaminioi

9 Plut. *Solon* XXIV, 2: γενέσθαι πολίταις οὐ δίδωσι πλὴν τοῖς φεύγουσιν
ἀειφυγίᾳ τὴν ἑαυτῶν ἢ πανεστίοις ᾿Αθήναζε μετοικιζομένοις ἐπὶ
τέχνῃ

10 *Ath. Pol.* XIII, 4–5; they are called 'those whose *genos* was not pure' (οἱ τῷ
γένει μὴ καθαροί); the revision of the rolls was conducted 'since many
were sharing in the citizenship who ought not to have been'; Cleomenes,
the Spartan king, drove out 700 families (οἰκίαι) from Athens (or perhaps
merely proclaimed their disfranchisement or banishment as accursed
(ἠγηλάτει, *Ath. Pol.* XX, 3)). They were Cleisthenes' supporters; they
can hardly all have been Alcmaeonidae. *Cf.* Hdt. V, 72, who calls them
'households' (ἐπίστια, Attic ἐφέστια), a word which implies families,
gods and all, like Plutarch's πανεστίοις (note 9 above)

11 Arist. *Pol.* III, 1, 10 (1275B): 'he enrolled many residents who were
foreigners and slaves' (πολλοὺς ἐφυλέτευσε ξένους καὶ δούλους
μετοίκους). J. H. Oliver (*Historia* 1960, 503 ff) has argued that Cleisthenes
did not incorporate a large number of outsiders into the citizen-body. This
seems hard to accept, since it depends (a) on an arbitrary addition to the
text of Aristotle, *loc. cit.*, in a hitherto unnoticed lacuna, (b) on refusing to
believe that νεοπολίτας in *Ath. Pol.* XXI, 4, bears the meaning it bears
elsewhere—that of those newly enfranchised. If he is right in accepting F. R.
Wüst's view that 'no investigating men's tribes' means a prohibition
on perpetuating the 'Thesean' castes of *eupatridai, geomoroi* and *demiourgoi*,
and that the enrolment in the *Politics* passage above means 'he formed
them into a φυλή or caste', then we must assume that Cleisthenes formed
these quasi-citizens into a new (temporary) φυλή, and then did his redistribution of the (now 4) 'caste φυλαί' among the demes—a move that would
certainly make the demand not to investigate men's tribes much more
strident. There is no evidence that the *metoikoi* enfranchised were not those
who had come to Athens under Solon's law, who had come with their
whole family and cult. It might also be suspected that the 'slaves' said to be
enfranchised may have been the descendants of those Athenians whom
Solon had liberated or repatriated from bondage abroad, who must have
lost their status in their tribes at their enslavement, and may have had
difficulty in obtaining reinstatement in their phratries, and not genuine
(barbarian) slaves. For a citizen as one who has judicial and political (as
distinct from merely personal) rights, Arist. *Pol.* III, 1, 4–5 (1275A)

12 *Ath. Pol.* III, 1; the archons were chosen by birth and wealth: ἀριστίνδην
καὶ πλουτίνδην.

13 *Ath. Pol.* III, 5 states categorically that there was none: κύριοι δ' ἦσαν καὶ τὰς δίκας αὐτοτελεῖς κρίνειν καὶ οὐχ ὥσπερ νῦν προανακρίνειν.

14 *Ath. Pol.* II, 2, ἡ δὲ πᾶσα γῆ δι' ὀλίγων ἦν; *cf. id.* IV, 5. Forrest, *EGD*, 148 ff

15 J. Boardman, *BSA Papers* 1955, 51 ff, *q.v.* (p. 51) for the dating, a little over a century from the last quarter of the seventh century, and their purely Attic provenance

16 G. M. A. Richter, *Archaic Gravestones of Attica* (1961), 1 ff, from whom this whole account is taken; *q.v.* for the change, some time after the middle of the sixth century, into a simpler form of *stele* of more modest size

17 Plut. *Solon* XX, 4, H. J. Wolff, *Marriage Law and Family Organisation in Ancient Athens* (*MLAA* hereafter), Traditio II, (1944), 57–8

18 The aristocrats led the party of the Plain, the Alcmaeonidae that of the Coast; *Ath. Pol.* XIII, 4, Hdt. I, 59, Plut. *Solon* XXIX, schol. on Aristophanes, *Wasps*, 1223 etc. Cleisthenes the Alcmaeonid was defeated by the noble Isagoras in the aristocratic (or oligarchic) clubs, *Ath. Pol.* XX, Hdt. V, 66 ff; *cf.* also the attack on the Alcmaeonidae for medism, *id.* VI, 121, and Pericles' leadership of the popular party in the later fifth century

19 It can scarcely be doubted that Megacles intended that the children of this marriage should inherit Peisistratus' position, and not the children of his former wife. For the marriage, *Ath. Pol.* XIV, 4–XV, 1, Hdt. I, 60–1

20 Plut. *Solon* XXI, 2; before Solon ἐν τῷ γένει ἔδει τὰ χρήματα καὶ τὸν οἶκον καταμένειν. For Solon's law, Gernet, *D. et S.*, 121 ff, the maintenance of the *oikos* was the main object of the will, which was in intention a means of procuring an heir by adoption, and, we may add, a means of providing alternative successors if the first choice failed

21 The group known as *anchisteia* (ἀγχιστεία): see above pp. 28–9. Dracon's homicide law (*IG*, I², 115) shows that the *anchisteia* was pre-Solonian, MacDowell, *Homicide*, 16 ff, 118 f etc.

22 For such a law to be guaranteed to succeed, the limits of the *genos* must be infinite, therefore the *anchisteia* cannot have been relevant to property before Solon; in *Iliad* V, 158, the χηρωσταί, whoever they may be, divided up the property of a man whose sons were all killed

23 Isaeus VI, 28, J. W. Jones, *Law and Legal Theory of the Greeks* (1956), 192

24 For this as a normal primitive way of obtaining an heir, *cf.* the Roman announcement of *heres in procinctu*, Gaius, *Inst.* II, 101. There are also traces in Homer, Gernet, *D. et S.*, 135, but see Chapter I and note 40

25 Dem. XLIV, 68 and XLVI, 14; I understand XLVI, 14 to mean 'any person who had not already been adopted when Solon became Archon in such a manner as to prevent their renouncing their adoption or entering a claim for an estate (ὥστε μήτε ἀπειπεῖν μήτε ἐπιδικάσασθαι), may make a will'; *i.e.* the law is speaking of those whose adoptive parent is dead, and who, having entered upon their inheritance, cannot therefore go back. The words ὥστε ... ἐπιδικάσασθαι are omitted in XLIV, 68,

but, whatever view be held of the genuineness of laws quoted verbatim in the orators as a general rule, these words look most unlikely to have been fraudulently inserted since they have not the least relevance to the case being argued. For other views on the meaning, Wyse, *S.I.*, note on II, 13

26 Plut. *Solon*, XXI, 2, Dem. XLVI, 14, Isaeus VI, 9; *cf. id.* III, 1

27 *E.g.* Isaeus VI, 28 and X, 9

28 Such an accumulation robbed the state of manpower, the impoverishment of the military classes robbed it of soldiers. This provides a satisfactory explanation for the urgent need for action, and the acceptance by the rich of the action taken by Solon. If the *genē* did not lose the land now legally owned by the poor they had no cause for complaint on grounds of cult

29 This was particularly likely to happen among the rich, Plato, *Laws* 773 A–D. Megacles was extremely rich before he married Agariste, the daughter of Cleisthenes of Sicyon; he became even richer by the marriage, Hdt. VI, 125–6. She was probably an *epikleros*, as Busolt (*e.g.*) thought; R. W. Macan, note on Hdt. VI, 126, 5 (1895 edn.). At the end of his account Herodotus says, 'The marriage was accomplished for Cleisthenes' (ἐκεκύρωτο ὁ γάμος Κλεισθένεϊ), VI, 130; this strongly supports such a view, since Cleisthenes would be particularly concerned with his daughter's marriage if through her, and only through her, could he obtain descendants. Her son bore his name

30 Plut. *Solon* XX, 2–3. The choice of her father's next of kin on the male side as her husband was no doubt dictated by the belief of ancient biology that a male planted his seed in a woman, who provided merely the materials for enabling it to grow. A family was therefore more actively continued through the father than through the mother. Aristotle (*Gen. An.* 729A) calls the male part the form (εἶδος) and first cause (ἀρχή), as opposed to the material (σῶμα and ὕλη), which came from the female. The mammalian ovum was not discovered until the early nineteenth century, A. L. Peck, introd. to Aristotle, *G.A.*, Loeb edn. (1943), xii

31 It is important to distinguish what Plutarch implies that the law said— *viz.* that the *epikleros* may have intercourse (ὀπύεσθαι) with her husband's next of kin—from his own comments, and those of others he reports. The fact that the later Athenian law differed from this suggests that the one cited here was genuinely Solonian

31A *Cf.* K. Freeman, *The Work and Life of Solon* (1926), 115–16

32 Hdt. I, 59, 3, *Ath. Pol.* XIII, 4, Plut. *Solon* XXIX. Herodotus believed that Peisistratus' party came late on the scene, after Solon's settlement. *Ath. Pol.* has no awareness of these particular parties before Solon. Schol. on Aristophanes, *Wasps* 1223 indicates that all are post-Solonian. Only Plutarch makes them antedate Solon

33 *Ath. Pol.* suggests that their lands lay in different parts of Attica (ἐγεώργουν), but Plutarch says that Peisistratus' party embraced the

poor (ὁ θητικὸς ὄχλος), and Herodotus implies that Hillsmen (ὑπεράκριοι) was merely a title for Peisistratus' party, not an all-embracing description (συλλέξας δὲ στασιώτας καὶ τῷ λόγῳ τῶν ὑπερακρίων μηχανᾶται τοιάδε). For the view that local rivalries impelled the parties, R. Sealey, *Historia* 1960, 155 ff

34 *Ath. Pol.* XIII, 2: δῆλον ὅτι μεγίστην εἶχεν δύναμιν ὁ ἄρχων. φαίνονται γὰρ ἀεὶ στασιάζοντες περὶ ταύτης τῆς ἀρχῆς

35 The sphere defined in *Ath. Pol.* LVI, 6–7. True, *Ath. Pol.* describes the situation at the end of the fourth century; no doubt many of the specific actions are not ancient, but the sphere of activity must be as genuine as the obviously primitive survivals in the duties of the other archons, the Basileus and the Polemarchos, *id.* LVII–LVIII. P. Vinogradoff, *Outlines of Historical Jurisprudence*, II, (1922), 203; 'The Archon Eponymos had to watch over this distribution (of *kleroi* distributed as far as possible permanently among a set of *oikoi*), and to guard against the disappearance of any of these ancient households'

36 He did not bring confusion into the archons' functions, Hdt. I, 59, 6: οὔτε τιμὰς τὰς ἐούσας συνταράξας, or change the laws: οὔτε θέσμια μεταλλάξας. His actions as recorded in *Ath. Pol.* show a deep concern for the *oikoi* of rural Attica

37 νόθον πρὸς τὴν μητέρα, Plut. *Themistocles* I, 1, who also relates that there was a Gymnasium of Heracles at Cynosarges for bastards, to which Themistocles persuaded legitimate youths to come and train, thus removing the barrier between νόθοι and γνήσιοι; for the one-time registration of bastards at Kynosarges, Dem. XXIII, 213. Athenaeus XIII, 576C, claims that Abrotonon was an *hetaira*; Hdt. VII, 143, merely says that Th. was a newcomer; whether there was an insinuation in 'he was called the son of Neocles' (παῖς δὲ Νεοκλέους ἐκαλέετο) must remain a matter of personal opinion. G. T. Griffith has suggested that the traditions about Themistocles derive from the propaganda of his numerous, powerful and aristocratic enemies; this is impossible to disprove, especially in the light of the confusion about Peisistratus' 'bastard' sons, p. 263, note 75

37A For the demes, Hignett, *HAC* 134 etc. (150 in the late fourth century); *cf.* von Schoeffer, *RE* V (1903), 1 ff (who knows of 166), Busolt/Swoboda *Griechische Staatskunde* II, (1925), 873, note 4

38 Dem. XLIV, especially 38–42, 46–8, provides the clearest evidence that an *oikos* belonged to a deme, since the essence of this argument is that a man was entered on the roll of a deme as belonging to the *oikos* of his natural or adoptive father. The evidence that a child on his adoption into an *oikos* assumed a new phratry and deme points in the same direction

39 First published by G. Daux in *BCH* 1963, 603 ff under the title *La Grande Démarchie*. Discussed by S. Dow in *BCH* 1965, 180 ff, whose conclusions are here adopted

40 Dem. LVII, 63 speaks of rent for *temenē*—lands attached to a cult

41 M. I. Finley, *SLC*, 14 and notes, has denied the existence of a land-register in Athens. There was no single civic register, but it seems impossible to deny that there were registers of the *oikoi* kept by the demes, however inefficiently, and that citizens were registered in them. Apart from anything else, the *temenē* must have been recorded somehow, and we know that non-members who owned land in a deme had to pay a rent (τὸ ἐγκτητικόν), SIG 912, 27–8. Cf. Dem. L, 8

42 Linked for example with προσήκοντες (kinsmen by blood) and *phrateres*, Isaeus VI, 10. Note also the deme's responsibility for ensuring the burial of the corpse of a man whose relatives had failed to take appropriate action, Dem. XLIII, 57–8. For a deme's solidarity in the fifth century, Aristophanes, *Acharn. passim*; for arousing prejudice against an opposing claimant to an estate on the grounds that he belongs to a different deme, (*e.g.*) Dem. XLIII, 64–5, 77–8, XLIV, 34–9 etc. For their religious community, note 39 and the very fragmentary inscription, perhaps of the deme Teithras, J. J. Pollitt, *Hesperia* 1961, 293–6

43 *SIG* 921, 32–42 for the *oikos* of the Deceleans

44 Though membership of a *thiasos* was not a necessary requirement, since the whole deme could approve a candidate rejected by the *thiasos* to which he had applied, *SIG* 921, 94–100

45 Identified with *orgeones* in *CIA*, IV, 2, 620b (third century) = *BCH* 1883, 68 ff

46 Hdt. IX, 73

47 Dem. XLIII, 11. *Ibid.* 77–8 for the adoption of Macartatus into his mother's brother's *oikos*

48 *Ibid.* 12; for severance, *e.g.* Isaeus IX, 2: 'Cleon's father was adopted into another *oikos* (εἰς ἄλλον οἶκον), and they are still in that *oikos* (ἐν ἐκείνῳ τῷ οἴκῳ), so that (because of the law) they have no kinship with Astyphilus in *genos* (ἐν γένει)'; Isaeus X, 4: 'Cyronides . . . was adopted into another *oikos* so that he had no longer any claim to any of the moneys.' (ὥστε αὐτῷ τῶν χρημάτων οὐδὲν ἔτι προσῆκεν). As an example of an adoption ending: 'Leocrates had left the house' (ἐξεκεχωρήκει), Dem. XLI, 5; *cf. id.* XLIV, 26: 'when his father returned to the deme of the Eleusinians he no longer retained for himself his kinship under the law' (τοῦ ὁ πατὴρ ἐπανεληλυθὼς εἰς τοὺς Ἐλευσινίους οὐκέτι τὴν κατὰ τὸν νόμον οἰκειότητα ἔλιπεν αὐτῷ)

49 Dem. XLIV, 33–42; the *oikos* remained, according to our speaker, that of Archiades because successive generations of the family of Leostratus had returned to their own *oikos* leaving a son in the *oikos* of Archiades; hence they had failed to establish a new *oikos*. For the *oikos* as renewed each generation, Gernet, *D. et S.* 149

50 Dem. XLVII, 53: γεωργῶ πρὸς τῷ ἱπποδρόμῳ καὶ οἰκῶ ἐνταῦθα ἐκ μειρακίου; *cf. id.* 60, where a witness is said to have stood on the plot (χωρίον) of a neighbour

50A As the word *oikos* means both a piece of real property (meaning much the same as *kleros*), and the family who made their living on it, it provides a typical example of that lack of exact terminology which confuses the study of Greek society

51 This is not entirely agreed; Wolff (*e.g.*) has grave doubts, *MLAA* 78 f (this article contains a valuable discussion of *oikos*, phratry and deme in connexion with marriage and family succession). Hignett, *HAC* 56 and references cited, regards the lists of phratry-members as the means by which women and minors were recorded as members of the state. For the presentation of girls, Isaeus III, 73–9, especially 75, *q.v.* for εἰσάγειν used for presenting girls as for boys

52 ληξιαρχικὸν γραμματεῖον; there was also a roll (πίναξ ἐκκλησιαστικός) entitling a citizen to payment for attending the assembly and festivals in the fourth century, which seems to have been less carefully kept; Dem. XLIV, 35–6. Even the ληξιαρχικὸν γραμματεῖον was not always carefully kept; Dem. LVII, 26 speaks of a deme's as having been lost

53 *Ath. Pol.* XLII, 1–2. If only youths of the hoplite class were trained, we should have to assume that *thetes* who rose to the ranks of the *zeugitae* (or, in Periclean Athens, became cleruchs and thus no longer *thetes*) thereupon underwent ephebic training. This seems quite impossible. It is not only quite unattested, but inherently unlikely that the state would have included some older men among the epheboi undergoing their training

53A Alice Brenot, *Recherches sur l'Éphébie Attique* (1920), 30, 41, the form described by Aristotle dates only from about 336/5, when it was founded by Epicrates

54 Some became oarsmen; for the fourth century, Dem. L, 6–7: 'The assembly voted that the councillors and demarchs should make lists of the demesmen and hand in lists of sailors . . . but when no sailors who had been listed came, except a few in number who were incompetent . . .'

55 *Ath. Pol.* XLII, 1–2; a similar procedure was employed when the rolls were revised and men were struck off; Dem. LVII is such a challenge to the demesmen, the fragmentary Isaeus XII part of another

56 *Wasps* 578. This particular interpretation of the passage is, I believe, new

57 *E.g.* Tod, *GHI*, I, 86, 14 ff and II, 178, 21 f; *cf.* Pericles' bastard son by Aspasia (Plut. *Pericles* XXXVII, 5), but in this case certainly it was to enable him to succeed to his father's *oikos*, and only when the statesman's sons by his Athenian wife were dead, as Plutarch makes clear

58 Dem. LIX, 104. For the admission of the Plataeans to ἰσοπολιτεία in 431, when the major part of the citizens was evacuated, rather than in 427, when the city fell, Gomme, *Comm. Thuc.* II, 339–40 (note on III, 55, 3). According to Tod, *GHI*, I, 96, 33–4, when the Samians were granted Athenian citizenship in 405, their envoys present in Athens were enrolled only in tribes, not in demes or phratries; obviously their 'deme' would be 'Samos', since that was where they lived at the time of their enrolment

59 Isaeus IX, 30; for *orgeones* in different demes, *SIG* 1096, 1–6

60 Dem. LIX, 61; to Hignett (*HAC*, 64) this means that in pre-Cleisthenic times the ancestors of those here named had separated; it is also possible that a man's deme could be changed when an *oikos* in the sense of a *kleros* of land was acquired by purchase, as it was when one was obtained by adoption. On this, see below, p. 98

61 It is generally believed that members of the Demotionidae belonged to several different demes, *SIG* 921, note 10 and line 119

62 Aeschines II, 147. Hignett, *HAC*, 61 ff

63 For *naukrariai* (naukraries), Hignett, *HAC*, 67–74. That they were pre-Cleisthenic is the important issue for this discussion

64 Dem. LVII, 46; note that this was a priesthood of Heracles, a hero of the trade-guilds, not of the land. Demeswomen also elected their presidents for the Thesmophoria, Isaeus VIII, 18–19; Isaeus II, 42, also mentions service as γυμνασίαρχος ἐν τῷ δήμῳ

65 *Ath. Pol.* LXII, 2; these numbers were in proportion to the size of the demes; if they did not alter (and there is no clear evidence that they did before 306), the size of the demes must have remained constant, and this implies some control on the constituent parts of the demes, the *oikoi*. For differences in the sizes of the demes, and the resultant differing attitudes, Dem. LVII, 57 etc. In the early (perhaps post-403/2) arrangements for election by lot, all the officers selected by lot except the archons were selected from the demes, but this was abandoned before Aristotle's day owing to bribery—perhaps not very long before, if this is the purport of Aeschines' jibes at Demosthenes (III, 62 and 73); *cf. Ath. Pol.* LXII, 1

66 For the demarch, Hignett, *HAC*, 136 and notes; for sailors, Dem. L, 6; for soldiers ἐκ καταλόγου Thuc. VI, 43, VII, 16 and 20, 2, VIII, 24, 2; *cf.* Xen. *Mem.* III, 4, 1, and for making up the lists, Thuc. VI, 26 etc.

67 Isaeus VI, 60; for another list, Xen. *Oec.*, II, 5–6. For the demes' part in the state-religion, *SIG* 1078, the *fasti* for the Dionysia, in which the deme of the *choregos* is often included, especially when the name of the tribe is prefixed to the liturgy, and in the festivals παίδων and ἄνδρων; *cf. id.*, 1084–92 for the deme's appearance on choregic memorials, *id.*, 912, in which the men of (the deme) Peiraeus conducted the Dionysia, but this is a third century inscription

68 *SIG*, 921, and commentary, note 5 etc.; *cf.* Pollux VIII, 107 (quoted *ibid.* note 6), Isaeus, VII, 16, and Wyse's note (*S.I.*) on Isaeus III, 73, 6. For the Apatouria, L. Deubner, *Attische Feste* (1932), 232 ff, (*AF* hereafter)

69 *SIG* 921, 22–24 *et al.*; *cf.* Isaeus III, 37, for a man who got in by four votes, *id.* VI, 21–3, for a corrupt bargain to gain admission

70 *SIG* 921, 97–8, Dem. XLIV, 42; there is no real distinction between introducing (εἰσάγειν) sons to the *phrateres*, and enrolling (ἐγγράφειν) them amongst the demesmen. Both bodies had written lists

71 Dem. XLIV, 41, XLIII, 13 etc. Isaeus VII, 13 and 27–8 etc.

72 For sons, Isaeus VIII, 19, implies at a very early age; for *epikleroi*, *id*. III, 73–9

73 γαμηλίαν ὑπὲρ τῆς γυναικὸς τοῖς φράτερσιν εἰσφέρειν, *id*. VIII, 18, *id*. III, 76 and Wyse, *SI*, 363 f

74 Dem. XXXIX, 4, XL, 11, XLIV, 41–2

75 *Id*. LVII, 46 etc.

76 *Id*. XXXIX, 5

77 *Id*. L, 8. The decree said that demesmen and ἐγκεκτημένοι were to be assessed, *i.e.* all the owners of land in a deme, whether or not they belonged to it for political purposes

78 *SIG* 912, 27–8, τὸ ἐγκτητικόν

79 Dem. LV, 13–14, 35

80 *Id*. XVIII, 312, Aeschines I, 96–101, III, 173 etc.

81 Known as the δίκη παρανοίας, Chapter VI below, notes 2–3

82 Dem. XLIII, 77 *et al*., XLIV, 28, XLII, 21, Isaeus VII, 45, XI, 47 (the opponents' allegation); *cf*. the abuse in *id*. VIII, 40–2, X, 25. Most of Isaeus' clients were in fact rascals who were themselves liable to that accusation

83 Isaeus VII, 38–42 *et al*.

CHAPTER V

MARRIAGE AND THE FAMILY IN ATHENS

1 *MLAA* 65 ff, *q.v.* for formal and informal marriage

2 Dem. LIX, 112–13

3 Plut. *Cimon* IV

4 Thuc. VIII, 6, 3. He speaks of family (πατρικοί) *xenoi*; this would not imply kinship of itself, and there cannot have been kinship within the degrees recognized for the *anchisteia*, but to name an only child with a foreign name without any associations of kinship would be surprising, even if the name was already in the family, as it certainly was

5 Chapter II, pp. 41–3; Democoön (*e.g.*) was Priam's bastard son by a concubine, *Iliad* IV, 499. For other examples, Chapter II, note 45

6 Especially Odysseus' Cretan, *Od*. 14, 199–213

7 *Od*. 14, 10–14; note that Megapenthes is not called a bastard anywhere

8 Chapter III, p. 67 and note 74

9 Chapter I, p. 20 and note 12

10 Chapter IV, note 37, his mother might have been both, an *hetaira* who became Neocles' concubine when she became pregnant by him. For a comic parallel, Aristophanes, *Wasps* 1351–4: the drunk Philocleon promises to

make the (slave) flute-girl his (free) concubine when he gets control of his property (λυσάμενος ἔξω παλλακήν)

11 Dem. XXIII, 53, Lysias I, 30–31, Plut. *Solon* XXIII, 1. It is stated by Lysias that it is one of the 'laws on a *stele* on the Areopagus', therefore probably in fact ancient

12 Chapter IV, p. 89, and note 31

13 The use of this word to describe them is a reminder that *xenos* is not essentially an outsider, but rather the one who is admitted to the family circle though not a kinsman by birth or marriage

14 Isaeus VIII, 43; 'If our mother was not a citizen (πολῖτις), we are not citizens'

15 For Pericles' law, Hignett, *HAC*, Appx. X, 343 ff, *q.v.* for earlier work. It cannot be proved that formal marriage—*i.e.* marriage following *engye*— was necessary before 403/2, and the restoration of the democracy; it can be inferred (perhaps) from the relaxation of the law after the Sicilian disaster in 413 (below, p. 113 and note 95), and from the implication of Aristophanes, *Wasps* 718. In this passage Bdelycleon points out that Philocleon and the chorus of fellow-jurymen (*heliastai*) have to submit to challenges ξενίας to substantiate their position as citizens and jurors; nobody ever suggests that they were not the sons of Athenians—true 'Attic' wasps (1075 ff); they must surely have been liable to a challenge only on the question of whether their parents were formally married, which was perhaps less easy to refute. A challenge ξενίας appears to be the only possible challenge; there was no γραφὴ νοθείας. However, it must be admitted that Aristophanes might not be consistent about the Attic pedigree of the jurors. After 403/2, *pace* Hignett, it is all but certain; it is not satisfactory to maintain that in phrases like γέγονε κατὰ τὸν νόμον, ἐγγυητὴ κατὰ τοὺς νόμους and others, which are by no means uniform, the expression 'lawful' is invariably pleonastic. Generalizations on the supposed habits of the proletariat in societies in which citizenship does not depend on legitimacy are quite irrelevant. It was in the large 'city' demes in which frequent challenges to men's right to be citizens may be inferred to have taken place, Dem. LVII, 57. *Id.*, 40–1, is designed to prove that Euxitheus' parents were not only citizens but married; the whole point of Isaeus III is to prove that Phile's parents were not married. Dem. XLIII, 51 quotes a law prohibiting bastards of either sex from having any kinship-rights from 403/2, νόθῳ δὲ μηδὲ νόθῃ μὴ εἶναι ἀγχιστείαν μήθ' ἱερῶν μήθ' ὁσίων, but that it was not retrospective is proved by what Euxitheus says of his father, *id.* LVII, 30

16 Pericles' own son from Aspasia for example (Plut. *Pericles* XXXVII, 5), Conon's son by a Thracian *hetaira* (*Athenaeus* XIII, 577A), the bankers Pasion and Phormion, Dem. XXXVI, 30, XLV, 78, etc.

17 Date unknown, but before 405, Lysias, XXXIV, 3

18 Chapter IV, p. 95 and note 58. For the slaves who fought at

Arginusae, Aristophanes, *Frogs* 692–4, and scholiast *ad loc.* (from Hellanicus). Isocrates (VIII, 88–9), claims that the Athenians made wholesale importations to replace war-casualties

19 For this law see below p. 113

20 Many writers use the term *engyesis* (ἐγγύησις) which is equally good Greek; I prefer *engye* (ἐγγύη) with Wolff (*l.c.*). Hence ἐγγυητὴ γυνή is frequently used to mean 'legitimate wife'

21 Dem. XLVI, 18 cites a law which defines her *kyrios* as 'father, brother by the same father and father's father', and goes on to say that 'if there are none of these, if she is *epikleros* her *kyrios* is to have her; if she is not *epikleros*, her *kyrios* is to be he to whom her *kyrios* has entrusted her'. Examples of the latter might be her late husband before his death (as Demosthenes' father on his deathbed betrothed his widow to Aphobus); it might also be an adult guardian of a minor, as Theophrastus, stepfather of Astyphilus and his sister, made the *engye* for his stepdaughter with the consent of her (minor) brother Astyphilus, Isaeus IX, 29. The meaning of the phrase ὅτῳ ἂν ἐπιτρέψῃ τοῦτον κύριον εἶναι has been disputed; I have supplied ὁ κύριος as subject of ἐπιτρέψῃ, from the previous sentence. L. Gernet, Budé Demosthenes *ad loc.* has proposed ὁ πατήρ, which seems rather arbitrary. For other discussions, Gernet *op. cit.* (*Plaidoyers civils*) I, 28. It scarcely seems possible to accept A. T. Murray's (Loeb) translation of 'may entrust herself'. The phrase as here interpreted implies that a woman with no brothers might still not be an *epikleros*—if for example she were a widow with a son, especially an adult one—and this is known to be the case, see pp. 141–2. For ἐγγύη by brothers, Dem. XLVI, 19, Isaeus II, 3–5, Dem. XLIV, 9 etc.

22 Hypereides, *Athenog.* 16 on the need for formality

23 Isaeus III, 25–6, Demosthenes LVII, 41, uncles of the bridegroom were witnesses; *id.* XLI, 6, speaks of witnesses, but does not describe them

24 ἐπὶ δικαίοις, Dem. XLVI, 18; *cf.* ἐπὶ ταῖς ὀγδοήκοντα μναῖς, *id.* XXVIII, 16, ἐπὶ τετταράκοντα μναῖς, *id.* XLI, 6; *cf.* Andocides IV, 13 ἐπὶ δέκα ταλάντοις. For an excellent recent treatment of the whole question of dowries, H. J. Wolff, *R.E.* XXIII, (1957), 133 ff, s.v. προίξ

25 Dem. XXVII, 5; it was paid before the elder Demosthenes died, immediately after *engye*

26 Isaeus VI, 22–4, Euctemon, Demosthenes XXVII, 17, Aphobus to Demosthenes' mother

27 ἐγγυῶ . . . . νόμοισι τοῖσι Ἀθηναίων · φαμένου δὲ ἐγγυᾶσθαι Μεγακλέος ἐκεκύρωτο ὁ γάμος Κλεισθένεϊ. Chapter III, p. 66, and note 64. Dracon's code (*Ath. Pol.* IV, 2) speaks of a requirement that high military officers should have legitimate children by a legal (γαμετῆς) wife. Even if the code is a forgery, this particular requirement cannot have seemed incredible to a contemporary (late fifth- or early fourth-century) audience

28 Demosthenes XLI, 6, LVII, 41; Isaeus III, 25-7, VIII, 14

29 Isaeus III, 18-20

30 προδήλους; Wyse (SI), note ad loc., against LSJ

31 Themistocles' daughter Mnesiptolema married her half-brother, Plut. *Themist.* XXXII, 1-2; so did the grandparents of Euxitheus, Dem. LVII, 20, and perhaps Demosthenes' parents, *id.* XXVIII, 1 and 3

32 E.g. *id.* LIX, 1-2, Theomnestus married his sister's daughter; *cf. id.* XLIV, 10

33 Isaeus XI, 16 ff; this family has four marriages at least between cousins. *Cf. id.* VIII, 7, the family of Ciron. Another of Themistocles' daughters, Nicomache, married her first cousin, Plut. *loc. cit.*; Demosthenes' sister was betrothed to her first cousin, Dem. XXVII, 4-5

34 Isaeus VII, 11-12. Contrast Aeschylus, *Supplices* 333 ff; hatred makes Danaus' daughters regard themselves as slaves, mere property, easily disposed of, when marriage to their cousins is proposed

35 Dem. XLIV, 10

36 Isaeus II, 18, but the speaker implies it was not unusual for natural fathers to do the same

37 Dem. XL, 12-13; it is implied by this speaker too that the father took the initiative in procuring his son a bride. *Cf. id.* 56, a result was that men mistook his daughter for his sister

38 Plato, *Laws* 721B, 785B; *cf. ib.* 772D, *Republic* 460E (25 or over); Arist. *Politics* VII, 14, 6 (1335A) (37 or a little before; girls at 18)

39 Isaeus II, 18 and 36; on old age, see below, pp. 116-8. This arrangement, whereby the young man was ready to take over from his father the management of the *oikos* and marry was approved by Aristotle, *loc. cit.*

40 They then were said to be ὑπὲρ τοῦ καταλόγου or ἔξω τοῦ καταλόγου. They became arbitrators (διαιτηταί) for one year (*Ath. Pol.* LIII, 4), but did not necessarily retire into oblivion—Socrates was even a member of the Council, and president of the Assembly after that age, since he was aged 70 in 399 and had been president in 405 (Xen. *Mem.* I, 1, 18 with Plato, *Apology* 32B–C). He was also married rather late in life, since his three sons were still under age in 399, two being described as merely little children (παιδία) at his death (Plato, *id.* 34D.)

41 See note 38 above. Hesiod, *W. and D.* 695 ff and in art, *Pl. 24*

42 Plut. *Lycurgus* XV, 3; they were … οὐ μικρὰς οὐδὲ ἀώρους πρὸς γάμον … ἀκμαζούσας καὶ πεπείρους

43 Pollux VIII, 107 (s.v. φράτορες). 'They brought boys (κόρους) and girls (κόρας) to the *phrateres*, and at the age of young adulthood (εἰς ἡλικίαν προελθόντων) on the so-called *koureotis* day they sacrificed, for the boys the boys' sacrifice (τὸ κούρειον), for the girls the wedding sacrifice' (τὴν γαμηλίαν). For the association with the cutting of the hair, *SIG* 921, and commentary. Deubner, *AF* 232 ff for an account of the Apatouria

44 See further Chapter VII below. For a modern illustration in primitive parts of the Peloponnese, Sheelagh Kanelli, *Earth and Water* (1965), 121/2

45 Hdt. VI, 122. The fact that the chapter is generally condemned as spurious does not affect this argument much, since, even if it was not Herodotus who thought it most unusual, it was another writer

46 Plut. *Cimon* IV, 7; *cf. ib.* 9 for Cimon himself, and Dem. XL, 27 for a man said to be in love with his wife (probably a second one in this case)

47 Chapter III, p. 69 and note 84

48 Isaeus I, 39 on the obligation to see to the marriage of cousins had they been left orphans by their father's death. In Athens it would be taken as a mark of his miserliness if a man did not procure husbands for his daughters or sisters; *cf.* Lysias XIII, 45, XII, 21 for deprivation of marriage as a grievous wrong

49 Elpinice, Plut. *Cimon* IV, 7; Dem. LIX, 8, 'Who would ever have married the daughter of a state debtor who was utterly without means—and she without a dowry?'; *cf. id.* XXVIII, 21, XL, 56, XLV, 74. Lysias XIX, 14–16, choosing a poor but honest bride; for *epikleroi*, Chapter VI below

50 Suggested by the comic fragment in Athenaeus XIII, 572A

51 Dem. LIX, 75–6; *cf. Ath. Pol.* III, 5. The shrine was at Limnae and open only once a year, on the occasion of this women's rite at the Anthesteria

52 Dem. XXVII, 13–15, *id.* XXIX, 26

53 Hypereides, *Lycophron* I, 7 with *ib.* 3

54 Demosthenes' mother is an example, also Hagnias' mother, Isaeus XI, 8; *cf. id.* VII, 7–8, IX, 27 etc.

55 By ἀπόλειψις; see (*e.g.*) Isaeus III, 8, 35, 78; Dem. XXX *passim*, Plut. *Alcibiades* VIII, 3–5. The only legal provision was that the woman must get the divorce registered in the Archon's court, Dem. XXX, 17 and 26, Plut. *loc. cit.*, Andocides IV, 14 etc.

56 By ἀπόπεμψις; *e.g.* Dem. LIX, 81–3; the speaker claims the reason was her illegitimacy. For varying formulae in divorce, Wyse, *S.I.*, note on III, 8, 5

57 Dem. XLI, 4

58 Isaeus II, 7–9; Dem. LVII, 40–41; see further Chapter VI, pp. 142–4

59 Isaeus III, 28; *cf. ib.*, 49–51: less than one tenth of an estate is 'outrageously small'

60 Isaeus XI, 40 (in effect), III, 49 *et al.*

61 Dem. XXVII, 42–5; *cf.* Archippe's huge dowry, *id.* XLV, 28

62 Isaeus XI, 38–9, Dem. XXVII, 69, law quoted in *id.* XLIII, 54

63 Aeschines, III, 258; *cf.* Plut. *Aristeides* XXVII, 4; Aristogeiton's grand-daughter was given a dowry by the state (fifth century). For Timosthenes, *SIG* 496, 18: ὅσα ἂν βούληται (in 229/8)

64 Examples above; *cf.* Isaeus VIII, 8, V, 26, Dem. XLI, 5. For money secured by real property as a form of dowry, Finley, *SLC*, 79 ff *et al.*

65 Wolff, *MLAA*, 61–2. Examples of widows' dowries, Dem. XXVII, 5, 13–4, 13 with *id.* XLV 28, Isaeus VIII, 8; Lysias XXXII, 6; Hypereides, *Lycophron*, I, 5—an exceptionally interesting case in that her *kyrios* (her brother)

arranged her marriage, but her child's guardian, who had charge of her first dowry, provided her with a dowry

66 Dem. XLVII, 56–7

67 Plut. *Solon* XX, 4; that this is the meaning of the passage, Wolff, *MLAA*, 58

68 Isaeus III, 35. For gifts of garments and jewels as a mark of goodwill, Isaeus II, 9: 'When Menecles (who had divorced his young wife by consent) paid back (ἀποδίδωσι) the dowry, and gave to her (δίδωσι) the garments she had when she came to the house and the jewels which there were . . .' Isaeus VIII, 8, should be punctuated in this sense as well: ἐκδίδωσιν αὐτὴν Ναυσιμένει Χολαργεῖ σὺν ἱματίοις καὶ χρυσίοις, πέντε καὶ εἴκοσι μνᾶς ἐπιδούς

69 Dem. XXVII, 53–5; he describes her as in control of them (κυρία), and says: 'If he distrusted his son's guardians, it was sheer madness to tell them about what lay concealed if he had no intention of putting the property into their charge. If he trusted them, surely he would not have given into their hands the bulk of his money without giving them charge of some more. Nor would he have given my mother this money to look after and given her herself to one of the guardians to be his wife; it is not rational to try to preserve the money through my mother and to put one of those whom he did not trust in charge of her and the money alike.' G. E. M. de Ste. Croix, *Classica et Mediaevalia*, 1953, 34, note 17, provides examples of concealment of wealth

70 Or he might provide her with a new dowry, as in Hypereides, *Lycophron* I, 13

71 Dem. XLI, 9 and 21; *cf. ib.*, 11

72 For the ceremonies at a marriage, 'Hans Licht', *Sexual Life in Ancient Greece* (1932), (*SL* hereafter) 42–56

73 Dem. XXVII, 45 says of Demophon's betrothing his infant sister that Demophon got possession of her dowry (2 talents) 'though he was not yet going to live with my sister': οὔπω μέλλοντι . . . συνοικήσειν. Cf. Pollux, III, 44–5

74 Xen. *Mem.* II, 2, 4: φανεροὶ δ' ἐσμὲν σκοπούμενοι ἐξ ὁποίων ἂν γυναικῶν βέλτιστα ἡμῖν τέκνα γένοιτο· αἷς συνελθόντες . . . τεκνοποιούμεθα. I doubt if *LSJ* is right in translating συνελθεῖν as 'have sexual intercourse'; it is equivalent to συνοικεῖν rather, which, it is true, implies this, but has prime reference to the establishment of an *oikos*. *Cf.* what Ischomachos says (Xen. *Oec.* VII, 11–12, 18–19)—he and his wife's parents both sought 'the best partner in the *oikos* and children'

75 Dem. LIX, 122; *cf.* Isaeus VI, 2–4, where; despite the husband's age, children were to be sought

76 Isaeus II, 7–9; *cf.* Xen. *Mem.* I, 4, 7: the desire for children is natural alike in men and women. On this question I should regard the evidence of tragedy as useful support; it is unequivocal, *e.g.* Sophocles, *Electra* 164–5

and 959–62, *O.T.* 1492 ff, *Antigone* 810 ff and 916–18, whether the latter is spurious or not, as Dindorf amongst others thought. See Jebb *ad loc.*

77 Isaeus VIII, 36

78 Aristophanes, *Wasps* 568–71, 976–8 etc. Plato, *Apology* 34D–35B; *cf.* Dem. LIII, 29, XXI, 99 etc. for accusations that the opponent will do this

79 *Id.* XLIII, 81–4; *cf.* XL, 56–7; Mantitheus' daughter was clearly in court

80 *Id.* XXVII, 65, reading γυναῖκας with the MSS. *Id.* LIII, 28 shows a mother claiming that part of an estate was not liable to be confiscated by the state

81 Xen. *Mem.* I, 5, 2

82 Isaeus VIII, 18, *id.* III, 75, 79; Pollux VIII, 107

83 Dem. XXXIX, 22, XL, 28; Isaeus III, 30, relatives (uncles) attended; Aristophanes, *Birds* 494, 922; *cf.* the comic fragment in Athenaeus XV, 668D for an all-night celebration. For family names, Dem. XLIII, 50, 74 and 77 etc.

84 *Id.* LVII, 54; ἀστὸν ἐξ ἀστῆς ἐγγυητῆς ἑαυτῷ γεγενημένον εἰδώς; Isaeus VIII, 19, suggests it was very early in life, *id.* XII, 3, somewhat later. Adopted sons were also introduced at their adoption, Dem. XLIII, 13, etc., Isaeus VII, 13 and 27–8 etc.

85 1000 drachmae = 10 minae = τὰ νοθεῖα, the bastard's portion. This meant that other (citizen) relatives could claim the rest of their family property, Dem. LVII, 53; *cf.* Hypereides, *Lycophron* I, fr. 5 and Isaeus III, *passim*, a speech which is intended to prove the rival claimant a bastard. For religious rights, Dem. XLIII, 51, citizen rights, Wolff, *op. cit.* 76–8

86 This is the point of the joke against Heracles in Aristophanes, *Birds* 1641–69. In Dem. LVII, 53–5, it is clear that bastards (νόθοι) were not the same as *xenoi*, but from the point of view of claiming citizens' estates, they had similar disabilities. *Xenoi* were themselves of several classes: ξένοι (true *xenoi*), who were merely temporarily in Athens, ξένοι μετοικοι (metics) who lived semi-permanently in Athens, ξένοι *isoteleis*, and *proxenoi* who were specially privileged metics. In what spheres bastards were under-privileged citizens, and in what they were exceptionally-privileged *xenoi* we do not know. It is important to remember that *xenos* means 'the out-sider who has been allowed into the circle though not a member of it'

87 *Ath. Pol.* LVIII, Dem. XLVI, 22

88 For metics, *e.g.* Thucydides II, 31, 2, 3000 metic hoplites. Among bastards, Themistocles certainly served, so did Ctesias son of Conon, Demosthenes LIV, 26 with 3 and 7. Poorer metics might have had to serve in the fleet; no doubt bastards did the same

89 Hommel, *RE*, XV, (1932) 1413 ff. sv. μέτοικοι; metics paid a special tax of 12 drachmae a year (μετοίκιον) unless they were raised to the status of *isoteleis* (*i.e.* those who (only) pay the same taxes as citizens). *SIG* 346, an inscription in honour of Nicandrus and Polyzelus, records payments of 10 talents in *eisphorai* between 347/6 and 323/2 (lines 14–18), as well as

military service (lines 37–41); in return they were made *isoteleis* and granted γῆς καὶ οἰκίας ἔγκτησις, leave to purchase real-estate, and to pay *eisphorai* and serve on campaign with the Athenians—*i.e.* only when the citizens were called out

90 Dem. LVII, 55; 'What have I done of the things that those who are not genuinely citizens are always revealed as having done, and where did I do it?' From this speech it may fairly be deduced that they bribed the officer in charge of the deme's roll of citizens (ληξιαρχικὸν γραμματεῖον) to insert their names, giving them a spurious parentage; they may also have tried a number of different demes

91 See above p. 95

92 Dem. LIX, 16–7; in his next sentence Apollodorus makes it clear that the point of the law was to prevent illegal pseudo-marriages: 'the law does not allow a foreigner to live with a citizen or *vice versa* nor to procreate children'—οὐκ ἐᾷ . . . συνοικεῖν . . . οὐδὲ παιδοποιεῖσθαι. Men who openly kept a concubine were not said συνοικεῖν and παιδοποιεῖσθαι, though concubines had a fully-recognized status under the law, *id.* XXIII, 55–6, etc.

93 Dem. LIX, 51–53; she cohabited (συνῴκει) with her husband, pretending she was a citizen

94 *Id.* LIX, 118–122. For a wife as higher in standing than a concubine or courtesan, *cf.* Plut. *Solon* XXII, 4, Lysias I, 30 Xen. *Mem.* II, 2, 4, *Oec.*, I, 13, Menander, *Dyskolos* 58–66 etc. This testimony across three centuries should be sufficient evidence to deny the validity of the traditional interpretation

95 Diog. La. II, 26 (à propos Socrates): γαμεῖν μὲν ἀστὴν μίαν . . . παιδοποιεῖσθαι δὲ καὶ ἐξ ἑτέρας

96 Lycurgus, *in Leocr.* 41; *cf. id.*, 100. He regards both as minor disasters, contrast the attitude of Aristophanes (*Frogs* 687–702) to the incorporation as citizens of all who fought at Arginusae, and the simultaneous refusal to reinstate the disfranchised

97 It is legitimate to wonder how far the remarkable ease with which Homeric and heroic ladies (except Penelope) could be seduced influenced men's thought. Dem. XLVII, 53, for the extreme impropriety of even entering the presence of an Athenian woman in the absence of her husband—the opponents (of course) did not hesitate, whereas a witness would not do so (*id.* 60), and of course the speaker did not do himself; though he entered the opponent's house 'he knew he was not married' (*id.* 38). See also p. 158 ff below

98 *Id.* XXIII, 53–6; *cf. Ath. Pol.* LVII, 3 for lawful killings

99 Lysias I, 2; Plut., *Solon* XXIII, says that Solon prescribed a fine of 20 drachmae for seduction of a free woman, 100 drachmae for rape; this hardly agrees with Demosthenes. The likeliest explanation is that Plutarch has either misunderstood his source, or expressed himself badly, and free but non-citizen women are in question here. The fact that his next sentence is

about prostitutes adds to this impression, since kept women are virtually always slaves or freedwomen, Isaeus VI, 19–22, Dem. LIX, *passim*, Lycurgus, fr. 96 (= Stobaeus II, 30) (we must remember that fragments lack their context), Xen. *Mem*. II, 1, 4–5

100 Plato, *Laws* 838E–841E

101 Lysias I, 33; *cf.* I, 4: 'He corrupted my wife, he brought shame on my children, he insulted me myself'

102 Implied by Plut. *Solon* XXIII, 2, a virgin could not be sold; Hypereides, *Lycophron* I, 12–13; the seducer is accused that [πολλὰς μὲν γ]υνα[ῖκας ποιῶ] ἀγάμου[ς ἔνδον κα]ταγηρ[άσκειν] and the same is said to happen to widows: ἀνέκδοτον ἔνδον καταγηράσκειν. Aeschines I, 183, shows that it was deprivation of the pleasure of dressing-up for festivals that was what 'made life not worth living'. Was this more savage than Victorian fathers putting their seduced daughters out on the street? Aeschines, *loc. cit.*, knows of even more barbarous punishments, but they may well be apocryphal, as Hans Licht is inclined to think (*SL* 62)

103 Kallias, frag. 1; κέρδος αἰσχύνης ἄμεινον. ἕλκε μοιχὸν ἐς μυχόν. *Cf.* Aristophanes, *Plutus* 168, *Ach.* 849 (shaving), *Clouds* 1079–1084 (depilation and ῥαφανίδωσις); Xenophon, *Mem.* II, 1, 5 for his Socrates' view

104 Dem. LIX, 86–7

105 Hypereides, *Lycophron* I, 12

106 Dem. LIX, 64–71

107 Isaeus III, 39; the passage has been hotly disputed, Wyse, *SI*, note *ad loc.* —but quite unnecessarily, unless we start with preconceptions as to what the Athenians ought to have done. The girl in this speech was married ὡς ἐξ ἑταίρας οὖσα with a dowry of 10 minae (τὰ νοθεῖα)—according to the speaker. He may be lying, but what he says must have sounded credible at least

108 Hypereides, *Athenog.* 29 (a very fragmentary passage) shows a metic marrying his daughters off; the orator employs the word (ἐξέδωκε) which is used for citizen-fathers also

109 *Ath. Pol.* LVIII. Dinarchus (*in Dem.* 23) also cites examples of Athenian courts punishing citizens severely for personal offences against non-citizens—keeping a free boy imprisoned, raping a Rhodian lyre-girl, sending an Olynthian maidservant to a brothel—but there may have been more in the cases than we are told

110 Xen. *Mem.* II, 8, 5–6, for Socrates' advice

111 Dem. XLVI, 14; alluded to in Isaeus II, 14–5: ὑγιαίνων ... εὖ φρονῶν ... εὖ νοῶν ... and he lived another 23 years. *Cf. id.* VI, 21, Wyse, *SI*, note on II, 13. Many refs. in comedy, *e.g.* Aristophanes, *Wasps* 67–135; Philocleon is sick (νοσεῖ), 71, 87, 114 etc., won't sleep, 91–6, does crazy things, 97–110; his family tried to cure him, 114–24, to keep him at home, 126–30, and eventually had to lock him up within, 69–70, 131–2 and the

horseplay of 138–210. *Cf.* Aeschines III, 251–2, the whole people in its dotage

112 Thuc. II, 44, 4. 'You who have passed the age for obtaining new children should think the greater part of your life in which you have been happy to be a blessing (κέρδος), and the life that is now yours will be short— and you should have your grief lightened by the fame of the dead', which would not by itself be so unsympathetic did it not follow immediately upon the sentiment that 'it is not possible for those who have no stake in the country and have no children of their own too to put into danger along with everyone else to give honest (ἴσον) or unprejudiced counsel to the state'. Nor does Herodotus seek longevity among the blessings of his 'happiest' men (I, 30–1); Tellus of Athens' own age is rather played down, though what we hear of his grandsons must mean that he was not young himself; however, he was still a soldier and there-fore not over 60

113 γονέων κάκωσις, *Ath. Pol.* LVI, 6; parents included grandparents (Isaeus I, 39), and all ascendants who might possibly be living (*id.* VIII, 32); the most distant the orator can conceive are greatgrandparents, who are defined as the starting-point of the clan (ἀρχὴ τοῦ γένους). *Cf.* Dem. XXIV, 103–7, XXV, 65 ff

114 Dinarchus 2, 17–18: τοὺς τῶν κοινῶν τι μέλλοντας διοικεῖν, *Ath. Pol.* LV, 3, Dem. LVII, 70, Aeschines I, 28

115 Xen. *Mem.* II, 2, 1–13 gives 'Socrates'' version of why the law is right; we owe an obligation to our parents who created us out of that which was not (οὓς οἱ γονεῖς ἐκ μὲν οὐκ ὄντων ἐποίησαν . . . εἶναι), and our obliga-tions are based on returning good deeds; Xenophon includes not only the need to feed our parents but also mentions legal action if a man does not look after them (ἐάν τις γονέας μὴ θεραπεύῃ). Demosthenes XXIV, 107 says that the laws compel the living to support their parents (τοὺς γονέας τρέφειν). For the law, Diog. La. I, 55: ἐάν τις μὴ τρέφῃ τοὺς γονέας ἄτιμος ἔστω. For comic treatments, Aristophanes, *Wasps* 341, 729–59, Philocleon will not accept his son's offers, 1004–6, new promises when he has submitted; *q.v.* for τρέφειν (737 and 1004, θρέψω); *id.* *Birds*, 1347–69: the point here is that a chick who pecks his father when he is the stronger is brave, 1349–50, but when the chick is old enough to leave the nest he must feed his father (1357). It is also to be noted that the father-beater is not allowed to live with the birds, but is sent off to win a living as a mercenary (1367–9). For another view, V. Ehrenberg, *People of Aristophanes* (1951) (*People* hereafter), 208–9

116 Plut. *Solon* XXII, 1 and 4; those to whom their father had not taught a trade, and bastards—children of *hetairai*, because their fathers had taken a woman merely for pleasure and not to rear a family; see the echo in Xen. *Mem.* II, 2, 2–4. Aeschines I, 13 includes those who had debauched their sons, or allowed others to do so

117 Xen. *Oec.*, VII, 12, Isaeus II, 10–12, etc.

118 Maintenance was σῖτος; a suit for the provision of it was δίκη σίτου; Photius (s.v. σίτου δίκη) also mentions divorcées who had initiated the divorce by ἀπόλειψις; it was the claim for maintenance which accounts for their appearance before the Archon, since any suit for σῖτος came before him; the expression σίτου δίκη was almost certainly ancient, preceding a monetary economy

119 9 obols per month (sc. per mina)—*i.e.* 18%

120 Isaeus VII, 7 and IX, 27–9; *id.* VI, 51; this widow must have been at least middle-aged

121 Isaeus II, 18 and 36 etc. *Cf.* the description of Bouselus' disposition of his property among his sons (Dem. XLIII, 19); it is strongly hinted that the father was still alive at the time

122 Lycurgus, *in Leocratem*, 40

123 Aristophanes, *Wasps*, esp. 441–52 (Philocleon was once master of the slaves now restraining him), 67–70 (Bdelycleon is master (δεσπότης)), 605 ff (the juror's 3 obols are pocket-money with which Philocleon can get some fun, whereas he can get bread from his son's steward, however grudgingly); Bdelycleon repeatedly undertakes to look after the old man, 341–2, 737–40, 1003–6 etc.; the drunk Philocleon behaves like an irresponsible youth not yet old enough to have control of his property, 1351–7

124 Xen. *Mem.* I, 2, 49 ff

CHAPTER VI

PROPERTY AND THE FAMILY IN ATHENS

1 The Athenian law of succession is a mixture of statute law and ancient custom; P. Vinogradoff, *Outlines of Historical Jurisprudence*, II (1922) 72 ff, 206 ff for the archaic elements in the law; pp. 139 ff below for *epikleroi*, for *oikos orphanikos*, note 61

2 *Ath. Pol.* LVI, 6: (ἐάν τις αἰτιᾶταί τινα παρανοοῦντα τὰ ὑπάρχοντα ἀπολλύναι (ὑπάρχοντα is a supplement in a lacuna); the action seems to have been taken by a son, Plato, *Laws* 928E, 929D, Aristophanes, *Clouds* 844 ff, Xen. *Mem.* I, 2, 49; if anyone could take action, it is odd that Chaerestratus made no attempt to restrain Euctemon, if his account of the old man's proceedings bears any resemblance to the truth, Isaeus VI, 29 ff

3 Dem. XLVI, 14: ἂν μὴ μανιῶν ἢ γήρως ἢ φαρμάκων ἢ νόσου ἕνεκα ἢ γυναικὶ πειθόμενος ὑπὸ τούτων του παρανοῶν, ἢ ὑπ' ἀνάγκης ἢ ὑπὸ δεσμοῦ καταληφθείς. *Cf.* Plato, Xenophon, Aristophanes *ll. cc.*, *Wasps*, 71, 87 ff, Philocleon is diseased (νόσον νοσεῖ).

4 Wyse, *S.I.*, 234 ff and note on II, 19–22

5 Xen. *Mem.* II, 3, 1–5, assumes that having a brother will result in a smaller, because divided, inheritance

6 Adoptions, p. 145 f, disinherison, Th. Thalheim, *RE*, 1 (1894), 2836–7, *s.v.* ἀποκήρυξις

7 Plut. *Themist.* II, 6, Dem. XXXIX, 39, Plato, *Laws* 928D–E: ἐν παγκάκων ἤθεσιν ἀνθρώπων . . . ἐν ἄλλῃ πολιτείᾳ παῖς ἀποκεκηρυγμένος οὐκ ἂν ἐξ ἀνάγκης ἄπολις εἴη. Aristotle, *E.N.* VIII, 14, 4 (1163B)

8 Dem. XLIV, 10: τὴν οὐσίαν ἀνέμητον διὰ ταῦτα συγχωρήσας εἶναι

9 Isaeus II, 28

10 Dem. XXXVI, 8–11. The land must be included in 'other property' here, since we know that Pasion owned land worth 20 talents, *id. 5. Cf. id.* XL, 14–15, where the house and the slaves, part of the inherited property (τὰ πατρῷα), was left undivided pending a settlement between half-brothers of claims arising out of their mothers' dowries

11 Isaeus I, 4, grandfather's wishes; *id.* 1, 12 ff, 28 etc. for their living with their maternal grandfather when their paternal uncle died

12 Dem. XLVII, 34–6 and 53

13 ἄνδρες ἐγένοντο, *id.* XLIII, 19; for a disputed division, Isaeus IX, 17; the Archon appointed the arbitrator of disputes, *Ath. Pol.* LVI, 6

14 Isaeus VI, 3–7, 38 (liturgies), 36 (attempted posthumous adoptions)— μισθοῦν ἐκέλευον τὸν ἄρχοντα τοὺς οἴκους ὡς ὀρφανῶν ὄντων; *cf.* 44. It is probable that Sauppe's emendation of para. 44 is correct, and that Philoctemon has been substituted for Hegemon by a scribe using his initiative, and that what Euctemon had planned was that he should be succeeded by three adopted sons, one in the *oikos* he had created for each of his three dead sons. This Chaerestratus would not accept, but tried, as Philoctemon's adopted son, to obtain the *oikoi* of all Euctemon's three sons, all of whom were his uncles. Comparable divisions of *oikoi* are traceable at Gortyn (code IV, 23–31) and in the 'Testament of Epicteta', K.M.T. Chrimes, *Ancient Sparta* (1949) (*A.S.* hereafter), 239 ff, where it is shown that if one son succeeds in his father's lifetime, all do so. It seems clear from para. 10 that all Euctemon's sons attained their majority, and they would therefore have had their property assessed at their *dokimasia*. Euctemon would, of course, be *kyrios* of the property of the *oikoi* of his dead sons, since they had no heirs, but this would perhaps not extinguish them unless he procreated new sons

15 Isaeus VI, 30; the daughters could not become *epikleroi* if Philoctemon had an adopted son. Most modern commentators seem to think that Chaerestratus did not claim because Euctemon and Philoctemon had some sort of joint ownership of the property, and therefore Philoctemon's estate did not amount to much. It seems to me more likely that at Philoctemon's death Chaerestratus' parents did not want Euctemon to become *kyrios* of Chaerestratus, who will then have still been a minor. They were probably on bad terms with him, and may have reckoned that since Euctemon was

old (more than 80 years old) it would be better to await his death and claim on the two grounds, one that Chaerestratus' mother was *epikleros*, along with her sister, to Euctemon and all his sons, and two, that Chaerestratus was Philoctemon's adopted son, and thus also heir at law to his childless (adopted) uncles and to Euctemon. By claiming as Philoctemon's heir he gained the advantage of denying the opposition the chance of accusing him of trying to get possession of two *oikoi*, since he would thereby relinquish his claims to his father Phanostratus' *oikos* (see below, p. 147)

The family tree, after Philoctemon's death, is as follows:

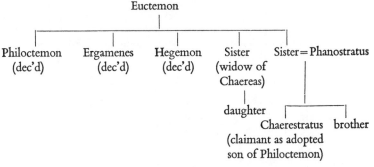

Euctemon was *de facto kyrios* of the *oikoi* of his three dead sons as long as he lived, since he might (in law at least) procreate other sons, as he had threatened to do before Philoctemon's death (para. 22). His daughters were not yet *epikleroi* for the same reason, but their sons' prospects were good, since the old man was past procreation and the women were both probably past child-bearing

16 The date of the speech was 364 (*id.* 14), Philoctemon died perhaps shortly before 373/2 (*id.* 27, with Wyse, *SI*, note *ad loc.*)

17 Chapter V, p. 118, and note 123, unless the whole thing is meant to be farcical, which is most unlike the tone of the situation

18 Isaeus VI, 19–24; for Callippe, below p. 143

19 *Id.* 30–4, 36–7; note 14 above for the *oikoi* of Ergamenes and Hegemon. Wyse's useful note on *id.* 44 ignores the fact that Athenian litigants might gain their ends by degrees, as the case of Hagnias' estate proves (Isaeus XI, Dem. XLIII)

20 Wyse, *SI*, 483 ff. However, Wyse fails to explain why the estate under dispute was that of Philoctemon, the long-deceased son, not Euctemon, the newly deceased father. The jury cannot have been so stupid as not to know whose *oikos* was in dispute

21 This implies that every man belonged to an *oikos* (in a deme); this I would accept, even for the poorest of the *thetes*, though it cannot be proved (Chap. IV above, p. 93), since it would not imply that the *oikos* had any

material possessions. Contrariwise *oikoi*, *kleroi* that is, of property, might lack an owner owing to the lack of a son to succeed his father; they were then vacant (ἐρημοί, or some such phrase) and under the care of the Archon. Rich men had *oikoi* in both senses, poor men only in the citizenship sense

22 Lysias XIX, 37—a father would want to have independent means; that does not mean that he always had it. Aeschines' simile (III, 251–2) of the state in its dotage illustrates the point

23 *Philotimia*—φιλοτιμία—a word for which there is no equivalent; the nearest perhaps being the oriental notion of 'face', but it is wholly Greek, and still survives today—Kanelli, op. cit., 27–8

24 Pollux VIII, 104, s.v. ληξίαρχοι: ὁ δ᾿ εἰς τὸ ληξιαρχικὸν γραμματεῖον ἐγγραφεὶς ἤδη τὰ πατρῷα παρελάμβανεν. ἡ δὲ πατρῷα οὐσία καὶ λῆξις ἐκαλεῖτο. For λῆξις as a land-holding, Harpocration s.v. ληξιαρχικὸν γραμματεῖον: λήξεις δ᾿ εἰσὶν οἵ τε κλῆροι καὶ αἱ οὐσίαι ὡς καὶ Δείναρχος (sc. φησίν.) Hdt. IV, 21 (λᾶξις) (Scythia), Plato, *Laws* 740A.

25 Dem. XLIII, 70–2; Lysias VII is the defence of a man accused of this offence

26 Pp. 117–18 above, and for Bouselus' five sons, p. 127

27 *Laws* 664C–D for example; παῖδες to 30 are all the same age-group, 666A–B etc. Council-membership, Xen. *Mem.* I, 2, 35, jury service, *Ath. Pol.* LXIII, 3; marriage, above pp. 106–7 and note 38

28 *Republic* 497E–498A: μειράκια ὄντα ἄρτι ἐκ παίδων τὸ μεταξὺ οἰκονομίας καὶ χρηματισμοῦ. In *Ath. Pol.* XLII, 1, παῖδες include all youths until they were accepted as physically ready to start military training, at the age of 18, as ἔφηβοι; μειράκια is the word always used by Plato for ἔφηβοι, and was perhaps general till the reorganization of the ἐφηβία in about 336: the word ἔφηβος does not occur in Plato's genuine works, though it appears in the spurious Axiochus

29 Isaeus VI, 35; cf. for drugs, disease or some such cause, *id.* 21; contrast *id.* 9, *id.* II, 14–5, where the speaker harps on his adoptive father's sanity

30 *Pol.* III, 1, 3–5, (1275A) γέροντας ἀφειμένους; the customary bracketing (as in OCT) of 1275A, 10–15 (τοῦτο . . . κοινωνίας) seems designed to obscure the fact that φατέον εἶναι πολίτας has reference also to those others who are not fully citizens without reservation. It is surprising how many commentators have taken δικάζεσθαι (going to law) as δικάζειν (sit as a juror). Cf. Teles, *ap.* Stobaeus XL, 8, 'those who are above age for service cannot govern', but this is third century

31 Aristophanes, *Wasps* 508 ff, 750 ff, 763 etc., *id.*, *Acharn.* 179–81, 210 ff etc.

32 Thuc. II, 44, 3; their activity was βουλεύεσθαι—attending assembly

33 See Chapter VII, p. 169 and note 107

34 *Laws* 755A–B, *Republic* 498B–C, 540A–B

35 Dem. XLVI, 14, though, even if it is genuine, it is only a partial quotation, as is usual in the orators, Isaeus VI, 9 *et al.*

36 Isaeus III, 68, X, 13; *cf.* note 57 below

37 Dem. XLVI, 24; *id.* XXVII, 4-6; Lysias XXXII, 4-6, the will of Diodotus. For a parallel to Demosthenes' detailed dispositions, Diog. La. III, 41-3, Plato's will

38 All minors had by law to have a guardian until they were of age and had passed their *dokimasia* by their demesmen (ἕως ἐγὼ ἀνὴρ εἶναι δοκιμασ-θείην, Dem. XXVII, 5); the Archon appointed (or ratified the appointment) and supervised the guardians, *Ath. Pol.* LVI, 6-7

39 Dem. XXVII, 44-5

40 Pasion, Dem. XXXVI and XLV-VI, Conon, Lysias XIX, 34-40

41 Dem. XXXVI, 22, and *id.* 37 with 10 (Pasicles was a minor 8 years)

42 *Id.* 5-6; *id.* 8 for the guardians

43 *Id.* XLV, 34; *id.* 83-4, XLVI, 20-1 for his residing with the family; XLV, 3 *et al.* for the marriage; it took place while Apollodorus the adult son was away serving as a trierarch. Clearly he much resented the marriage, as he indicted Phormion for wanton injury (ὕβρις), by which he clearly meant having sexual relations with his mother; this was a method of challenging the validity of the marriage (*id.* 4). It was indeed open to challenge, since citizens were not allowed to marry non-citizen women, and *vice versa*. The likeliest explanation of why the situation was allowed to stand is that, as Phormion's sons would make no claim on Pasion's *oikos*, which already had heirs, the widow (who perhaps had no citizen relatives) could best be provided for in this way. When (10 years later) Phormion was granted Athenian citizenship, his two sons by her were also made citizens, and the marriage became fully regular again. When she died, all her sons inherited a share of her property, *id.* XXXVI, 32, and by accepting this arrangement Apollodorus tacitly accepted the validity of the marriage (*ibid.*)

44 Dem. XXVII, 9; the other factory employed couch, or sofa, makers. Other examples in the orators include Pasion's shield-makers, *id.* XXXVI, 4, etc., and Comon's two factories, one at the house where he lived, in which sackcloth was made, the other elsewhere where grinders of either colour-pigments or drugs worked under a particularly trustworthy slave, *id.* XLVIII, 12-14. Xenophon *Mem.* II, 7, 6 mentions slaves employed by a miller, a baker, makers of outer garments (*chlamydes*) and underclothes (*exomides*), the latter in Megara. *Cf. Pl. 46* which shows slaves listed with real property and furniture as possessions which could be confiscated and valued

A slave could also be a source of profit by purchasing his or her freedom; Neaira's mistress had seven girls whom she had trained as *hetairai*; they all got their lovers to buy them their freedom, Dem. LIX, 18-20, 30-2. For many aspects of slavery, *Slavery in Classical Antiquity*, a recent collection of articles edited by M. I. Finley (1960)

45 Xen. *Oeconomicus*, XII-XIII; he had bailiffs and a system of rewards for

good work, and of punishments, *cf. id.*, *Mem.* II, 1, 16; *id.* II, 5, 5, nobody would sell a good slave. For slave-owning in Athens, A. H. M. Jones, *AD*, 12–13, whose view is slightly different from that here expressed; it largely turns on the view one takes of Euphiletus' circumstances (Lysias I)

46 *Id.*, *Oec.* IX, 5

47 Dem. XLVII, 53–6; how the πύργος could be closed the orator does not explain

48 Xen., *Oec.* III, 4, VII, 37

49 Xen., *Mem.* II, 4, 2–3; men you recruit for harvest-work and other hired labourers are not φίλοι καὶ ξένοι, Dem. XVIII, 51. For slaves as fellow workers (συνεργοί) Xen. *Mem.* II, 3, 3, A. Zimmern, *Greek Commonwealth* (1931), 380 ff

50 Dem. XXIX, 25–6; Diog. La. III, 41–3 (Plato), V, 11–6 (Aristotle), V, 55 (Theophrastus), V, 63 (Strato), V, 72–3 (Lyco), X, 21 (Epicurus)

51 Dem. XXXVI, 28–9; in the instances named the master had also provided that his widow should marry the liberated slave

52 *Id.* XLIII, 44, where the half-brother of the *epikleros* who had a different mother made no claim to her inheritance

53 *Ath. Pol.* II, 2, Plut. *Solon* XIII, 2–3; in the *Ath. Pol.* passage, 'they were in servitude' (ἐδούλευον) is used to describe the condition of the poor men, women and children; *cf.* Arist. *Pol.* II, 9, 2, which shows that ἐδούλευον does not mean 'were slaves'; the wives however are conspicuously absent from the following passage, describing the sales into slavery. From the fourth century, Lysias XII, 98, Isocrates XIV, 48, enslavement of children for petty debt

54 Isaeus VII, 18–21; *cf. id.* VI, 4, 46 and 56, where the widow with an only daughter was unsuccessfully claimed as *epikleros*, but her sister, who had two adult sons, was not even claimed

55 Dem. XLVI, 22 quotes the law

56 *Ath. Pol.* LVI, 6–7, Dem. XLIII, 75; for advertisement, *Ath. Pol.* XLIII, 4, Dem. XLIII, 5, Wyse, *S.I.*, note on Isaeus III, 43, 2

57 Isaeus III, 68, X, 13; estates (*kleroi*) and *epikleroi* were covered by the same rules, *Ath. Pol. loc. cit.*, Dem. XLVI, 22 etc.

58 *Id.* XLIII, 54, Isaeus I, 39, Andocides I, 118–21

59 See note 56 above; the Archon is to look after orphans and *epikleroi* and *oikoi* which are bereft of a *kyrios* and any women who remain in the *oikos* of their deceased husband claiming to be pregnant

60 Thuc. II, 46; they were (at least in the fourth century) presented by the city with a set of hoplite armour on attaining their majority, and paraded before the citizens after enrolment in their deme and tribe, Plato, *Menexenus* 248D–249B, Arist. *Pol.* II, 5, 4 (1268A), as being also the custom elsewhere; attributed to Solon, Diog. La. I, 55

61 κάκωσις was the charge, *Ath. Pol.* LVI, 6–7; Dem. XXXVII, 45–6 for ἐπικλήρου κάκωσις, Pollux VIII, 35 for ὀρφανῶν κάκωσις, *Ath. Pol.*,

loc. cit. for οἴκου ὀρφανικοῦ, and Dem. XLIII, 75 for οἴκων ἐξερημ-
ουμένων κάκωσις

62 ἐπιτροπῆς κατάστασις and διαδικασία, *Ath. Pol.*, *loc. cit.*

63 *Loc. cit.*; μισθοῖ δὲ καὶ τοὺς οἴκους τῶν ὀρφανῶν καὶ τῶν ἐπι[κλήρων
ἕως ἄν τις τέτταρ]α καὶ δε[κέ]τις γένηται. At 14 the *epikleros*
would be married. It seems quite unnecessary to suppose that ὀρφανῶν
(sc. boys) is also governed by the clause ἕως ἄν ... γένηται; the gram-
mar indeed forbids it, since δεκέτις is feminine. The normal phrase for
the ending of a guardian's charge is 'two years above puberty', ὅποτε ἐπὶ
διετὲς ἥβησαν, Isaeus VIII, 31; *cf.* Harpocration, *s.v.* ἐπὶ διετὲς
ἡβῆσαι, Isaeus, fr. 26 (Loeb), *id.* X, 12; by analogy from the girls'
age this has been put at 16, but Hypereides (fr. 192 (Kenyon), quoted
by Harpocration) seems to make it clear that it coincided with the com-
mencement of military training, *i.e.* at 18 (nominal), though Harpocration
thought it coincided with the end of service as ἔφηβος. Demosthenes'
guardians mismanaged his estate for 10 years (XXVII, 6); he was 7 years
old at his father's death, and began his suit as soon as he had passed his
dokimasia as a citizen; he would thus have claimed to be 18, and we should
not quibble over the missing months (which need not in fact have been
missing at all if he were well over 7 at his father's death, and 10 years a
rough estimate). Wyse's suggestion (*S.I.*, note on VIII, 31), that the legal
definition of puberty (16) and the natural (14) differed, may well be right

64 Isaeus VII, 7 ff shows it was not always very effective

65 *Ath. Pol.* XLII, 5. Claiming priesthoods was also permitted

66 Isaeus III, 64, with Wyse *SI*, 347 ff

67 Isaeus VIII, 31

68 Isaeus X, 19

69 As Wyse thinks, *SI*, 275 ff

70 Dem. LVII, 41

71 Isaeus VI, 12–4 and 21–4

72 Plangon's oath, Dem. XXXIX, 3–4, XL, 10–1; her father and brothers,
id. XL, 20–23, her good looks, *id.* XL, 27. Both her sons bore names of
members of her family, XXXIX, 2 and 32, etc.

73 Isaeus XI, 37–9, V, 35, VI, 59, Hypereides, *Euxenippus* 32, Dem. XLIV,
3; *id.* 28, XLII, 21–3, XLIII, 77, for two *oikoi*

74 Isaeus I, 39, Andocides I, 119, but *cf.* the whole of 117–123

75 Dem. XLI, 3

76 Wyse, *S.I.*, note on. Isaeus VIII, 36, 8, *q.v.* for Plut. *Moralia* 843A, Dem.
XLII, 21 and 27, *id.* XLIII, 37, Isaeus X, 4, 5 etc. Neocles, father of Themistocles, adopted one of Themistocles' sons, probably the eldest surviving
one, and almost certainly after his son had been exiled, Plut. *Themist.*
XXXII, 1. Some nephews and nieces appear in Isaeus VI, 6, *id.* XI, 41–2,
id. 8, Dem. XLIII, 77, and many other places

77 Dem. XLVI, 22, Isaeus X, 9

78 Isaeus III, 42–3, *id.* V, 6

79 *Id.* II, 10–2

80 *Id.* IV, 18; for family feuds and hatred, Dem. XLIV, 63, LIX, 55 ff, Isaeus IX, 16–21, I, 9 ff

81 Isaeus XII, 2, *id.* VI, 63; compare Dem. XL, 13 and 48, where it is clear that all Mantias' sons shared equally in his estate despite the fact that he tried not to acknowledge those of Plangon, and they were, in the words of our speaker, 'adopted' by him

82 Dem. XLIV, 19–24, *cf. id.* 36–7, 39–42. For the law, Isaeus VI, 44, Dem. XLIII, 77–8 with 13–4; for repudiation, *id.* XLI, 4

83 Foreigners granted citizenship by the state are described as having been adopted by the state, *id.* XLV, 78

84 We know of revisions in 445/4, schol. on Aristophanes, *Wasps* 718, Plut. *Pericles* XXXVII, (Hignett, *HAC* 345), and in 346, Harpocration, *s.v.* διαψήφισις, Aeschines I, 77 and 114 and scholia *ad loc.* Dem. LVII and Isaeus XII are appeals against being struck off, Wyse, *SI*, 714 ff. Admission for money, Isaeus XII, 2, Dem. LVII, 25 and 52 etc.

85 *Ath. Pol.* LVIII, 2–3, Dem. XLVI, 22. *Cf.* Plato, *Republic* 331D, where it is said that Polemarchus will be heir to his father Cephalus; κληρονόμος, the normal word, is used, though they were metics

86 *Ath. Pol.* LVIII, 3 refers to the δίκη ἀπροστασίου, the prosecution of a metic for not having a patron or προστάτης; Isaeus V, 37, a metic's successful claim

87 Isaeus X, 4, Dem. XLIV, 26; both these speeches show attempts to keep an *oikos* in existence by posthumous adoption, *cf. id.* XLIII, 12–14, 77–8

88 Dem. XLIII, 83–4, from the peroration of the speech. The 'dreadful creatures' (ὑπὸ τῶν μιαρῶν τούτων θηρίων) were second cousins

89 Isaeus II, 46, also from a peroration

90 *Ath. Pol.* LV, 3; *cf.* Xen. *Mem.* II, 2, 13: 'If a man does not care for the tombs of his parents when they are dead' he fails his *dokimasia*

91 Deubner, *AF*, 93 ff for Anthesteria

92 MacDowell, *Homicide*, 8 ff, shows that no vengeance could be taken for a man who forgave his killers, Dem. XXXVII, 59; Aeschylus, *Choephoroe* 37–41 *et al.*, the anger of the dead

93 Dem. XLIII, 57 ff, and as a legal obligation, *id.* XXIV, 107. For the importance of the rites, Wyse, *SI*, note on Isaeus II, 25, 4; Aeschines I, 13–4, Lysias XIII, 45–6, *id.* XII, 96 on this as one of the crimes of the 'Thirty Tyrants'; Plato, *Hippias Major* 291D–E as the crowning success in a good life; *cf.* tragedy *passim, e.g.* Sophocles, *Antigone*, Euripides, *Medea* 1032 ff, *Supplices* 168–75, 524 ff, 538–41, *Troades* 387–90 etc. *Cf.* also *Pls. 21, 22*

94 Isaeus I, 10, preventing an enemy conducting one's funeral; perhaps the truth behind *id.* VI, 39–42. *Cf.* Plut. *Lysander* XXIX, 3

95 Isaeus II, 25 and 36–7, IV, 19, VI, 40, VIII, 21–7 and 39. Dem. XLIII, 65. *Cf. id.* XLIV, 32 ff, where blood is said to have been allowed to count for

more than legal rights derived from adoption; not to trust one's heir to do it was a grave insult, Lysias XXXI, 21

96 Dem. XLIII, 62. In Mytilene, Pittacus forbade all non-relatives to attend, Cicero, *de legibus* II, 66

97 *Id.* 79–80; an old one now disused, *id.* LV, 13–4; for proof of relationship, *cf. id.* LVII, 28, Plutarch's argument in *Themistocles* I, 3

98 Jacoby, *JHS* 1944, 37 ff, 'The cult of the dead was particularly deep-rooted in Attica . . . where the foundations of material and spiritual life reached back far into the second millennium', *ibid.*, 52

99 τὰ τρίτα καὶ τὰ ἔνατα, Wyse, *SI* 264; *cf.* A. T. Bradshaw, *CQ* 1962, 200 ff on Antigone's burial of Polyneices

100 30 days was the limit of mourning; people were expected to observe it as a minimum as well as a maximum, Lysias I, 14, Aeschines III, 77 for not doing so. Dedications (ἐναγίσματα) were made at the tombs, Wyse, *SI*, 269, often mentioned in tragedy, *e.g.* Aeschylus, *Choephoroe* 84 ff, esp. 93–5, with the striking exchange of κακῶν (evil) for καλῶν (good); the most well-controlled (σωφρονεστάτη) burial—no show, but leaving nothing undone—was approved by Plato, *Laws* 717D–E. The rites are known from all over Greece, and so well known to all that they are known merely as 'what is customary' (τὰ νομιζόμενα), Wyse, *SI*, note on Isaeus II, 4, 5

101 *E.g.* Lycurgus, *in Leocr.* 97, 147, *cf. id.* 131 for the hearth

102 F. Jacoby, *CQ* 1944, 65 ff, *JHS*, 1944, 61 ff. Deubner, *AF*, 232–4 for the Apatouria, at which there were drink-offerings (χόαι) for the dead

103 Plutarch, *Solon* XXI, 4–5, who remarks that in his day (second century AD) similar prohibitions were still in force in Chaeroneia, Cicero, *de legibus* II, 64–6; Phormion is accused of extravagance for spending more than two talents on a monument, Dem. XLV, 79: Plato, *Epistle* XIII, 361E, not more than 10 minae for his mother's tomb; for his views, *cf.* Cicero *l.c.* 67–8, from *Laws* 958D–959D; Dem. XL, 52, 10 minae borrowed for father's funeral

104 *Acharnians*, 241 ff, in a comic version

105 Isaeus VIII, 15–6, Wyse, *SI*, 600; *IG* II¹, 578, 36–7, Theophrastus, *Characters* III, 5 for the date, which was in December

106 Dion. Hal., *Ant. Rom.* I, 67, 3; Isaeus VIII, 16, Antiphon I, 16–8; Dem. XXI, 53 for the state festival

107 *Anth. Pal.* XI, 249

CHAPTER VII

WOMEN IN DEMOCRATIC ATHENS

1 Some of the contributors in English have been F. W. Cornish and J. Bacon in *Companion to Greek Studies* (1931), 610 ff; A. Zimmern, *Greek Commonwealth* (1931) especially Part III Chapter XII; A. W. Gomme, *Classical Philology* XX (1925), = Chapter V in *Essays in Greek History and Literature*, took a different view; for more recent views, V. Ehrenberg, *People of Aristophanes* (1951) (the most valuable treatment), especially Chapter VIII; H. D. F. Kitto, *The Greeks* (1951), Chapter XII, which suffers from being based too much on tragedy; R. Flacelière, *Daily Life in Greece at the time of Pericles* (1959, English Translation by Peter Green 1965), Chapter III

2 Dem. XLI; the citations are from paras. 8–21: in para. 9 the speaker states that he bought things from Polyeuctus, and received things from his wife (ἦν ἐωνημένος and παρὰ τῆς γυναικὸς εἶχον), the contrast is probably intentional, since a wife would not sell, but give, to her daughters' husbands

3 Aeschines I, 95–99

4 Andocides I, 124–127

5 In Homer we meet only the poor woman who spun wool and managed to support her children, although in poverty (*Il.* XII, 433–5), and Achilles' picture of the most wretched life on earth—that of an agricultural labourer working for a man of small means (*Od.* 11. 488–91)

6 Dicaiogenes (Isaeus V) and his father Menexenus fell in the Peloponnesian War: so did Diodotus (Lysias XXXII, 4 and 7), whose children were ruined by their guardian; so were Thrasyllus' children (Isaeus VII, 5–8): he fell in Sicily; Pistoxenus' daughter was left destitute in Euctemon's house when he fell in Sicily (Isaeus VI, 13). Hagnias (Isaeus XI), Astyphilus (Isaeus IX), Philoctemon (Isaeus VI), were all killed in the many struggles of the fourth century. For the severity of these casualties, Isocrates VIII, 88–9, even if exaggerated, must have struck a comprehensible note

Aeschines II, 147, claims that the Peloponnesian War impoverished his father; *cf.* Lysias XX, 33, XXVI, 22, Isocrates XV, 161. Lysias XXVIII, 2–3 contrasts the 'former times', *i.e.* before the Peloponnesian War, with its large state revenues and private fortunes, with the fourth century's constant demands for taxes—εἰσφοραί. G. E. M. de Ste Croix has argued (*Classica et Mediaevalia* (XIV) 1953, 69) that these averaged not more than $\frac{1}{4}$ of 1% per annum for 20 to 23 years after 378–7, which is equivalent to income-tax at 6*d.* to 1/– in the pound; but see note 160

7 Lysias XIX *passim* for liturgies and other services performed at this period; *cf.* Lysias XXI, 1–5, XXV, 12–13, XXVI, 3 ff etc. *SIG*, 346 lists *eisphorae* amounting to 10 talents from two individuals in the period 347/6–323/2

8 Isaeus' remark (VI, 38) that Euctemon and Philoctemon could perform the most expensive liturgies without making inroads on their capital cannot be without significance

9 The Old Oligarch (so called) may hardly be called an unbiased witness, but he can say that the people had introduced the liturgies in order to get something for themselves and to impoverish the rich (Ps.-Xen., *Ath. Pol.*, I, 13–14), and that in the courts they are quite unconcerned for justice, only for that which is to their advantage; οὐ τοῦ δικαίου αὐτοῖς μᾶλλον μέλει ἢ τοῦ αὐτοῖς συμφόρου

Aristophanes too represents the jurors as delighting in pleasing themselves, and giving verdicts against the rich regardless of the laws; see *Wasps* 240–1, where Laches' wealth is their target, 287–9 (with which *cf. Peace* 639–40), 575, 626–7 etc. For the period of the Thirty Tyrants, Lysias XII, 6–7, XIX etc., Isocrates XXI, 11 ff etc. In XV, 159–60, Isocrates claims that in the mid-fourth century it was more dangerous to be rich than criminal

10 Such as digging up an old olive-stump, Lysias VII, *passim. Cf.* Dem. XXI, 182, 10 talents' fine

11 For Timotheus' borrowing to finance his expedition of 374–3, Dem. XLIX *passim*; *q.v.* 9–10 also for his ill treatment at the hands of the people, and the death-sentence and confiscation of property imposed on his faithful treasurer Antimachus

12 Dem. L; *cf.* Dem. XLVII, 28–33 etc.

13 Demosthenes' speeches now numbered XXVIII–XXXI were all necessitated by the court's failure to ensure that Aphobus complied with the judgement given against him

13a For inflation, Jones, *A.D.*, 135, note 1 *et al.* Losses of old families, Isocrates VIII, 88–9

14 Conon's estate was 40 talents, Lysias XIX, 39–40; for Aristophanes (not the comic poet), *id.* 18–29; his fortune was made in a little over 5 years

15 His fortune at his death was nearly 14 talents, Dem. XXVII, 4; Aeschines III, 171–2, declares that she was a Scythian—if in fact her parents were domiciled on the north coast of the Black Sea they were probably Athenians engaged in commerce there

16 Dem. XLVIII, 12–14, Xen. *Mem.* II, 7, 6, a miller, a baker, two clothing-manufacturers

17 Plato, *Republic* 330B, Lysias XII, 6–20. Some bankers actually failed in business, Dem. XXXVI, 50

18 Pasion's property, Dem. XXXVI, 4–6, 36–8, Phormion's wealth, *id.*, 43–4, 57 etc. 'Now the mouse has a taste of the [bitter] medicine; he wanted to be an Athenian' was Polycles' reaction to the friends of Apollodorus, Pasion's son, when he complained of the drain of money in his trierarchy, Dem. L, 26. Jones, *AD*, 91 for further examples of non-Athenian rich business-men

19 Arist. *Pol.* I, 3, 22–3 (1258 A–B); his word is οἰκονομία, but he must mean management of landed property, Xen. *Oec.* IV–VI, especially VI, 4–10; *cf.* Dem. XXII, 65, where the picture of the virtuous citizens is one of small farmers who live economically (γεωργοῦντες καὶ φειδόμενοι), repeated in *id.* XXIV, 172

　　Note how both Aristophanes (Lysias XIX, 29) and Apollodorus (Dem. L, 8) had put their money into land

20 Dem. *ibid.*, Lysias XX, 23; accusing opponents of keeping wealth liquid to avoid paying taxes, Dinarchus, *in Demosthenem* 70, Dem. XLV, 66, etc.

21 Jones, *AD*, 57: *cf.* Thuc. VI, 30–1 on the competition to make a show in the Sicilian expedition, and for the fifth century, Isocrates, XV, 159–60 (though this is of dubious value because of the argument), and for the fourth, *id.*, VII, 53

22 Isocrates XVIII, 52–4; the evidence was a slave maidservant alleged by the opposing party to have been killed; *cf.* Isaeus VI, 42; the demand to search was refused. For seizing disputed goods, Isocrates XVIII, 5–6 (money), Lysias III, 11–12 (a slave) Dem. LIX, 40 (a mistress); as security for a debt, Dem. LIII, 15, XLVII, 37–8, 52 ff; *id.* XXII, 54–5 for the state's doing so to public debtors

23 Lysias XXIII, 8–9, claiming a slave, Dem. XXX, 2, a piece of land; *cf.* Isocrates XVIII, 52, a battle took place (μάχης δὲ γενομένης) over a piece of land

24 Dem. XLVII, 34, 36, 64–5, etc.

25 Lysias I, 23–4

26 *E.g. Acharnians* and *Wasps. Cf.* Isocrates XVIII, 9 for a man going around canvassing for support, and notes 27–9 below

27 Lysias III, 6, IV, 5, Dem. XXI, 16, 79; *cf. id.* XLVII 54, 63, to obtain security *et al.*

28 Dem. LIV, 7–14, Lysias IV, 7, III, 12–20, Plato, *Symposium* 212C–213A, Plut. *Alcibiades* IV, 5 etc.

29 Dem. *loc. cit.*, Lysias III, 8 ff etc.

30 For friends and neighbours, see *e.g.* Xen. *Mem.*, II, 2, 12 (neighbours), II, 4–6 *et al.*, Plato, *Lysis*, Aristotle, *E.N.* IX. etc.

31 Thuc. VIII, 65, 2 and 92, 4 for the use of ἕταιροι as the word for oligarchic conspirators; *cf.* Lysias XII, 43: ὑπὸ τῶν καλουμένων ἑταίρων. Thucydides VIII, 54, 4, also speaks of sworn brotherhoods (συνωμοσίαι) as previously existing in the city to cope with law-suits and magistracies undertaken (ἐπὶ δίκαις καὶ ἀρχαῖς). In the fourth century there were laws against forming them, Hypereides, *Euxenippus* 8, *cf.* Ziebarth, *RE*, VIII, (1913) 1374, *s.v.* ἑταιρία; hence Demosthenes accuses Meidias of having a *hetaireia* of bought witnesses, XXI, 139–40; 'many of Aristogeiton's aristocratic kinsmen' will plead for him, *id.* XXV, 78

32 ζῆν ὅπως τις βούλεται: Arist. *Pol.* V, 7, 22 (1310A); *cf. id.* VI, 2, 4 (1318B (fin.)) *et al.*; *cf.* Thuc. II, 37, 2 and VII, 69, 2 Plato, *Republic* 557B, and

the whole discussion of democracy (as based on liberty) to 564A, Isocrates, XII, 131, etc. Jones, *AD*, 44, *q.v.* (Chapter 1) for a demonstration that the majority of the Athenian citizens were quite poor and worked hard for a living

33 Ps.-Andocides IV; Plut., *Alcibiades* XVI, XX, XXXIV, 6, XXXV, 1-3, XXXVII, 1-2 all speak of his allies and enemies. Compare the attack on his son, whose morals, sodomy, drunkenness and keeping a mistress as a teenager are all mentioned, together with his father's career, as reasons for prejudice against him, Lysias XIV, 25 *et al.*

34 XXI (*in Meidiam*), 143-6

35 Plut. *Pericles*, *passim*, Aristophanes, *Acharn.*, 524-34. For the attacks on his friends, Plutarch, *op. cit.* XXXI-II, and *cf.* Diod. XII, 39

36 *Wasps* 1024-8

37 L. Versenyi, *Socratic Humanism* (1963), 147-67 for a recent discussion of Socrates' trial, discounting anti-aristocratic prejudice; contra, Jones, *AD*, 44, citing Xen. *Mem.* I, 2, 12 ff, and Aeschines 1, 173 (a very dubious support). In Lysias XVI, 18, a young aristocrat apologizes for his long hair, characteristic of *hippeis*, Aristophanes, *Knights* 579-80, *Clouds* 14 *et al.*; Xen. *Symposium* IV, 29-32, lost wealth brings freedom from fear; Isocrates XV, 140-3, the jurors' envy and poverty make them take revenge on the successful. In the fifth century, ps-Xenophon (*Ath. Pol.* I, 14) accuses the democratic courts of prejudice against the leading men among the allies; *cf.* Aristophanes, *Peace* 639-40, Thuc. VIII, 48, 5-6, where ἐκείνων might be allied or Athenian would-be oligarchs. G. Grote, *History of Greece* (1862 (8 vol.) ed.), IV, 124-7, dealing with the rich and powerful was always a major problem; *cf.* Lysias II, 56, Dem. XXI, 112. Bonner and Smith, *Justice* II, 288 ff, for an overall assessment of the courts; Jones (*AD*, 36) has argued that in Demosthenes' day the jurors were middle-class; this, if it is true (and Isocrates VII, 54 (355 BC) contradicts it), reflects a change from the Peloponnesian War period and Aristophanes' picture, as exemplified by the chorus in *Wasps*, Jones, *AD*, 50; *AD*, 58-61 for the view that prejudice against the rich belongs almost entirely to the early fourth century

38 To be κόσμος was the claim, Lysias XXVI, 3; *cf.* to obtain κόσμοι as relatives by marriage, Lysias XIX, 16

39 *e.g.* Isaeus X, 25 (sodomy), Dem. LIV, 14-7, immorality and dissolute behaviour of aristocrats (καλοὶ κἀγαθοί)

40 Aeschines I, 6-12

41 Plato, *Symposium* 183C; *cf.* 217A-219D: Alcibiades' attempts to seduce Socrates into sodomy began with the dismissal of the attendant who had always accompanied him up to that time

42 Aeschines I, 19-20; adult Athenians who acted as catamites were excluded from all offices in public life, administrative, judicial and diplomatic; they were even forbidden to address the assembly. This presumably explains

the insults in Aristophanes' plays levelled at orators; *Knights* 878–80, *Wasps* 687–91, *Eccl.* 112–13—*cf.* Plato Comicus fr. 186; also at speakers in the courts, *Acharn.* 716, and the wild farce of *Clouds* 1086–1101 at the expense of the audience, which has even been taken as a serious proof that there was nothing wrong with being εὐρύπρωκτος. Insulting the audience was part of the fun of comedy (as of modern music halls); for other examples, *Frogs* 276–9 and 783, *Wasps* 73 ff, *Peace* 962 ff. For the fourth century, Dem. XXI, 30, 61, Aeschines III, 174 etc.

43 Aeschines I, 13–14; boys prostituted are said to have been freed from the normal obligation to maintain their aged parent or guardian; the guilty parent or guardian was liable to be treated as a pander, and punished; so was he who paid money for the use of the boy—and hiring boys (says Aeschines) is surely also covered by the heading 'wanton injury' (ὕβρις) (*id.* 15–7), for which the maximum penalty was death

44 Lysias III, 4 and 26, where it is implied that both the boy's lovers were ashamed of their conduct; this particular catamite seems to have been a slave (*ib.* 33), though some modern writers have thought that paederasty was only practised with noble youths

45 Because oligarchic. For a demanding boy, *Anth. Pal.* XII, 212 (second century AD). *Cf.* the stories of *Alcibiades*, Plutarch, *Alcib.* IV and V. For male prostitution, Licht, *S.L.*, 436 ff

46 *Laws* 838E–839A for 'the best'; *cf.* 840C–D. For 'the second best', 841C–842A. *Cf.* Aristotle, *Politics* II, 6, 6 (1269B); the tone is critical

47 Xen. *Oec.* VII, 5–6

48 Lysias III, 6: αἱ οὕτω κοσμίως βεβιώκασιν ὥστε καὶ ὑπὸ τῶν οἰκείων ὁρώμεναι αἰσχύνεσθαι

49 Isaeus III, 13–14, Lysias I, 22

50 As perhaps the victory-celebration described in Dem. LIX, 33–4; even Apollodorus admits that Phrynion's conduct was too much for Neaira, *id.* 35

51 Lysias III, 43; *cf.* Dem. LIV, 14 for riotous behaviour of sons of καλοὶ κἀγαθοί who are in the habit of drinking and fighting over *hetairai*

52 Athenaeus II, 36B, quoting Eubulus, a fourth-century comic poet: 'Three bowls only for the sensible: . . . then wise guests go home: the fourth is of drunken sport, the fifth of shouting, the sixth of riot, the seventh of fighting, the eighth of locking-up, the ninth of sickness, the tenth of madness and throwing things about', etc.

53 Dem. XLVII, 19; contract (συμβόλαιον), revels (κῶμος), an affair (ἔρως), a drinking-bout (πότος) are things which might cause a quarrel, and lead to a man's going to a house to get his own back, or pursuit of pleasure (ἡδονή), Lysias XVI, 11

54 *Symposium* 176 A–E. It is almost certain that Plato's picture is not of a normal symposium, and that Xenophon (in his *Symposium*) provides a much more typical picture, as does the merry party enjoyed by Sophocles in Chios,

Athenaeus XIII, 603E–604D. Compare Aristophanes, *Wasps* 1197 ff, and what Philocleon says: (*ib*. 1253–5) 'From wine come breaking of doors and brawls and throwing things, then paying fines of money out of your hangover'

55 Isaeus III, 13f, Dem. LIX, 24, 33, 48 etc.

56 Lysias XXXII, 11–18

57 Lysias XIII, 39–42 (in effect); *cf*. Dem. XXXVI, 14; 'As long as Apollodorus' mother lived, she who knew exactly all these facts (*i.e.* about her husband's will and the moneys he had left), he made no complaint'

58 The opponents of Lysias III (see 6 and 23) and Demosthenes XLVII, Lysias XII, 30: 'You (the restored democracy) were angry with those who had entered men's houses to seek for their victims.' *Cf*. Dem. XXXVII, 45–7, XXI, 79

59 *Id*. XLVII, 53, 60, 34–8 and 80

60 Hypereides, *Lycophron*, *ap*. pap. Oxy. 1607, 40 ff; he had ἐξουσία καὶ τὰ παρ' ἐκείνης εἰδέναι καὶ τὰ παρ' αὐτοῦ λέγειν, *i.e.* full permission to converse with her sociably; *cf*. Lysias XIV, 28, where it is assumed that a brother could visit his sister

61 Lysias I, 36

62 *Ath. Pol.* LVI, 7; the figure is part of the restoration of a lacuna in the papyrus, but is generally accepted, as by Oppermann (Teubner, 1928), *et al.*; in Gortyn the age of marriage of such girls was 12 or over, code XII, 33–5

63 Xen. *Oec.*, VII, 5; she might have been fifteen; the Greek is slightly ambiguous. I assume that the consensus of opinion among commentators is correct, and that Ischomachus is Xenophon himself. His bride was timid and shy, he says (*id*. 10); their conversation took place when she 'felt sufficiently at home to talk': ἐτετιθάσευτο ὥστε διαλέγεσθαι.

64 Xenophon, *Lac. Pol.* I, 3–4, Hesiod, *W. and D.* 695 ff, Plato, *Republic* 460E (20), though in the *Laws* he advocated 18–20 (833D), or even 16–20 (785B), Arist. *Pol.* VII, 14, 6 (1335A); the biologist also produces physical reasons why girls should not marry too young; they have small babies he says, more trouble in labour and more of them die—and an example from Troezen is quoted, *ibid*. 4; Plut. *Lycurgus* XV, 3. Art, however, shows brides as fully grown-up (*e.g. Pl. 24*), and maidens, such as those on the Parthenon friezes are also adult (*Pl. 41*). The so-called 'dancing maiden, putting on her *chiton* (*Pl. 35*) is at least past adolescence, as is the girl on the swing (*Pl. 34*) and the girl who died unmarried (*Pl. 26*). Writers objected to marriages where the partners were too unequal in age; Aristotle, *ibid*. 1 (1334B) remarks that for one partner to be capable of procreation and the other incapable causes quarrels; it evidently offended Solon too, and commentators on him quoted by Plutarch (*Solon*, XX, 2); *cf*. the farce of Aristophanes, *Ec.* 877–1111, and Athenaeus XIII, 559F–560A etc.

65 Sheelagh Kanelli, *Earth and Water* (1965), 109–114

66 *Memorabilia* I, 1, 8, Dem. LIX, 113; for the match-maker, *cf.* Xen. *Mem.* II, 6, 36, Plato, *Theaetetus* 149D–150B, Aristophanes, *Clouds* 41–2, Kanelli, *loc. cit.*

67 Aristotle, *E.N.* VIII, 10, 4–12, 8 (1160B–1162A); note especially the contrast between 12, 4f, the 'fraternal' affection of coevals, and 12, 7, the affection of husband and wife based not on age, but on natural instinct

68 Xen. *Oeconomicus, passim,* especially III, 11–14 and VII, 5–30, though he often speaks of the husband and wife as partners (κοινωνοί), and of their material possessions as communal (τὸ κοινόν)

69 F. A. G. Beck, *Greek Education* (1964), 85 ff; Plato, *Laws* 658D, remarks that educated women, like the general mass of the people, think tragedy the best form of entertainment

70 For Aspasia, who was a Milesian, A. W. Gomme in *OCD* (1948), 108; for fuller refs. to the sources, Judeich, *RE,* II, (1896) 1716 ff, *s.v.* Aspasia. For Theodore, Xen. *Mem.* III, 11; that she was a foreigner is implied. Diotima is introduced by Plato (*Symposium* 201D) as a foreigner also. For Hipparchia, Diog. La. VI, 96–8

71 Xen. *Oeconomicus* III, 11–15: ἔστι δὲ ὅτῳ ἐλάττονα διαλέγει ἢ τῇ γυναικί; εἰ δὲ μή, οὐ πολλοῖς γε, ἔφη (12). . . . νομίζω δὲ γυναῖκα κοινωνὸν ἀγαθὴν οἴκου οὖσαν πάνυ ἀντίρροπον εἶναι τῷ ἀνδρὶ ἐπὶ τὸ ἀγαθόν (15)

72 *Republic* 454D–456C, *Timaeus* 42A, 90E, and, less certainly, *Laws* 804E–806C, etc.

73 Athenaeus V, 186D ff; *Odyssey* 16, 110–1, for the pointless expenditure in Ithaca

74 Hdt. VII, 102, 1: Greece has always had poverty as foster-sister; *cf.* Xen. *Oec.* VII, 15–21 for the economic objectives of the family; for the mass of the people, Jones, *AD,* 12. The poverty-stricken became day-labourers—μισθωτοί, Wyse, *SI,* note on V, 39, 5; *cf.* Xen. *Mem.* II, 8, 1–3, Ehrenberg, *People,* Chapter IX

75 Aristophanes, *Wasps* 291–316; it must be noted though, that the chorus had only 3 mouths to feed, the juror, his slave and (presumably) his wife, and no other dependants, but *cf. Eccl.* 460–4

76 La Rue van Hook, *Transactions Am. Phil. Assoc.* (1920), 134–45, for a summary of earlier views; supported by H. Bolkestein, *Classical Philology,* XVII (1922), 222–239, in denying its prevalence; they ignore, however, Plato *Theaetetus* 151A–D (note 83 below); contra, A. Cameron, *CR* 1932, 105 ff. Plato, *Republic* 372B, provides the clearest statement that the right number of children for a man was the number his *oikos* was able to support

77 Aeschines I, 102–4. He had bad eyesight. Plato and Aristotle are specific in their view that deformed children should be exposed, Plato, *Republic*

459D–460C, Arist. *Pol.* VII, 14, 10 (1335B). Hdt. I, 59, 2: don't marry; if you are married, divorce your wife; if you have a child, repudiate it

78 *W. and D.* 376–7; note that there is no mention of rearing daughters, but there is one in the house, 519–21

79 Menexenus, 4 daughters, 1 son (Isaeus V, 5); Polyaratus of Cholargus, 3 sons, 2 daughters (Wyse, *SI*, introd. to *id.*); Euctemon, 3 sons, 2 daughters from the daughter of Mixiades, probably 2 more sons from Callippe (Isaeus VI); in Bouselus' family Bouselus himself had 5 sons, Stratocles 1 son, 4 daughters, Sositheus and Phylomache 4 sons, 1 daughter (Wyse, *SI*, introd. to Isaeus XI). Menexenus, Euctemon and Bouselus were all at least comfortably off. Cleon's son Cleomedon had 1 son, 3 daughters from one of Menexenus' granddaughters; Euthymachus had 3 sons, 1 daughter (Dem. XLIV); Themistocles is said by Plutarch to have had no less than 10 children, 5 sons, 5 daughters; he also says he had been fabulously wealthy (*Themist.* XXXI–XXXII). Peisistratus the tyrant had not less than 4 sons, 1 daughter: Isocrates had two brothers and one sister; his family was comfortably prosperous, making flutes (Plutarch, *Moralia*, 836E). Aristeides, who is said to have been very poor, had 2 daughters, 1 son (Plut. *Aristeides* XXVII); Socrates, who was also poor, had three sons. Even these were only those who survived infancy; those who died within a week of birth were not even named, and were very numerous, Aristotle, *Historia Animalium* VII, 588A

80 Aristophanes, *Thesm.* 446–52; her deceased husband might have been a merchant. He died in Cyprus

81 Hdt. V, 48. For the modern custom, Sheelagh Kanelli, *op. cit.,* 120, *cf. id.,* 85

82 Euripides, *Medea* 228–51, Aristophanes, *Lys.* 493 ff etc.

83 Plato, *Theaetetus* 151A–D, the fury of a woman whose firstborn child is exposed; it seems however that Plato has merely failed to make explicit here what he makes clear next time the subject was raised (160E–161A), that Socrates will reject Theaetetus' first-born only if it is not worthy of rearing; the tone of the passages strongly suggests that examination of a new-born baby was part of the midwife's job. In the *Republic* it is only unhealthy children, or those born outside the conditions of legal procreation, who are to be exposed; in *Laws* 740 Plato seems to have been more reluctant to adopt exposure as a means of population control, and Aristotle, *Pol.* VII, 14, 10 (1335B), shows that there was some feeling against exposure in his day. Against this, Terence, *Heauton Timoroumenos* 626–7, if it is a literal translation of Menander, Poseidippus (Kock, *C.A.F.* III, p. 338), frag. 11 (late third century), and Oxyrhynchus Papyrus 744 (first cent.) provide the clearest evidence for the exposure of legitimate children in the period after Alexander; 'if the child is a girl', the writer says, 'expose it'

84 Xen. *Mem.* II, 2, 4, Aristotle, *Historia Animalium* VII, 1 (581B), *Pol.* VII, 14, 5 (1335A)

85 Other hints, such as the use of the ὄλισβος (Aristophanes, *Lysistrata* 106, Cratinus etc, Licht, *SL* 314 ff), also suggest that husbands may have imposed this form of birth-control

86 Aristophanes, *Clouds* 530–2; the schol. on 531 clearly understood the child to be illegitimate. In *id.*, *Thesm.* 502–16, it is said that it took 10 days to find a child to smuggle into the house as a supposititious baby; there can hardly have been several exposed daily even in a place as big as Athens. Dem. LIX, 38–42 etc. for Neaira; the speaker of Isaeus VI always maintains that Callippe's children were really a prostitute's (20, *et al.*); the allegation must have been credible

87 Diog. La. V, 11–16; they were a boy and a girl

88 Menander, *Perikeiromene* 369–82, provides an exception; a man exposed his twins because his wife died the day after they were born, and he himself had lost his ship, his only source of income. It does not prove the rule invalid, because the circumstances were so exceptional. For the survival of the practice of exposing bastards into modern Greece, J. K. Campbell, *Honour, Family and Patronage* (1964), 187

89 A very large number of child-slaves are found in Aristotle's family for example (Diog. La., *loc. cit.*); some child-slaves will have been made available when cities were taken in war and their women and children enslaved when the men were butchered, but, in general, this was less common in the fourth century than in the fifth; however see the story of Agesilaus, Xenophon, *Ages.* I, 17–21. For the training of *hetairai*, Dem. LIX, 18: Nicarete had obtained seven girls as small babies, having the knack of seeing—even at that age—which were good looking. For temple-slaves serving the temple of Aphrodite Melainis in Corinth, Schneider, *RE* VIII (1913), 1333, *s.v. hetairai*; Strabo (VIII, 6, 20, C 378) says there were more than 1000, Athenaeus XIII, 573B–574B mentions dedications, such as the 100 dedicated by Xenophon of Corinth in the fifth century (called 1000 by Schneider)

90 *Lac. Pol.* I, 3–4

91 Aristophanes, *Ec.* 446–9, *Plutus* 450–1, Ehrenberg, *People*, Chapter IX

92 Lysias 1, 7: οἰκόνομος δεινή ... φειδωλός ... ἀκριβῶς πάντα διοικοῦσα; Aristophanes, *Ec.* 600. Cf. also Xen. *Oec.* VII, esp. 13 ff: the *oikos* is common (κοινός) to husband and wife; he brings things in, she guards them (20–22); for marriage, σωφρονεῖν means seeing as well as possible to existing property (τὰ ὄντα) and winning honourably as much more as possible (15)

93 Dem. LIX. 122: τῶν ἔνδον φύλακα πιστὴν ἔχειν. Cf. the implications of Aristophanes, *Lys.* 894–7

94 Cf. Xen. *Oec.* VII, 30–31, 35–6. Xenophon was, of course, comparatively well off. Ehrenberg must surely be right to protest (*People*, 201 note 8) against the often-propounded view that because the social rule kept women at home they were generally despised; cf. Kanelli, *op. cit.*, 65, 'I had made

my appeal to the highest authority, to a servile woman who alone had the power to break tradition'

95 Dem. XLIII, 29–46, Isaeus VIII, 9–10. Pistoxenus' daughter, Isaeus VI, 13–16, Stephanus' wife, Dem. LIX, 120–1

96 Aristophanes, *Lys.* 16, *Th.* 823; the σκιάδειον, or parasol, must have been for use out of doors; *cf. Lys.* 531–5; *Frogs* 1346–51 is a parody of Euripides

97 *Id.*, *Frogs* 1158–9; *Ec.* 446–9, etc.; Lysias I, 14 etc., Xen. *Mem.* II, 2, 12

98 Aristophanes, *Ec.* 528–9, Plato, *Theaetetus* 149A–D

99 Aeschines I, 183; dressing up (κοσμεῖσθαι) for festivals was one of a woman's great pleasures; to be basket-bearer at the Panathenaic festival was the greatest honour a maiden could obtain, Aristophanes, *Lys.* 641–8, *Birds* 1551, *Eccl.* 730–2. For the rustic Dionysia, *Acharn.* 242–262, Deubner, *AF*, 134–8

100 For marriage ceremonies, Licht, *SL*, 41–56

101 For funeral rites, pp. 147–9 above; Dem. XLIII, 62 for those entitled to attend; Lysias I, 8 for a funeral as the start of a seduction

102 It did not even have a stair, only a ladder leading up to the women's quarter on the first floor

103 Dem. XLVII, 53–55, Xen. *Oec.* IX, 3 ff. E. Delebecque, *Essai sur la vie de Xénophon* (1957), 367 ff, etc., assuming Ischomachus to be Xenophon

104 And there was a law against idleness, ascribed to Solon, Thalheim, *RE*, II, (1896), 717, *s.v.* ἀργίας γραφή. Thuc. II, 40, the disgrace of not trying to be quit of poverty: Dem. LVII, 32, Plut. *Lycurgus* XXIV, 3, show the law was still in existence in the fourth century

105 οἰκουρός is the orator's word, Dem. XLVII, 56

106 Plato, *Laws* 805A, Arist. *Pol.* I, 5, 12 (1260B)

107 Xen. *Mem.* II, 2, 5–10. *Cf.* Aristotle, *E.N.*, VIII, 12, 3, (1161B) mother-love is even stronger than a father's: φιλοῦσι μᾶλλον αἱ μητέρες; *cf. id.* IX, 7, 7 (1168A); 'all women love children', Lycurgus, *in Leocratem* 101

108 Lysias I, 6. 'Bear down on' (λυπεῖν) clearly indicates the supposition that the husband was master; 'paid attention to' (προσεῖχον τὸν νοῦν) probably has sexual undertones, as it is used of newly-married husbands, Plato, *Laws* 783E; *cf.* Hdt. V, 40, 2

109 Aristophanes, *Thesm.* 502–16, 564–5, etc.

110 Lysias I, 9–10 and 11–13; unfortunately Lycurgus, frag. 99 (= Stobaeus LXVIII, 35) is only a fragment; 'when a woman loses sympathy with her husband (ὁμόνοια), life becomes not worth living' (ἀβίωτος)

111 II, 7, 2–14

112 Xen. *Lac. Pol.* I, 3–4; see note 64 above. To sit still is to behave δουλικῶς, *Oec.* X, 10–12; for kissing the maid on the sly, Aristophanes, *Peace* 1127–39, *cf. Acharn.* 271 ff. Many illustrations in Greek art, however, show that women in fact frequently stood up both to weave and to spin, as modern Greek country folk may often be observed to do. See *Pls. 37–39*

113 P. Herfst, *Le travail de la femme dans la Grèce ancienne* (Utrecht, 1922) for a collection of the source-materials. M. N. Tod, *BSA Journal*, 1901/2, 204 ff for freedwomen in trade

114 Aristophanes, *Thesm.* 446–52, Dem. LVII, 31–4; her poverty, *id.* 45; other citizen-women were driven by war conditions to act as wet-nurses, wool-workers and fruit-pickers, *ibid.* Wet-nurses were well thought of, and often freed, if slaves, Tod, *loc. cit.*, see also below

115 Apart from greengrocers, Aristophanes, *Wasps* 497, *Thesm.* 387 etc., and bread-sellers, *Frogs* 858, *Wasps* 238, more specialized trades include fig sellers, *Lys.* 564, honey-sellers, Pollux VII, 198, sesame-sellers, frankincense-sellers etc., Tod, *op. cit.* 206, and others, perhaps purely comic, as in Aristophanes, *Plutus* 426, 427, 435 etc. Café-owner, *Frogs* 549 ff, retailer of wine, *Plutus* 1120; *cf.* Athenaeus XIII, 566F, Plato, *Laws* 918D for their low repute

116 Herfst, *op. cit.*, 103. Wool-workers, Aristophanes, *Frogs* 1346–9, Plato, *Alcibiades* I, 126E, *Lysis* 208D, *Republic* V, 455C etc. Common among freedwomen, Tod, *loc. cit.* For vase painting, *Pl. 42*, a fifth-century vase. Aristophanes says (*Thesm.* 839–43) that Hyperbolus' mother was a money-lender, but we have no idea whether this is true

117 Aristophanes, *Eccl.* 1024–5, Isaeus X, 10; L. J. Th. Kuenen-Janssens, *Mnemosyne*, 1941, (series III, 9), 199–214

118 Such parties are the mark of courtesans (ἕταιραι), and 'nobody would serenade a married woman', Isaeus III, 13–14; *cf.* Dem. LIX, 24, 33–4, 48 etc. for Neaira's colourful career. Popular opinion of *hetairai* was low, and they had to be registered and pay a tax, Aeschines I, 119, Pollux VII, 201–2

119 The trade of πορνόβοσκος, Dem. LIX, 30; *cf.* Aeschines III, 214, where it is used as an insult, Aristotle, *E.N.* IV, 1, 40 (1121B), where they are proverbial acquirers of property, suggesting perhaps that their charges were exposed babies, or stolen. Procurer or go-between, Plato, *Theaetetus* 150A, Aristophanes, *Frogs* 1079, *Wasps* 1028, *Th.* 341; *cf. id.* 558, Xenophon, *Symposium* III, 10, Athenaeus X, 443A. A business-woman, Hypereides, *Athenogenes* 2; her name was Antigona

120 Dem. XLVII, 56; feelings of responsibility to nurse and *paidagogos*

121 Tod, *loc. cit.*; other nurses are kindly remembered in inscriptions: *IG* II³, 3111, 4050, 4109, *cf.* 3522, 4039, 4139, 4260, III, 1457 etc. Plato, *Protagoras* 325C–D

122 ὅτι δὲ φίλοινον τὸ τῶν γυναικῶν γένος κοινόν, Athenaeus X, 440E–442A; examples from (lost) comedies follow; *cf.* Aristophanes, *Thesm.* 733–38 etc. For lovers, *Birds* 793–6, *Peace* 978–85, *Thesm.* 339–46, 395–7, 479–501 etc.

123 Diog. La. II, 36–7: for his children's ages, Plato, *Apology* 34D. For his wife's pride in her household management and unwillingness to serve a dinner not up to the standard expected by his rich guests, Diog. La. II, 34. A critical wife, Plato, *Republic*, 549C–D

124 Isaeus VI, 21

125 Plut. *Alcibiades* VIII, Andocides IV, 14 etc., Dem. LIX, 22

126 Dem. XXXVI, 45, Dem. XLVIII, 53–6; *cf.* Lycurgus, *in Leocr.* 17

127 Aristophanes, *Clouds* 46–55, 60–74

128 Dem. XLIII, 74–8: of the 4 sons of Sositheus and Phylomache, 2 were called after her kinsmen. In a noble family, Agariste's son was called Cleisthenes after her father, her grand-daughter (who was Pericles' mother, Hdt. VI, 131) was Agariste

129 It is clear that this was the nub of the opponent's case in Isaeus II; Wyse *SI*, 251 *et al.* For the law, Dem. XLVI, 14; for other allusions, Wyse, *SI*, note on II, 13, 2; *id.* VI, 21 is the only one specifically alleging women's influence

130 *E.g.* Plato, *Laws* VIII, 840D-E, animals' mating is in accord with their pleasure (κατὰ χάριν), both for male and female, and human beings should be better than animals (ἀμείνους), Aristotle, *E.N.* VIII, 12, 7 (1162A)

131 Ehrenberg, *People*, 192 ff

132 Dem. XL, 29

133 *Id.* XXI, 79

134 Plut. *Alcibiades* II, 2. The Euripidean fragment, πάντων δυσμαχώτατον γυνή (544 Nauck), being out of context, cannot be taken seriously; on the other hand, is the Sophoclean portrait of Electra impossibly unrealistic? or that of Antigone? *Cf.* Aristophanes, *Lys.* 160–6. The satirical epigram, *Anth. Pal.* XI, 79, is of the Roman period, and Alexandrian

135 Lysias I, 14; neighbours as a source of good services, Xen. *Mem.* II, 2, 12–13; summoned as witnesses, Dem. XLVII, 60–1; they enquired anxiously what was wrong when they heard screams, *id.* LIV, 20

136 *Ecl.* 446–50; *cf. Frogs* 1158–59; Demosthenes XLVII, 52 for the loan of a bronze *hydria*. For neighbours in general, Ehrenberg, *op. cit.*, 214 f, Lysias VII, 18 for neighbours' proverbial curiosity

137 Dem. LV, 23; *Cf. id.* LIII, 4–7, where a neighbour is said to have been more help to a man than his relatives were, and to have looked after his neighbour's property when he went off to serve as trierarch

138 Isaeus VIII, 19

139 Isaeus XII, 5, in effect

140 Dem. LIX, 110–11

141 *Lys.* 507–20; it is impossible not to believe that this dialogue is essentially true to life; the husband's unwillingness to talk was also no doubt fairly typical, and his attitude that war is none of the women's business, *id.* 1126–7

142 Chapter VI, pp. 109–10 above. Plato even thought that a woman's burial-ceremonies should be commensurate with her means, *Laws* 719D-E

143 Isaeus VIII, 8

144 They (at least the successful) had servants too: Theodote, Xen., *Mem.* III,
    11, 4, Neaira, Dem. LIX, 35, 42 etc.

145 Dem. XL, 11; another mother is said to be ready to swear a similar oath,
    Isaeus XII, 9; Diogeiton's daughter would swear 'anywhere her father
    wanted', Lysias XXXII, 13

146 *E.g.* Dem. XXIX, 26; *cf.* the business transactions of *id.* XLI, XLIII, 37, 46

147 Isaeus XII, 5

148 οἰκεῖοι, as in Isaeus VI, 15; συγγενεῖς in Isaeus XII, 1; *cf.* Dem. XLIII,
    35–7 for evidence given by relatives

149 Isaeus VIII, 9–10—*cf.* VI, 15

150 Isaeus VI, 10 also speaks of *phrateres* and many of the demesmen knowing
    who a man's children were

151 Hypereides, *Lycophron* I, 7 and I, 3. For Demosthenes' widowed mother,
    Chapter V, p. 108

152 Hypereides, *ap.* pap. Oxy. 1607, 80 ff

153 Hypereides, as preserved by Stobaeus LXXIV, 33: 'A woman who goes
    out of the house ought to be at a stage of life at which those who meet her
    do not ask whose wife but whose mother she is.' Note that Euripides
    dressed as an old woman in Aristophanes' *Thesmophoriazusae*; it was
    presumably the absurdity of the idea which made Aristophanes fond of
    depicting them as over-sexed—*e.g. Eccl.* 976 ff, *Plutus* 975 ff, *Thesm.*
    344 etc.

154 Aristophanes, *Eccl.* 542–6, speaks of wearing men's clothes for protection
    at night; a law of Solon is said to have compelled women not to travel by
    night except in a carriage with a torch-bearer preceding them, Plut. *Solon*
    XXI, 4

155 Midwives should be women who have had children, but are too old to
    have more, Plato, *Theaetetus* 149B–D, *cf.* Aristophanes, *Thesm.* 505, 512,
    Eccl. 528–42 etc.

156 Lysias I, 15; Dem. XLIII, 62

157 Athenaeus XIII, 592E–F, Dem. XXVIII, 20; *cf.* Dinarchus, in *Demosth.* 65,
    99, 109, etc., in *Phil.*, 2, Lycurgus, in *Leocr.* 2, 141, Lysias IV, 20 etc.

158 Dem. L, 60–2

159 Lysias VII, 41, Dem. LIII, 29, *id.* XXVII, 65; *cf.* Lysias XXVIII, 14, who
    bids the jury pity themselves, their children and their wives

160 As Mr Griffith has pointed out, Athenian taxation was much lower than
    modern (British) when there was no crisis. However, it was this variability
    which made their taxation so harsh, and makes talk of averages over the
    years meaningless for comparison. Income tax at 8/3 in the £ (*e.g.*) for
    two years is in theory heavier than tax at nil in one year and 15/- in
    the £ the next, but there is little doubt about which is the harder to
    pay. Modern landowners do not mortgage their farms to pay their taxes

CHAPTER VIII

THE FAMILY IN PLATO'S STATE, SPARTA AND CRETE

1 Certainly, if that of Phaleas of Chalcedon was an ideal rather than an actual polity, as Aristotle half suggests, *Pol.* II, 4, 12-13 (1267B)

2 Plut. *Lycurgus* XXXI, 2, *Lyc.* hereafter in this chapter

3 Diog. La. VI, 72, 97

4 *Cf.* H. C. Baldry, *The Unity of Mankind in Greek Thought* (1965), 104-11, especially 108: 'Ultra-individualism is the main theme behind Cynic statements on human society'

5 The first part of *Republic* Book V, which needs to be read as a whole, treating as it does first of women, and their education, 451B-457C, and leading on from there to marriage, 457C-461E, and then to property and its problems, 461E-464B, with remarks like 'divergence of interest is shown when men use the words "mine" and "not mine"' (462C)

6 Arist. *Pol.* II, 2, 11-14 (1264A-B); 'Plato', says Aristotle, 'made the farmers (*georgoi*) owners (κύριοι) of their produce if they paid a part of it over, but he did not make it clear whether they had community of wives or not; if they do have wives in common and private farms, who will manage the *oikos* (τίς οἰκονομήσει) in the way that their men manage the farm work?' (this is an abridged version)

7 Lands and houses, *Republic* 416D-417B, marriages, 457C-461E

8 *Laws* 720E-21A: ἀρχὴ δ' ἐστὶ τῶν γενεσέων πάσαις πόλεσιν ἆρ' οὐχ ἡ τῶν γάμων σύμμειξις καὶ κοινωνία; it should not be forgotten that the meaning of γαμεῖν includes the sexual act without marriage

9 *Ibid.*; *cf.* 773E, where begetting children is said 'to hand over to god servants to take one's own place'—a concept in which the family is even further from the centre of the picture

10 Rather than 'head of a family', as some commentators, *e.g.* Glenn R. Morrow, *Plato's Cretan City* (1960), 103. If marriage was at 30, as is twice suggested (not 25, as suggested once), and the age of service 20-60, there will be a maximum overlap of 10 years in the father's and the son's liability to service. In view of the life expectation of ancient society (Jones, *AD*, 82-3), few families will have had two active soldiers simultaneously. 'Head of a family' is a Roman Law concept

11 This is one of Plato's inconsistencies. Elsewhere, 721B, 785B, it is laid down as 30, but the maximum age before punishment ensues is 35 in all 3 contexts

12 The reason for dowries, at least as expressed in modern Greece, *e.g.* Sheelagh Kanelli, *Earth and Water*, 30 *et al.*

13 One was in the part of the *kleros* near the city, the other in the more

distant parts; there are traces of similar arrangements at Gortyn (code IV, 32 ff), and possibly in Sparta, where it is hard to believe that the citizen had no house on his *kleros* when he had food-stores there, note 69 below. It was a highly convenient arrangement for a society in which accommodation was required for young adults while it was not certain whether they would obtain a *kleros* (or husband) or not, and for the old, those past military age, and widows

14 The existence of these is proof that the family was only very partially reinstated; the *syssition* under whatever title and the family are incompatible, M. P. Nilsson, *Die Grundlagen des spartanischen Lebens*, *Klio* XII (1912), 315 ff

15 By implication, sexual misdemeanours

16 L. Gernet, *Platon, Lois, Livre IX* (1917), arguing from these homicide laws, stresses family associations more strongly than in the views here expressed

17 Morrow, *op. cit.*, 123

18 *Laws* 828B: μία γέ τις ἀρχὴ θύῃ . . . ὑπὲρ πόλεώς τε καὶ αὐτῶν καὶ κτημάτων

19 Hestia is mentioned first of all the gods, even before Zeus, *Laws* 745B 848D. Temples to Hestia and Zeus and Athene are to be put up in every village, and they are to be surrounded by a wall and called 'acropolis'; other gods get shrines only where they are patron (ἀρχηγός). Hestia is the guardian of justice in the gravest trials (854C–856A), in which we note that even here the punishments are such as to ensure the integrity of the *kleros*

20 Genesia may have been peculiarly Attic, Apatouria was purely Ionian, which may adequately explain their absence, but it is hard to believe that there were no Dorian counterparts

21 Morrow, *op. cit.*, 450; the *chthonioi* are less honoured than the Olympian gods (*Laws* 717A–B); Plato's view of the relation of soul and body makes this not surprising, Morrow, *op. cit.*, 463–4. For the distinction *Chthonioi*/ Olympian, W. K. C. Guthrie, *The Greeks and their Gods* (1950), 209 ff

22 διάδοχον καὶ θεραπευτὴν θεῶν καὶ γένους καὶ πόλεως. For ἐγ-χώριοι θεοί, Guthrie, *op. cit.*, 28–9

23 729C, Morrow, *op. cit.*, 462, note 210, for Pollux III, 5, and other refs. to this belief

24 Plut. *Lyc.* XXXI, 2

25 Morrow, *op. cit.*, 42 ff. F. Ollier, *Le Mirage Spartiate* (1933) for an extended treatment of 'laconism'; in Athens, the first clear evidence is in the early fifth century (p. 142), especially noteworthy in Cimon (pp. 144 ff). Thuc. IV, 40, comments on the shock caused by the surrender at Sphacteria in 425; it shattered illusions, perhaps Thucydides' own

26 Pindar, *Pythian* I, 75–8, Aristophanes, *Birds* 1281–3, *q.v.* for Socrates as a 'laconizer', Ollier, *op. cit.*, 211 ff, E. N. Tigerstedt, *The Legend of Sparta* (1965), 242

27 He was also a cousin of Plato's mother. H. Diels—W. Kranz, *Die Frag-mente der Vorsokratiker*, (1951–2 edn.) II, 378–80, 391–94. It was one aspect of Critias' bitter feelings towards the Athenian democracy, Ollier, *op. cit.*, 168–174

28 Aristotle (*Pol.* VII, 13, 11) speaks of 'Thibron . . . and each of the other writers about their polity'; Xenophon's work (*Lacedaimoniorum Politeia, Lac. Pol.* hereafter) survives; *cf.* also his *Agesilaus*

29 Xenophon comments on the failures of the harmosts (the officers put in charge of the Greek cities in the period after the defeat of Athens in 404), *Lac. Pol.* XIV, 1–7; earlier, Herodotus had commented on the Spartans' susceptibility to bribes (III, 148), and Thucydides on a variety of failings, Morrow, *op. cit.*, 44, note 21

30 As Lysias puts it (XXXIII, 7, probably 388): 'the Spartans are the only Greeks who are now living without damage to their lands, without walls, without *stasis*, without suffering defeat, and having institutions which have always been the same'. *Cf.* Plato, *Laws* 628B, 'everyone hates *stasis* and wants it to end as rapidly as possible'

31 Ollier, *op. cit.*, 44, *et al.*

32 Thuc. II, 65, 11–12; for a criticism of the critics, Jones, *AD*, Chapter III

33 Plato, *Gorgias* 515E *et al.*; Plut. *Lyc.* XVIII, 3, XIX–XX, and the collections of Spartans' and Spartan women's sayings in *Moralia* 208B–236E, 240C–242D

34 A. Fuks, *The Ancestral Constitution* (1953)

35 Above, notes 25–8. For the fourth century, Dem. LIV, 34, Plato, *Protagoras* 342A–343C, where 'laconizers' are mocked for attention to the outward, not the real, features of Spartan life; *Republic* 544C, the Spartan state is the imperfect state 'nearest' to the ideal; Isocrates VIII, 95–6, XII, 41, 65, 155, 200, 235 ff, *et al.* for admirers of Sparta

36 Thuc. II, 65, 13, etc.

37 400 years, according to Thucydides, before the date of his work (I, 18, 1); Isocrates in the fourth century favours 700 years before his day, *e.g.* VIII, 95; the correct date is immaterial for this purpose, and disputed by scholars

38 Cinadon is said to have headed an abortive revolt of all those of less than full Spartan citizenship in 398, but he was betrayed, Xen. *H.G.* III, 3, 5–11. The total omission of this attempt from the records (*e.g.* of Plutarch) shows the overwhelming power of the tradition of freedom from *stasis*. Aristotle also mentions attempts by Lysander to abolish the kingship and by Pausanias to abolish the ephorate, as examples of internal strife (*stasis*), *Pol.* V, 1, 5 (1301B)

39 Hdt. VII, 104, 4. For a satire on this, Plato (*Hippias Maior* 285A–B) makes Hippias prove the Spartans the least law-abiding of men

40 Arist. *Pol.* II, 6, (1269A–1271B), V, 6, 1–2 (1306B–1307A), VII, 13, 10–13 (1333B) (*cf. id.* 20, 1334A–B), VIII, 3, 3–4 (1338B) *et al.*, Plato, *Laws* 628E

ff: the legislator should legislate for peace, not war; the Spartan laws produce valour but not self-control (633A–634C); the *syssitia* lead to factions and sodomy (636B–C), the lack of rules for women leave them idle and luxury-loving (637C, 806C). Perhaps, too, as Morrow suggests, Plato's description of oligarchy in *Republic*, 548A–B, may reflect his view of Sparta; Plato has been talking about Sparta (545A), as the community of the man who is 'competitive and covetous of honour', and again in 547B–D, though here not by name. *Cf.* Isocrates, to whom comparison of Athens and Sparta is a favourite theme; see *e.g. Panathenaicus* (XII), 41–71, 89–118, 176–198. In this work, completed in 339, the comparisons are all favourable to Athens, the Spartan merits being solely those of courage and *homonoia*—avoidance of internal dissension. Ephorus on the other hand (*c.* 405–330), whose account appears in Polybius and Plutarch, remained favourable; however we cannot date this part of his work

41 Plut. *Lyc.* VIII, 3; that the lots were equal is supported by Polybius VI, 45, though the two authors differ as to what this meant—viz. that the lots produced equal crops (Plutarch), that the area of the *kleroi* was equal (Polybius); Plutarch also reports two other, divergent, theories of how 9000 *kleroi* came to be created. The question of Spartan land-tenure is highly perplexing, and there is no agreement amongst scholars; two facts, however, should always be borne in mind, one, that the system was intended to be the economic basis on which the army was supported (Aristotle, *Pol.* II, 6, 12 (1270A), the other, that the word *kleros* need not necessarily bear the meaning of 'individual's allotment', if we may argue from the Gortyn code V, 25–8, where the *klaros* (= *kleros*) is a body which steps in when the kinship-group fails to provide an heir. Equality of individual land-holding may well be a fifth-century fiction of Spartan panegyrists, F. W. Walbank, *Commentary on Polybius*, I (1957), 728 ff, on the right lines, if not necessarily right in every detail. The name *homoioi*, however, as a description of citizens shows that equality was a conceivable ideal, and perhaps (so Forrest, *EGD* 131) indicates considerable inequality at an earlier date

42 Plut. *Lyc.* XVI. 1. This implies that the land was originally vested in the tribes (φυλαί), and that the *kleroi* were assigned to the tribes; there were always tribes in Sparta—since they appear in the so-called Great Rhetra in *Lyc.* VI, 1–2—and the 3 Dorian tribes based on birth must be inferred from Tyrtaeus, frag. 1, 12 (Diehl). Whether the Spartans always remained so divided for land-tenure and military organization is disputed. A recent view (Forrest, *EGD* 131) is that *obai*, units based not on ancestry but on residence, determined a man's place in the organization. By Aristotle's day private (*viritim*) ownership of land by individual Spartans was so firmly established that he assumes that the birth of a number of sons will involve physical division of the *kleros*, and hence impoverishment (*Pol.* II, 6, 13 (1270B)). In one fragment however (fr. 611, 12), if the scribe has reported

Aristotle properly, we hear of two kinds of land, that belonging to an individual, and land belonging to his ancient *moira* (ἀρχαία μοῖρα), which was inalienable; the '*moira* ordained from the beginning' appears also in a passage of Plutarch (*Mor.* 238E), which implies that the Lycurgan reform incorporated *xenoi* into the Spartan system by this means. If trust may be founded on these shaky props, it might be concluded that the *moirai* were military subdivisions of the tribes from an early date, but they appear in the light of day only from the fifth century, when the *mora* (μόρα) (philologically of the same root) appears as a regular Spartan unit in the field, and hence *moirai* were perhaps connected with the original *kleroi*, which did not embrace all land. All Spartans belonged to a *mora* according to Diodorus XV, 32. For a discussion of *morai*, Chrimes, *AS*, 317 ff, though her assumption that locally-based tribes must have had all their land in the same area is hard to credit in a state which had expanded into Messenia; were the lands of any tribe all in Messenia? Surely not. There was always private land at Sparta, since there were always cavalry, and Thucydides (V, 72, 4) and Ephorus (Strabo X, 4, 18, (482C)) suggest that the name of ἱππεύς (cavalryman) was merely a title (Chrimes, *AS*, 246, note 5); cavalry involve some people in more expense, and hence in more property; both Tyrtaeus (during the second Messenian War) and Alcaeus (a generation later) know of divergences in wealth in Sparta (Walbank, *op. cit.*, 730). There was state land too, which was allocated both to individual mercenaries like Xenophon, and to the class known as *neodamodeis*, who were professional soldiers, Xenophon, *Agesilaus* I, 7, *H. G.* V, 2, 24 etc, and may sometimes have been ex-helots, or (R. F. Willetts, *C.P.* XLIX, 1, 1954, 27 ff) men who would have been helots had they had a Spartiate master to pay tribute to; having none, they paid the state by personal service as hoplites instead. Xenophon, *H.G.* VI, 5, 24, mentions two colonies of *neodamodeis*; it is evident from Cinadon's revolt that they were not always content, and were inferiors, *id.* III, 3, 6, Willetts, *op. cit.*, Chrimes, *AS*, 38-41

43 Confirmed, for what it is worth, by Plutarch, *Agis* V, 1. Why some writers imagine that a newly-born baby requires a *kleros* producing enough grain to support a man and his wife I do not know

44 Plut. *Lyc.* III, 3

45 Phratries managed the education (Forrest, *EGD* 130); for a satirical view of it, Plato, *Hippias Maior* 285A-D; they were interested only in stories of the genealogies of heroes and men, and foundation-legends of cities

46 Competition and surveillance, Plut. *Lyc.* XVI-XVIII, Xen., *Lac. Pol.* II, 2 and 10-11, IV, VI, 1-2 etc.; the function of 'lovers' was purely educational, Plut. *Lyc.* XVII, 1, XVIII, 4, Xen. *Lac. Pol.* II, 12-13; it is clear that both writers are on the defensive against popular aspersions on the moral aspect. Plato thought the Spartans notorious for sodomy (*Laws* 636B-C),

and *cf.* (perhaps) the fiction that a bride was a boy (but see note 56); Aristotle, however, *Politics* II, 6, 6–7 (1269B), seems to suggest that the Spartans were excessively influenced by women for sexual reasons. That the lover (ἐραστής) was a survival from pre-Lycurgan Sparta, with military implications for the *syssitia*, Chrimes, *A.S.*, 223–7. For black-balling, note 122 below; however, there must at some stage have been a formal act of approval, since Xenophon (*Lac. Pol.* III, 3) refers to a disgrace which fell on those who did not undergo the Spartan training. That the *syssitia*, like the Cretan *andreia*, evolved out of nobles' gathering bands of followers, is shown by Chrimes, *op. cit.*, 219–245, arguing from Cretan analogies (see also pp. 211 ff below), supported by the traditions of nobles' feuds in Crete, Aristotle *Pol.* II, 7, 7–8 (1272B), and of civic disharmony in early Sparta, Thuc. I, 18, 1, Hdt. I, 65, etc.

47 Plut. *Lyc.* X, XII: this latter passage (XII, 2), mentioning as it does a small sum of money being contributed each month, is quite anomalous for the seventh century; *cf.* XXV, 1, and the reference to men below 30 getting their necessities bought for them by kinsmen or other people in the market, but see further p. 200 below. The meals were notoriously frugal, Athenaeus IV, 138B–D

48 Plutarch, following his belief in Lycurgus' mildness, says he believes it belongs to the period of the revolt of Messenia, following the earthquake of 464, *Lyc.* XXVIII, 6

49 Plut. *Agis* XI, 2, an 'ancient law' against begetting children from a foreign wife; *cf.* Leonidas' leaving his Persian wife and children behind when he returned to Sparta in the third century

50 Plut. *Lyc.* XV, 1–2. Pollux (III, 48, VIII, 40) mentions never marrying as punishable in many places, marrying 'badly' or 'late' as punishable in Sparta. 'Bad' marriage is defined by Plutarch (*Lysander* XXX, 5) as trying to obtain a rich bride instead of one from 'good men' of a man's own circle—ἀγαθῶν καὶ οἰκείων. 'Late' marriage presumably means deferring marriage beyond the age at which the rest of a man's age-group married, perhaps in the expectation of a richer bride, or one especially desirable for other reasons. As a Spartan generation was 27 years (Chrimes, *A.S.* 341), the marrying age may have been in the 25th year, in the winter between a man's 25th and 26th (our 24th and 25th) birthdays

53 ἐγάμουν δι' ἁρπαγῆς (Plut. *Lyc.* XV, 3): Athenaeus XIII, 555C, quoting Hermippus, a writer of the late third century

54 Hdt. VI, 65. The fact that it was the royal family may be significant, but *cf. id.* 57, 4, fathers may promise daughters, if they have no son; Plutarch, *Lysander*, XXX, 5, early fourth century

55 Plut. *Lyc.* XV, 3–5. At 30, men ceased to be of the class σφαιρεῖς, a word whose meaning is disputed, H. Michell, *Sparta* (1952), 172, Chrimes, *A.S.*, 132, M. N. Tod, *B.S.A. Papers*, 1903/4, 72 ff

56 And in Greece at Argos, where the bride put on a false beard for her

wedding-night (Plut. *Mor.* 245F). E. A. Westermarck, *History of Human Marriage* (1921), I, 509, note 3, suggests it is merely symbolic of chastity, but *ibid.*, p. 72 ff for examples of the trial marriage which is not consummated till a birth, or at least a pregnancy, occurs

57 ἐν ἀκμαῖς τῶν σωμάτων for men, Xen., *Lac. Pol.* I, 6; ἀκμαζούσας καὶ πεπείρους for girls, Plut. *Lyc.* XV, 3

58 Plut. *Lyc.* XIV, 2–XV, 1. Spartan girls even learned to manage horses; they drove wicker carts at the festival of Hyakinthia, Athenaeus IV, 139 F, Xen. *Agesilaus* VIII, 9, Plut. *Ages.* XIX, 5

59 οὐκ ἰδίους . . . τῶν πατέρων τοὺς παῖδας, ἀλλὰ κοινοὺς τῆς πόλεως, Plut. *Lyc.* XV, 8

60 Hdt. V, 39–41

61 Hdt. VI, 61–63

62 Plut. *Lyc.* XV, 6–8, Xen. *Lac. Pol.* I, 7–9; Nic. Dam., fr. 103z (F. Jacoby, *FGH*, IIA, 387), includes foreigners, but this is unlikely. I assume that Xenophon's 'man who does not wish to live with a wife' was a widower, not a bachelor

63 On this possibility, p. 203 below. Plutarch's words are ' it was legal to adopt what was born of noble seed as their own' (ἴδιον αὐτοῖς); he does not specify whose *kleros* the baby would be heir to, nor that the elderly husband was childless, *Lyc.* XV, 7

64 Polybius XII, 6; he also speaks of polyandry, 3 or 4 men sharing a wife, 'or even more if they were brothers', and having their children in common

65 Plut. *Lyc.* XV, 9, implies that the accusation was familiar, though he denies its truth in respect of Lycurgus' day. *Cf. Moralia* 228B; the ancient evidence in fact does not go beyond hints, and the custom of provocative dress at the festivals, to encourage the men to want to marry (Euripides, *Andromache* 595 ff; Plutarch, *Lycurgus and Numa Comparison*, III, 3–4). Aristotle, *Pol.* II, 6, 5, (1269B) does imply libido if ἀκολάστως is the correct reading, but this has been questioned

66 Hdt. VI, 67–69

67 This was presumably in the bride's family home, though Plutarch does not say so, specifically, Plut. *Lyc.* XV, 4

68 Plut. *Lyc.* XVI, 3

69 Plut. *Lyc.* VIII–IX. Tradition spoke (as Xen., *Lac. Pol.* VI, 3–4) of their free use of one another's property, slaves, dogs and even stores of provisions in the country. *Cf.* Aristotle, *Pol.* II, 2, 5, (1263A), Plut. *Mor.* 238E–F

70 Especially the sophists, who did not appear till late in the fifth century; for a fifth-century soothsayer (μάντις) who made a good living, Isocrates XIX, 5–7. Xen, *Lac. Pol.* VII, 6, says that there was liable to be a search for gold and silver, though on what basis he does not say; harlots in Sparta are attested by Athenaeus (XIII, 574C–D, 591–2)

71 Plut. *Lyc.* XXVII, 3, quoting also Thuc. II, 39, 1. They also discouraged

their own citizens from foreign travel, Plutarch, *Agis* X, Xen., *Lac. Pol.* XIV, 4, Aristophanes, *Birds* 1012–3, Aristotle, fr. 543 etc.

72 Plut. *Lyc.* XIII, 3–5, *id.* XXVII, 1–2. However, the burial of Lysander 'in the first friendly and allied territory they came to' shows the common Greek attitude, Plutarch, *Lysander* XXIX

73 See Burn, *LA*, 77. The tradition that they were bastards, Ephorus, *ap.* Strabo VI, 3, 2–3 (C 278–80), Aristotle, *Pol.* V, 6, 1 (1306B), and W. L. Newman's note *ad loc.* (vol. IV, 367); Lyctus in Crete also claimed to be a Spartan colony, Aristotle, *Pol.* II, 7, 1 (1271B)

74 Hdt. V, 42, 2ff; they failed to found one despite several attempts, Hdt. *loc. cit.*

75 *Id.* IX, 10. The order of succession here is a clear example of a succession within a kinship-group (κατ' ἀγχίστειαν), not within a single patriarchal family. The oldest member of the group succeeds unless the succeeding generation is adult

76 συμβολαῖα, Plut. *Lyc.* XIII, 2; in the absence of trade the only contracts which would be common would be those between the Spartiate owner of the *kleros* and his helots for the supply of foodstuffs, but Plutarch (*Mor.* 239E) says that it was not permissible to change the terms of supply; *cf.* Athenaeus XIV, 657D

77 *Politics* II, 6, 9 (1270A); *cf.* Plato, *Laws* 781A, 806C (total failure to regulate women's lives). See also below, pp. 203 ff

78 Hdt. VI, 57, 4; it might have been for the purpose of augmenting the citizen-body, see pp. 204–5 below

79 Gaius II, 101; that the installation of a successor (*heres*) was the essential foundation of all Roman wills is universally agreed

80 The Spartans were conscious of their descent from Heracles as Dorians, a consciousness which seems to have grown in the fifth century

81 It might also be significant that the sixth and fifth centuries saw a great weakening in the power of the kings. The Spartan kingship is 'the position of a sort of perpetual commander in chief with supreme powers' οἷον στρατηγία τις αὐτοκρατόρων καὶ ἀΐδιος, Arist. *Pol.* III, 9, 2 (1285A), *cf. id.*, 10, 1 (1285B)

82 Hdt. VII, 205, 2, V, 41, 3

83 See the stories above, pp. 198–9 and notes 60–61

84 Collateral relatives of the kings were still within the royal house, as Leotychidas, despite the fact that he was in the 8th generation from a ruling king, Hdt. VI, 65, VIII, 131. *Cf. id.* VI, 75, 2, for kinsmen who put the 'mad' Cleomenes in the stocks. Marriages within the royal house include Anaxandridas and his niece (*id.* V, 39), Archidamus and Lampito, *id.* VI, 71, Leonidas and Gorgo, *id.* VII, 205, 1, and in later generations, Cleonymus and Chilonis (Plut. *Pyrrhus* XXVI), Cleomenes and Agiatis (*id.*, *Cleomenes* I). It is probable that the older Cleomenes' mother was great grand-daughter of the famous Chilon (Hdt. V, 41, 3)

85 Thuc. V, 15 and 34, Arist. *Pol.* II, 6, 15 (1270B); *cf.* Isocrates VI, 55

86 Convincingly argued by Chrimes, *A.S.*, 220 ff, 107 ff; for wealth, note 42 above; *I.G.*, V, I, 213 (C. D. Buck, *Greek Dialects* (1955), 268–9 (no. 71)) for the victories of Damonon in chariot-races. For long hair, Plut. *Lysander* I, *Lyc.* XXII; *cf.* the dead warriors on a cup of the sixth century, *Pl. 48*

87 Hdt. VI, 60, and How and Wells's notes *ad loc.* The cooks (μάγειροι) were not merely butchers, but baked the Spartan bread, presumably for the *syssitia*, as well, since they had heroes, Matton (kneader) and Keraon (mixer), whose statues stood in the *syssitia*, Athenaeus I, 39C; Nic. Dam. (fr. 103Z, 15, F. Jacoby, *FGH* IIA, 387) mentions doctors (ἰατροί) in place of cooks. It was more commonly held that the Spartans undertook no work for pay—*e.g.* Xen., *Lac. Pol.* VII, 1–6, Plut. *Ages.* XXVI, 4–5 *Mor.* 214A, 239D, Aelian *V.H.* VI, 6 etc.

88 As. R. M. Cook, for example, believes, *CQ* 1962 (N.S. 12) 156 ff; for Spartan pottery, E. A. Lane, *BSA Papers* XXXIV (1933–4), 99 ff; in the mid-sixth century parties and revels were a common feature of Laconian pottery; literary sources (Plut. *Lyc.* XII, 7, Xen., *Lac. Pol.* V, 4–7) emphasize the Spartans' sobriety; the cups may be more truthful

89 Plut. *Lyc.* IX, 4–5. For other crafts, Xen. *H.G.* III, 3, 7, *Agesilaus* I, 26–7

90 Plut. *Agesilaus* XXVI, 5 (fin)

91 Hdt. VI, 57, 4. 'Engaged' translates ἐγγυήσῃ; the Spartan word, if Herodotus' text is sound (which is doubtful), is πατροῦχος

92 Arist. *Pol.* II, 6, 11 (1270A); the kings had lost their power to the heir-at-law (κληρόνομος), who was obliged to get her a husband, not, apparently, to marry her himself (*ibid.*)

93 Plut. *Lyc.* XV, 7

94 Chapter VII, p. 171; for nurses, Plut. *Lyc.* XVI, 3, woolwork, Xen., *Lac. Pol.* I, 3–4 etc.

95 *Politics* II, 6, 6–8 (1269Bf), claimed by Plutarch to be incorrect (*Lyc.* XIV, 1–2). Chilon, the seventh-century Spartan sage, is said to have said: 'do not threaten, it is womanish'. Diog. La. I, 70

96 Cynisca, the sister of King Agesilaus, was also wealthy; according to Xenophon (*Agesilaus* IX, 6) he persuaded her to breed race-horses and show by victory in the games that this is the mark of wealth, not of manly achievement (ἀνδραγαθία). For her victories, Pausanias V, 12, 5, III, 15, 1, *id.* 8, 1, *q.v.* for the victories of other women afterwards

97 Aelian (*V.H.* VI, 6) says the exact opposite, but Plut. *Lysander* XXX, 5 for an engagement in which a dowry was at least expected

98 Plut. *Agis* IV, VII, 3–4, XIII, 2–3

99 *Lac. Pol.* IX, 4–5; V. Ehrenberg, *RE* VIA (1937), 2292 ff, *s.v.* τρέσαντες; Nic. Dam. adds that they were shunned by friends too, fr. 103Z, 12, (F. Jacoby, *FGH* IIA, 387); *cf.* Hdt. VII, 229–32

100 *E.g.* Plut. *Lyc.* XIV–XVII, XXI, XXVI

101 Plut. *Lyc.* XIII, 2; in Aristotle's day there were still no written laws governing lawsuits, *Pol.* II, 6, 16 (1270B)

102 Aeschines I, 180–1

103 *Pol.* II, 6, 10 (1270A): ὠνεῖσθαι μὲν γὰρ ἢ πωλεῖν τὴν ὑπάρχουσαν
ἐποίησεν οὐ καλόν, ὀρθῶς ποιήσας

104 Thuc. IV, 38, 5; 112 fell in the battle, and unstated numbers in the previous
engagements; of the 112 we do not know how many were Spartiates; of
the 308 prisoners, about 120 were Spartiates. The survivors were disfranchised and prohibited from office and the right to dispose of property,
but they were later restored, *id.* V, 34. Contrast the story in Herodotus
(I, 82, 8) of the suicide of the sole survivor of the 300 champions' battle
with the Argives, and of the fates of those who were not with
Leonidas at Thermopylae (*id.* VII, 229–32); a change of attitude is very
apparent

105 Arist. *Pol.* II, 6, 10 (1270A): for an opposite view about early times, note
41 above

106 *Pol.* II, 6, 11 (1270A); he implies that they were in the form of land

107 Cicero, *Tusculan Disputations* II, 15, 36, quoting an unknown play

108 Hdt. III, 148

109 Plato, *Laws* 633A–634C; *cf.* note 40 above

110 *Pol.* II, 6, 22, *et al.*; note 40 above

111 Isocrates VIII, 95–6; *cf.* XI, 20 for their 'sloth and greed'

112 Plut. *Lysander* XVII, *cf. Mor.* 239E–F

113 Plut. *Agis* V

114 *Pol.* II, 6, 10 (1270A)

115 Arist. *Pol.* II, 6, 5–11 (1269B–1270A)

116 Plut. *Agis* V, 3–4; only 100 of the 700 were still landowners; for lands
pledged for debt, *id.*, XIII, 3

117 Xen. *H.G.* III, 3, 5 ff. Forty Spartan *homoioi*, four thousand others

118 Plut. *Agesilaus* VI, 2

119 *Pol.* II, 6, 12 (1270A); in 425, of the 308 hoplites captured on Sphacteria
only about 120 were full Spartiates. *Cf.* Plut. *Agesilaus* XXXII, 7, *et al.*,
and, for later times, Stobaeus XL, 8 (from Teles, who wrote *c.* 240,
O. Hense, introd. to the fragments, 1889, xxvii), Plut. *Mor.* 238E: as 'the
report of some people' (ἔνιοι ἔφασαν) that anyone, whether *xenos* or
helot who submitted to Spartan discipline could share land and become a
homoios, but there were certainly some periods when the Spartans' attitude
was exclusive

120 *Lac. Pol.* X, 7

121 *Pol.* II, 6, 21 and 7, 4 (1271A, 1272A)

122 Plut. *Lyc.* XII, 4–6, though Chrimes, *AS*, 245, 161–2, has cast doubts on its
veracity

123 For Crete, pp. 211–12 below; *cf.* Chrimes, *AS*, 111–6

123a G. H. Morrow (*op. cit.*, 22–31) thinks that Plato knew Crete well, and was mainly responsible for later knowledge of what, to Herodotus and Thucydides at least, was an almost unknown island. H. van Effenterre, *La Crète et le monde Grec* (1948), (*Crète* hereafter), 68, thinks that Plato was in Crete, but not long, 70–2, that Plato's source of information was visitors to the Academy. It is more usually thought that Dosiades, said by Diodorus (V, 80, 4) to be reliable, and Ephorus (mid-fourth century) are the basic sources for our surviving literary evidence, in Aristotle, *Politics* II and fragments of *Cretan Constitution* (*frag.* 611, 14–15), Strabo and Athenaeus

124 Cretans managed to avoid servile revolts, Arist. *Pol.* II, 6, 3 (1269A–B). Crete is omitted from Plato's list of serf-owning communities who have difficulties, *Laws* 776C–D

125 Certainly in education: Homer and foreign poets other than Tyrtaeus were neglected, mathematics and physics ignored, Plato *Laws* 629B, 680C, 818E, 886B–E; young men were not allowed to go abroad, *id.* *Protagoras* 342C–D. Herodotus' failure to go there must be significant, and so must the fact that the Cretans played almost no part in fifth century history. Yet Crete was not isolated, and Cretans travelled abroad, van Effenterre, *Crète*, 38–42

126 Military education, Plato, *Laws* 625D–626B, including gymnastic exercises in the nude, *id.*, 673B–D, which were invented in Crete, *id.*, *Republic* 452C (though Thucydides declares the practice came from Sparta, (I, 6, 5)); specializing in archers and light troops, *Laws* 625D, 834A–D

127 None of the 'Seven Sages' was a Cretan, though some people admitted Epimenides to the list (Diog. La. I, 13); Herodotus says that the Spartan Lycurgus got his laws from Crete, a tradition accepted by virtually all writers except Polybius, for whose polemical attack (in VI, 45–7) see F. W. Walbank, *Commentary ad loc.* Strabo, reporting Ephorus (in X, 4, 17–19), and Aristotle (*Pol.* II, 7, 1 ff (1271B)) also recognise similarities. For the growth of the legend, Aristotle, *id.* 9, 5, (1274A) reports (but does not believe) that Thaletas of Gortyn taught Zaleucus and Charondas, the two lawgivers of Western Greece. The Cretans' own laws were excellent, Plato, *Republic* 544C, *Laws* 631B, 693E; like the Spartans they enjoyed *eunomia*, *id.*, *Crito* 52E; their lawgiver made them obedient to their laws, Aristotle, *E.N.* I, 13, 2–3 (1102A). Politically, Crete was not united at any period in ancient times, but the belief that their institutions were uniform seems well founded

128 Plato, *Laws* 708A; 'people' translates γένος; it is interesting that Gortyn is called a γένος, a family unit, not a *polis*

129 R. F. Willetts, *Aristocratic Society in Ancient Crete* (1955), 3–6, a description and dating. He points out that the inscriptions are clearly complete in themselves, despite their incompleteness as a code

130 Arist. *Pol.* II, 7, 4 (1272A)

131 P. Vinogradoff, *op. cit.*, II, 208; the Gortyn code has nothing to do with the *klaros*. Code IV, 31 ff; the list is in two categories, houses (στέγναι),

except for those in the country (κόρα = χώρα) which are being lived in by *oikeis*—the serf cultivators who belonged to the *oikos*—and flocks and large animals (πρόβατα καὶ καρταίποδα), and other property (κρήματα, code V, 29–41), subdivided into livestock (τνατῶν = θνητῶν), produce (καρποῦ), clothing (Fήμας = εἵματος), ornaments (ἀνπιδήμας = ἀμφιδήματος), furniture (ἐπιπολαίων κρημάτων)

132   Successors at law, ἐπιβάλλοντες, appear particularly in the sections about succession to property, V, 10–29, and in those affecting the marriage of *epikleroi*, VII, 15–IX, 24, where the word also includes the statutory husband

133   Code VIII, 47–53. The *epikleros* who has no ἐπιβάλλων 'statutory husband', shall live with her mother; if she is dead, with her mother's kin, who, by implication, are not eligible to be ἐπιβάλλων

134   *CIG*, II, 2448, *IJG* XXIV; Chrimes, *AS*, 239–44, whose account I follow except where indicated

135   τὸ κοινὸν τοῦ ἀνδρείου τῶν συγγενῶν. On the meanings of *Andreion* see below

136   Code IV, 23–31, VIII, 24–36, IX, 1–24, and, by analogy, VI, 31–6

137   The following are not conclusions drawn by Miss Chrimes

138   Athenaeus IV, 143A–D (from Dosiades—Jacoby, *FGH*, 3B, 394–6), Strabo X, 4, 16 (C480) ff (from Ephorus), *q.v.* for οἱ ἐπιφανέστατοι τῶν παίδων καὶ δυνατώτατοι, X, 4, 20 (C483)

139   Strabo, *loc. cit.* This custom may lie behind the story that the Cretans were perpetually occupied with feuds between noble families and their followers; but for Cretan solidity, van Effenterre, *Crète*, 27 ff

140   Or perhaps seventeen; Hesychius (from whom the definition comes) says 'those up to seventeen years'; a Greek's 'seventeenth birthday', was the end of his sixteenth year of life (H. Michell, *Sparta* (1952)), 167

141   ἐβίον = ἡβῶν, also known as boys (παῖδες), Strabo, *loc. cit.*, and as ἀπάγελοι (Hesychius); *cf.* Willetts, *op. cit.*, 7 ff. According to Plato (*Laws* 660B) they had laws about poetry and the dance

142   Schol. on Euripides, *Alcestis* 989, but Willetts (*e.g.*) *ASC* 14, disagrees

143   ἀπόδρομοι, code VII, 35–6, known also as ἀγέλαστοι by Hesychius, who defines them as *epheboi* (ἔφηβοι). The law on not discussing the merits of laws in front of the young (Plato, *Laws* 634D–E) points in the same direction, since public business was discussed in the *syssitia*

144   Chrimes, *AS*, 224–7. Whether the designations of 'lover' and 'beloved' had their origin in a widespread habit of paederasty, or whether it represented a continuance of the custom we do not know; popular report in Greece believed the latter, *e.g.* Plato, *Laws* 636B–D, 836B–C, but it may not be correct, Van Effenterre, *Crète*, 84 ff. 'Comrades in arms' translates παρασταθέντες.

145   Cretan hospitality is also praised in various passages—*e.g.* Aristotle, *Cretan constitution* (fragments) (fr. 611, 15): this accords ill with hostility to

strangers. The explanation may be that the *xenoi* hospitably treated were other Cretans, members of another *andreion*

146 Aristotle's text (*Pol.* II, 7, 5 (1272A)) as usually printed then reads: 'providing for their association with the men, about which, whether it is good or bad, there will be another opportunity to investigate'. There must be a lacuna of at least one word before 'association' (ὁμιλίαν) such as 'infrequent' or 'restricted'—ὀλίγην or σπανίαν; there might even have been the otherwise unknown ὀλιγομιλίαν in the original text. There might be a larger gap, of a line or more, but Aristotle did not write egregious nonsense, as the customary text implies

147 πατρωίωκοι; Code XII, 32–34, the last provision of all—and very evidently added to clear up what is earlier merely described as 'being of youthful maturity' (ἐβίονσα = ἡβῶσα)

148 Code VII, 35–VIII, 8

149 Ephorus, *ap.* Strabo, *loc. cit.* Gortyn code, II, 20–24. Willetts, *ASC*, 86, disputes the view that the first two would be classed as seduction, not adultery in modern society

150 It would also tend to support the view that the *andreion* was the centre of the man's life, and not the home, which the wife was mainly responsible for running. In paternity cases however, the mother must bring her baby to the man's house (στέγα); but if he is not there, she has done her part, code III, 44–6, *cf.* IV, 14–17

151 If her statutory husband will not marry her, and there are no successors, code VII, 47–52; if she is unwilling to marry him, or to wait till he is of age, VII, 53–VIII, 8; if she has no one entitled, VIII, 8–12

152 Code VIII, 13–20 'Servants of the *oikos*'; Ϝοικεύς is the word used in the code. ἀφαμιῶται, Strabo XV, 1, 34 (701C); for discussion, Willetts, *ASC*, 46–51, van Effenterre, *Crète*, 93 ff

153 Code X, 33–9—ἄνπανσις is the word

154 Code X, 48 ff

155 Code X, 33–4; ὅπο κά τιλ λῆι = ὅποθεν ἄν τις ἐθέλῃ.

156 Apetairoi (ἀπέταιροι) are known in the code, *i.e.* those outside the circle of *hetairoi*; Willetts, *ASC*, 45, suggests some who might fall into that category, but we should add the rejected adopted sons, since all non-*hetairoi* were *xenoi* in a legal sense

157 *ASC*, 68, but see last note. He was equivalent to the Polemarch in Athens—who dealt with all legal business affecting *xenoi* of all sorts. Plato believed that disinherison, since it involved removal from the list of those owning *kleroi*, involved removal from the citizen-body, *Laws* 928D–929A

158 Aristotle, *Pol.* II, 7, 4 (1271B), has been thought to say that they attended the *syssitia*. In fact the passage indicates clearly that the *klaroi* of land and flocks supporting the citizen-body were regarded as public property, which means that *klaroi* were not the private possession of individual

families as has been supposed, but that the families corporately enjoyed no more than the usufruct of them

159 Aelian (*VH* XII, 12) reports that by his day (second to third century AD) disfranchisement and exclusion from public employment were added

160 It was the fact that it was only an attempt which made the difference: even a slave girl who was not a virgin (the least highly valued class) could name the father of her child if she were pregnant, and her oath prevailed over the man's denials, code II, 13-6

161 Code III, 44 ff, IV, 9 ff

162 Adultery, code II, 20-45; divorce and widowhood, II, 45-III, 44—κήρευσις, the same word is used for both; children born to those not living with a husband, III, 44-IV, 17

163 Code II, 52-4; II, 2-5

164 This was half as much as a son's portion in the property other than houses and large animals, code IV, 37-V, 1; for things to be divided, note 131 above

165 Code II, 45 ff, III, 24 ff, III, 31 ff. The wife retains half the καρπός of her property and half what she has woven (if anything) if she is divorced, and her kin receive the same if she dies without children; if a widow without children remarries she receives only a share (μοῖρα) of the καρπός.

166 τὰ Fα αὐτᾶς.

167 Code IV, 29 ff, XI, 31-45

168 Code XI, 18-9. Oddly enough, however, she was allowed to have free children by a slave if she took the slave to live in her house, but this does not mean that they would be *hetairoi*

169 Code III, 31-7

170 Code III, 17-22; if she has no children, a widow may remarry and take anything her husband has given her in writing

171 Code III, 37-40, X, 14-20; the successors-at-law (*epiballontes*) may, if they wish, allow the gift if more is given, but they are not obliged to

172 Most strikingly shown by the fact that it was a woman's husband's kinsfolk (her *kadestai*) who took action against adulterers and rapists

173 Her successors-at-law succeed if a wife dies childless (III, 31-7), a mother's possessions go to her children (IV, 43-6); but (III, 17-22), if a widow remarries, her property is separated from her late husband's, which is given to their children; VIII, 33-36, a childless *epikleros* who loses her husband must marry the successor-at-law; if the *epikleros* is a widowed mother, she may marry any of the tribe (*phyle*) she can, but there is no obligation, *ibid.* 30-33

174 Code X, 39-47; in *Cretan Cults and Festivals* (1961), 8, R. F. Willetts has been unable to find evidence of a well-developed family and ancestor cult of the sort found in Athens

175 It should be noted (especially in the section on sexual offences) how the state played little or no part in actions at law

CHAPTER IX

THE FAMILY IN OTHER STATES

1 Arist. *Pol.* II, 9, 7–9 (1274B): 'getting of children' translates παιδοποιῖα, 'placing' translates θετικοί (sc. νόμοι); it is usually thought (*e.g.* by Newman, *op. cit.* II, 381, note on 1274B4) to refer to adoption; see Newman for refs. and below, p. 231

2 Dem. XXIV, 210

3 Hearth, hestia (ἑστία or ἱστία) means *oikos* in Tod. *GHI* 1, 24, 8 *et al.*, Hdt. I, 176, V, 40, VI, 86 and many other places; *cf.* Süss, *RE*, VIII (1913), *s.v.* Hestia, especially 1277 ff.; Burckhardt, *HGC*, 109–10

4 *Id. HGC* 3, associates monogamy with ancestral cult; polygamy in Persia, Hdt. III, 68–9, 88 etc.

5 Hdt. I, 216, 196, IV, 104, 172, V, 6, *et al.* Nic. Dam. in Stobaeus XLIV, 25, (F. Jacoby, *FGH* 90, 103) etc., for marriages; Hdt. II, 85 ff, IV, 26, 71–3, III, 38 etc. for funerals

6 Hdt. I, 4 and 136

7 Hdt. I, 108–19, 34–8; *cf.* tales of revenge in III, 11, 14 etc., or the dying Persian king Cambyses' prayer for blessings on his associates: 'may your land be fruitful and your women and flocks bring forth offspring, and may you be free for ever' (III, 65, 7)

8 *Pol.* III, 2, 8 (1277B), VI, 4, 5 (1321A), ἀποσχομένοις . . . . . . βαναύσων ἔργων; Finley, *SLC*, 53, *q.v.* for more refs.

9 Hdt. IV, 108–9

10 Burckhardt, *HGC*, 3, and 8; Burckhardt's translators actually write 'imposed the right', but this is un-English in thought

11 After the purification of Delos in 426, when all corpses were exhumed and it was forbidden for the future for parturition or death to take place on the island. I accept Jebb's emendation κείσεται in Plut. *Mor.* 230D, *Essays and Addresses* (1907), 215, note 2

12 Text and translation of the foundation decree, A. J. Graham, *Colony and Mother-City* (1964), Appx. II, 224 f

13 Graham, *op. cit.*, 14–15, *q.v.* for references

14 Text in Tod, *GHI*, I, 24 *et al.*, translation and discussion, Graham, *op. cit.*, 226 ff

15 'Household' translates ἱστίᾳ = ἑστίᾳ, *i.e.* hearth

16 *Op. cit.*, 68

17 As the Messenians and Chalcidians at Rhegium, Graham, *op. cit.*, 17–19; he is too kind to improbable conjectures which fly in the face of Strabo's evidence

18 Arist. *Pol.* V, 2, 10–11 (1303A–B); Cyrene was organized by Demonax into three tribes: 1, emigrants from Thera and their neighbours, 2, Pelo-

ponnesians and Cretans, 3, men from 'the islands'; later they were re-organized 'more democratically', Hdt. IV, 161, 3. Aristotle, *Pol.* VI, 2, 11 (1319B) says that democracy was established (*c.* 401) 'by increasing the number of tribes and phratries'. Thurii, Diod. XII, 10 ff, ten tribes initially, on a national basis, though there was a measure of reorganizing here too, V. Ehrenberg, *AJP* 1948, 149 ff

19 Aristotle, Diodorus, Ehrenberg, *loc. cit.*, last note

20 Hdt. I, 82, 7; *cf.* Theognis 829 f, an expression of bitter grief over the city's lost lands

21 Thuc. II, 27, IV, 56, 2–57; the Aeginetans were condemned to die, the prisoners from Cythera, and the Spartan commander, were kept prisoners. But there was a particularly virulent feud between Athens and Aegina

22 For the individual character of homicide courts, Aristotle, *Pol.* IV, 13, 2–3 (1300B), *cf.* II, 5, 2 (1267B), III, 1, 7 (1275B); implications of II, 9, 9 (1274B) for their general existence. For revenge, *e.g.* Plut. *Pelopidas* IX, 5–6; *cf.* Periander's attempt to revenge himself on the nobles of Corcyra for murdering his son; he sought to cut off their chance of obtaining descendants, Hdt. III, 48

23 Isocrates, *Ep.* VII, 8–9

24 Xen. *H.G.* V, 2, 10, (Phlius, *c.* 385) where real property τὰ ἐμφανῆ κτήματα may be what is intended, as it is distinguished in the late fifth century at Selymbria, Tod. *GHI*, I, 88, pp. 217 f, 265, Finley *SLC*, 55 and notes. The restoration of exiles ordered by Alexander produced similar decrees, as the law from Tegea found at Delphi, E. Schwyzer, *Dialectorum Graecarum Exempla Epigraphica* (1923), no. 657, p. 317, Tod, *GHI* II, 202; *cf. id.* 201 (from Mytilene)

25 Many states in early times (τὸ ἀρχαῖον), Arist. *Pol.* VI, 2, 5 (1319A); for Sparta, Chapter VIII above

26 Arist. *Pol.* II, 3, 7 (1265B), II, 4, 4 (1266B); some modern commentators think that Aristotle means only the Italian Locrians

27 Arist. *Pol.* II, 5, 2 and 7–8 (1267B–8B), criticized for being confused; for Phaleas, *id.* II, 4, 2 (1266A–7A), criticized for dealing only with land, not touching animals or other property

28 Burckhardt, *HGC*, 93–4

29 *SIG*, 45, 167, 169: purchases are made κυρίως.

30 J. D. Rogers, *AJA* 1901, 159 ff; 174 for text (two versions) and translation; the inscription is very much restored, but the references to πάματα (goods) and οἱ Ϝοι (i.e. αὐτῷ) ἐ[γγύτατα γένει seem fairly certain; C. Waldstein *et al.*, *The Argive Heraeum*, I (1902), 206–7, Inscription No. 9. For πάματα as ancestral property, *i.e.* real property, Schwyzer, *loc. cit.* (note 24), line 6 *et al.*

31 Th. Thalheim, *RE*, V, 2 (1905), 2584, *s.v.* ἔγκτησις; in Athens, the first example is from 410/9, *IG* I 59; the fourth century has a fair number, including a corporate grant to the Acarnanians who fought with the

Athenians at Chaeroneia (*IG* II, 121); outside Athens, two examples, at Oropus, *IG* VII, 4250–51, are of the mid-fourth century. The Hellenistic examples come from many different sites

32 Hdt. IX, 35 and I, 54; Delphi was peculiarly unable to be exclusive

33 Dem. XXIII, 211–3, Isocrates, *ep.* VIII, 4

34 Hdt. VII, 156. *Cf.* N. G. L. Hammond, *History of Greece* (1959), 271 *et al.* for the dangers of this policy, well illustrated for the fourth century in Plut. *Timoleon* XXV, 2

35 40,000 are said to have come to Syracuse, 10,000 to Agyrium, Diod. XVI, 82 etc; 60,000 *in toto*, Plut. *Timoleon* XXIII

36 Diod. XIII, 48, 7; the veracity of the passage has been questioned

37 Hdt. VI, 76–83; the date of the battle has been disputed, both in ancient times, by Plutarch, *Mor.* 245E, and in modern; for a discussion, W. W. How and J. Wells, *Commentary on Herodotus*, II (1928 ed.), 350 ff with references: 6,000 Argives fell, says Herodotus, 5,000 says Pausanias (III, 4, 1)

38 Slaves (δοῦλοι) is Herodotus' word. Plutarch, *Moralia* 245F, attacked Herodotus, saying that those made citizens were 'the leading *perioikoi*' (τῶν περιοίκων . . . τοὺς ἀρίστους); *cf.* Arist. *Pol.* V, 2, 8 (1303A). Modern scholars tend to believe that both writers were in fact speaking of the Gymnetes (γυμνῆτες), compared by Pollux (III, 83) to Spartan Helots, a view strengthened by the fact that Cretan *perioikoi* were sometimes serfs (Willetts, *A.S.C.*, 37–9, 47), and Crete and Argos had close connections (van Effenterre, *Crète* 29, note 4); Plato, *Laws* 707E–708A, Argive colonies in Crete

39 Plut. *Mor.* 245F; the women despised their husbands. P. A. Seymour, *JHS* 1922, 24–30, for the view that δοῦλοι means 'overseers of farms, estates etc.' He thinks that the Argives also enlarged the citizen-ranks by incorporating Dorian aristocrats from the small towns of the Argolid in a sort of synoecism referred to by Pausanias VIII, 27, 1, where however, the *perioikoi* are clearly not the same as the members of these towns

40 Note 18 above for Thurii; Miletus was sacked by the Persians after the battle of Lade in 494, Melos was captured by Athens in 416, Aegina in 431, though the population of the last was expelled, not massacred. For reinforcing colonies, Arist. *Pol.* V, 2, 10–1 (1303A–B), V, 5, 6 (1306A), Graham, *op. cit.*, 64–7 *et al.*, and references

41 Graham, *op. cit.*, 226 ff *et al.*

42 Isocrates XIX, 50–1; see further below

43 Finley, *SLC*, 6 and note 17; for *horoi* see further below

44 Isocrates XIX, 13–15

45 Stobaeus XLIV, 24; for its spurious character, Niese, *RE*, III (1899), 2182, *s.v.* Charondas; it ranks injury to parents with sacrilege and contempt for the laws, preaches against sodomy and all sexual intercourse except with a wife, commends chastity for women, and piety towards the dead, not with wailing and lamentation, but with a good memorial and the seasonal

offerings. Even Diodorus' account (XII, 12 ff) is thought to be neo-Pythagorean by many scholars

46 Hdt. III, 124; Arist. *Pol.*. V, 3, 3–4 (1304A), quoting family quarrels as causes of political strife; Dem. XXXVI, 29

47 Diog. La. VIII, 73; Diod. XII, 18, 3–4

48 Finley, *SLC*, 6 and note 17

49 Finley, *SLC* 83, 30 of the surviving *horoi* (about ⅓), including stones from Amorgos and Naxos, *SLC*, 162–3; *id.*, 46–7 for *apotimema*, *cf.* Wolff, *RE*, XXIII.1 (1957), 159 ff, *s.v.* προίξ.

50 *SIG*, 1215; *IG*, XII, 5, 873, from Tenos; *SIG*, 364, 55 ff, Ephesus in the third century. The inscriptions raise many problems, Wolff, *op. cit.*, 144

51 Arist. *Pol.* II, 4, 2 (1266A–B); we do not know Phaleas' date, but he wrote before Aristotle. Plut. *Pelopidas* III, 1–4, the rich marrying the rich—Thebes, fourth century; his γάμος λαμπρός must mean a 'splendid (in the rich sense) match'

52 All England Law Reports, 1960, I, 778 ff, Phrantzes vs Argenti. I am grateful to Mr. S. J. Papastavrou for this reference

53 Hdt. III 125, 129–137 for Democedes' exciting career. *JHS* 1966, 55 ff for the two marriage-patterns

54 Isocrates IX (*Evagoras*), 50

55 *Id.* XIX, 7–9; *ibid.*, 18–20 for Paros

56 Thuc. VIII, 21

57 Isocrates XIX, 6–7 and 42–6: διαιτηθεὶς ἐν πολλαῖς πόλεσιν ἄλλαις τε γυναιξὶ συνεγένετο, ὧν ἔναι ... καὶ παιδάρι᾽ ἀπέδειξαν ἃ κεῖνος οὐδὲ πώποτε γνήσια ἐνόμισε. Note how he avoids the use of γαμεῖν or συνοικεῖν, which would imply legitimate marriage. γυνή of course means both 'woman' and 'wife'

58 Athenaeus XIII, 608–9, quoting the sophist Hippias (contemporary with Socrates)

59 Diod. XII, 14–15. Disfranchisement seems an unlikely penalty; the remarrying father might have been disbarred from making a will. For divorce, *ibid.* 18

60 Heracleides Ponticus XIV (in C. Müller, *FHG* II, 217), Nic. Dam. in *id.* III, 461–2; Heracleides XXX, 3, *id.* II, 221, with Aelian, *V.H.* XIII, 24. *Cf.* the ferocity of Darius' punishment of a Persian noble for raping another noble's virgin daughter; he was impaled, Herodotus IV, 43

61 Arist. *Pol.* V, 3, 1 (1303B), *id.* V, 5, 10 (1306A–B): I have used Ross's translation of στασιωτικῶς

62 Xen. *H.G.* VI, 4, 7, Diod. XV, 54, Plut. *Pelopidas* XX, 3, Strabo VI, 1, 8 (C 259–60), from Ephorus; they revenged themselves in a brutal and disgusting fashion. For revenge *cf.* Plut. *Timoleon*, XXXIII, Xenophon *H.G.* V, 4, 12

63 Diod. XII, 18; the case was a famous one

64 K. Freeman, *Greek City States* (1950), 60

65 Diod. XIII, 89, 3; *id.* 55, 4, 56, 7 at Selinus in 409, *id.* 108, 8 at Gela in 406; the Argive women are said to have armed themselves and opposed Cleomenes after his victory at Sepeia, Plut. *Mor.* 245D–E; for the Spartan women, Arist. *Pol.* II, 6, 7 (1269B)

66 'Superintendents of women' translates γυναικόνομοι, Arist. *Pol.* VI, 5, 13 (1322B–1323A), *id.* IV, 12, 3 (1299A), IV, 12, 9 (1300A)

67 Diod. XII, 20–1; a man may not wear a gold ring nor a garment of Milesian style unless he is intending adultery or is a sodomite

67a Xen. *H.G.* V. 4. 7

68 Plut. *Pelopidas* XVIII, Plato *Laws* 636B; it is uncertain how far the political uniformity imposed by Thebes, and attested by Hellenica Oxyrhinchia XI (F. Jacoby, *FGH* IIA, 26), was accompanied by uniformity in social institutions

69 Arist. *Pol.* VII, 9, 6 (1330A), VII, 10, 8 (1331A), V, 9, 2 (1313B): φρόνημα καὶ πίστις, VII, 9, 2–4 (1329B); VII, 11, 2 (1331A) for separation of the citizens for athletics

70 Hdt. III, 45, 4, Plut. *Pelopidas* XXVII, 4; Aelian, *V.H.* X, 2; Arist. *Pol.* VII, 14, 4 (1335A)—though Troezen was an unhealthy place according to Isocrates XIX, 22, Plut. *Mor.* 249D–E

71 T. W. Beasley, *CR* 1906, 249 ff

72 Arist. *Pol.* II, 9, 9 (1274B), V, 3, 3–4 (1304A); Diod. XII, 18, 3 ff; Thucydides' account of the origins of the revolt of Mytilene omits this detail (III, 2–3)

73 Polybius XII, 5, who corrects Timaeus, preferring Aristotle's account (now lost), Strabo VI, 1, 7–8 (259C), who corrects Ephorus on the origins of the city, but has nothing to say about matrilinear descent. Herodotus I, 173, speaks of the Lycians as unique in this respect

74 Finley, *SLC* 155–6, 43–4

75 Aelian, *V.H.* III, 26, *SIG* 364, 53–64

76 At Hestiaea in the early sixth century, *Pol.* V, 3, 2 (1303B)

77 Graham, *op. cit.*, 224 f, Isocrates XIX, 50–1; *ib.*, 13, only ὁμοῖοι may be adopted, Arist. *Pol.* II, 9, 7 (1274B)

78 Aelian, *V.H.* II, 7; in cases of extreme poverty it was permissible to sell a child under the supervision of the magistrate. The story may be a mere myth derived from the Oedipus legend

79 ἔρημος, Isocrates XIX, 3; *cf. id.*, 34–5

80 Thrasylochus' funeral, *id.* 31 f; Sopolis' death, 38–41

81 Thrasyllus, *id.* 7, festivals, 10–1, the women's death ἐπὶ ξένης καὶ παρ' ἀλλοτρίοις, 21–3

82 Thuc. V, 11, Plut. *Timoleon* XXXIX; *cf. id.*, *Aratus* LIII, (died in 213), *Cimon* XIX, 4, *Themist.* XXXII, etc., though in the latter two cases it was disputed where the corpse actually was

83 Hdt. III, 55. For the public funeral of Agathon of Abdera (sixth century), *A.P.* VII, 226, Burn, *LA* 316

84 Thuc. III, 58, 4–5, Isocrates, *Plataïcus* (XIV), 60–2

85 Thuc. III, 67, 2–3

86 Thuc. I, 26, 3, Strabo VI, 1, 8 (C 259–60), from Ephorus

87 *SIG*, 1218 (*c.* 420 B.C.); *cf. ibid.* 1219, from Gambrion, near Pergamum (third century). Plutarch (*Mor.* 249B–D) has an extraordinary tale of how threatening to bury them naked stopped Milesian girls from committing suicide

88 *SIG*², 438, 132 ff, Dittenberger's dating. Note the distinction between πριάμενον, bought, and Ϝοίκω (= οἴκου), of the *oikos*; all were to go home after the funeral except ὁμέστιοι, those of the same *hestia*, fathers' brothers, brothers-in-law and daughters' husbands, *ibid*, 155–9. *Cf.* the introduction to Charondas' laws, Stobaeus, XLIV, 24, where piety to the dead is enjoined by offerings and not by wailing and lamentation

89 Theophrastus, Diog. La. V, 53, Strato, *id.*, 61, Lyco *id.*, 70, 74

90 *Id.* 16

91 *Id.* X, 19, Pliny, *Nat. Hist.* XXXV, 5

92 P. I. Zeppos, *Greek Law* (Athens, 1949) *passim*, with references; *cf.* All England Law Reports, 1960, I, 780 f

SOURCES OF ILLUSTRATIONS

APPENDIX

INALIENABILITY OF LANDS

RECENT WRITERS, notably W. G. Forrest (*E.G.D.*) and A. Andrewes (*The Greeks*), have argued that, in communities in which there never was a division (or a redivision) of lands in historical times, at no time or place that we know of was the land ever inalienable. In this context 'inalienable' means that a man could not sell his land in his lifetime to another person who wanted to buy it. Land could never be alienated by a man at his death in ages before the freedom of testamentary disposition was established, since there was no possibility of anyone other than the entitled kinsmen, however distant, inheriting it. By 'historical times' is meant times subsequent to the Dorians' settlement in Greece and the migrations of the Dark Ages. As thus defined, the question can be discussed (from lack of evidence elsewhere) only in regard to Attica, and since the implied view that land never was inalienable there seems likely to become standard dogma, a word of caution may be timely.

A passage in Aristotle (*Politics* II, iv, 4 (1266b)) is sometimes quoted (*e.g.* by A. French, *The Growth of the Athenian Economy*, 178, note 1 to Chapter II); to the present writer, however, this means only that Solon refused to allow the rich to take over their debtors' land (that on which the *horoi* had been planted) when he cancelled debts. We know from his poems, and from Aristotle's understanding of them, that Solon refused to countenance a redivision of land, so the passage cannot mean that Solon equalized estates in Attica by division. The passage is therefore probably irrelevant to this issue, or, if relevant, militates in favour of inalienability before Solon's day.

The only other possibly relevant example, therefore, which can be cited to support the 'alienability' view is that of Hesiod and his father; Hesiod's father was an immigrant into Boeotia, where he bought a farm, and Hesiod in his poem speaks of an improvident man having to sell his land. Is this example relevant to Attica, however? There are two reasons for doubting it, one general, one particular. The former concerns the character of the land in question, the latter concerns Boeotia. The Boeotian population did not claim to be autochthonous in the same way as did the Athenian. According to a Theban spokesman in Thucydides (III, 61, 2) it had been a hotch-potch of a population until the Thebans organized it, long after Hesiod's day. A hotch-potch population would be more likely to accept an outsider than would a racially-conscious and integrated one like the Athenian.

The more important factor, however, is probably the character of the land. Ascra is in the southwestern corner of Boeotia, and Hesiod's father's farm was an upland farm, on poor soil, as Hesiod explicitly states, and not a farm on the 'deep-soiled' plain, the sort of land that the original (and less numerous) settlers will have occupied. Such uplands will have originally been used as common or grazing lands, and have been brought into cultivation only when the pressure of population grew, or new immigrants arrived, and thus they will have become accepted by the community as the 'private' property of a family much less readily than the lands of the most ancient and longest-established families.

The ancient families had their tombs on their lands; even in the fourth century in Athens there was a strong objection to the sale of ancestral lands, especially those containing tombs. It is inconceivable (at least to the present writer) that village communities would tolerate the purchase of such lands by an outsider in an age before there was a written law of the city to say that he might do so. The written law, when it came into being, might say that it was 'the law' (νόμος) that men could purchase land, but the law of the family and clan, which preceded that of the city, certainly will have said that it was not 'right' (θέμις). As long as 'right' prevailed there will have been the strongest opposition from other members of the group to sales of family lands.

Moreover, who sold lands? Arguments from silence are notoriously dangerous, but we must note that in Solon's poems no debtor in Athens ever had to sell his land. Debtors had to sell themselves and their children, and to pledge part of their produce, but never do we hear that they had to sell or pledge their land. If the poor did not sell their lands, who did? Surely not the rich? Land was at all times much the most valuable and much the safest form of property; men would hardly be willing to exchange land for cattle or for any other sort of commodity which a would-be purchaser might have to offer, especially before the introduction of coined money, that is, on the current view, not till after Solon's reforms in Athens.

Hence, it seems to the present writer that while it may be true in theory that land was never inalienable in that there never was a law that said 'thou shalt not sell thy land to a stranger', such a law was unnecessary, because use and custom made the land inalienable *de facto* until long after men had started to think in terms of 'that which is legal' rather than 'that which is right'. The fact that colonial and similar societies passed laws to prevent the sale of lands is merely an illustration of the need of such societies to supply by law the sanctions which the ancient, family-based communities supplied by tradition.

INDEX

NAMES AND PLACES

References to authors are mainly confined to places where their views are given in the text. Where a city's name is used merely to define a person (as in Cleisthenes of Sicyon), or a date (as in Battle of Chaeroneia), it is not included on every occasion.